M000227501

The Providence of God

The concept of providence is embedded in the life and theology of the church. Its uses are frequent and varied in understandings of politics, nature and individual life stories. Parallels can be discerned in other faiths. In this volume, David Fergusson traces the development of providential ideas at successive periods in church history. These include the early appropriation of Stoic and Platonic ideas, the codification of providence in the Middle Ages, its foregrounding in Reformed theology and its secular applications in the modern era. Responses to the Lisbon earthquake (1755) provide an instructive case study. Although confidence in divine providence was shaken after 1914, several models were advanced during the twentieth century. Drawing upon this diversity of approaches, Fergusson offers a chastened but constructive account for the contemporary church. Arguing for a polyphonic approach, he aims to distribute providence across all three articles of the faith.

DAVID FERGUSSON is Professor of Divinity at the University of Edinburgh. He is the author and editor of more than fifteen books, including *Faith and Its Critics*, based on the Gifford Lectures delivered at the University of Glasgow. A Fellow of the British Academy and a Fellow of the Royal Society of Edinburgh, he is co-editor (with Mark Elliott) of a three-volume *History of Scottish Theology* (forthcoming).

CURRENT ISSUES IN THEOLOGY

General Editor:

Iain Torrance
Pro-Chancellor of the University of Aberdeen

Editorial Advisory Board:

David Ford   *University of Cambridge*
Bryan Spinks   *Yale University*
Kathryn Tanner   *Yale Divinity School*

There is a need among upper-undergraduate and graduate students of theology, as well as among Christian teachers and church professionals, for a series of short, focussed studies of particular key topics in theology written by prominent theologians. *Current Issues in Theology* meets this need.

The books in the series are designed to provide a 'state-of-the-art' statement on the topic in question, engaging with contemporary thinking as well as providing original insights. The aim is to publish books which stand between the static monograph genre and the more immediate statement of a journal article, by authors who are questioning existing paradigms or rethinking perspectives.

Other titles in the series:

Holy Scripture   John Webster
The Just War Revisited   Oliver O'Donovan
Bodies and Souls, or Spirited Bodies?   Nancey Murphy
Christ and Horrors   Marilyn McCord Adams
Divinity and Humanity   Oliver D. Crisp
The Eucharist and Ecumenism   George Hunsinger
Christ the Key   Kathryn Tanner
Theology without Metaphysics   Kevin W. Hector
Reconsidering John Calvin   Randall C. Zachman
God's Presence   Frances Young
An Incarnation Model of the Eucharist   James M. Arcadi

DAVID FERGUSSON
University of Edinburgh

The Providence of God

A Polyphonic Approach

CAMBRIDGE
UNIVERSITY PRESS

CAMBRIDGE
UNIVERSITY PRESS

University Printing House, Cambridge CB2 8BS, United Kingdom

One Liberty Plaza, 20th Floor, New York, NY 10006, USA

477 Williamstown Road, Port Melbourne, VIC 3207, Australia

314-321, 3rd Floor, Plot 3, Splendor Forum, Jasola District Centre, New Delhi - 110025, India

79 Anson Road, #06-04/06, Singapore 079906

Cambridge University Press is part of the University of Cambridge.

It furthers the University's mission by disseminating knowledge in the pursuit of education, learning and research at the highest international levels of excellence.

www.cambridge.org
Information on this title: www.cambridge.org/9781108466578
DOI: 10.1017/9781108683050

© Cambridge University Press 2018

First published 2018
First paperback edition 2019

A catalogue record for this publication is available from the British Library

Library of Congress Cataloging in Publication data
Names: Fergusson, David, author.
Title: Th e Providence of God : A Polyphonic Approach /
David Fergusson, University of Edinburgh.
Description: New York: Cambridge University Press, 2018. |
Series: Current issues in theology | Includes bibliographical references and index.
Identifiers: LCCN 2018015094 | ISBN 9781108475006 (hardback)
Subjects: LCSH: Providence and government of God –
Christianity – History of doctrines.
Classification: LCC BT 135.F38 2018 | DDC 231/.509–dc23
LC record available at https://lccn.loc.gov/2018015094

ISBN 978-1-108-47500-6 Hardback
ISBN 978-1-108-46657-8 Paperback

To Margot

Contents

Acknowledgements

This study of providence has been some years in gestation, and I am glad to record my gratitude to many people and institutions for their input. The project began as the Warfield Lectures (2009) at Princeton Theological Seminary, and reappeared in modified form in the Birks Lectures (2013) at McGill University and the Ferguson Lecture (2014) at the University of Manchester. Its completion was made possible by a period of research leave funded by the UK Arts and Humanities Research Council which I spent happily as a visiting fellow at Princeton Theological Seminary in 2016–17.

I am indebted to many friends and colleagues for invitations, hospitality and conversations, particularly in Princeton, Montreal and Manchester. The list is long, and without their input this work would be greatly impoverished and more deeply flawed than it is. In no particular order, I am glad to express my appreciation to Jay Brown, Iain Torrance, Alex Chow, Will Storrar, Jolyon Mitchell, Makoto Fukimura, Simon Burton, Naomi Appleton, Mona Siddiqui, Craig Barnes, Cynthia Rigby, Grant Macaskill, Bob MacLennan, Tom Oord, Andreas Losch, Mark Elliott, Fred Simmons, Doug Ottati, Gerald McKenny, John Bowlin, Robin Lovin, Joshua Mauldin, Jessie van Couenhoven, Shane Berg, Jane Dawson, Ryan Mullins, Mark Harris, William Johnstone, Lydia Schumacher, Alastair McIntosh, David Searle, George Hunsinger, Kate Timoney, Eric Gregory, Gordon Graham, Bruce McCormack, Kathryn Tanner, Gordon Mikoski, Naoki Yajima, Paul Munday, Malan Nel, Robert Adams, Dan Migliore, Ed Turner, Michael Solomon, Ellen Aitken, Douglas Farrow, Susan Hardman Moore, Peter Scott, David Law, Hugh Goddard and George Brooke. My thanks also to Cory Brock for his support in compiling the bibliography and indexes and Makoto Fujimura for generously permitting use of his painting 'Luke – Prodigal God' on the cover design – I was privileged to visit his studio outside Princeton. Last, but not least, I am indebted to two anonymous referees commissioned by Cambridge University Press, whose constructive and critical remarks offered further encouragement.

In some of what follows, I have drawn upon a succession of earlier publications on the theology of providence.

Creation (Grand Rapids: Eerdmans, 2014).

'Providence' in Paul Dafydd Jones and Paul T. Nimmo (eds.), *Oxford Handbook of Karl Barth* (Oxford: Oxford University Press, in press).

'Providence and its secular displacements' in George Pattison, Graham Ward and Nick Adams (eds.), *Oxford Handbook of Theology and Modern European Thought* (Oxford: Oxford University Press, 2013), pp. 655–74.

'Natural theology after Darwin' in Andrew Robinson (ed.), *Darwinism and Natural Theology: Evolving Perspectives* (Newcastle: Cambridge Scholars Publishing, 2012), pp. 78–95.

'The reformed doctrine of providence: from Calvin to Barth' in Theo Boer, Heleen Maat, Alco Meesters and Jan Muis (eds.), *Van God gesproken: over religieuze taal en relationele theologie* (Zoetermeer: Uitgeverij Boekencentrum, 2011), pp. 233–45.

'Theology of providence', *Theology Today*, 67 (2010), 261–78.

'Providence after Darwin' in Michael Northcott and R. J. Berry (eds.), *Theology After Darwin* (Milton Keynes: Paternoster: 2009), pp. 73–88.

'Epilogue' in Francesca Murphy and Philip Ziegler (eds.), *The Providence of God* (London: T&T Clark, 2009), pp. 326–33.

'Divine providence and action' in Michael Welker and Miroslav Volf (eds.), *God's Life in Trinity* (Minneapolis: Fortress Press, 2006), pp. 153–65.

The book is dedicated to Margot, who has accompanied me along the way with her generous and unfailing support.

Introduction

I realize I have always believed there is a great Providence that, so to speak, waits ahead of us.[1]

In the history of the church, the concept of divine providence has been widely deployed. Its scope includes the order of nature, the direction of history, the ways in which the lives of persons are subject to divine guidance, the problems of evil and suffering, the language of politics, the constructions that we place upon our individual life stories, and the final outcomes of nature and history. A capacious theme, God's providence is illustrated by the stories of Scripture and has been theorised by theologians throughout the history of the church.

The term 'providence' refers literally to divine foresight and provision but its historic meanings are broader – these encompass purpose, direction, rule and vocation. Within Christian theology, providence is the sequel to creation. After creating the world, God preserves and directs it to fulfil God's purposes. This has been read maximally, particularly in the Latin west. Everything that happens is willed by God and serves some end – nothing lies outside the scope of divine volition and intentionality. This generates several virtues – confidence, patience, gratitude and expectation. Although providentialism is closely associated with Reformed thought and piety, it is powerfully expressed in medieval theology. Despite some popular misconceptions, the doctrine of providence is not a Calvinist franchise.

[1] Marilynne Robinson, *Lila* (London: Virago, 2014), p. 76.

The term 'providence' hardly features at all in the Bible. Borrowed from Platonic and Stoic philosophy, it was inflected by Christian thinkers. Parallels can be found in other philosophies and religions, though languages such as Chinese and Japanese have no readily available equivalent term. Judaism has a more flexible account of providence and Islam a stronger reading, though these are generalisations which conceal disputes and variations surrounding the compatibility of divine determinism and human freedom. Indeed, the range of positions in the other Abrahamic faiths seems as diverse as those within Christianity.[2] In Indian traditions, there is a corresponding sense of a *karma* governing the universe. The way the world works ensures that in the long run we reap what we sow – we get what we deserve. Our *karma* determines previous and future lives, unless one finds release. This may explain physical appearance, social station and span of life. In attempting to affirm human responsibility together with cosmic order, Buddhist and Jainist teachers inveighed against forms of fatalism and materialism which disrupted the necessary equilibrium.[3] Within Daoism, a similar acknowledgement of cosmic balance can readily be discerned. This moral and spiritual order resembles some aspects of the providentialism of Christian thought, particularly as reflected in the wisdom literature. For later theorists, it raised the question of whether these ideas are embedded in the human psyche. Freud famously postulated a universal projection arising from primordial fear.

> And so a rich store of ideas is formed, born of the need to make tolerable the helplessness of man, and built out of the material offered by memories of the helplessness of his own childhood and

---

[2] See the essays in Karl W. Giberson (ed.), *Abraham's Dice: Chance and Providence in the Monotheistic Traditions* (New York: Oxford University Press, 2016), and also David Burrell, *Freedom and Creation in Three Traditions* (Notre Dame, IN: University of Notre Dame Press, 1993), pp. 75–83 and 115–28.

[3] See for example Naomi Appleton, *Narrating Karma and Rebirth: Buddhist and Jain Multi-Life Stories* (Cambridge: Cambridge University Press, 2014), p. 7.

the childhood of the human race ... Over each one of us watches a benevolent, and only apparently severe, Providence, which will not suffer us to become the plaything of the stark and pitiless forces of nature.[4]

Ideas of divine providence can be discerned in different ecclesial contexts and appropriated to a variety of purposes. The myriad details of personal life were to be decoded to detect God's hand. This is particularly evident in the diaries of pilgrims who travelled to the new world. Empires were viewed as providentially ordained to transmit the benefits of religion, education, trade and culture from the west to other parts of the world. This was almost an intuitive assumption of imperial rhetoric, particularly in the nineteenth century. On the one hand, the laws of nature and of economics were regarded as providentially ordered – these were to be respected and allowed to work their natural course for our benefit. On the other hand, exceptional events, particularly catastrophes, could also be seen as providentially directed for the sake of punishment, repentance and correction. As we shall see, the Lisbon earthquake of 1755 proved a hinge event in shifting European reactions to divine providence.

Many of us probably live according to some theology of providence, at least an inchoate or implicit one.[5] Indeed, we may have several theologies of providence inside our heads, our particular moods and circumstances determining which of these is dominant at any one time. Pastoral work repeatedly exposes diverse convictions and confusions about divine providence, some of these profound and moving, others verging on the superstitious, others – perhaps the majority – an admixture of these. I was once asked to bless the new home of a young couple who

---

[4] Sigmund Freud, *The Future of an Illusion* (London: Hogarth Press, 1928), p. 32.

[5] Vernon White explores the ways in which notions of providence continue to surface in contemporary 'secular' literature. See *Purpose and Providence: Taking Soundings in Western Thought, Literature and Theology* (London: T&T Clark, 2015), pp. 39–70.

were experiencing fertility problems. Although it was obvious that some transaction was intended, this was never admitted or explored. Perhaps that represented a failure on my part. A spurious deal was being done with God, a bargain in which a modicum of sacrifice would elicit the outcome of an appropriate reward. This manipulation of the supernatural by some natural means at our disposal is close to one standard description of magic. The people of the church may hold a host of assumptions and beliefs that do not reflect those of any mainstream or recognisable theological position; this is an uncomfortable thought for those who are theologians or pastors. Perhaps this has generally been the case – and study of popular religion may increasingly confirm this. Within the domain of providentialism, we are confronted by a range of half-formed assumptions and hopes that are difficult to justify on any serious theological reckoning. At the same time, we need to recognize that church teaching has often reinforced some bad ideas about providence. This has led to a surfeit of guilt, anxiety and anger which might have been alleviated by a more honest account of the matter. The faithful who have 'defected in place' may have been more discerning than their teachers.[6]

Many of us need some notion of providence by which to lead our lives, both in good times and in bad, though others seem to eschew any notion of a unifying narrative pattern.[7] But we are also conscious of the formidable difficulties that surround the standard

---

[6] Charles Wood, *The Question of Providence* (Louisville: Westminster John Knox Press, 2008), p. 65.

[7] Galen Strawson contrasts 'narrativists' and 'non-narrativists', arguing in favour of the latter, though also citing some moving examples in support of the former. His claim is that our history as selves has neither unity nor the sequential coherence that could intelligibly be rendered in the form of a single story. 'I concede it. Consideration of the sequence – the "narrative", if you like – may be important for some people in some cases. For most of us, however, I think self-knowledge comes best in bits and pieces.' *The Subject of Experience* (Oxford: Oxford University Press, 2017), p. 135.

accounts that have been given. This is captured by some remarks of David Martin in surveying religion in England in the late 1960s.

> [V]ast numbers of people work on the assumption of two basic principles: one is the rule of fate or chance, conceived as rooted in a kind of symmetry (such as disasters occur in threes), and the other is a 'moral balance', rooted in a universal homeostasis whereby wicked deeds eventually catch up on those who perpetuate them.[8]

Research undertaken on the religion of soldiers during wartime reveals a deeply ingrained sense of providence, even when most other vestiges of faith have disappeared. This is hard to distinguish from fatalism, a persistent feature of army life, and perhaps one that is even more apparent in modern times on account of the range and indiscriminate fire power of artillery. Writing from the front during the First World War, a Scottish army chaplain stated of the infantry battalions:

> Almost every solider in the lines has become an Ultra-Calvinist – if not a man of faith, at least a man of fatalism. He believes that he will die only 'when his number's up' and that this bullet has his name on it. I have had more talks on Predestination and on God's ordering of lives with soldiers than with Christian people during all my ministry.[9]

Michael Snape describes the attention that was devoted in wartime to dreams, premonitions and lucky charms.[10] Fortune-tellers flourished and were regularly consulted by troops preparing to leave for the front. Alarmed at these trends, the churches inveighed against all forms of fatalism, seeing these as displacing a proper trust in a personal God. This antithesis of belief in divine providence with abandonment to fate may also have contributed to the traditional Protestant hostility to

---

[8] David Martin, *A Sociology of English Religion* (London: Heinemann, 1967), p. 76.

[9] Quoted by Michael Snape, *God and the British Soldier: Religion and the British Army in the First and Second World Wars* (London: Routledge, 2005), p. 28.

[10] Ibid.

gambling, even to the extent of proscribing raffles and games of chance at fund-raising events (guessing the weight of the cake or the number of sweets in the jar).[11] While such attitudes are easy to lampoon, they reflect a laudable concern to protect people from addiction and exploitation in ways that remain all too evident.

What we see here may represent only a very visible manifestation of deep-seated trends in human nature. The terms 'magic' and 'superstition' are not easy to define and have often been used to create a binary opposition either with proper, mainstream religion or with reliable, scientifically informed belief. But we need to consider that historically one person's superstition may have been another person's faith. Attempts by powerful elites to suppress popular practice and belief by castigating these as superstitious may never have been entirely successful. The Latin term and its Greek counterpart were used to denounce practices and beliefs adjudged unfounded, disruptive or even dangerous. So Pliny the younger could complain in his letter to the emperor Trajan of the immoderate superstition of Christians. The body politic should be protected from this contagion as it was leading to a neglect of temples, festivals and the purchase of sacrifice animals. Yet, as Dale Martin notes, by the time of Eusebius in the fourth century, the tables were turned when Hellenic religion and philosophy were denounced by Christian writers as superstitious.[12]

---

[11] 'In the Divine Providence and through the limitations of human knowledge, life brings us uncertainty, risk, hazard, and adventure: these are to be cheerfully and courageously accepted, not for gain or personal advantage, but for the ends of the Kingdom of God and in reliance on the Divine Providence. The Christian motive must determine all our life and service, including economic effort and the acquisition and use of money. Gambling is contrary to an acceptance of the Divine will and providence. Belief in luck cannot be reconciled with faith in God.' *Minutes of the Annual Conference of the Methodist Church* (London: Methodist Publishing House, 1936), p. 390.

[12] Dale B. Martin, *Inventing Superstition: From the Hippocratics to the Christians* (Cambridge, MA: Harvard University Press, 2004), pp. 206–25.

Another popular pastoral assumption is that everything is ordained by the will of God. This has some warrant both within Scripture and *a fortiori* within the traditions of western theology after Augustine. We can find some heavyweight authorities to cite in support of this view – Aquinas and Calvin, to name but two – yet it is one that requires careful handling. In dealing with sin, suffering and evil, exponents of this view have generally attempted to distinguish between the active and the permissive will of God. Even within Reformed orthodoxy with its strong determinism and insistence upon the sovereignty of the divine will, there is a belated leaning in this direction. But whether this tradition is in good order is seriously doubted by significant bodies of opinion today. Does the biblical narrative of salvation history make much sense unless we assume that the world is not the way God wants it to be? We are enjoined not to meek acceptance but to complaint and protest. A useful doctrine should mobilise us rather than demand our resignation to injustice. Our prayers and actions are enlisted in the cause of transformation, as opposed to the recognition that everything is as it is meant to be. Can we face our suffering (and that of others) with the gloss that it comes from the hand of God and is foreordained? Alternatively, can we discern our good fortune as the outcome of divine blessing, if this entails viewing someone else's misfortune as the absence of such blessing or (still worse) the result of a divine curse? Or if we deny this and allow aspects of nature and history to run apart from God's rule, do we then postulate a form of dualism in which there are powers, forces and agencies at work in the cosmos outside the sovereignty of God? I shall argue that one of the tasks of a chastened doctrine of providence is to offer a more circumscribed description of what constitutes the will of God.

The rhetoric of divine providence has often found its way into political discourse, whether pagan, Christian or secular. It is not hard to see why. If the citizens of a republic or the subjects of a realm are asked to subordinate their own private and domestic interests to that of a wider social cause, then they be must be motivated accordingly. This will require a good story, powerful symbols and a set of concepts that create a vision of a cause and ends that are worthy of our allegiance. Alasdair MacIntyre has shown how this generates a problem for modern liberal democracies that seek to establish the rationale for the state on purely procedural grounds. The state as a guarantor of individual freedoms and the arbiter of disputes about equality and justice may manage to persuade us in good times of the reasonableness of paying our taxes. But to demand of us – or our children – that we lay down our lives in hard times, the state will have to furnish us with a better story. Otherwise, as MacIntyre says, it is as if we are asked to fight to the death for our telephone company.[13] In exploring the ways in which this problem has been faced, we should note how much of the post-Christian politics of the twentieth century has continued to retain the discourse of divine providence by harnessing this for ideologies, some of which have had sinister outcomes.

A further challenge to the doctrine of providence came in the form of Darwinism. Indeed, soon after the publication of *The Origin of Species* in 1859, some critics, notably T. H. Huxley, claimed that natural explanation had now supplanted divine providence. God was no longer needed to explain the creation of complex organs such as the human eye or the ways in which forms of life were so beautifully adapted to the environment in which they flourished. The old worldview of William Paley, which saw divine providence everywhere active in nature, now lay in ruins. Or so it was argued. Instead of God's wise ordering of means to ends throughout nature, we have an algorithmic formula which can explain, given enough time and space, how the world has come to be as it is. Whether this indeed displaces providence altogether or simply leads to its restatement and relocation is a question for consideration.

---

[13] Alasdair MacIntyre, 'A partial response to my critics' in John Horton and Susan Mendus (eds.), *After MacIntyre* (Notre Dame, IN: University of Notre Dame Press, 1994), pp. 283–304 at p. 303.

Tackling the theology of providence can also be a frustrating and elusive exercise for other reasons. It is difficult to identify many classical loci on the subject that command the field and provide an obvious point of reference. What are the best works on providence? Almost all the leading theologians of the church tackled this subject – Schleiermacher, who regarded it as a pagan import, is one possible exception – but none of them is renowned for a treatise on providence. One can find important accounts in Aquinas and Barth, but these do not stand out as the obvious high points of the *Summa Theologiae* or the *Church Dogmatics*. A sifting of Augustine provides influential materials but this is hard work and does not lend itself to the teaching of providence from an accessible source. Some theologians – Theodoret of Cyrus and Zwingli – wrote individual treatises but these were largely defensive and did not set out lines of enquiry that others developed to any significant extent.

A further frustration surrounds many of the standard textbook treatments of the subject. These often begin by spelling out what providence is not – it is neither fate, nor fortune, nor determinism, nor caprice. But then when we come to the substantive material, the theology of providence begins quite quickly to lean in the direction of those proscribed notions, doubtless as the result of real pressure to avoid other unwanted associations.

Despite its scope and existential significance, the subject of providence is less widely treated than other doctrinal loci. There may be accidental reasons for this. After all, some doctrines are more fashionable than others at different times. Who would have guessed fifty years ago that so much would have been written about the doctrines of the Trinity or the Eucharist? But one reason why providence has suffered some neglect may be its standard textbook location as a subdivision of the doctrine of creation. Through reduction to an account of how God continues to preserve and shape the world after its initial creation from out of nothing, providence has been downsized to a minor element in Christian theology. This sub-theme has been stressed, partly to avoid a deist construction of the relationship between God and the world and partly to articulate scriptural claims about God's wise oversight of creation and provision for its creatures. The difficulty here is that providence is too narrowly presented in terms of the general outlay of the natural world. Other themes relating to redemption, sanctification and eschatological consummation are squeezed by location within the first article of the faith. To put it another way, the work of providence tends historically to have been appropriated to the first person of the Trinity, with too little attention given to the enhancement of providence by the work of the Son and the Spirit, whom Irenaeus described as the two hands of God in the economy of creation and salvation. These two hands have not featured sufficiently in standard accounts with their exclusive focus on the sovereign will and rule of God as Father.

Not all theology has treated providence in the context of the doctrine of creation. In much medieval theology (including Aquinas), it is located within the doctrine of God, rather like a divine attribute, or a deduction from other essential properties. Yet this also has a constricting effect, by a relative absence of reference to the work of the Son and the Spirit. Here providence is something that God must necessarily have by virtue of the divine being. It is placed alongside or even prior to the divine decree that precedes creation – Zwingli seems to have assumed this in his treatise on providence, as did some of the later rationalists such as Samuel Clarke in his 1704 Boyle Lectures. Here maximal providence is a function of divine omnipotence.[14] God must have foresight, control and a will that disposes every actual outcome across the whole creation. Without

---

[14] 'And when and whilst things are in being, the same moral perfection makes it necessary that they should be disposed and governed according to the most exact and most unchangeable laws of eternal justice, goodness, and truth because while things and their several relations are, they cannot but be what they are.' Samuel Clarke, *A Demonstration of the Being and Attributes of God and Other Writings* (Cambridge: Cambridge University Press, 1998), p. 88. See also the discussion in Heinrich Heppe's *Reformed Dogmatics*, trans. G. T. Thomson

providence of this totalising variety, God could not be God. Yet, despite its impressive antecedents, this location of the concept of providence is deeply problematic. It pre-empts the doctrine almost by virtue of a transcendental argument that demonstrates the necessary conditions for God's government of any created world. As an *a priori* account, this secures the right outcomes but largely on philosophical grounds, without reference to Scripture, empirical observation or the Christian life. Although confirmation is doubtless sought from these, the die is already cast. God could not be God without a maximal providence conceived in terms of rule and control at every micro- and macroscopic level. Much of this thinking can be discerned already in classical philosophy.

A case can be made for the revisiting of providence under each article so that it is spread across the exposition of the faith as a recurrent theme requiring a multi-dimensional exposition. One benefit of this may be that divine action is not thus restricted to any one single model or type. God's agency may be viewed as pluriform and differentiated, so that no one form of engagement with creation is privileged to the detriment of others. A further benefit may be a more nuanced story of providence which can construe the action of God as variously determining, interacting, permitting and improvising. With its plurality of providential forms, such an account may lose some systematic coherence. But it may be better positioned to accommodate the diversity of scriptural materials that are reflected in the liturgical life of the church.

This project is one of criticism and recovery. I seek to explore the origins, problems and abuses of providentialism, particularly in the west, while also attempting reconstruction to rescue it from earlier distortions and wrong turnings. This involves some retrieval of classical elements and an adaptation of several twentieth-century models. To that extent, much of the reconstruction involves a

(London: Allen & Unwin, 1950), pp. 251–80, for the ways in which the Reformed orthodox also incorporated this view.

borrowing and reshaping of materials that lie to hand. The argument of Chapters 1 to 5 is rehearsed largely through an engagement with historical forms of providentialism. Despite the inevitable risks of excessive breadth, this contextualisation of the subject is important for the sake of an informed appraisal of its political and pastoral outcomes. Here, as elsewhere, the work of systematic theology requires closer interaction with the study of lived religion.

Readers who wish to review the main conclusions of the study will find these at the outset of Chapter 6.

1 | Sources of Providentialism

The Christianizing of providence came at a cost; its reconciling power would henceforth carry the moral ambiguities of an omnipotent divine will answerable for its purposes.[1]

1.1 Hinterland of Ancient Philosophy

To set the scriptural account of providence in context, some initial comparison with the thought of the ancient world is required.[2] The term 'providence' itself (*providentia* in Latin, *pronoia* in Greek) is imported from the philosophy of Plato and the Stoics, where its development can already be discerned. While the Epicureans denied providence and Aristotle restricted it to the heavenly regions, both Plato and the Stoics viewed it more comprehensively and favourably. As we shall see, the adaptation of providence in the early church largely represents a modified form of its expressions in Platonism and Stoicism. In addition, many of the philosophical arguments relating to human freedom and the presence of evil in the world would reappear in subsequent Christian theology.[3]

---

[1] Genevieve Lloyd, *Providence Lost* (Cambridge, MA: Harvard University Press, 2008), p. 149.

[2] For a valuable overview of providence in ancient philosophy, see Myrto Dragona-Monachou, 'Divine providence in the philosophy of the empire', *Aufsteig und Niedergang der Römischen Welt, Teil II*, 36.7 (1994), 4417–90.

[3] These include evil as necessary, pedagogical, retributive, instrumental, incidental by-product, or the result of voluntary agencies. See A. A. Long and D. N. Sedley, *The Hellenistic Philosophers*, vol. I (Cambridge: Cambridge University Press, 1987), p. 332.

For Plato, there is a natural order to the world which is attributed to the gods. This is a theme of the *Timaeus* with its account of cosmic order, though even here there is a sense in which the gods themselves are acting in accordance with some deeper natural necessity by which they are bound. Despite an imprecision in its account of the relations between reason, the world soul and the demiurge, the theology of Plato's later *Dialogues*, especially the *Laws*, moves towards affirming a divine providence that governs the cosmos and human beings. This is rational, spiritual and godlike.[4] Much of the discussion in Book x of the *Laws* argues that the gods must care not only for the general order of the world but also for the affairs of human beings. A wise ruler will attend to the details and order these according to the principles of justice for the good of the whole. This requires attention to all the parts.

> Let us not, then, deem God inferior to human workmen, who, in proportion to their skill, finish and perfect their works, small as well as great, by one and the same art; or that God, the wisest of beings, who is both willing and able to take care, is like a lazy good-for-nothing, or a coward, who turns his back upon labour and gives no thought to smaller and easier matters, but to the greater only.[5]

Given the proximity of this idea to the teaching of Jesus on the Sermon on the Mount, it is not hard to see why the theologians of the early church often perceived the Platonists as their allies in this and other matters. 'There are none who come nearer to us than the Platonists.'[6]

---

[4] See Robert Mayhew, 'The theology of the *Laws*' in Christopher Bobonich (ed.), *Plato's 'Laws': A Critical Guide* (Cambridge: Cambridge University Press, 2010), pp. 197–216.

[5] Plato, *Laws*, 10.902e–903a. Citation from Edith Hamilton and Huntington Cairns (eds.), *Collected Dialogues of Plato, Vol. IV* (Princeton: Princeton University Press, 1961), p. 474.

[6] Augustine, *City of God*, 8.5, cited from the translation by Henry Bettenson (Harmondsworth: Penguin, 1972), p. 304.

For the Stoics, whose theology is generally pantheistic, materialist and impersonal, this is extended to a single cosmic organisation by which all things are ruled. Although there are differences among the Stoics as to the degree of determinism entailed by this vision, it is agreed that human life is best lived by submission and acceptance of these cosmic laws, which are evident from a contemplation of the universe and the destiny of human beings. God, nature and fate are closely aligned by the Stoic philosophers; these can be identified as constituting a single force by which all events are determined. This position is evident in the extant writings and comments on Stoic thinkers from Cleanthes and Chrysippus onwards. While some outcomes are co-fated by our will, even these seem to be predetermined. This is argued on the basis of three types of claim: a metaphysics of sufficient reason; a logical commitment to causal pre-determinism as the only alternative to the positing of uncaused events; and the empirical observation of both organic unity in the world and the seeming success of divination.[7]

In Plato, the cosmos is likened to a single organism, whose movements, interacting elements and actions are ordered according to an idealised plan. Hence seemingly discordant elements can, from a more distant perspective, be viewed as belonging to a harmonious pattern. Against Epicurean notions of chance and randomness, the Stoics developed this Platonic account of providence by deploying an organic metaphor. The gods are unified and identified with a world soul or reason (*logos*) that is the animating and controlling principle of the cosmos.[8] As rational and ensouled, the cosmos is ordered by laws which govern its functions. The virtuous person, a microcosm of the whole, is the one who will accept and adopt the order of nature in their being. While Stoic thinkers could differ on

---

[7] This is argued in A. A. Long and D. N. Sedley, *The Hellenistic Philosophers*, vol. I, p. 343.

[8] See for example Christopher Stead, *Philosophy in Christian Antiquity* (Cambridge: Cambridge University Press, 1994), pp. 46–7.

how freedom is to be constructed on this model, they tended to view the happy life as one which recognises and internalises the cosmic order. Identified with an impersonal fate, the harmony and purpose of the world impose on us so that our only significant choice is to align ourselves with it.

Some Stoic philosophers, such as Chrysippus, offer softer forms of determinism in which individual choices are influenced but not wholly fixed by antecedent conditions. Stoicism clearly faced some major challenges in this area arising from the dominance of its organic model.[9] Yet Stoic choice should not be regarded as passive submission to an external force – we might better construe it as a patient acceptance of one's nature and one's place in the wider scheme of things. The Stoic cosmopolitan ideal situates the human person in the earthly city, as one committed to its common good. To identify oneself with one's natural fate is to go with the flow of the world; in this respect, Stoic ethics can be liberating and emotionally fulfilling. 'The acceptance of necessity lends a grace and smoothness of movement that is lacking in the rough actions of the wise.'[10]

In his *Didaskalikos*, Alcinous provides a benchmark for the Middle Platonist position. Writing in the second century CE, he offers a standard account of providence which is set apart from Stoic philosophy in ways that can also be detected among Christian thinkers in the east. Fate is only a general law that operates conditionally. The natural consequences of particular decisions are determined, but the content of the decision is down to human freedom rather than fate. So Alcinous can hold that, while everything is bounded by fate, not everything is fated. 'Fate consists rather in the fact that if a soul chooses a given type of life and performs such-and-such actions such-and-such consequences will follow for

---

[9] See David Furley, 'Cosmology' in Leimpe Algra, Jonathan Barnes, Jaap Mansfeld and Malcolm Schofield (eds.), *Cambridge History of Hellenistic Philosophy* (Cambridge: Cambridge University Press, 1999), pp. 412–51.

[10] Genevieve Lloyd, *Providence Lost* (Cambridge, MA: Harvard University Press, 2008), p. 96.

it.'[11] This hypothetical character of fate is an aspect of providence that is prevalent in Middle Platonism. Alcinous elucidates it further by adapting an Aristotelian distinction between the 'possible' and the 'potential'. The possible is undetermined by nature since it requires the operation of the free will to become determinate. By contrast, the potential describes a capacity that will eventually be realised, as a boy will become a flautist or a scholar or a carpenter.[12]

A blending of Plato's account of providence with Judaism appears in Philo's *De Providentia*, a first-century work that adumbrates much Christian reflection on this topic. Surviving in Armenian and the Greek fragments of Eusebius, the treatise attests a divine providence that disposes of the world in such a way that the righteous are rewarded and the wicked punished. In this sense, their actions are ruled by God's providence, though not caused by it, with respect to their free decisions to comply with or to resist God's law. Philo's sense of providence pervades his entire theology on account of its links with the concepts of God and creation. Here Platonic themes are allied to Jewish theological convictions. The power and wisdom of God entail providential oversight, just as the maintenance and direction of creation are governed by divine care. This includes the history of individuals and nations, which are overruled by the justice of God.[13]

Plotinus blends several ideas from Platonism and Stoicism in his account of providence in the third *Ennead*. While maintaining the causal significance of human freedom, he also argues that the sensible world is ordered in all its details according to rational principles. This is not the result of the intention of a divine agency, but rather a consequence of the world's participation in the reason from which it emanates. Even in the material world, far removed from the One,

---

[11] Alcinous, *Handbook of Platonism*, ed. John Dillon (Oxford: Oxford University Press, 1993), p. 35.

[12] For commentary on the use of this distinction, see Dillon in ibid., p. 164.

[13] For further discussion, see Peter Frick, *Divine Providence in Philo of Alexandria* (Tübingen: Mohr Siebeck, 1999).

there is a providential ordering which is described through a series of analogies with the healthy body, a play of contrasting characters, and a musical score with discordant notes. Evil has no independent reality apart from its contribution to an enriched whole; in itself it can only be seen as deficient in goodness.

> We are like people who know nothing about the art of painting and criticise the painter because the colours are not beautiful every-where, though he has really distributed the appropriate colours to every place; and cities are not composed of citizens with equal rights, even those which have good laws and constitutions; or we are like someone who censures a play because all the characters in it are not heroes but there is a servant and a yokel who speaks in a vulgar way; but the play is not a good one if one expels the inferior characters, because they too help to complete it.[14]

Plotinus' portrayal of divine providence has a powerful emotional and spiritual appeal. Although his influence upon subsequent Christian thinkers was sporadic, nevertheless as representative of Platonism his work points to ways in which Christian theology could be harmonised with philosophy.[15] While insisting upon the place of human freedom, he discerns a majestic harmony in the profusion of material things and in the diversity of characteristics. Even evil, suffering and base deeds are finally given their fitting place in the total scheme of the universe which reflects the reason and goodness of its source and final end.

For classical philosophy then, the concept of 'providence' increasingly plays a vital role for understanding both God and the world. In designating a spiritual and moral order, divine superintendence and a circumscribed freedom, providence became an indispensable

---

[14] Plotinus, *Ennead*, 3.2.11. Citation from A. H. Armstrong translation in Loeb Classic Library edn (London: Heinemann, 1967), pp. 79–80.

[15] See John Rist, 'Plotinus and Christian philosophy' in Lloyd P. Gerson (ed.), *Cambridge Companion to Plotinus* (Cambridge: Cambridge University Press, 2006), pp. 386–414.

theme for thinking of the cosmos and the place of human beings in relation to God. The concept was also closely implicated in discussions surrounding human responsibility, sin, evil and creaturely destiny.

1.2 Scripture

As already noted, the word 'providence' does not itself feature in the Hebrew Bible or the Greek New Testament with reference to God, although we begin to see the emergence of the term in the Septuagint, and especially in the later deutero-canonical works. The verb προνοέω and the noun πρόνοια appear nine times each in the Septuagint. For example, the Wisdom of Solomon and 3 & 4 Maccabees reflect on divine πρόνοια, in ways that anticipate the reflections of early church writers on the subject. By divine providence, a frail wooden vessel can make its ways across the seas (Wisdom 14:3), thus suggesting a wise ordering of creation.[16] Commentators discern here the influence of Platonic and Stoic terminology. At 3 Maccabees 4:21, which speaks of an invincible providence, the stress falls on a particular divine overruling of human wickedness by which the exiled Jews in Egypt are preserved. This sense of overruling is repeated at 5:30. A divine and all-wise providence is affirmed at 4 Maccabees 13:19 with respect to the affection of family ties, as is the providence by which the death of the martyrs preserves Israel (17:22). The closest approximation to the term 'providence' in the Hebrew Bible is the term *providebit* in the Latin Vulgate translation of Genesis 22:8. The Hebrew root is the verb 'to see' (*r'h*), which carries a sense of divine involvement and resolution, rather than merely viewing from afar.[17]

---

[16] The conceptual background in classical philosophy is noted by David Winston, *The Wisdom of Solomon*, Anchor Bible vol. XLIII (New York: Doubleday, 1979), p. 265.

[17] See W. Schotroff, 'R'h – to see' in Ernst Jenni and Claus Westermann (eds.), *Theological Lexicon of the Old Testament*, vol. III (Peabody, MA: Henrickson, 1990), pp. 1176–83.

Here Abraham assures Isaac that the Lord will provide (i.e. see to) a sacrifice.[18]

In the New Testament, πρόνοια appears just twice, and in connection only with human foresight (Acts 24:2; Romans 13:14). The verb, προνοέω, is also confined to human activity (Romans 12:17; 2 Corinthians 8:21; and 1 Timothy 5:8). Nevertheless, we can identify other terms which have close conceptual links with divine providence. These include the verb 'to foreknow' (προγινώσκω), of which there are five occurrences (Acts 26:5; Romans 8:20, 11:2; 1 Peter 1:20; 2 Peter 3:17), and the noun foreknowledge (πρόγνωσις), which occurs twice (Acts 2:23; 1 Peter 1:2). A further notion with providential links is οἰκονομία, denoting stewardship, administration or plan.[19] With its stress on breadth and comprehension, this is used with some theological significance at Ephesians 1:10, 3:2 and 3:9, and Colossians 1:25 to signify a single overarching plan, hidden and mysterious, that is being worked out cosmically, historically and now ecclesially.[20] Similarly, the term βουλή (counsel, purpose) also denotes a divine strategy with strong providential overtones (Acts 2:23, 4:28, 5:38, 13:36; Ephesians 1:11; Hebrews 6:17). These related themes express a divine ordering of nature and history 'in which all things hold together' (Colossians 1:17). The historical enactment of

---

[18] Within later Judaism, the scope of God's activity could be viewed as providential although specific terms for providence emerged only in medieval discussions, largely through translation of Arabic concepts. The distinction between *hanhagah* and *hashgachah* corresponds to that between general governance and individual acts of providence. See Alexander Altmann, 'Providence: in medieval Jewish philosophy' in Fred Skolnik (ed.), *Encyclopaedia Judaica*, 2nd edn (2007), vol. XVI, pp. 649–51.

[19] This range of meanings is reflected in the different English renditions of οἰκονομία. For linguistic analysis see Andrew T. Lincoln, *Ephesians: Word Bible Commentary*, vol. XLII (Dallas: Word Book, 1990), p. 32. In using the term οἰκονομία to refer to his own ministry in Colossians 1:25, Paul appears to signify his own providential locus in the spread of the gospel. See Paul Foster, *Colossians* (London: Bloomsbury T&T Clark, 2016), p. 221.

[20] Christopher R. Seitz notes the providential connotations of Colossians 1:15–20 with its extensional sense of the gospel. See *Colossians* (Grand Rapids: Brazos, 2014), p. 91.

a single divine purpose is then developed in patristic theology and in the church's *regula fidei*.

Hence, notwithstanding the infrequency of πρόνοια in Scripture, there is a profusion of materials that point us to different forms of divine provision, care and purpose.[21] These provide canonical support for the emphases of later theological traditions. Every account of providence can draw upon scriptural support, many seeking a systematic resolution of tensions within the text by allowing one model to dominate or exclude others. In what follows, I shall identify a diversity of approaches to divine providence in Scripture. These should not be forced into one single form or theory but acknowledged as a plurality of ways in which God relates to the creation. If providence is a way of capturing important aspects of divine action, then we might expect this to reflect the relational complexity of God's dealings with the world. Accordingly, we might do better to narrate the ways of providence from the outset, rather than to propose a definition that will prove constrictive in scope and distortive in outcome.

1.2.1 General Providence

At first glance, there is evident scriptural support for general providence. This appears unproblematic. The ordering of creation is celebrated as beneficial and majestic. Attesting the glory of God, the universe – considered both as a totality and in microscopic detail – is recognised as good for creatures. Not only a feature of the opening creation narratives in Genesis 1–2, this order and harmony are frequently attested in the Psalter (e.g. Psalms 8, 19, 65, 104, 148) and integrated with other elements of Israel's faith. With its promise of annual seasons and the succession of day and night, the covenant

---

[21] Mark Elliott notes that a range of Hebrew verbs might be appropriated under the concept of providence. See *The Heart of Biblical Theology: Providence Experienced* (Farnham: Ashgate, 2012), pp. 150–4.

with Noah is a sign of divine faithfulness to all creatures on the face of the earth (Genesis 8:22). So far, so good. This regularity of nature has appealed to almost forms of providentialism, including the more minimalist accounts of those on the far side of deism.

Yet two further aspects of creation theology need to be noted. The first is the way in which the order of the world is sometimes depicted as threatened and mysterious. Surd elements are already evident in the 'face of the deep' and the 'formless void' in the opening verses of Genesis. Elsewhere, God is required to contain unruly forces while humans are frequently threatened by the hazards of creation, including famine, earthquake, flood and disease. Such surd-like components are less easily accommodated in a cheerful theology of nature. Images of evil are deployed to depict the ways in which creation continues to be menaced by hostile forces (Psalm 74:12–17; Isaiah 51:9–10).[22] God struggles to overcome these. The temptation is to suppress this imagery in the interests of a monotheism predicated on the sovereignty of God (Isaiah 40:25–6). Here the serpent, Leviathan and even Satan can be domesticated through either creaturely status or membership of the heavenly court (Genesis 3:1; Job 1–2; Psalm 104:26). In the whirlwind speeches in Job, God rules over creation, even its most unfathomable reaches and dangerous animals (Job 38–42). The determination in those passages to avoid dualism generates the problem of God willing evil. The Old Testament lives with this unresolved tension. Yet the determination of God to overcome evil and thus not to abandon the project of creation is a persistent theme. This generates notions of partnership, solicitude and a constancy of being and purpose. The forces of evil

---

[22] 'Two and a half millennia of Western theology have made it easy to forget that throughout the ancient Near Eastern world, including Israel, the point of creation is not the production of matter out of nothing but the emergence of a stable community in a benevolent and sustaining order.' Jon D. Levenson, *Creation and the Persistence of Evil: The Jewish Drama of Divine Omnipotence* (San Francisco: Harper & Row, 1988), p. 12. Further comment is offered by Walter Brueggemann, *Theology of the Old Testament: Testimony, Dispute, Advocacy* (Minneapolis: Fortress, 1997), pp. 534–42.

are not dismissed by divine fiat, so much as overcome from within creation by God's redemptive activity, a theme that resonates with Paul's discourse on the foolishness of the cross. The serpent and Satan have a scope for action that requires counteraction by God. To this extent, divine providence has a reactive dimension in Scripture which should not be dissolved or explained merely as a concession to human ways of thinking.

1.2.2 *Continuous Creation by the Two Hands of God*

This leads to the second and correlative feature of Hebrew creation theology. God's work does not cease on the sixth day. This is merely the first of a sequence of diverse actions that continue in nature and history. Divine provision is not restricted to the initial endowment of nature; the action of God continues to make provision and to offer direction.[23] Here two bridge concepts became important in the development of theological expressions of the continuous creative activity of God – these are wisdom (*ḥokmah*) and spirit (*ruaḥ*). Both connect God and the world by denoting forms of divine agency that extend beyond the making of the world. Throughout Proverbs, wisdom is celebrated not only in the natural world but also in domestic and social life. As universal, pervasive and active, divine wisdom permeates the created order. While evident in nature, its reach includes ethical and political forms of life. Yet wisdom is also mysterious.[24] In Job and Ecclesiastes, there is a reaction against ideologies that too readily claim to possess wisdom or to assume a simple correlation between virtue and

---

[23] Brueggemann suggests that divine providence is most obviously captured in the Hebrew Bible by verbal constructions that suggest divine provision: 'This is no absentee ruler, but one who plans ahead, thinks ahead, works ahead, and acts ahead, so that the world of real possibility is ready and waiting in Yahweh's enormous generosity.' *Theology of the Old Testament*, p. 353.

[24] See ibid., pp. 685–9.

worldly prosperity. The race is not always to the swift, nor the battle to the strong (Ecclesiastes 9:11). The familiar pieties of Job's friends no longer have traction: 'Have windy words no limit?' (Job 16:3). Similarly, new social circumstances may sometimes require deconstruction of earlier platitudes. 'The parents have eaten sour grapes, and the children's teeth are set on edge.' Here an assumption of transgenerational punishment needs to be contested and even rejected. Such teachings are neither as timeless nor as unassailable as was formerly claimed (Ezekiel: 18:2–4; Jeremiah 31:29–30). This process of discerning wisdom is never complete but presents itself afresh to each generation.

The speeches of God at the end of Job point to a grandeur and beauty in creation. But they also teach that this is not a risk-free world or one that is devoid of suffering and misfortune. Purposes that altogether elude human understanding are suggested. There are creatures who contribute to the goodness and harmony of the world but have little relation to human concerns of utility. The animals include Leviathan and Behemoth (Job 40:15ff). Although symbols of evil forces in ancient near eastern mythology, these are fearsome creatures known by God. Presumably they belong among the animals that were named by Adam in Eden (Genesis 2:19–20). Yet Job is given a reminder that they are dangerous and that human beings can suffer from them. No sudden or easy resolution is to be expected on God's part. The world is created, ordered and constrained but without a tight control or immediate interposition by its Maker to ensure those outcomes that human beings might prefer. No answers are offered to Job. Instead God's perspective is offered. Divine wisdom requires Job to see a bigger picture, although not one that can be fully comprehended or rendered free of flaw and ambiguity.[25]

---

[25] See Norman C. Habel, 'In defense of God the sage' in Leo. Perdue and W. Clark Gilpin (eds.), *The Voice from the Whirlwind: Interpreting the Book of Job* (Nashville: Abingdon, 1992), pp. 21–38.

These wisdom themes are present also in a different context in the teaching of Jesus, particularly the oft-quoted passage in the Sermon on the Mount about unnecessary worry (Matthew 6:25–34). Here God's parental care governs the flowers of the field and the birds of the air. So, how much more, reasons Jesus, must God be concerned with human lives. Again, there is no promise of sudden relief from suffering or accident or premature death – only the assurance that the reign of God will come upon us. The Authorised Version translates the closing verse of this section rather memorably: 'Sufficient unto the day is the evil thereof' (Matthew 6:34). Put more prosaically, today's troubles will be enough to worry about for the time being. This is neither a counsel of despair or resignation nor a declaration of divine determinism. The troubles that befall us must be set in their place. We should understand them and deal with them only by reference to the commonwealth of God already breaking upon us.

One clear implication of this approach is that the relationship between God and creation is not exhausted by a single act of origination. The world continues as the arena in which the work and wisdom of God are evident. This is a place of divine concern and oversight, of knowledge, rule and attention, even if these do not take the form of micro-management and total control. Creatures are given their time and space, and allowed to be under the providence of God. Creation is both original and continuous.

More elusive, and later partially eclipsed by wisdom, the term 'spirit' is also frequently used by Old Testament writers to describe the presence and action of God in ways that include the gift of life (Psalm 104:29–30), charismatic empowerment (1 Samuel 16:13–14), the inspiration of prophets (Micah 3:8) and messianic appointment (Isaiah 11:2). The spirit of God is everywhere present (Psalm 139:7). Divine transcendence does not imply absence. Its power is life-giving, energising and directional. This notion is developed extensively in the New Testament, with its images of the dove of peace (Mark 1:10), tongues of fire (Acts 2:3–4), an advocate

(John 14:16), gifts for the upbuilding of the church (1 Corinthians 12:1) and fruits of Christian living (Galatians 5:22–3). Despite the relative neglect of the spirit in the church's theology, such profusion of scriptural reference alerts us to the multiple ways in which God is present, active and apparent in the life of the world. One of the deficits of classical theology is its tendency to appropriate providential action to the first person of the Trinity only. In subsequent chapters, I shall argue for a better distribution across all three articles of the faith.

This survey of scriptural materials already suggests a multiplicity of forms of divine action in making the world, pervading its life, and acting in the course of history. The division between a general and a special providence is thus blurred. Although the distinction has some residual uses, we should not divide these too rigidly, as if the providence of God were limited to two discrete forms. This is neither a hard and fast division, nor is divine action reducible to only two types. Providence has original, universal and pervasive forms, as well as particular manifestations which themselves reflect some diversity. In relation to history, this raises further questions about the mode of divine activity, particularly with respect to human autonomy.

Among the books of the Bible, the Psalter offers the richest reflections on providence. Here divine actions are invoked, attested and celebrated both individually and collectively. In praising and celebrating these, the Psalmists convey their providential benefits. Amid the diversity of forms, a consistency in God's ways is discovered and trusted. These comprehend the establishment of creation, the abundance of nature, the presence of wisdom throughout the world, the preservation of humans and animals, the positive functions of law, the blessings of political justice, the punishment of evil, and the protection and guidance of individual people. At the same time, God's praise is sung within a world that is experienced as dangerous, frustrating and conflicted. Enemies are seldom far away, and often there is a descent into vituperative rhetoric. In reading Psalm 36, to take one example, we find these strands woven together in ways that resist any simple systematisation.

1.2.3 Divine Sovereignty and improvisation

In much of the way that the history of Israel is read, there is support for a strong divine determinism and overruling of human affairs. What appear on one reading to be contingent and fluctuating military outcomes, can be regarded on another as the outworking of divine wrath, judgement and mercy. In some places, this might resemble a utilising of worldly affairs to a greater end, for example the adoption of Cyrus as God's anointed in Isaiah 45:1ff. This action of God does not abrogate creaturely causes so much as work through them, though divine sovereignty is intensified in subsequent passages: 'I form light and create darkness, I make weal and create woe' (Isaiah 45:7). In other places, God's will appears to operate in ways that sustain the counterfactual conditional; that is, if God had not willed these outcomes, then the creaturely causes would not have obtained. This is not merely an adapting of materials that lie to hand but rather a determining of specific outcomes.

Many passages do not flinch from this strong determinist line, even when it generates some serious moral and theological problems. This applies especially to the Deuteronomistic history. The people of Ashdod are struck with terror, tumours and death. The primary agent is God, whose 'hand was very heavy there' (1 Samuel 5:6). Later in the narrative we learn that it is the Lord who gives Israel the victory (1 Samuel 14:23). And yet soon within the same sequence of events, the possibility of an alternative modality appears with references to a repenting and changing of mind on God's part: 'I regret that I made Saul king, for he has turned back from following me, and has not carried out my commands' (1 Samuel 15:11 – see also Genesis 6:6; Amos 7:3; Jonah 3:10). Embarrassed by such seeming anthropomorphism, commentators from Philo onwards have interpreted these texts in different ways. Calvin, for example, insisted that all references to a change of mind were merely expressions of speech intended to accommodate the capacities of a human audience – there could be no question of God's lacking foreknowledge or having to alter course on account of unexpected creaturely choices.[26] On the other side, some recent philosophers of religion have appealed to these texts as authorising a more improvised approach to divine providence which requires an abridgement of the traditional account of omniscience.[27]

Such passages provide support for a more synergist reading of biblical history. Given the conditions of creation, God must wrestle with recalcitrant material to bring about intended outcomes. For much of the time, the rule of God is deferred, though registered in sign, promise and down payment. This eschatological direction-ality is central to New Testament understandings of how God's purposes are being enacted in history. Divine providence is not perfectly instantiated everywhere. It follows a narrative shape and is temporally distributed. The creation will only fully be under the divine sway at the end of time, though this is not the outcome of a linear progression. This generates an account of providence in which the wisdom of God's continual action is maintained and revealed along a sequence of events marked by threats, setbacks and disruption. This involves reference in Paul to both past and future events. When the time was right, Christ was born (Galatians 4:4). Yet the full mystery of God's plan awaits some further mani-festation with the gathering together of Israel and the church (Romans 11:26).

These tensions in Scripture are vividly telescoped in Jeremiah 18:1–11, where we are presented with the image of the potter at his wheel. The material is at the disposal of God to be reworked in any

---

[26] John Calvin, *Institutes of the Christian Religion*, trans. Ford Lewis Battles (Philadelphia: Westminster Press, 1960), I.17.13.

[27] For example, John R. Lucas, *Freedom and Grace* (London: SPCK, 1976).

way that God judges fit. 'Can I not do with you, O house of Israel, just as this potter has done? says the Lord' (v. 6). The emphasis here is firmly on divine control and the effective will of God, though the artistic analogy may allow some scope for notions of constraint in relation to the materials at hand.[28] And yet, curiously, this image is immediately followed by a sense of the conditionality of divine action. If a nation or kingdom turns from its evil, then God's mind may be changed (v. 8). Or, vice versa, if a nation or kingdom does evil, then God may repent of the good that was originally intended. The verb *niham* generates some difficulties here for translators, yet it is clear that, whatever equivalent is used, some connotations of change, turning and adjustment attach to God's agency in response to creaturely wills. The interpretive tactic of reading the text as composite and so reflecting the different theological perspectives of two authors is hardly useful in this context, since we are left with a canonical registering of both perspectives. Either we must choose one or else we must find a way of holding both together in some creative tension.

Alongside the texts of divine repentance, others in the Hebrew Bible explicitly rule that there is no inconstancy or fickleness on God's part. These can appear in close proximity to the idea of divine repentance. 'Moreover the Glory of Israel will not recant or change his mind, for he is not a mortal, that he should change his mind' (1 Samuel 15:29). Similarly, Numbers 23:19 asserts that 'God is not a human being, that he should lie, or a mortal, that he should change his mind.' The tendency of such passages is to outlaw any suggestion that the being of God is subject to fluctuations in mood or character. There is a singularity of purpose and action on the part of Israel's God. Though this may take account of creaturely outcomes, the divine rule is consistent in all its dispensations.

[28] This is noted by R. W. L. Moberly, *Old Testament Theology: Reading the Hebrew Bible as Christian Scripture* (Grand Rapids: Baker, 2013), p. 123. In what follows, I am indebted to his reading of Jeremiah 18.

This tension between divine sovereignty and creaturely contingency is apparent in the prophetic literature. Predictions of the future reflect the priority of God's purpose and action. But there is an element of conditionality built into these, which is consistent with that divine priority. God says 'I will do x', meaning that, unless you repent, x is going to happen to you. Or 'I will do y' is a promise that can be revoked in the event of human weakness. This appears to be the logic of Jeremiah 18. 'Prophetic announcement of coming disaster can be seen to have the logic and dynamics of *warning* ... Comparably, prophetic announcements of coming good have the logic and the dynamics of *invitation*.'[29] Yet this does not reflect caprice on God's part; on the contrary, the adaptation of divine action reflects an underlying consistency of intention. Hence an element of responsiveness and mutuality marks the divine–human relationship, though this remains asymmetrical owing to God's character and prevenient action.

In general, the theological tradition, particularly in the west, has tended to side with the more determinist exegesis of such passages in Scripture. Through resonating with philosophies of providence in the ancient world, these readings became closely linked to a traditional account of the divine attributes. This tendency was no doubt reinforced by the need to exclude the obvious alternative, namely that some events happen outside the scope of God's sovereign rule. A world that was improvidently constructed seems unworthy of a God who creates, rules and disposes. Such notions are more akin to Epicurean approaches to chance and randomness, which have never sat comfortably alongside Christian theology.

My argument is that the reading of Scripture in the church's theology of providence has been generally inadequate to the diversity of biblical materials, especially the preponderance of those passages which testify to divine interaction, creaturely causality, contingency and eschatological deferral. In the life and teaching

[29] Ibid., p. 120.

of Jesus, we find abundant reference to the hiddenness of God's reign, its germination and subsequent growth in concealed ways. Providence is more like a work in progress than a project that is complete and perfect *ab initio*. This is further accentuated in the theology of the cross, which is foolishness when measured by Greek philosophical conventions. Although this is primarily an epistemological observation about our discernment of providence, there are some ontic antecedents. The world is not as it should be in every respect – far from it. And to speak of each event as willed by God is problematised by recognition of the partial, hidden and counter-intuitive ways in which the reign of God is fulfilled. A more dynamic and future-oriented account of providence is required to make sense of these features of biblical history. Divine sovereignty should take anticipatory and promissory forms, as opposed to a full and perpetual realisation. So we proceed here with an initial hermeneutical decision about how to read divine providence across the Bible. Its success or otherwise will require extensive argumentation in the chapters ahead.

Here is an initial hypothesis. Providence in Scripture narrates an account of the God–world relationship that has general, pervasive and particular features which are characterised in covenantal terms. Although asymmetrical, this relationship between God and creatures is one of co-dependence. Even while threatened by human failure and the turbulence of natural and historical forces, the world is overruled by God's good purposes, which are directed towards a future resolution. For the New Testament writers this is decisively expressed in the crucifixion and resurrection of Christ. For the church, God's providence continues in the indwelling and inspiration of the Holy Spirit. In some ways, this must generate a dissonance with the dominant accounts of providence in ancient Hellenistic philosophy. Notions of struggle and resistance have to be incorporated, together with the stronger historical, pneumatic and eschatological sense that the world needs to be redeemed and remade by the creative action of God. This seems far removed from

Plotinus' image of the entire world as ordained by a single radiating gaze. By contrast, in the scriptural witness, the Spirit of God works to express itself in the life of the world. Often faced with opposition, its manifestations are generally hidden, surprising and discerned only by 'those with eyes to see'. This contrast with the wisdom of the ancient world is most marked in the Pauline epistles. Later Christian appropriations of ancient philosophy accommodated Stoic notions of patience, fortitude and perseverance, while also insisting upon the importance of viewing divine providence in its wider cosmic setting. But, in so doing, they did not fully reflect these scriptural themes and so set the theology of providence in a default position now in need of some revision.

1.2.4 Divine Relationality

Much that is embedded in the later church doctrine of providence can be called into question on grounds of scriptural adequacy. This has become particularly apparent through recent encounter with Jewish exegesis of the Hebrew Bible. The assertion that God is in some sense dependent upon creation is in tension with much of what has traditionally been held concerning God's aseity and impassibility. Divine self-sufficiency and immutability have sometimes been taken to imply that there is no real relation between God and the world. The creation cannot act upon God to change or modify or harm God, so ontologically dissimilar are creatures and their Creator. This element of the tradition is important in pointing to ways in which the faithfulness, constancy and serenity of God are quite unlike creaturely attributes; for this reason, the Creator–creation relation is an asymmetric one of like and unlike. Nevertheless, the surface narrative of Scripture strongly suggests that these relations are marked by co-dependence and a relative though different autonomy of parties. At the very least, we should not allow this to be ignored on account of philosophical scruples.

Here I follow the recent scholarship of writers who concentrate on the relationality of God with respect to creation, a relationality that is often expressed though not exhausted by the language of covenant.[30] References scattered throughout the Hebrew Scriptures suggest that God is a relational being by virtue of the divine community that God inhabits. Later Christian theology has been nervous around these allusions, particularly since they seem to threaten an exclusive monotheism. However, we read of the divine council, the sons of God, heavenly messengers and a celestial wisdom (Genesis 1:26; Isaiah 6:8; Jeremiah 23:18–23; Proverbs 8: 22–31). Whatever their ontological status or function, it is clear that they underscore the strong scriptural sense of God existing in a communicative relationship with other conscious beings and as being properly characterised in personal and relational terms. Biblical metaphors for God are generally personal rather than impersonal, often making use of quite anthropomorphic and anthropopathic language. Fretheim classifies these metaphors as personal, ordinary, concrete, everyday and secular.[31] In other words, they typically draw upon the mundane world of social life to characterise the identity of God in relation to the world. Fretheim notes that even non-personal metaphors tend towards a relational aspect: 'I bore you on eagles' wings and brought you to myself' (Exodus 19:4). The giving of the divine name to Israel also intensifies the covenant relationship, entailing further possibilities of encounter and communication. At the same time, however, it makes God's honour vulnerable to the misuse of that name.

The Hebrew prohibition of images is not cited to protect God's ineffability or unknowability so much as to avoid misrepresenting God's relatedness. The idols 'have mouths, but do not speak; eyes, but do not see. They have ears, but do not hear; and there is no

---

[30] In what follows, I have drawn especially from Terence E. Fretheim, *God and World in the Old Testament: A Relational Theology of Creation* (Nashville: Abingdon, 2005).

[31] Ibid., pp. 17–19.

breath in their mouths' (Psalm 115:5–7). Unlike the false gods in the contest on Mount Carmel, Israel's God is one who lives and therefore can speak, hear and act. As such, this God is also the creator of the world, living in relation not only to Israel but to all the families of the earth (Genesis 12:3). The affirmation that 'God is' or 'God lives' is explicated in dynamic, personal and relational terms by the Old Testament. Here God is not approached by a philosophical *via negativa* or an abstract account of the most perfect being, so much as through a tradition of divine–human exchange.

The relationship of God to creatures is expressed, moreover, through a system in which all creatures are interrelated in a cosmic whole. God does not relate to us merely as individuals but as persons who exist in relation to one another and to the wider environment. The social and natural orders of the world are deeply connected in ways that affect God also, a point that has some urgency given our acute awareness of environmental despoliation. This is a recurrent theme in the Psalms and the prophets. 'The land mourns and all who live in it languish; together with the wild animals and the birds of the air, even the fish of the sea are perishing' (Hosea 4:1–3). One feature of this web of life is that we have a system that is neither chaotic nor deterministic. There is a rhythm that is natural to it in the regularity of the seasons, the succession of day and night, the movement of the planets and the universal patterns of life and death. The world is God's good creation. At the same time, however, there is 'no little play in the system'.[32] Within the order of the cosmos, there are events that appear random, surprising and surd. There are forces, sometimes within us, that threaten the harmony and delicate complexity of life. Although good and worthy of celebration, the world is not yet a finished project; it remains a site under construction. The closing speeches of the Book of Job explore this duality of divinely bestowed order threatened by untamed forces. This ambivalence of God's world needs to be registered by

---

[32] Ibid., p. 19.

an adequate theology of providence. It is a world created good, but not yet perfect.

If we think of an interconnected world established in a continuing relationship with its Maker and Redeemer, then we can attribute a proper place to creaturely action, initiative and power in ways that reflect the co-dependence of God without lapsing into lamented forms of synergism or Pelagianism. The divine–human relationship is asymmetric in terms of its setting, yet it is one in which God becomes reactive and in important respects dependent upon what has been made. Within this conceptual space, activities such as prayer, obedience, rebellion, forgiveness, redemption and blessing become possible. Fretheim writes,

> God works from within a committed relationship with the world and not on the world from without in total freedom. God's faithfulness to promises made always entails the limiting of divine options. Indeed, such is the nature of this divine commitment that the relationship with Israel (and, in a somewhat different way, the world) is now constitutive of the divine identity. The life of God will forever include the life of the people of God as well as the life of the world more generally.[33]

For Scripture, providence is not confined to a general setting of the terms in which life is lived, although this is part of it. There are also notions of guidance, presence, protection and blessing that determine individual actors and particular episodes in the history of peoples and individuals. The stories of the patriarchs, for example Jacob at Bethel, are marked by a strong sense of divine oversight and direction. Frequently this takes the form of promise, even if the promises are not fulfilled in quite the ways that might be expected.

---

[33] Ibid., p. 20. Levenson writes of a covenantal theonomy which gives Israel a choice and a role, but these are given in such a way that a choice against is really no choice at all. The option of refusal is a possibility that can scarcely be considered. See *Creation and the Persistence of Evil*, pp. 140–8.

The seed of Abraham is not always as successful and triumphant in subsequent history as a straight fulfilment of this promise would imply. The story of Joseph concludes with a strong sense of the wise rule of God overriding the sins of his brothers in selling him into slavery. Provision is made for the survival of Jacob's family during the years of famine. The Book of Genesis concludes on this note of provision as Joseph is reconciled with his brothers: 'Even though you intended to do harm to me, God intended it for good, in order to preserve a numerous people, as he is doing today. So have no fear; I myself will provide for you and your little ones' (Genesis 50:19–21).

This theme of special providence informs the history of Israel as it is narrated, and it continues into the New Testament in much of what is said about the history of the church in Acts. The Spirit sustains, preserves and guides the spread of the faith, even while we read elsewhere of division, factionalism and frequent failures to live the gospel. Again there is both human confusion and divine oversight, the latter supervening the former in some mysterious way. This dialectic of divine faithfulness and human shortcoming is also apparent in the Psalms. The protection of God is affirmed repeatedly (e.g. Psalm 121) yet sin has to be confessed (e.g. Psalm 51), while misfortune and suffering result in frequent complaint and lament (e.g. Psalm 42).

John Rogerson has warned against imposing nineteenth-century ideas of historical progress and unity upon Old Testament texts. For most of the Hebrew writers, there is little sense of a single world history that is unfolding according to a divine plan. The prophets have little to say about other nations except when they impinge upon Israel's history. Elsewhere, we find a series of historical episodes that become occasions for judgements or deliverance. But these do not constitute a single organised whole.[34]

---

[34] John Rogerson, 'Can a doctrine of providence be based on the Old Testament?' in Lyle Eslinger and Glen Taylor (eds.), *Ascribe to the Lord: Biblical and Other Studies in Memory of Peter C. Craigie* (Sheffield: JSOT, 1988), pp. 529–43.

1.2.5 *The Cruciform Pattern of Providence*

In interpreting God's ways in the New Testament there is much that fits this same pattern, particularly in Paul's remarks about the foolishness of the cross. The means by which God's wisdom is displayed is not through standardised norms of power, such as those depicted in Greek philosophy. Instead, the world is redeemed through the death of the Messiah, the paradigmatic image of divine weakness and dependence upon the created world. It is worth reminding ourselves that Paul speaks of this as folly to those schooled in ancient philosophy. The providential ordering of the cruciform lifestyle is unlikely therefore to be continuous with other approaches or outlooks. This folly represents a clash of epistemologies, albeit one that has frequently been sidestepped.[35] How then might we think again about divine providence? What are the implications for our understanding of God's presence and rule in the world of Jesus' taking upon himself the lament of Psalm 22 in his hour of death? At least one conclusion that we should draw from this is that the providence of God is not universally perspicuous. As we shall see, this may have been a mistake that Calvin made in occasionally treating providence as an article of natural theology. If Paul's words to the Corinthians are close to the mark, then the wisdom of God's rule is apparent only as we enter the life of faith empowered by the Spirit. It cannot be deduced from the pages of history or the observations of philosophy, as many of the great thinkers of pagan antiquity had sought to do. Providence is here represented not as a speculative vision or intellectual insight but as a practical perspective that makes sense in the light of other commitments. As such, this reverses many natural assumptions, including some that continue to threaten the account of providence offered in later Christian history.

The divine interruption of cosmic processes is accentuated in Galatians with its criticism of the earthly powers (στοιχεία τού

---

[35] This is described by A. C. Thiselton, *First Epistle to the Corinthians* (Grand Rapids: Eerdmans, 2000), pp. 157ff.

κόσμου). These should be identified with the primal forces which Stoic philosophers believed comprised the four elements of the physical universe.[36] By insisting upon their defeat, Paul criticises all forms of religious observance that acknowledge or venerate the rule of these elemental forces. With the appearance of Christ at the right time, these are no longer worthy of our devotion. 'Now, however, that you have come to know God, or rather to be known by God, how can you turn back again to the weak and beggarly elemental spirits?' (Galatians 4:9). Continued religious observance of the στοιχεῖα is a retreat into false practice. The God of Jesus is proclaimed apart from the elemental forces; with his resurrection from the dead, believers are now liberated from previous forms of enslavement. How this generates a new theory of providence is not altogether clear, yet it must include reference to the advent of the Son of God, his crucifixion and resurrection, and the liberating experience of the Spirit. From those core ingredients of faith, there arises an understanding of divine rule in ways that signal a departure from the standard approaches in the ancient philosophical world.

The reference at Galatians 4:4 to the birth of Christ when 'the fullness of time had come' (see also 1 Timothy 2:6) is developed by Augustine and later theologians in the context of their providential thinking. The economy of salvation betokens the foresight and wisdom of God, rather than a sudden scrambling to initiate a recovery process. Thomas Aquinas reflects at length on why the incarnation came neither at the beginning nor at the end of the world but at some mid-point in its history.[37] This was altogether fitting for the purposes of redemption. As he continues his

---

[36] See for example Martinus C. de Boer, 'Cross and cosmos in Galatians' in David J. Downs and Matthew L. Skinner (eds.), *The Unrelenting God: God's Action in Scripture, Essays in Honor of Beverly Roberts Gaventa* (Grand Rapids: Eerdmans, 2013), pp. 208–25.

[37] Thomas Aquinas, *Summa Theologiae*, 3a.1. All citations are from the Blackfriars edition.

exposition of the incarnation, he stresses that the precise time was fitting because the world was at peace and under one ruler when Christ was born.[38] Although this speculation goes beyond the precise terms of Scripture, it might be seen as following a pattern of interpretation deeply ingrained in Pauline theology. Here a retelling of the scriptural story of creation and redemption is crucial to Paul's description of the Gentile church. The gospel is not just about the sin and forgiveness of the individual; its proper expression requires attention to a much wider cosmic and historical context in which God is provident.[39] This is part of an unfolding plan intended by God but only now unveiled with the coming of Christ. Although the term *pronoia* is not invoked, it seems clear that notions of foreknowledge, plan, wisdom and scriptural fulfilment are thoroughly providential in communicating God's purpose for Israel and the nations.[40] Hence Romans 9–11 is not a sudden digression into a philosophy of history but instead a sub-plot that is crucial to the wider narrative that Paul seeks to rehearse throughout Romans. In affirming at 8:28 that God works in everything for good, Paul reiterates the sense of providence that emerges throughout the course of his extensive argument. This does not commit us to a total predetermination of each event, or the platitude that everything will be all right, so much as the conviction that in and through all events God is steadfastly active in fulfilling the divine will. The good is that towards which

---

[38] Ibid., 3a.35.8.

[39] In making this point, Beverley Gaventa points out that the terms 'repentance' and 'forgiveness' have little place in the Pauline lexicon by contrast with broader notions of 'deliverance'. See Beverley Roberts Gaventa, *When in Romans: An Invitation to Linger with the Gospel According to Paul* (Grand Rapids: Baker, 2016), p. 42.

[40] Here I am indebted to Grant Macaskill, 'History, providence and the apocalyptic Paul', *Scottish Journal of Theology*, 70.4 (2017), 409–26. Macaskill argues that closer attention to the theology of providence may help to overcome the impasse between those rival interpretations of Pauline theology in which the predominance of apocalyptic or salvation-history categories is contested.

everything is moving, rather than an inherent quality of the status quo.[41] In this context of Romans 8:18–39, it carries a strong promissory element set in the future tense and directed towards the liberation of the created order.

What emerges is a new understanding of the steadfast purposes of God emerging amid the vicissitudes of history, though likely to remain obscure outside the perspective of faith.[42] This is strongly underscored by those passages in Ephesians and Colossians which describe a divine plan temporally extended from creation to the eschaton (Ephesians 1:3–14, 3:1–13; Colossians 1:15–29). Although these reflections are often cited in support of a cosmic Christology, their providential import is also significant. The Christ event is continuous with all God's work, so that it can be viewed as central and pivotal to the enactment of a single economy of creation and salvation. This, however, is hidden, mysterious and not apparent except with the eye of faith, that is, to the saints (Colossians 1:26).

Recognising the element of mystery here, we should also respect the plurality of scriptural voices and themes, together with other Jewish possibilities of interpretation. An over-systematising of the text for the sake of demonstrating a meta-narrative is to be avoided. There are figurative ways in which earlier patterns and themes can resonate with the cross and resurrection as the index to God's purposes in and through the world. This process is already underway in the New Testament writings and continues in the theological exegesis of the church. But these should be seen as permitting

---

[41] See Luke Timothy Johnson, *Reading Romans: A Literary and Theological Commentary* (New York: Crossroad, 1997), p. 132. Johnson explicitly identifies this passage as an expression of divine providence.

[42] See for example N. T. Wright, *Paul and the Faithfulness of God* (Minneapolis: Fortress, 2013), pp. 456–537. Wright's project has been challenged for over-schematising salvation history. See John M. G. Barclay, 'Article review: *Paul and the Faithfulness of God*', *Scottish Journal of Theology*, 68.2 (2015), 235–43.

a Christian providential reading of Scripture rather than driving all other possibilities from the field.

Together with the aforementioned themes from the Hebrew Bible, an account of providence that is cruciform in its shape must be significantly different in two key respects from the philosophies of providence that characterised Platonist and Stoic philosophy. Considered ontically, the providential rule of God sometimes works against nature and history. The resurrection of Christ from the dead is a disruption of the natural order of death, and the sign of a new age that is already breaking upon us with the outpouring of the Spirit. Considered noetically, this providential pattern that irrupts within the world is an article of faith believed by the church rather than an aspect of a speculative philosophy. The need to bring religious and philosophical tendencies into a single configuration is a task bequeathed to later generations. But whether we find sufficient differentiation of these trajectories in the traditions of the church is at least an open question.

physical (order)

intellect

1.2.6 The Multiple Forms of Providence in Scripture

On the basis of all this, we might further refine the hypothesis by stating that providence in Scripture is *general* (it signifies the way the world is made), *universal* (it is neither occasional nor intermittent but pervasive in all societies through the agency of wisdom), *particular* (it determines the individual circumstances of people and communities, including Israel and the church, where some patterns and shapes can be discerned), *hidden* (it requires the discernment of faith and even then is often inscrutable), *contested* (the presence of evil, suffering and misfortune create obstacles and crises for our more naïve intuitions) and *incomplete* (an eschatological resolution is promised and anticipated).

As a proposal to be developed, I offer the following as ways in which these trajectories of Scripture appears to diverge significantly

Mathematics ?
planets ?

from the leading treatments of providence in antique philosophy. These differences are of both a theoretical and practical nature. First, the created order is seriously disrupted by surd elements and therefore in need of redemptive and eschatological resolution. This prevents any simple equation of the present or past condition of the cosmos with the perfect ordering of a divine providence. The 'not yet' character of God's reign requires a providential reserve which works against Stoic *apatheia* as a response to the way the world is. The invocation 'Thy will be done' is not a strategy of resignation but a petition for a re-ordering of earth according to the ways of heaven. Its parabolic corollary is the importunate widow's assailing of the unjust judge. Second, the differentiated forms of divine action require a corresponding account of providence in which there is a blending of general, particular, interactional and universal themes. Providence cannot be assimilated to a single model of divine agency, as for example an account of general providence in which the world is shaped according to rational principles. This may be part of the story but it needs to be enhanced by reference to the universal and particular actions of God's two hands – the Word and the Spirit – in cosmic history. Third, the affirmation of divine providence is an act of faith. Several of the parables indicate that the kingdom of God is hidden even while it is present and spreading. The apprehension of divine providence is often in the ordinary, the provincial and the insignificant, at least from a Roman imperial perspective.

This is further accentuated by Paul in 1 Corinthians. The gospel has the character of promise for those who receive it. For example, in the conviction that the resurrection of Christ is a token of what will happen, this promise is a vital ingredient. Given this promissory dimension, the awareness of providence must lack the fullness of complete vision; it is received 'through a glass darkly' so that its wider discernment remains incomplete and necessarily tentative. As a component of faith, the belief in providence retains this occluded character, which should prevent the confident interpretation of each event as an element of a single divine blueprint.

1.3 The Early Church

In studying the doctrine of providence in the early church, we encounter a series of reflections, often underdeveloped, that borrow in some measure from ancient philosophy, particularly Stoicism, while at the same time articulating more distinctive themes that are derived from reflection upon Scripture. Unlike Trinity, Christology and pneumatology, providence was never a central item of sustained theological reflection. In the writings of Justin Martyr, Theophilus of Antioch, Origen and Clement of Alexandria it is treated occasionally and unsystematically. Providence did not become the focus of major dogmatic controversy. The classical creeds are silent on the concept, though one might reasonably claim that they are organised in a quasi-temporal sequence to convey a providential purpose.   *opposite of paranoia*

The linguistic prominence of *pronoia* in Christian theology owes a great deal to the influence of ancient philosophy. This has also had a significant effect upon its material content. Here an account of providence was offered, largely in conscious opposition to notions of chance and randomness. A later Stoic work, Seneca's *De Providentia*, written in the middle of the first century CE, exhorts its readers to trust in a cosmic order of which they are a part.

> This much I now say, – that those things which you call hardships, which you call adversities and accursed are, in the first place, for the good of the persons themselves to whom they come; in the second place, that they are for the good of the whole human family, for which the gods have a greater concern than for single persons; again, I say that good men are willing that these things should happen and, if they are unwilling, that these things happen thus by destiny, and that they rightly befall good men by the same law which makes them good.[43]

---

[43] Seneca, 'De providentia' in *Moral Writings*, ed. John Basore, Loeb Classical Library (London: Heinemann, 1928), 3.1–2, 15.

Two features of the Stoic account are relevant in assessing its appropriation by Christian theology. First, it is an austere account in which an impersonal moral purpose is fulfilled through everything that happens.[44] Within this worldview the sufferings that befall us are to be accepted as our fate, which, if we willingly assent to it in the proper manner, will lead to an increase in virtue. Second, this account tends towards a radical determinism in the role that is assigned to human freedom and responsibility. Both Zeno and Chrysippus liken the human situation to that of a dog tied to a cart. The dog can willingly run along keeping pace with the cart, or else it will be dragged. Either way its destination remains the same.[45] By this account, every event serves a purpose. Foreseen by the gods, the total system of causes governing the universe can be described as 'fate'. Nevertheless, the pronounced resignation that is suggested by this image needs to be tempered. For the Stoic sage, it is what we feel within ourselves that is important. Freedom is realised by learning to will what must happen. By accommodating our inner being to the exterior world, we can learn to live more serenely. For this reason, the distinction between the dog that is dragged and the dog that runs is important. There is a qualitative difference for the Stoics between the smooth-flowing life and one of turmoil.[46]

These tendencies are undoubtedly present in the writers of the early church, particularly in resisting Epicurean trends. But they are also adapted, and at times checked and corrected. There are repeated denials of fatalism and also a stress upon the parental, personal and specific provision of God for human creatures. In her valuable

---

[44] There is some variety within Stoicism on this point. Epictetus, for instance, accentuates a more personal account of providence that pays heed to the circumstances of each individual. See Dragona-Monachou, 'Divine providence in the philosophy of the empire', p. 4445. This may explain why Epictetus was influential among some Christian deists in the eighteenth century.

[45] See John Rist, *Stoic Philosophy* (Cambridge: Cambridge University Press, 1969), p. 127.

[46] See A. A. Long, 'Freedom and determinism in the Stoic theory of human action' in A. A. Long (ed.), *Problems in Stoicism* (London: Athlone Press, 1971), pp. 75–113.

study of the literature, Silke-Petra Bergjan notes the recurrence of several themes: the retributive character of divine providence, its pedagogical function, its eschatological ordering and its particular concern for individuals.[47] While much of the thought and language is borrowed, it reflects an attention to scriptural themes. For example, Theophilus of Antioch can write as if pagan and Christian teachers say much the same thing: 'The Sibyl, then, and the other prophets, yea, and the poets and philosophers, have clearly taught both concerning righteousness and judgement, and punishment; and also concerning providence, that God cares for us, not only for the living among us, but also for those that are dead.'[48] However, the Scriptures provide clearer and deeper insights into the workings of God's providence. Justin Martyr sees neither an iron necessity nor an impersonal fate governing the affairs of human beings, but a God with foreknowledge, oversight and provision for individual men and women.

> So that what we say about future events being foretold, we do not say it as they came about by a fatal necessity; but God foreknowing all that shall be done by all men, and it being His decree that the future actions of men shall all be recompensed according to their several value, He foretells by the Spirit of prophecy that He will bestow meet rewards according to the merit of the actions done, always urging the human race to effort and recollection, showing that He cares and provides for men.[49]

Clement of Alexandria seems to split the difference by arguing at some length that providence is a widely accepted and ineluctable truth throughout the nations of the world, but that its finer details

---

[47] Silke-Petra Bergjan, *Der Fürsorgende Gott* (Berlin: De Gruyter, 2002).

[48] Theophilus of Antioch, *To Autolycus*, 2.38, in Alexander Robertson and James Donaldson (eds.), *Ante-Nicene Fathers*, 10 vols. (Edinburgh: T&T Clark, 1985–7), vol. II, p. 110.

[49] Justin Martyr, *First Apology*, 44, in Robertson and Donaldson, *Ante-Nicene Fathers*, vol. I, p. 177.

are understood only by Christian philosophers. Here it emerges as an *articulus mixtus*. God is understood as the 'invisible and sole, and most powerful, and most skilful and supreme cause of all things most beautiful', but to know the implications of these truths requires the teaching of the church.[50]

While Christian formulations of providence reveal affinities with both Platonism and Stoicism, a much clearer distinction is drawn with fate. Providence and fate may have been viewed as largely convergent in Stoic philosophy, but Christian writers generally sought to distance themselves from associations of fatalism. The concept εἱμαρμένη is widely criticised on account of its links to immoral practice, astrology and philosophical absurdity. Given its failure to do justice to human freedom and the clear sense of Scripture, Christian writers felt compelled to note its differences from divine providence. This is particularly apparent in Origen and Clement of Alexandria, who distinguish God's providential care from the impersonal force detected in Stoicism. Two considerations appear to be at work here. The first is a desire to affirm human freedom and responsibility, partly in order to attribute evil to the human rather than the divine will. A second concern is to accentuate the personal and parental care of God over the world. We are not bound by an undiscerning necessity but ruled by a just and gracious Maker whose goodness is apparent in the works of creation and redemption. This construction of providence is

---

[50] Clement, *Stromateis*, 5.14, in Robertson and Donaldson, *Ante-Nicene Fathers*, vol. II, p. 474. See also Origen's Stoic-like description of providence in *De Principiis*, 2.1.3: 'Although the whole world is arranged into offices of different kinds, its condition, nevertheless, is not to be supposed as one of internal discrepancies and discordances; but as our one body is provided with many members, and is held together by one soul, so I am of opinion that the whole world also ought to be regarded as some huge and immense animal, which is kept together by the power and reason of God as by one soul.' Robertson and Donaldson, *Ante-Nicene Fathers*, vol. IV, p. 269.

particularly evident in the Greek tradition as it develops in later Byzantium.[51]

Two later examples, both from the early fifth century, illustrate further some of the tensions already latent within second-century teaching on providence. In a treatise dedicated to the subject, Theodoret of Cyrus advances a series of rather engaging apologetic arguments for providential order. In many ways, these anticipate the design arguments of William Paley in the early nineteenth century. The providence of God is apparent in the regulation of the planetary system, the seasons of the year, the harmony between species and environment, and the physiognomy of the human body. Even our buttocks are happily arranged, he argues, to provide a natural couch for sitting on the ground or on stone.[52] In his later discourses, he reflects at length on the ordering of society, arguing that the division between master and slave is providentially ordered for the benefit of a post-lapsarian world. This results in an instruction to respect the hierarchies that we find in every social institution, including the church: ⌊fallen

> A father rules his family, correcting the children that are unruly and praising those that are well-behaved. The teacher rules his pupils, and the husband his wife. The master rules his slaves, regarding the better-disposed as worthy of honor, encouragement, and often of freedom. On the other hand, he corrects those who are slothful and inclined to do wrong, and he teaches them manners. The God of the universe has established this same order in the priesthood. Some He has deemed worthy to be priests, and he has appointed others to rule them. He has also set up other orders of inferior clergy.[53]

---

[51] See Andrew Louth, 'Pagans and Christians on providence' in J. H. D. Scourfield (ed.), *Texts and Culture in Late Antiquity: Inheritance, Authority, and Change* (Swansea: Classical Press of Wales, 2007), pp. 279–98.

[52] Theodoret of Cyrus, *On Divine Providence*, trans. Thomas Halton (New York: Newman Press, 1988), 3.21.

[53] Ibid., 7.36.

Like much of the Hellenistic tradition on providence, Theodoret's work describes the cosmic dimensions of providence as well as the ordering of animal bodies and the regulation of human affairs. Much of this detail, however, does not engage historical processes, which are relatively absent from much of his reflection. With Augustine, in contrast, we find a stronger historical reading of God's providential ways. This is less apparent in his earlier reflections on divine providence in *De Ordine*, a work written shortly after his conversion. Here he views the world as properly ordered in every aspect by a divine providence that can be discerned through reason and revelation. The apparently dissonant elements in creation are made to serve God's purpose: the hangman, the brothel and the excesses of climate all make their contribution to a divinely ordained *telos*. While evils do not originate in God, they are ruled by the hand of providence and made to serve an order that is everywhere present. Augustine appeals to the testimony of Monica:

> I think that nothing could have been done aside from the order of God, because evil itself, which has had an origin, in no way originated by the order of God; but that divine justice permitted it not to be beyond the limits of order, and has brought it back and confined it to an order befitting it.[54]

Although the greater stress on the purposive and personal rule of God may set Augustine apart from Platonist philosophers, there remains a sense of a serene and fully ordered cosmos in each moment and aspect of its existence. Within this setting, attitudes of wonder, gratitude and acceptance appear to be the dominant practical responses.

---

[54] Augustine, 'Divine providence and the problem of evil' in Robert P. Russell (ed.), *Writings of St Augustine*, vol. 1 (New York: CIMA Publishing, 1948), p. 300. For an overview of Augustine's several writings on providence, see Mark W. Elliott, *Providence Perceived: Divine Action from a Human Point of View* (Berlin: de Gruyter, 2015), pp. 37–45.

In the *City of God*, Augustine offers a more sombre and chastened reflection on the ways of providence, while continuing to affirm the rule of God throughout the cosmos. He inveighs against all forms of astrological fatalism. The constellation of the stars has no causal influence upon life on earth. These are not determined by remote events. As in Theodoret, much of the discussion has a curiously modern ring, particularly in Augustine's extended analysis of twins. Their similarities and differences must be accounted for by proximate causes of parentage, diet, upbringing, external circumstances and so on. None of these can be explained by the identical constellations at the time of their birth. And yet we can also affirm that God through these secondary causes, including voluntary agents, executes an overarching purpose.

As with earlier Christian thinkers, Augustine places his account of providence in close proximity to Stoic philosophy. Although both chance and a blind determinism are firmly rejected as governing causes in nature and history, he is willing to concede that the Stoic description of destiny can be transposed into the language of Christian theology. In some ways, this resembles a rebranding of an earlier philosophical tradition. But the accent is now placed both on the transcendent will of God as ordaining everything that happens and also on the reality of human freedom as divinely foreknown and so assured. Before quoting Seneca with approval, he writes, 'What they mean by "destiny" is principally the will of the supreme God, whose power extends invincibly through all things.'[55] Augustine insists that this does not abrogate free will. The necessity that attaches to God's foreknowledge – without this, God could not be God – does not transfer to human actions so as to rob these of their freedom. Since God necessarily foreknows our free choices, his foreknowledge guarantees the freedom of the will.

Augustine views the course of human history as ordained by God. He reasons that, since God has ordained the health and

55 Augustine, *City of God*, 5.8, p. 189.

constitution of even the lowliest creature, so *a fortiori* God must will the rise and fall of every imperial power: 'It is beyond anything incredible that he should have willed the kingdoms of men, their dominations and their servitudes, to be outside the range of the laws of his providence.'[56] What emerges from this is the conviction that everything must in its own way serve a single cosmic purpose. So the earthly city, despite its many imperfections and lust for power, is instrumental to the city of God. The vindication of goodness and the punishment of evil are already taking place, although these are only complete and finally ordered at the end of history. Much of this thinking was already present in *De Ordine*. God must foreknow and foreordain everything that comes to pass. There is nothing that can be placed outside of the order intended and created by God in both nature and history. To understand this, we need to think of evils as lesser goods or privations which belong to an order which could not be accomplished without them. While God does not desire evil, nevertheless the wisdom of God is such that evils can be used to serve a purpose that is altogether good. Hence, the rational order, evident in the constitution of even the lowliest creatures, can be discerned in human affairs.

In one important respect, this seems to move beyond Scripture into the realm of metaphysical explanation. The evils and imperfections of the world are ordained by God as part of the majestic tapestry of creation and redemption. There is a single divine blueprint that is enacted in the history of the world, each event and entity being assigned its proper place. This produces patterns of redemption and punishment whereby the truly virtuous are rewarded in heaven while the sinful mass are consigned to their righteous damnation. Divine providence is perceived in a single chiaroscuro of light and darkness, good and evil, melody and discord. With its stress on the aesthetic harmony of the world,

---

[56] Ibid., Book 11, p. 156.

Book 3 of Plotinus' *Enneads* expounds a similar doctrine of providence. This is already taken up in *De Ordine*.

Augustine's later thought, however, becomes more determinist. This arises partly as a result of the struggle with Pelagianism and partly through his reflections on the difference between divine eternity and creaturely temporality, the former being construed in terms of timelessness. A comprehensive account of how the will of God becomes effective through temporal causes thus emerges. God works both intrinsically and extrinsically through natural and voluntary agents. Within the orders of creation, all creatures are sustained in being, while an inward illumination and grace are given to voluntary agents. This sets the scene for later medieval accounts of double agency. As transcendent, God does not belong to the system of creaturely causes. But as constantly involved in creaturely processes, God works everywhere through the created order.[57] Considered extrinsically, divine action can be discerned in the guidance of the total set of natural causes and in the ruling of free agents (angels and human beings) to serve God's purpose. This latter governance of voluntary causes includes first the permission and then the overruling of evil wills to God's greater glory.[58] The fine-grained providentialism and determinism of the Stoics remain in Augustine, but these are now set under the sovereign will of the eternal God.

Within the Christian east, however, a different trajectory emerges which decisively shaped Orthodox reflection upon divine providence. Much of this tradition has been largely absent from western discussions of providence, yet it merits greater attention for the sake of registering the ecumenical diversity that has long existed

---

[57] Simon Oliver notes the ways in which Augustine avoids both deism and pantheism in his account of divine providence working in and through the *rationes seminales*. See 'Augustine on creation, providence and motion', *International Journal of Systematic Theology*, 18.4 (2016), 379–98.

[58] Here I am indebted to the outlining of these in Eugene TeSelle, *Augustine: The Theologian* (New York: Herder and Herder, 1970), pp. 219–21.

on these matters. The Greek writers of the fourth century already looked back to the work of Origen. Appealing to Plato's myth of Er, Origen regarded misfortune and suffering in this life as sent to remedy the evils chosen in a pre-existent state. Here divine providence can be discerned in the outcomes that attend our free choices. A pedagogical function is evident in the blending of moral training with punishment. Human autonomy is given greater scope, while remaining steadfastly fixed within a divinely ordained moral order. As a result of this tendency, a sharper distinction emerges between divine willing and permission. Although nothing escapes the scope of divine providence, there is an important difference between those things which God wills and those things to which God consents. Our human choices belong to this latter category. Although the exercise of free will produces a multiplicity of outcomes ranging from imitation of God to abject failure, Origen argues that each rational creature is created alike. Differences arise 'not from the will or judgment of the Creator, but from the freedom of the individual will'. Yet 'divine providence continues to regulate each individual according to the variety of his movements, or of his feelings and purpose'.[59] Although Origen's account of the migration of souls is not followed by subsequent theologians, his distinctive coordination of divine willing, permitting of freedom and providential ordering of its outcomes became well established in the eastern tradition.

In the development of these strands, a key source is Nemesius' *On the Nature of Man*, a late fourth-century work by the Bishop of Emesa (in Syria). Nemesius is significant not only for his reception of the Platonic tradition (and what he reveals about lost sources) but also for his influence upon later Byzantine writers including Maximus the Confessor and John of Damascus. Inveighing against Stoic notions of fate, Nemesius insists that these undercut both human responsibility and the foresight of God. Here he resists any

---

[59] Origen, *De Principiis*, 2.9.6, in Robertson and Donaldson, *Ante-Nicene Fathers*, vol. IV, p. 292.

alliance with Stoic fatalism.[60] Even 'the wise amongst the Egyptians' claimed that the fate written in the stars could be averted by prayer and sacrifices. Unlike other theologians who harmonised fate and providence, Nemesius regards these as mutually exclusive. Plato comes closer to the truth, though he must be criticised for not allowing sufficient scope for divine interaction in the creation. According to Plato, some actions are genuinely up to us, but the laws governing their consequences are fixed under the providence of God. For example, it may be up to us to decide whether to set sail, but having done so whether we are shipwrecked is determined by a natural order established by God. Yet Nemesius will not allow even this measure of necessity in the cosmos. Shipwreck may be averted by prayers and divine intervention. Hence the world created by God permits a free and particular providence within its natural order.

> In order that this should be shown to be, he once stopped the course of the sun and the moon which travel of necessity and are always the same, to show that nothing comes about for him of necessity, but everything contingently according to his authority ... Also he preserves some men alive, such as Elijah and Enoch, who are mortal and subject to passing-away, in order that we should recognize through all these acts his authority and unfettered will.[61]

Human freedom is established for Nemesius on the basis of two considerations. First, actions which are evil and unjust must have their origin in us, since we cannot ascribe them to God, fate, luck or nature. And, second, the process of deliberation which sometimes precedes our actions makes no sense except on the assumption that such actions are genuinely owned and willed by us. Similar remarks are applied to activities such as encouragement, advice, praise and blame which both influence and evaluate our deliberations and

[60] Nemesius, *On the Nature of Man*, trans. R. W. Sharples and P. J. van der Eijk (Liverpool: Liverpool University Press, 2008), 35.184–5.

[61] Ibid.

voluntary choices. A disposition to virtue is genuinely up to us, and is not to be attributed to external causes, even though these can exercise an influence on us. Yet divine providence still exercises a care over all things.[62] Although this is most clearly shown in the incarnation, it is also evident in ways that are discernible to pagans. Owing to our constitution, we are inclined to seek God's providence in moments of crisis. Even the sceptical and unreflective find themselves constrained. 'For also in sudden disturbances and fear we involuntarily call upon God without even thinking.'[63]

Nemesius rehearses familiar arguments, already noted in Theodoret, about the rhythms of nature, the harmony of bodies, the flourishing of species, and a moral order in which the wicked receive their deserts. These are symptoms of a general providence, to which he adds a special providence that superintends human affairs. Here his discussion moves in a more problematic direction by affirming that everything is made to serve some overarching purpose which we could discern if only we were able to see the bigger picture. This temptation to over-stretch the theology of divine providence is a besetting one throughout its history, for both theologians and pastors. 'Surely also poverty has often been to our advantage, as has the burial of our children and the flight of our servants. For the preservation of worthless children or servants who became robbers would be more bitter than their loss.'[64]

Maximus the Confessor draws upon Nemesius' description of providence in *Ambiguum* 10.[65] He notes that by natural inclination

---

[62] 'Providence, then, is care for things by God. It is also defined as follows: providence is the wish of God by which all thing receive a suitable way of life.' Ibid., 42.208. This description of providence is later quoted approvingly by both John of Damascus and Maximus the Confessor. See Peter C. Bouteneff, 'The two wills of God: providence in St John of Damascus', *Studia Patristica*, 42 (2006), 291–6 at 294.

[63] Nemesius, *On the Nature of Man*, 43.217.

[64] Ibid., 43.215.

[65] Maximos the Confessor, *On Difficulties in the Church Fathers: The Ambigua, Vol. 1*, ed. Nicholas Constas (Cambridge, MA: Harvard University Press, 2014), 10.100–5. For further discussion, see Andrew Louth, *Maximus the Confessor* (London: Routledge,

we tend towards a belief in God's providence since 'it prepares us to seek salvation through prayers in sudden emergencies, as if pushing us towards God in an untaught way'.[66] Divine providence governs every particular to ensure that it draws each into a fitting harmony of the whole. Even though we cannot see how the diversity of parts can cohere, we must acknowledge that this is merely the result of our epistemological limitation. At the same time, he wants to distinguish clearly what happens by God's providence from the outcomes of our rational agency. Although the setting and effects of our actions are circumscribed by providence, these actions are themselves willed by us, rather than by God. Here a distinction is maintained between what God wills and what God permits. This is later summarised by John of Damascus in his differentiation of the antecedent and the consequent will of God. In this important respect, the eastern tradition tends to side with the Middle Platonists against the Stoics. Fatalism is criticised for the threat that it poses to human freedom and responsibility. While the outcomes of choice are bound by a providential order, our free decisions are not themselves fated. As a broad generalisation, we might view the east as following Platonism with the west more inclined to appropriate Stoicism.

John of Damascus also takes his cue from the Nemesian definition. And, like Maximus, he argues that all the works of providence do not include those that are to be attributed to our free will.[67] These are conceded or permitted, rather than actively willed, though providence can use these concessions for its own ends, as in the salvation that was brought about through the cross. God's original wish is that all come to salvation – this is the antecedent will – but

---

1996), p. 144, and Bronwen Neil, 'Divine providence and the gnomic will before Maximus' in Pauline Allen and Bronwen Neil (eds.), *Oxford Handbook to Maximus the Confessor* (Oxford: Oxford University Press, 2015), pp. 235–52.

[66] Louth, *Maximus the Confessor*, p. 146.

[67] John of Damascus, 'Exposition of the Orthodox faith' in *Nicene and Post-Nicene Fathers*, 2nd series (New York: Scribner's, 1899), vol. IX, pp. 41–2.

by permission of our wicked deeds, God's consequent will can chastise, discipline and punish. Providence overarches our freedom. But to understand this we must maintain a strong distinction between the active and the permissive will of God. With this in view, John is able then to expound predestination, a more minor note in eastern theology, as a function of God's foreknowledge of our free choices. What emerges is an account of human freedom that maintains its autonomy, seeing this as passively permitted rather than actively willed by God. At the same time, our free actions are not outside the wider scope of providence. In the long run, God's purposes will draw these into a wider cosmic harmony, whether through recovery or through retribution.[68]

The development of this position took place in close proximity to parallel debates around fatalism in the early phases of Islamic theology. John of Damascus was well acquainted with these. The affirmation of a comprehensive divine decree (*qadar*) raised questions about the extent of human determination by God's will. On one reading, this resulted in the intrusion into Islamic thought of an earlier Arab fatalism which was balanced by the more nuanced position of the Qur'an. In terms characteristic of the criticism of Stoic philosophy in the early church, Montgomery Watt represents this as a contrast between the theistic predestinarianism of the Qur'an and the pre-Islamic concept of an impersonal fatalism.[69] At any rate, Islamic thought was divided around the time of John of Damascus. The Qadarites argued robustly for human freedom, even to the extent of denying divine foreknowledge. This contrasted with

---

[68] See Andrew Louth, *St John Damascene* (Oxford: Oxford University Press, 2002), pp. 140–3. In many respects, this Orthodox reading of providence is close to Jewish accounts of the matter which affirm a universal providence that leaves space for our free choices. As the Talmudic saying states, 'Everything is in the hand of heaven, except for the fear of heaven' (Berakhot 33b). Cited by Yehoshua M. Grintz, 'Providence: in the Talmud' in Skolnik, *Encyclopaedia Judaica*, vol. XVI, p. 649.

[69] W. Montgomery Watt, *Free Will and Predestination in Early Islam* (London: Luzac, 1948), pp. 19–29.

the teaching of the Jabriyyah, who posited a strong divine determination in which the human will is 'like a feather in the breeze without any power of one's own'.[70] The writings of John of Damascus appear to take a mediating position, as do other Islamic schools. Though divine foreknowledge is comprehensive, God's will is not the cause of our free actions except in its concessionary mode. Nevertheless, the outcomes of our free actions are governed by a wise providence that imposes an order even upon the waywardness of the human will.

1.4 Conclusion

The assumption that the church shared providentialist beliefs with the philosophies of the ancient world led much of its teaching in the direction of Stoic fatalism. This was especially pronounced, as we shall see in the next chapter, in the Latin west. By contrast, the eastern tradition with its stronger libertarianism insisted against philosophies of fate on a thicker distinction between divine willing and permission. Some things are generally up to us – in such cases, God permits rather than wills. But, in general, the struggle against theories of chance and fortune helped to forge an alliance with philosophies of providence. Elements of Platonic and Stoic philosophy proved useful and seemed to resonant with much of what Christian writers wished to affirm of divine sovereignty. At the same time, these underwent some adjustment under the impact of scriptural interpretation. Divine providence as purposive, particular and parental was not to be confused with fate or fortune, and it induced a different set of practical attitudes.

[70] See Louth, *St John Damascene*, p. 81. For further discussion of the range of positions on predestination (*qadar*) and free will in Islam, see Majid Fakhry, *A History of Islamic Philosophy* (New York: Columbia University Press, 1970), pp. 56–81, and M. Abdel Haleem, 'Early *kalām*' in Seyyed Hossein Nasr and Oliver Leaman (eds.), *History of Islamic Philosophy*, Part I (London: Routledge, 1996), pp. 71–88.

Yet, notwithstanding these critical notes, the axis with classical philosophy was especially evident whenever providence was discussed. This was hardly surprising given the prominence of the concept in all the great Stoic thinkers. And, as the theology of providence became systematised in the Latin church of the Middle Ages, so these philosophical influences became increasingly apparent. Despite gestures towards revision and criticism, the resultant disposition was overall towards a determinism and passivity in constructions of providentialism. And these tended to restrict the diversity of scriptural materials and the distribution of providence across all three articles of the faith. Elements of struggle, resistance and interaction were increasingly difficult to accommodate as the concept of providence became anchored either to the doctrine of God or to the doctrine of creation. Without stronger Christological and pneumatological expressions of divine providence, the polyphonic witness of the scriptural tradition was always in danger of diminution.

2 | The Latin Default Setting

There is no event in which it has been shown not to have taken place at its good time by command and ordination of God.[1]

During the Middle Ages, the Augustinian account of providence was developed by the Latin Church. By contrast with the occasional explorations of patristic theology, the theology of providence was now systematised in ways that ensured its centrality to the relationship of God to the world. As a result, the classical doctrine emerged in the west with its typical stress on divine sovereignty, double agency, a distinction between primary and secondary causes, and a compatibilism that affirmed both human freedom and divine determinism. Allied to the Augustinian doctrine of predestination, we find accounts of varying degrees of strength which postulate divine foreknowledge as a function of the primal decree. In this chapter, I seek to identify this approach to providence that became standardised in the Latin west during the Middle Ages. Carried forward at the Reformation, it reached its high point in seventeenth-century Reformed orthodoxy. The practical implications of this providentialism continue to reverberate.

In this paradigm, a maximalist tendency in which everything is attributed to the divine will becomes evident. This generated difficulties already identified by the theologians of the early church. Is God the author of sin and evil? How are human freedom and responsibility to be maintained? In what ways can petitionary prayer be considered effective? Are natural causes only illusory? A strategy for

---

[1] Huldrych Zwingli, *On Providence and Other Essays*, ed. William John Hinke (Durham, NC: Labyrinth Press, 1983), p. 216.

dealing with these problems was developed largely through articulating the distinction between primary and secondary causality. The relation and differentiation of these sets of causes both safeguarded the maximalist account of providence while also maintaining human freedom, creaturely contingency and divine goodness. The articulation of this high theology of providence represents a formidable effort. Its exponents include some of the greatest theological minds. While Protestants did not reinvent providentialism, nevertheless they could foreground its themes in ways that had deep practical significance. If we are to offer an adequate assessment of this element of church teaching, some attention to its spiritual, ethical and political effects will be required. Despite its extensive support and intellectual pedigree, I shall argue that in some important respects it is both theologically flawed and deleterious in outcome.

2.1 The Influence of Boethius

Unlike the Greek theologians hitherto examined, the medieval thinkers of the west tended to harmonise providence and fate. Following Boethius' *Consolation of Philosophy*, an influential text throughout the medieval period, fate is understood as the order inherent in things as a result of divine providence. In this respect, fate can be viewed as the instrument or outworking of the providence that closely adheres to God. 'The simple and ever-changing plan of events is Providence, and Fate is the ever-changing web, the dispositions in and through time of all the events which God has planned in His simplicity.'[2] Although God's providence is all-knowing and infallible, Boethius argues that it is consistent with human freedom. This is put forward in *Consolation* Book V by reference to three considerations: what God knows is not in and of itself necessary, although it is necessary that God knows everything;

---

[2] Boethius, *The Consolation of Philosophy*, trans. V. E. Watts (Harmondsworth: Penguin, 1969), 4.6, p. 136.

the act of knowing belongs to the subject rather than the object of knowledge, so does not interfere with the contingency of the latter; and, finally, God's foreknowing is represented in terms of an eternal perspective to which everything – past, present and future – is time-lessly present. 'If you wish to consider, then, the foreknowledge or prevision by which He discovers all things, it will be more correct to think of it not as a kind of foreknowledge of the future, but as the knowledge of a never ending presence.'[3]

This Boethian account is significant for our purposes in two ways. The first is its subordination of fate to divine providence. Though adjusted in significant ways from its Stoic legacy, the concept of fate is now integrated into Christian theology. This harmonisation of *providentia* and *fatum* is quite unlike their dialectical opposition in much eastern theology. And, second, the account of divine atemporality in terms of an eternal presentism establishes a conceptual relationship between God and the world which appears to be much more indebted to the legacy of Platonism than to anything mandated by the Bible. Everything is now seemingly held all at once by the impassible gaze of God.

A further indication of the Platonist hinterland is the way in which providence tends to be located within the doctrine of God by medieval theologians. By virtue of the divine essence, providence is something that God cannot lack. The dependence and ordering of everything upon God implies the exercise of an all-pervasive providence that radiates outwards from the divine being.

In his *Summa Theologica*, a twelfth-century Franciscan treatise, Alexander of Hales, the overseer rather than sole author, asserts that knowledge, wisdom and will belong to God's providence.[4]

---

[3] Ibid., 5.6, p. 165. These three ingredients in Boethius' reconciliation of foreknowledge and contingency are explored by Robert Sharples, 'Fate, prescience and free will' in John Marenbon (ed.), *The Cambridge Companion to Boethius* (Cambridge: Cambridge University Press, 2009), pp. 207–27 at pp. 216–20.

[4] In what follows, I am indebted to the guidance of Lydia Schumacher, who is preparing a critical edition of the *Summa Halensis*.

This involves seeing and causing as well as ordaining, governing and ruling.[5] Divine providence rules all things, although its operations allow for the freedom of intelligent creatures. Following Boethius, whom he quotes extensively, Alexander maintains that fate can be construed as an instrument of providence. In this way, fate is regarded as a subset of providence – it operates upon particular mutable things – but is not identical with it. Further distinctions are introduced which are standard for most Christian thinkers in the Middle Ages and Reformation. By virtue of being created, all things are subject to divine providence in terms of their regularity: for example, the sun will rise tomorrow. But there is also a providence according to concession (*providentia concessionis*) in the case of those free wills that resist providence. Here Alexander cites John of Damascus, whose distinction between divine will and permitting he approves, seemingly to a greater extent than Thomas Aquinas. Yet God's permission also displays its providence in ordering the actions of evil wills to some other good.[6] Following much of the patristic tradition, Alexander has redemptive or retributive outcomes in view. A further distinction that is apparent is the one between a general and a special providence. At the level of sustaining things in their appointed mode of being, providence operates generally upon all created beings. This is complemented by a more specific providence which takes account of rational creatures, for example by giving them the law.

---

[5] 'Quid sit providentia' in *Doctoris irrefragabilis Alexandri de Hales Ordinis minorum Summa theologica*, vol. I (Florence: Quaracchi, 1924), p. 285. See also Mikko Posti, 'Divine providence in medieval philosophical theology, 1250–1350', unpublished PhD thesis, University of Helsinki (2017), pp. 58–62, https://helda.helsinki.fi/bitstream/handle/10138/228641/DIVINEPR.pdf?sequence=1. I am grateful to Dr Posti for sharing his work with me. Its appearance at the completion of this present study has prevented me from fully absorbing his many historical insights.

[6] 'Quid sit providentia', p. 292: '*Sic ergo sub divina providentia sunt bona tamquam ab ipsa facta, et etiam mala tamquam ab ipsa ordinata.*'

2.2 Providence in Aquinas

The definition of providence offered by Thomas Aquinas reveals Platonic and Stoic influences, although the extent to which these determine his account is disputed. God has providence as creator, as source of being and goodness, and as the one who directs all things to their final end. 'It is not only in the substance of created things that goodness lies, but also in their being ordained to an end, above all to their final end, which, as we have seen, is the divine goodness.'[7] This providence governs not only the general course of events but every single particular. Since each thing owes its existence to God, its final end is bound to be directed by God. Aquinas here employs the model of God as artist: 'Since his knowledge is related to things like that of an artist to his works of art ... it must be that all things are set under his ordering.'[8] For Aquinas also, providence is something that necessarily attaches to God as the unconditioned source of all being – hence it is treated under the doctrine of God rather than the doctrine of creation. Furthermore, for Aquinas predestination tends to be one aspect of providence and thus subordinate to it, whereas the Reformed tradition sought to invert the order by prioritising predestination and viewing providence as its means.

Subsequent exposition suggests an understanding of the divine rule in which every event is determined by the prior (or eternal or timeless) will of God. This is confirmed by several features of his account, particularly where he follows Boethius. Nothing happens by chance, insofar as there are no uncaused or random events. The only sense in which chance can be said to occur within the created order is in the intersection of particular unrelated causal sequences. Nevertheless, these are governed by the universal cause. 'Thus the meeting of two servants, in their eyes unexpected because neither knew the other's errand, was foreseen by their master who

---

[7] Thomas Aquinas, *Summa Theologiae*, 1a.22.1. References are to the Blackfriars translation of the text.

[8] Ibid., 1a.22.2.

intentionally sent them where their paths would cross.'[9] The presence of evil in the creation is also ruled by divine providence. Though evils may conflict with the nature of some particular thing, these contribute to the overall *telos* of nature. 'Were all evils to be denied entrance many good things would be lacking in the world: there would not be life for the lion were there no animals for its prey, and no patience of martyrs were there no persecution by tyrants.'[10] The secondary causes which govern contingent entities are related to the primary cause of God's will, which is both their necessary and sufficient condition. 'Consequently the whole of their design down to every detail is anticipated in his mind.'[11] Although the integrity of secondary causes is guaranteed by the primary cause, their direction and outcomes are always willed by the primary cause. While emphasising the contingency of secondary causes, Aquinas is able to follow Boethius in describing everything as fixed by fate. In this sense, providence can be regarded as the universal plan in God's mind, while destiny or fate is the realisation of this plan in the world.[12] Furthermore, the Augustinian doctrine of predestination, as affirmed by Aquinas, reinforces the sense of an eternal foreordination of every temporal effect.[13] Predestination, as also reprobation, is an aspect of providence. It cannot be reduced to foreknowledge of free choices since it is gratuitous, fixed and certain.[14]

On one reading, Aquinas's view appears determinist and monistic. Everything moves according to an immutable divine plan. Although once removed from the creaturely arena through the mediation of secondary causes, the primary cause of all effects

---

[9] Ibid., 1a.22.2.

[10] Ibid.

[11] Ibid., 1a. 22. 3. Cf. Thomas Aquinas, *De Potentia* 3.7.

[12] Aquinas's relationship to Stoicism and his mediaeval predecessors is discussed in Gerard Verbeke, *The Presence of Stoicism in Medieval Thought* (Washington DC: Catholic University Press, 1983), pp. 71–96.

[13] E.g. Aquinas, *Summa Theologiae*, 3a.24.1.

[14] Ibid., 1a.23.

remains prior and controlling. Here the apparent combination of divine absence with total determinism suggests an austere Stoic-like vision. This has occasioned severe criticism of Aquinas among some commentators for developing a 'supreme being theology' that prevents any genuine interaction with the world.[15] Is this valid?

Undoubtedly, the order of the *Summa Theologiae* has suggested to some that a doctrine of God determined on Platonist philosophical grounds provides the underpinning of his subsequent doctrinal work. In his 'strict observance' Thomist reading of providence, Reginald Garrigou-Lagrange sets out an argument for divine existence by drawing upon cosmological and design arguments. As one to whom belong complete unity, sovereign goodness and simplicity, God as absolute cause of all other causes must be providential in relation to everything that is not God. 'The absolute universality of providence is deduced from the absolute universality of divine causality, which in this case is the causality of an intellectual agent.'[16] With some confidence, Garrigou-Lagrange describes the ways in which providence safeguards human freedom and works through creaturely causes by governing the lower creation through the higher. There then follows a chapter on the teaching of providence in which these conclusions are further amplified and extended. Although his exposition is clear, forthright, and not lacking in spiritual force and insight, one might reasonably conclude that a theology of providence has been determined primarily on philosophical rather than scriptural grounds. Yet whether Aquinas is guilty of such a manoeuvre is doubtful. The context of the *Summa*, its sustained engagement with Scripture, and other resultant features of his theology indicate that this criticism is at least overstated. The charge of philosophical captivity results in part from isolated readings of

---

[15] 'The remorseless logic of Aquinas left the prime mover incapable of real relation to the world.' Keith Ward, *Rational Theology and Creativity of God* (Oxford: Blackwell, 1982), p. 87.

[16] Reginald Garrigou-Lagrange, *Providence* (London: Herder, 1937), p. 159. I discuss this work in further detail in Chapter 5.

Aquinas that are dominated by the opening sections of the Prima Pars. Yet the Tertia Pars of the *Summa* and the goal of much else is Christology. It is by the mystery of Christ's incarnation that we come to blessedness. There are intimations of this throughout the *Summa*, the parts of which cannot be understood except in relation to the overall intention and vision of Aquinas, which are rooted in scriptural interpretation and church teaching.[17] Elsewhere, the attention to human freedom, miracles and petitionary prayer offers a more dramatic account of the God–world relationship in which divine initiative and creaturely response achieve a degree of mutuality.[18] This is reflected in Aquinas's insistence upon divine friendship, in which the common life of God and human persons is formed by mutual love.[19]

On the subject of freedom, Aquinas appears to stress one element of the Augustinian position by maintaining that divine agency guarantees rather than threatens our contingent freedom. God does not so much act upon human persons, so causing them to behave in the ways they do, but instead makes them to be what they are, thus enabling them to be free. In the exercise of human agency, divine and creaturely causes belong to different orders.[20] A similar justification of petitionary prayer is offered. In response to ancient anxieties about the efficacy and propriety of prayer, Aquinas argues that divine providence has ordered the world in such a way that the will of God is sometimes made effective through the agency of human prayer. Thus prayer is a natural and universal activity.

---

[17] This is argued, for example, by William C. Placher, *The Domestication of Transcendence* (Louisville: Westminster John Knox, 1996), pp. 21–36.

[18] These themes are treated in the context of divine providence by Brian Davies, *The Thought of Thomas Aquinas* (Oxford: Oxford University Press, 1992), pp. 169ff.

[19] Aquinas, *Summa Theologiae*, 2a.2ae.23.1.

[20] Ibid., 1a.105.5. Cajetan glosses this text with the remark '*Impotentis est non posse facere alia cooperativa sibi*' ('it is weakness not to be able to let others cooperate with you'). I owe this reference to Fergus Kerr. For further discussion of this topic, see Davies, *The Thought of Thomas Aquinas*, p. 177.

In the case of prayer, we do not pray in order to change God's plan, but in order to obtain by our prayers those things which God planned to bring about by means of prayers, in order, as Gregory says, that our prayers should entitle us to receive what almighty God planned from all eternity to give us.[21]

Petitionary prayer, it seems, is more about aligning ourselves with God's will than seeking to change it. Despite some difficulties inherent in this response, such passages do at least illustrate the central place accorded to human agency and divine response in Aquinas's account of the world order.

Yet much that we have identified in ancient philosophy persists in Aquinas. There is a tendency to see the entire nexus of causes in the universe as the single expression of a divine vision that is eternally comprehended and willed by God. Nothing can be situated outside this providential scheme. Nor is there any disruption or deviation. Evil, fortune and fate are all subsumed under the *providentia Dei*. Harm Goris has pointed to ways in which Aquinas is able to protect the contingency of creaturely causes and the voluntary nature of the human will, despite these being determined by the intellect and will of God. The eternal mode of the divine being is such that events which are future and indeterminate to us are fully present and therefore determinate to God. This should not be represented as the divine cognition of a reality that is apart from God. God's action in bestowing being upon the world also ensures that everything is preserved, ruled and directed to its appointed end. God does not make beings who subsequently function in an autonomous manner; their existence is governed by God, who directs them to a final destiny. As the source of all being, God wills only what is good for creation. With Augustine, therefore, we should view imperfect elements as privations which contribute to an overall harmony. All this is imparted to creation by the divine understanding which holds everything in view from an eternal perspective. 'Now, to rule

---

[21] Aquinas, *Summa Theologiae*, 2a.2ae.83.2.

or govern by providence is simply to move things towards an end through understanding. Therefore, God by His providence governs and rules all things that are moved toward their end, whether they be moved corporeally, or spiritually as one who desires is moved by an object of desire.'[22] The mode of existence imparted by God to creatures, moreover, determines the appropriate mode of secondary causality, whether that be necessary, contingent or voluntary. And because the divine cause is transcendent and eternal, and so only to be characterised analogically and negatively, we cannot posit any direct competition between creaturely and divine agency. These operate at complementary and incommensurate levels. We should regard them as answers to different sorts of question.[23]

Aquinas's account of divine action sits somewhere between earlier Islamic forms of occasionalism and later forms of deism. He maintains an account of double agency in which the activity of God and the activity of creaturely causes are complementary rather than mutually destructive. God's action determines and facilitates all creaturely causes, not so much by overruling or annihilating these as by ensuring that they can exist, function and complete their effective activity. As an Aristotelian, he resists the occasionalist argument, apparent in the writings of al-Ghazali, that the attribution of causal powers to nature in some way derogates from the sovereignty of God.[24] By distinguishing the primary causality of God from the secondary causality of created beings, we can both set these apart and view them as complementary types

Double
Ag

---

[22] Thomas Aquinas, *Summa Contra Gentiles*, 3.64.4, trans. J. F. Anderson (Notre Dame, IN: University of Notre Dame Press, 1975).

[23] See Harm Goris, 'Divine foreknowledge, providence, predestination and human freedom' in Rik Van Nieuwenhove and Joseph Wawrykow (eds.), *The Theology of Thomas Aquinas* (Notre Dame, IN: Notre Dame Press, 2005), pp. 99–122.

[24] See Alfred J. Freddosos, 'Medieval Aristotelianism and the case against secondary causation in nature' in Thomas V. Morris (ed.), *Divine and Human Action: Essays in the Metaphysics of Theism* (Ithaca: Cornell University Press, 1988), pp. 74–118.

of explanation. This has proved attractive to recent theologies of divine action which espouse both the involvement of God in creation and the integrity of creaturely causes, whether material or personal.[25] God can be described as ceaselessly and constantly at work in everything that happens so that nothing lies outside the scope of a single divine providence. Yet creaturely causes are guaranteed rather than annihilated by the mode of God's action as primary and enabling. By assigning divine and natural causation to different levels of description, these do not compete on the same explanatory terrain. Divine causation is entirely different from creaturely causation since the term 'cause' must be analogically applied to God as the self-existent and infinite first cause. Hence we do not need to abridge the account of either divine or creaturely causation because these can and must be viewed together, though as different categories of description. The contemporary appeal of this account is not difficult to discern. We are not left with the awkward task of finding gaps in scientific explanation to postulate the intermittent activity of God, as for example in intelligent design theory. We can let science provide a complete explanation in terms of natural causal processes while also affirming the involvement of God in everything that happens. In his sympathetic commentary on the text, Brian Davies notes that, for Aquinas, 'God makes things to be what they truly are.'[26]

---

[25] See for example Kathryn Tanner, *God and Creation in Christian Theology: Tyranny or Empowerment* (Oxford: Blackwell, 1988), pp. 81–119. Aquinas's account of double agency is also invoked in the context of recent work in science and religion. In particular, I have drawn upon the exposition of Ignacio Silva, 'Revisiting Aquinas on providence and rising to the challenge of divine action in nature', *Journal of Religion* 94.3 (2014), 277–91. For a vigorous defence of Thomist double agency, see also Alexander Jensen, *Divine Providence and Human Agency: Trinity, Creation and Freedom* (Aldershot: Ashgate, 2014).

[26] Brian Davies, *Thomas Aquinas's Summa Contra Gentiles: A Guide and Commentary* (New York: Oxford University Press, 2016), p. 264.

Aquinas's articulation of this position is also evident in Q3, Article 7 of *De Potentia Dei*, where he distinguishes four different ways in which God can be considered to be the cause of all creaturely outcomes. These range through notions of creating, sustaining and directing each cause in order to bring about the appointed effect. All are embedded in the single, eternal and indivisible power of God. Here Aquinas contests the occasionalism of those Islamic thinkers who believed that the power of God was the sole explanation for the transfer of properties from cause to effect. According to occasionalism, rather than residing in the inherent power of the cause, the effect can only be brought about by direct divine action. In this way, the appearances deceive. The burning of the wood in the fire is not the result of the fire's causing the wood to burn. This is no explanation at all. Instead, we must assume that God, as sole cause, brings about the consumption of wood by fire. In this respect, everything that happens can be considered a miracle.

Although he is open to the possibility of miracles as cases where secondary causality may be absent, Aquinas resists the case for a universal occasionalism. It is contrary to our sense experience and reason, which teach us that there is a transmission of property from cause to effect. There is no barrier to our believing that this is so. Our senses do not massively deceive us in relation to the cause–effect nexus in the natural world.[27] The processes that we see all around constitute a natural order endowed with a derived potentiality that God has created *ex nihilo*. The power to change actually resides in the fire itself; this is not an illusion that God generates. 'God is active in the nature or will that acts, not that he is active as if the natural things did nothing, and we need to show how we can understand this.'[28]

---

[27] In the *Summa Contra Gentiles*, 3.69, Aquinas tends to dismiss occasionalism as an 'absurd' doctrine.

[28] Thomas Aquinas, *The Power of God*, trans. Richard J. Regan (Oxford: Oxford University Press, 2012), p. 56.

The four respects in which God is the cause of other causes are as follows:

i) God confers upon natural things the power to act. This is an aspect of creation in which God brings about entities that have the capacity to act with causal efficacy.

ii) In preserving these powers to act, God may also be considered the cause of other causes. As constantly sustaining a world in which there are causal forces, God is the underlying cause or power. This again does not place God within a natural causal nexus so much as recognise God as its necessary and sufficient condition.

iii) The third way in which God brings about creaturely causes moves towards a stronger sense of a divine willing of powers to act. Aquinas notes the tendency of higher powers to order lower powers throughout the created order. He offers the example of a hand moving a knife to cut. The knife is the cause but only through its being moved by the hand. As the highest and transcendent power, God must also be understood not merely as enabling creaturely causes but as actively moving them in their exercise of powers.

iv) Finally, there is an order to be recognised in the movement of all causal powers. As first and final cause, God ordains the totality of higher and lower powers in creation. Though difficult to distinguish from the preceding, this last aspect of divine causality appears to secure the will of God as the single cause of everything that happens. Divine agency is not confined to setting the initial conditions for creaturely causes but empowers each and every one of these. Hence from a philosophical perspective, the divine will must be regarded as bringing about everything that happens but through secondary forms of creaturely causality.

Therefore, God causes each action inasmuch as he bestows the power to act, preserves it, and applies it to action, and inasmuch as every other power acts by his power. And when we have added to these things that God is his power, and that he is within each thing as what holds the thing in existence, not as part of the thing's essence, we will conclude that he acts directly in each active thing, without excluding action by the will and nature.[29]

We can now see the ways in which this Thomist account differs from later deist readings of creation, which tend to restrict divine action to the first two senses above. In creating and ordering a natural world inhabited by rational agents, God's work is restricted to a providential sustaining. In this world, natural causes and human agents are given their place but without much sense of their effects being willed or guaranteed by God. Standing foursquare in the western medieval tradition, Aquinas cannot allow any explanatory gap between the divine will and what comes about through created natures. Divine agency is strongly interpreted as a transcendent potency that brings about each created power and its consequences. Both deism and pantheism are excluded on this account.

Aquinas's account of double agency has a metaphysical elegance and religious appeal. Meticulously developed through the use of Aristotelian concepts, his theory also has the capacity to represent God as deeply involved in everything that happens. In this respect, it was an account that Calvin could readily deploy in the sixteenth century in opposition to any theology that rendered God idle as a spectator, unconcerned with the minutiae of the world, or not fully in control of the creation. Given that all these options had to be eschewed, this account of double agency offers an attractive alternative.

Yet the theory of double agency, at least in this form, comes with serious drawbacks for a theology of providence that intends to make sense of Scripture and much of our experience. A single act of primary divine causation that governs the universe sits uneasily with an account of God's wrestling with difficult and recalcitrant creaturely material. Notions of divine struggle and worldly resistance are harder to accommodate on this model. Moreover, the

[29] Ibid., p. 58.

particularity of divine providence is also threatened. If God is active in everything that happens, how can we think of divine action as producing some beneficial outcomes but not others? Despite its best intentions, critics have argued that, given the opacity of the link between primary and secondary causation, this account will tend to veer either towards an all-embracing determinism, as in occasionalism, or towards a mere setting of the initial conditions of creation, as in deism. The standard Thomist response is that considered in its totality the whole creation is consistently ordered to a single divine purpose. From our perspective, some events are more clearly expressive of that purpose than others. These are intended by God as disclosures to us. Nevertheless, the religious conviction that God is causally active in specific ways in some events, rather than others, seems to require an account of special providence which cuts across the divide between primary and secondary causality. Christians wish to acknowledge the action of the Holy Spirit as particular in some events that bear God's signature. In this respect, the classical account of double agency proves too much or too little. On the one hand, in explaining everything as caused or willed by God, the theory seems to over-determine much of what happens as in accordance with a single divine intention. This produces difficulties in relation both to what is trivial and to what is horrendously evil. On the other hand, with its different levels of explanation that can never compete or conflict, the account runs into difficulties in describing the more interactive and dialogical aspects of the relationship between God and creatures. To address these problems may not require the abandonment of all forms of double agency – I shall later argue, following Austin Farrer, that some accommodation of this notion is required for a theology of providence. But some significant adjustment and nuancing of its terms may be required if its difficulties are to be overcome.

Before leaving Aquinas, some attention to his scriptural commentaries is necessary. The accounts offered by Aquinas in the *Summa Theologiae*, the *Summa Contra Gentiles* and *De Potentia* do not readily reflect all the scriptural marks of divine providence that were noted earlier. Although the order and rhythms of the natural world and creaturely life are readily expressed, along with the sense of a final *telos*, it is harder to accommodate notions of creaturely recalcitrance together with the in-breaking and disruptive character of God's grace. There is something consoling in the doctrine that everything has a pre-ordained purpose. But it is less clear whether this is adequate to the magnitude of evil or the destructive randomness of what befalls (some of) us, and hence to the counteractive character of divine redemption. These themes are more evident in the scriptural commentaries of the classical theologians, where a nuancing of more systematic positions can be discerned. In expounding Matthew 24:45, where Jesus speaks about the importance of vigilance until the return of the head of the household, Aquinas interprets this as an ethical injunction set upon the church 'to give food in due season' to others whether that be the sacraments or a sharing of material resources. Commenting on this passage, Michael Dempsey writes, 'Clearly, then if we adhere to scripture as the norm and understand the philosophy for its greater manifestation, then the particular ordering of all things in Christ to their end in God is evident whenever superiors provide for their subordinates through their exemplary apostolic life and the distribution of their resources to the poor.'[30]

This reading of Aquinas points usefully to the ways in which human agents are not only the passive objects of divine providence but also those who can act providentially for others. Following Origen, Aquinas writes that 'to give food in due season calls for prudence in a man; not to take away the food of the needy requires faithfulness.'[31] Divine providence can be enacted in the love of our

---

[30] Michael Dempsey, 'Providence, distributive justice and divine government in the theology of Thomas Aquinas', *New Blackfriars*, 90 (2009), 365–84 at 379.

[31] Thomas Aquinas, *Catena Aurea*, ed. J. H. Newman, vol. I.III (London: J. G. F. & G. Rivington, 1842), p. 838. I owe the reference to this passage to Dempsey, 'Providence, distributive justice and divine government'.

neighbour, so that we become the instruments by which grace breaks into the lives of others. This deserves to be accentuated in any worthy account of providence. As capable of being activated by our own deeds through the power of God's Spirit, providence can be retrieved from the more passive and determinist constructions which construct us too readily as its victims.[32]

There are undoubtedly elements in Aquinas which offer much for a constructive theology of providence, not least in his scriptural commentaries. While constrained by the inheritance of Augustine's doctrine of predestination, he seeks to generate space for human freedom, cooperation with God, the agency of petitionary prayer, and a practical acceptance of God's mercy and justice.[33] Yet his theory of double agency with its account of secondary causes as instruments of God's primal agency leads to a single, all-determining act of providence. This tradition, especially when the links with predestination become more explicit, would produce a powerful though problematic rendition of the subject in the Reformed tradition. On this reading, Aquinas, for all his brilliance and deeply Christian sensibility, remains too enthralled to an earlier philosophical tradition mediated by Augustine and Boethius. Calvin and the Reformed orthodox relentlessly pursued the same course.[34]

---

[32] Ellen Charry points to the ways in which for Aquinas our human agency can act in a reciprocal analogical relation to God. 'Enacting our identity as instruments of God's intention for creation through wise self-use pleases the agent. Advancing creation's well-being is both enjoyable for its own sake and brings God joy.' *God and the Art of Happiness* (Grand Rapids: Eerdmans, 2010), p. 160.

[33] See for example his commentary on the closing speech of God in Job 40. Thomas Aquinas, *The Literal Exposition of Job: A Scriptural Commentary Concerning Providence*, trans. Anthony Damien (Atlanta: Scholars' Press, 1989), p. 445.

[34] Nevertheless, some other possibilities for the theology of providence are apparent throughout this period. For example, in his *De Visione Dei*, Nicolas of Cusa writes movingly of the divine gaze that sees everything with a paternal affection. He identifies this with providence. But though we are entirely dependent upon the face of God for our being, this generates a freedom that is itself a divine gift. 'Because you have placed this matter within my freedom, You do not coerce me: rather, You

In its reaction against Thomism, the Molinist tradition of the late sixteenth century adopted a different approach to divine providence by deploying the concept of middle knowledge. *Scientia media* is neither a knowledge of necessary truths nor knowledge generated by divine fiat about what will come to pass. Instead it is the knowledge that God possesses of what creatures will do under different sets of conditions. This assigns to creatures a greater measure of independence and autonomy, while remaining under the foreknowledge and rule of God. In creating this world from among other possible worlds, God's decision is partly dependent upon a knowledge of what voluntary agents will choose to do. What happens is in part up to us (to recall the language of the theologians of the east), though God's providence will always superintend our free choices. The Molinist modification is matched by departures within the Reformed tradition from the same standard account of divine predestination and human choices. These stem from shared anxieties about the seeming determinism and capriciousness of the default position of the western tradition in which the total system of causal outcomes is generated from a single, unswerving divine decision.[35]

Although some nuances and shifts of emphasis can be detected in late medieval developments, the reassertion of a strong and meticulous theology of providence by writers such as Thomas Bradwardine provides the context for the Reformed appropriation of the concept. Resisting more covenantal and synergist approach to providence, Bradwardine stresses the sovereign hand of God in everything that happens. This account has been described as 'self-evident, all-pervasive and intimate' and hence as foreshadowing the

---

await my choosing to be my own. The matter is up to me, then, not up to you.' Jasper Hopkins, *Nicolas of Cusa's Dialectical Mysticism: Text, Translation and Interpretive Study of De Visione Dei* (Minneapolis: Arthur J. Banning Press, 1985), p. 147. My colleague Simon Burton has pointed me to ways in which Cusa influenced later thinkers, including Comenius and C. S. Lewis, on this matter.

[35] See for example Thomas P. Flint, 'Two accounts of providence' in Morris, *Divine and Human Action*, pp. 147–81.

later Protestant conviction that every detail of our personal lives is governed by God's providential rule.[36]

2.3 The Sixteenth-Century Reformed Tradition

The Reformed tradition has typically placed a strong emphasis upon the doctrine of providence. This moving section of the Heidelberg Catechism (1563) is often quoted.[37]

Q.27 What do you understand by the providence of God?

A. The almighty and ever-present power of God whereby he still upholds, as it were by his own hand, heaven and earth together with all creatures, and rules in such a way that leaves and grass, rain and drought, fruitful and unfruitful years, food and drink, health and sickness, riches and poverty, and everything else, come to us not by chance but his fatherly hand.

Q28 What advantage comes from acknowledging God's creation and providence?

A. We learn that we are to be patient in adversity, grateful in the midst of blessing, and to trust our faithful God and Father for the future, assured that no creature shall separate us from his love, since all creatures are so completely in his hand that without his will they cannot even move.

Providence is also accentuated in many of the metrical psalms that emerged from the French-Genevan tradition, for example Psalm 23, 'The Lord's My Shepherd', or Psalm 121 'I to the Hills Will Lift Mine Eyes', that were found fitting for all occasions – birth, marriage

---

[36] Hester Goodenough Gelber, 'Providence' in Robert Pasnau (ed.), *The Cambridge History of Medieval Philosophy*, 2nd edn (Cambridge: Cambridge University Press, 2014), pp. 761–72 at p. 772.

[37] See A. C. Cochrane (ed.), *Reformed Confessions of the Sixteenth Century* (Philadelphia: Westminster John Knox Press, 2003), pp. 309–10.

and death could equally well be marked by psalms of praise which were powerful and passionate without lapsing into false sentiment. The school I attended in Glasgow required us to sing Psalm 121 at the beginning and end of every term. I could faithfully recite 'the moon by night thee shall not smite, nor yet the sun by day', even though I had no comprehension of its meaning. Many of the familiar paraphrases that emerged in the eighteenth century also focus repeatedly on divine providence. Best known among these might be 'O God of Bethel' (based on an earlier hymn by an English Independent writer, Philip Doddridge). Its penultimate verse blends maternal and paternal images of God's care.

> O spread thy covering wings around
> Till all our wanderings cease.
> And at our Father's loved abode
> Our souls arrive in peace.

Why did providence emerge as such a resonant article in the Reformed tradition? This is closely related to a similar question about predestination. One sort of answer will properly appeal to the theme of *sola gratia* as a reflection of divine sovereignty. Whatever good befalls us is a token of divine mercy, whether by creation or by redemption. Another type of answer is that the early Reformed communities in cities such as Strasbourg and Geneva were beleaguered. Comprised in part of refugees who had fled other parts of Europe, these were disparate and threatened groups that sought assurance, strength and comfort from their most cherished convictions. In the face of persecution, the assurance offered by the doctrines of election and providence became a source of comfort and fortification. Heiko Oberman notes that these ideas are important resources in the 'city Reformation'. Arriving from other parts of Europe in Zurich and Geneva, refugees were energised by the thought that their security was guaranteed by God's providence alone. Divine guidance and provision were consoling strategies for people driven from their homes and native lands. When combined with notions of the elect chosen by God from all eternity, the classical idea of providence proved to be of important practical force. In times of political uncertainty and upheaval, assurance was derived only from faith in the protection of God. Yet, as Oberman also notes, these ideas could become more oppressive and unsettling in different political circumstances such as those obtaining at Dordt the following century. The preaching and liturgical celebration of a theological idea can prove fruitful in one context, yet counter-productive in another, if elevated to the status of an organising principle.

> The limitations emerge when election is no longer the confession of the church-in-the-diaspora which, with only one patria left, cries out: 'We have no other place of refuge but his providence.' The doctrine of election becomes not merely a limitation but an abomination when it is uprooted and displaced in its turn, torn from its biblical context in the pilgrimage of the church.[38]

William Naphy has similarly argued that, although predestination worked much better for this group, it was received with less conviction by those who had grown up in the Genevan church. Many found it to be unnecessary and even baffling.[39] Similarly, providence emerges here as a constitutive theme of the Christian life that works best for those who are facing testing times. It is not so much a function of a serene and prosperous lifestyle as the refuge of those on the underside of history. Trust in providence is the mark of those who are persecuted, threatened and placed in hazardous circumstances. The *Scots Confession* (1560) illustrates this with its description of the Christian life.

---

[38] Heiko A. Oberman, *The Two Reformations: The Journey from the Last Days to the New World* (New Haven: Yale University Press, 2003), p. 150.

[39] William Naphy, 'Calvin's Geneva' in Donald McKim (ed.), *Cambridge Companion to John Calvin* (Cambridge: Cambridge University Press, 2004), pp. 25–37 at p. 33.

Others do not share this conflict since they do not have God's Spirit, but they readily follow and obey sin and feel no regrets, since they act as the devil and their corrupt nature urge. But the sons of God fight against sin; sob and mourn when they find themselves tempted to do evil; and, if they fall, rise again with earnest unfeigned repentance. They do these things, not by their own power, but by the power of the Lord Jesus, apart from whom they can do nothing.[40]

In his commentary on the confessions, Dowey notes that this approach is inverted by those modern forms of evangelical piety where the happy and untroubled life is seen as a sign of divine blessing. This earlier characterisation of the godly life is far from a contemporary gospel of prosperity. Today it is the ungodly who experience turmoil in contrast to the blessed fortunes of the faithful.[41]

Nevertheless, in many of its sixteenth- and seventeenth-century expressions, the theology of providence is an embattled and energising article of faith. People were urged to leave their homes and communities to make common cause with the faithful in Geneva or wherever they could be found. If not by Calvin, political theories of resistance were developed by Beza and Knox. Persuaded that God was on their side and was calling them to rebellion, Puritans and covenanters were sometimes willing to bear arms. Providentialism did not always display a demobilising tendency in its outcomes. In resistance and rebellion, one could equally well be animated by a

---

[40] *Scots Confession*, chapter 13. See Cochrane, *Reformed Confessions of the Sixteenth Century*, pp. 172–3.

[41] Edward A. Dowey Jr, *A Commentary on the Confession of 1967 and Introduction to the 'Book of Confessions'* (Philadelphia: Westminster, 1968), p. 182. Eleonore Stump has also noted the ways in which an untroubled life was to be viewed with suspicion in patristic spirituality. 'Chemotherapeutic regimens are withheld from people with cancer only in case they are so ill that the therapy cannot do them any good. That is why, when good things happen to good people, Gregory finds the ways of providence so hard to understand.' *Wandering in Darkness: Narrative and the Problems of Suffering* (Oxford: Oxford University Press, 2010), p. 400.

conviction that God was working in and through a just cause that would surely prevail. As Michael Walzer argues:

> The saints interpret their ability to endure this discipline as a sign of their virtue and their virtue as a sign of God's grace. Amidst the confusion of the transitional period, they discover in themselves a predestination, a firm and undeviating sense of purpose, an assurance of eventual triumph.[42]

Was this a misreading or a bold recovery of authentic scriptural insights for the times? To venture a judgement on this question, we will need to examine the outworking of providential convictions over several centuries.

2.3.1 Providence in Zurich

Zwingli's *De Providentia* (1530) is the most developed early Reformed treatise on providence.[43] Based on a series of sermons, it follows a rigorously determinist view of the divine rule based on classical philosophy and Scripture. In a text replete with references to Plato and Seneca, Zwingli assumes an alliance on this subject between ancient philosophy and Christian theology. Providence must exist, he argues, because the supreme good necessarily cares for and regulates all things. Zwingli even worries about the distinction between primary and secondary causes. God must superintend the latter and we must avoid any suggestion of creaturely autonomy. Secondary causes are instruments properly understood.[44] Despite his extensive citation of Scripture in the latter part of the treatise, it seems clear that Zwingli's initial articulation and defence of providence are primarily philosophical. Its meaning and

---

[42] Michael Walzer, *The Revolution of the Saints: A Study in the Origins of Radical Politics* (London: Weidenfeld and Nicolson, 1966), 317.

[43] Zwingli, *On Providence.*

[44] See W. P. Stephens, 'Election in Zwingli and Bullinger: a comparison of Zwingli's *Sermonis de Providentia Dei Anamnema* (1530) and Bullinger's *Oratio de Moderatione*

truth are presented in terms of arguments that require the postulation of a First Cause who is supremely wise, good and sovereign over all. There is little here with which Garrigou-Lagrange would have quibbled.

> [W]e shall see both that Providence must exist and that it cares for and regulates all things. For since it is of the nature of supreme truth to see through all things clearly, inasmuch as that which is divinity must see all things, and since it is of the nature of supreme might to be able to do what it sees, nay, to do all things, and, finally, since it is of the nature of the supreme good, to will by its goodness to do what it clearly sees and can do, it follows that he who can do all things, must provide for all things.[45]

This provision is interpreted in a determinist manner by Zwingli both through a series of arguments and through numerous examples drawn from Scripture. A binary opposition is assumed between divine sovereignty and randomness. Unless each event is willed by God towards some end, then it will be the result merely of random forces and therefore outside the scope of providence. This would generate a universe in which some things eluded the wise comprehension of God. A duality would then be established between divine causality and a creaturely contingency that lacked any adequate explanation. Providence must ordain everything that happens; if we cannot see any obvious purpose in each circumstance, this is merely the result of our human limitation. Yet Scripture is able to point to ways in which seemingly incidental events are ordained by God to assist us in our faith. The story of Joseph, according to Zwingli, provides the clearest evidence of this. The coat of many colours, Joseph's dreams, the crime of his brothers, his languishing in prison, his rise to high office in

Servanda in *Negotio Providentiae, Praedestinationis, Gratiae et Liberi Arbitrii* (1536)', *Reformation and Renaissance Review*, 7 (2005), 42–56.

[45] Zwingli, *On Providence and Other Essays*, p. 133.

Egypt – each of these events represents something of the wonderful wisdom of God imparted to us. So Zwingli concludes that, 'Joseph's life is nothing else than a testimony to the fact that all things are done by Providence. There is no event in which it has been shown not to have taken place at its good time by command and ordination of God.'[46] Zwingli is not inattentive to Scripture nor to the spiritual significance of the church's teaching on this matter. Indeed his own trust in the disposition of God's providence seems to have been a constant in his life, after he survived the plague in 1519.[47] Yet he shares the assumption of much of the early church and medieval traditions that providence is an article that can be stated and maintained in significant measure apart from Scripture, on grounds that are already established in ancient philosophy. On this matter at least, there can be a consensus between paganism and Christianity.

Several years later in Zurich, the young Heinrich Bullinger would offer a more moderate account that sought to avoid some of the harsher implications of Zwingli's predestinarianism. His approach is more thoroughly driven by scriptural examples, with a stress on divine mercy and also on the perceived need to attribute neither too much nor too little to God's action. His position mediates between Pelagianism and Manichaeism, whereas Zwingli's tends to be driven merely by hostility to the former.[48] Yet these differences in Zurich should not be exaggerated. In preaching on providence in the *Decades*, Bullinger sets out an account of both election and providence which is not significantly different from Zwingli and Calvin, except perhaps in its refusal to speculate much beyond the text of Scripture. Insisting that faith is 'a most assured sign that thou art elected', Bullinger seems aware of the capacity of the doctrine

---

[46] Ibid., p. 216.

[47] See the discussion in W. P. Stephens, *The Theology of Huldrych Zwingli* (Oxford: Clarendon Press, 1986), pp. 86–97.

[48] Here I am following Stephens, 'Election in Zwingli and Bullinger'.

to arouse fear and uncertainty. Yet its double aspect remains quite explicit in his teaching.[49]

These shifts in emphasis and presentation illustrate the ways in which the sixteenth-century Reformed tradition already included some diversity in this and other respects, a point that may offer some encouragement to those who seek to revise its standard account of providence.

2.3.2 Providence in Calvin

The most influential Reformed approach to providence is set out in John Calvin's *Institutes*.[50] For Calvin, divine providence is a necessary aspect of creation. Here there is a heavy stress on the attentiveness to detail in God's government of the world. It is not a general ordering or superintendence from a distance but instead a wise and all-pervasive action of ruling, willing and guiding. The doctrine of providence teaches the divine interaction with creation at the micro-level. Providence cannot be reduced to an initial determining cause which enables it to run programmatically in accordance with a divine blueprint. God's hand is to be detected in the operation of the laws of nature and in historical forces. Providence is not the infusing of nature with general powers but the particular care of every created thing. As Christ taught, the benevolence of God

---

[49] Heinrich Bullinger, *Decades*, vol. IV, ed. Thomas Harding (Cambridge: Cambridge University Press, 1851), Sermon 4, p. 187. The view that Bullinger represents a different emphasis rather than a new trajectory in Reformed theology is argued by Cornelis P. Venema, *Heinrich Bullinger and the Doctrine of Predestination: Author of 'The Other Reformed Tradition'?* (Grand Rapids: Baker, 2002).

[50] See John Calvin, *Institutes of the Christian Religion*, trans. Ford Lewis Battles (Philadelphia: Westminster, 1960), I.16–17, 183–209. Calvin's position had already taken shape in earlier editions of the text. For example, he writes 'Nevertheless let it remain unresolved in our heart that nothing will happen which God has not ordained.' *Institutes of the Christian Religion: 1541 French Edition*, trans. Elsie Anne McKee (Grand Rapids: Eerdmans, 2009), p. 446.

extends to the level of little birds, whose sustaining of themselves is 'virtually a miracle'.[51] John Leith argues that Calvin's horror of deism leads him to the brink of pantheism, a position he only avoids by repeated stress on divine transcendence.[52]

In his exposition of providence, Calvin rehearses several familiar themes. In almost all of what he writes in this context, he does not see himself as innovative or original. His intention is quite the reverse, since he strives to show the faithfulness of his reflections to the plain sense of Scripture and to the best of what we find in the traditions of the church, especially Augustine. Of the 3200 direct references to the church fathers in Calvin's writings, over half of these are to Augustine who is generally enlisted in support of his claims.[53]

Calvin sees the hand of God in everything that happens. Nothing takes place that does not contribute to the fulfilment of the divine purpose, even if much of this is by virtue of a divine overruling and therefore adapting of creaturely confusion. God does not sleep but is forever vigilant, energetic and active. We must rid ourselves of pagan notions. It is simply wrong to attribute bad or good outcomes to luck, chance or fortune; these are always the instruments by which God's secret purpose is advanced. What seems the consequence of good fortune should be acknowledged as a token of God's faithfulness, forbearance, grace and mercy. Conversely, ill fortune is the mark of divine displeasure, punishment, chastisement or discipline. So we are to be grateful in the midst of blessing and obedient in times of trouble. Several further features of Calvin's account should be noted.

---

[51] John Calvin, *A Harmony of the Gospels: Matthew, Mark and Luke*, ed. D. W. Torrance and T. F. Torrance, 3 vols. (Edinburgh: St Andrew Press, 1972), vol. I, p. 221.

[52] John Leith, *John Calvin's Doctrine of the Christian Life* (Louisville: Westminster/John Knox, 1989), p. 112.

[53] See Brian Gerrish, 'The place of Calvin in Christian theology' in Donald McKim (ed.), *Cambridge Companion to John Calvin* (Cambridge: Cambridge University Press, 2004), pp. 291–304 at p. 291.

i) Divine providence cannot be reduced merely to foresight. It is not simply that God foreknows what will happen to us. God surely possesses this prescience, but divine providence extends to an active willing of what takes place and not merely a foreknowing of outcomes with respect to which God's will is indisposed. The route favoured by Orthodox, Lutheran, Molinist and Arminian theologians is firmly blocked by Calvin at this juncture.

ii) The epistemological limitation of providence is repeatedly asserted by Calvin. The meaning of events is largely hidden in God's secret counsel. We cannot work out why this or that took place. For the time being, it is a mystery that awaits fuller disclosure. Nevertheless, Calvin qualifies this by adding that we are given some very clear signs. Indeed, so confident is he in this respect that providence becomes for him on occasion a piece of natural theology. Evident all around us, the great disparities in human circumstance can only have their explanation in the ways in which God disposes to act differently towards us. Here Calvin's doctrine tilts in a problematic direction: 'We must see that some mothers have full provision for their infants, and others almost none, according as it is the pleasure of God to nourish one child more liberally, and another more sparingly.'[54] This observation is later extended to the distinction between rich and poor, with Calvin urging a patient endurance upon the latter class, as opposed to a discontent resulting in a desire to shake off 'a burden that God has imposed upon them'.[55] Earlier in the *Institutes*, Calvin has already suggested that God's special providence can be observed from the course of human affairs. Just as general providence can be detected by the observations of the planets and the regularities of the seasons, so we can each see the daily signs of special providence. 'The righteous are the special objects of his favour, the wicked and profane the special

---

[54] Calvin, *Institutes*, I.16.3.

[55] Ibid., I.16.6.

objects of his severity.'[56] It is as if the fundamental separation of human beings into two classes can already be discerned from the page of history. God's favour or displeasure is registered by whatever befalls us amid the changes and chances of this life.[57]

iii) Despite the perpetual activity of God in ruling the world we cannot justifiably depict God as the author of sin and evil. Here Calvin eschews the distinction between divine willing and permitting. God does not sit in a watch-tower viewing what happens fortuitously. (Calvin seems to assume that a mere permission on God's part would betoken a lack of involvement or interest in the world, though this can be questioned.) Scripture is clear that what happens is finally to be explained by the will of God. Repeatedly, Calvin has recourse to passages in Job where suffering and seeming misfortune are held to come directly from the hand of God. This conclusion is inescapable. To avoid divine authorship of sin and evil, Calvin employs instead the medieval distinction between primary and secondary causality. The intermediate causes of sin are created agencies; these alone are culpable. God as the primary cause of everything may will all that happens, but since the divine agency is primary and not secondary we cannot attribute blame to God, whose purposes are always just and gracious. Employing a metaphor noted earlier, he points out that though the rays of the sun may cause the corpse to putrefy, it is the corpse which stinks, not the sun.

---

[56] Ibid., I.5.7.

[57] The hiddenness of God's providential order is accentuated in Calvin's exegesis of Job. Though this is relative to the revelation of God as judge and disposer, it remains a sombre theme in his existential struggles to discern the hand of providence in the world. See Susan E. Schreiner, *Where Shall Wisdom Be Found? Calvin's Exegesis of Job from Medieval and Modern Perspectives* (Chicago: University of Chicago Press, 1994), pp. 93–5. Describing the hiddenness of God in the Reformers, Brian Gerrish notes that the term 'secret' (*arcanum*) remains Calvin's most characteristic description of God's design (*consilium*). *The Old Protestantism and the New* (Edinburgh: T&T Clark, 1982), p. 141.

This same move enables him to make sense of voluntary action. Although our human deeds are overruled by God's providence, these are often performed as a result of voluntary causes. God can work through human wills as well as against them. In this sense, divine action can be said to guarantee human responsibility. The paradigmatic instance of this is Judas' betrayal of Jesus. This is the responsibility and fault of Judas but God wills it as the occasion of our redemption. So, as Augustine taught in his reflection on Psalm 11:2,[58] God can mysteriously will what in another sense contravenes the divine will so that good comes out of evil. Convinced that this is the clear teaching of Scripture, Calvin concludes his account of providence by observing the need for a 'meek docility'. For good measure, he adds that anyone who wishes to indulge their petulance in this matter is undeserving of a longer refutation.[59]

The psychological, spiritual and socio-political dimensions of this pronounced stress on providence require attention. Calvin is in no doubt that this doctrine is of inestimable practical value in the Christian life. It relieves us from unnecessary anxiety in the face of seemingly uncertain circumstances. As a result, the mind can be redirected to more useful concerns. All things come to pass by a divine dispensation. This elicits an attitude of trust that nothing can happen by fortune or chance. Everything is under the paternal care of God. There is good practical wisdom in this. A consideration of the evils which may befall can induce anxiety and paralysis. The ship may sink. There lurks danger on the streets and in the fields. One's house may burn. Even within a high-walled garden a serpent may lie in wait. In the face of possible misfortune we draw a feeble breath.[60] The remedy is to trust God and commit oneself to the knowledge that all things are ruled by a parental care. This doubtless affords

[58] Calvin, *Institutes*, I.18.3.

[59] Ibid., I.18.4.

[60] Ibid., I.17.10.

comfort, and promotes constancy throughout the Christian life. It may even energise one for secular action. (We are not far from the Weber thesis here.) If Joseph had allowed himself to be consumed by anger and thoughts of gaining revenge upon his brothers, then he could never have rediscovered his fraternal affection.

Acknowledgement of providence makes us teachable, obedient and patient even amid adversity. In good times, we are humbled, sobered and made 'unfeignedly thankful' (Book of Common Prayer) in the way that we live. In bad times, we learn endurance and strength of character. The rhetoric of determinism informs Calvin's account and it promotes a particular type of piety. Attacking Epicurean notions of chance, he insists upon everything being ordained by God. He speaks of those words of beautiful solitude, 'The Lord gave, and the Lord has taken away: blessed be the name of the Lord' (Job 1:21). Summarising the attitude of those who have made no little progress in their meditation on divine providence, he writes, 'The Lord willed it, it must therefore be borne; not only because it is unlawful to strive with him, but because he wills nothing that is not just and befitting.'[61]

This form of piety is confirmed by Calvin's Commentary on the Psalms, where he avows that faith, prayer and all the duties of religion depend upon the conviction that every single event happens by the personal rule of God.[62] All things are ruled by God. Therefore, we are required to view evils that befall us as signs of divine displeasure with our sins while also perceiving anything good as a token of God's unmerited favour. Patience and gratitude amid everything that befalls us are the hallmarks of a true piety. Here

---

[61] Ibid., I.17.8. See also Heinrich Heppe's compendium, Reformed Dogmatics, trans. G. T. Thomson (London: Allen & Unwin, 1950), pp. 251–80. Interestingly, this conjunction of intellectual and practical knowledge is similar to al-Ghazali's advocacy of trust in divine providence (tawakkul). See David B. Burrell, Towards a Jewish–Christian–Muslim Theology (Oxford: Wiley Blackwell, 2011), pp. 63–85.

[62] John Calvin, Commentary on the Book of Psalms, vol. IV, trans. James Anderson (Grand Rapids: Baker, 1989), pp. 205–45.

one might register again the criticism that the providential action of God tends to be appropriated to the first person of the Trinity in Calvin. All of the 270 uses of *providentia* in the *Commentary on the Psalms* seem to be attributed to God as Father. What is missing is any ascription of providential action to the Holy Spirit, whose activity is unpredictable, free, surprising and in dynamic interaction with creatures. B. B. Warfield may have been right for other reasons to label Calvin 'the theologian of the Holy Spirit' but his theology of providence reveals a serious pneumatological deficit.[63]

Despite its pastoral benefits, Calvin's doctrine has its practical downside. In the face of life's fragility, it has the dubious effect of suppressing complaint or questioning. There can be no interrogation of God. The Psalms of lament do not feature positively in Calvin's treatment of providence in the *Institutes*. Nor is there any trace of the importunate widow. Jewish themes of complaint and disputation with God tend to be suppressed, although these are not altogether excluded. Christian patience, he insists, is not the same as Stoic resignation.[64] One practical danger of this is that it renders the doctrine a demobilising force. By inducing acceptance, it generates resistance to change. Passivity instead of revolt is occasioned. The prophets' inveighing against injustice, poverty and the exploitation of the rich and powerful is not given sufficient coverage, at least at this juncture in Calvinist theology. One might also argue that the doctrine's close links to election ironically induced that very *uncertainty* that it was intended to banish. Providence, it seems, does not have a beneficial outcome for everyone. There are divergent tracks

---

[63] Charles Hodge insists upon distinguishing God's providence from the influences of the Holy Spirit. Somewhat confusingly, he equates this with the distinction between nature and grace. See *Systematic Theology*, 3 vols. (Grand Rapids: Eerdmans, 1989), vol. I, pp. 614–16.

[64] See Calvin, *Institutes*, III.7.8. Cynthia L. Rigby argues perceptively that Calvin does not allow sufficient scope for creaturely contingency and playfulness under God's providence. See 'Providence and play', *Insights: The Faculty Journal of Austin Theological Seminary*, 126.2 (2011), 10–18.

leading to contrasting destinations, though each attests God's justice and grace, albeit in different ways. While Calvin also taught that the doctrine of election was to be employed as a source of reassurance and strength, its double aspect inevitably rendered it a source of disquiet, unease and fear as individuals began to ask themselves whether they could know that they were numbered among the elect, rather than the reprobate. Under this pressure, the Reformed tradition tended to advertise the doctrine of predestination as a 'high mystery' to be handled with caution, rather than the occasion of unqualified evangelical proclamation.[65]

In defence of Calvin, one can point to commentaries and sermons where different themes are enunciated. These are more accommodating of notions of resistance, struggle and a divine wrestling with unruly creaturely forces. As with the writers of the early church, exegetical themes in Calvin may tug in a different direction. His attention elsewhere to the details of the scriptural text and its unfolding of the gospel through contingent historical events offers some surprising reflections. The theme of accommodation, which is found everywhere in his theology, is employed to show that God chooses individuals, gives laws and directs Israel in such a way as to accommodate human weakness and frailty.[66] Here the providence of God is presented as more reactive. It must wrestle with recalcitrant human material. The outcome is divine action which in order to prevail must improvise to a much greater degree than is conceded in the *Institutes*. Despite what Calvin says elsewhere in his Psalms commentary, there is a stronger sense of divine struggle, concession and perseverance when he deals with the history of Israel as narrated in

---

[65] See *The Westminster Confession of Faith*, chapter 3.

[66] I owe this insight to David F. Wright's study of Calvin on the Pentateuch: 'Calvin's Pentateuchal criticism: equity, hardness of heart, and divine accommodation in the Mosaic harmony commentary', *Calvin Theological Journal*, 21 (1986), 33–50. He comments, 'The distinctive element in this presentation seems not the gracious condescension of God but his malleability, even his vulnerability, indeed even his captivity to the passions and lusts of his rude people' (p. 46).

Psalm 106.[67] And in his social theology he argues that poverty is an offence against the honour of God which requires urgent remedy.[68] As with Aquinas, Calvin's exegetical work can incline him in other directions, though this is not properly integrated into his standard account of divine providence, which tends towards a more comprehensive divine control and a resultant human quietism.

2.4 Reformed Orthodoxy

Was Calvin a Calvinist? This was once a hot topic, although the debate has subsided in recent times. On the subject of providence, later writers tended to codify, develop and defend the account offered by Calvin, Bullinger and other sixteenth-century writers against later philosophical and theological trends. In doing so, the Reformed found ways to resist the synergism of Lutheran and Arminian theologians and also the arguments of Molinist and Socinian thinkers. But it is difficult here to disjoin later expressions of the tradition from earlier ones, as if Calvin might not have been numbered among the Calvinists. Attempts to distinguish an evangelical Calvinism from a desiccated Reformed orthodoxy have found little support in recent scholarship, which has drawn attention to the vitality of the tradition throughout the seventeenth century.

We find in Reformed orthodoxy a patient development of all the themes already noted in Calvin. The use of the threefold form of providence in preservation (*praeservatio*), concurrence (*concurratio* or *concursus*) and government (*gubernatio*) provides a more systematic treatment of the idea.[69] This threefold pattern proved useful in describing the scope of divine providence while also articulating

---

[67] Calvin, *Commentary on the Psalms*.

[68] See Nicholas Wolterstorff, 'The wounds of God: Calvin's theology of social justice' in *Hearing the Call: Liturgy, Justice, Church, and World* (Grand Rapids: Eerdmans, 2011), pp. 114–32.

[69] The origin of the threefold form of providence is hard to trace, though its attribution to the Lutheran dogmatician J. F. König in his *Theologia positive*

important distinctions, especially that between primary and secondary causality. These three forms of providence together express the conditions, means and purposes by which God governs the creation in a single continuous action according to the eternal decree.

i) The contingent status of the world as created out of nothing entails that it requires more than itself for its ongoing existence and sustaining. To hold the world in being, the conserving action of God is a constant requirement.

ii) The divine concurrence is not to be understood in terms of a causal partnership; instead, it is the way in which God as the primal cause works in and through secondary causes. These are willed as the means to the fulfilment of the primal cause – hence concurrence involves a divine willing that is more than mere enablement or permission. This does not restrict or loosen the control of divine providence so much as articulate its mode of operation.

iii) Finally, the divine government or overruling of all causal forces denotes the way in which everything that happens serves God's purpose for the whole creation – hence there is a divine governance and rule of the whole and the parts. According to the *Leiden Synopsis* XI.17–18 (1625), as the logs that burn in the hearth do not fulfil the end of each log so much as take care of the entire household, so God's providence must be seen with reference to the single economy of creation and redemption.

Two further features of the Reformed orthodox tradition merit passing comment. First, the distinction between primary and secondary causes facilitates a useful definition of the miraculous. Miracles are those forms of divine government which are

---

acroamatica (1664) seems too late. See Charles Wood, *The Question of Providence* (Louisville: Westminster John Knox Press, 2008), p. 27. The distinction is already employed in Reformed theology by Johannes Wollebius in the *Compendium Theologiae Christianae* (1626). See John W. Beardslee III (ed.), *Reformed Dogmatics* (New York: Oxford University Press, 1965), p. 59.

not reliant upon secondary causes or their normal operation, but which in unusual ways attest the divine rule. It is not that miracles alone are acts of God or serve God's purposes apart from everything else that happens. Miracles are merely those elements in the world process that contribute to the divine rule in a particular way. Second, the distinction between God's active willing and permitting is reintroduced, albeit within this more determinist framework. Although God does not withdraw from the world by allowing some events to take their course, one can still speak of a difference between an *actio efficax* and a *permissio efficax*.[70] As sin, it is permitted in the sense of not being prevented by God but it is not the end that God wills. It is a means that God permits or 'wills to allow' in order to exercise judgement and righteous vengeance.[71] Whether the distinction is entirely coherent within this framework is not clear, but it is significant that it had to be reintroduced to preserve the divine character and purpose.

Lutheran dogmatics followed a similar pattern in affirming a threefold divine providence over all the works of creation. Nothing lies outside the scope of this wise providence, though greater stress is accorded to human freedom. In dealing with the concursus, the accent falls on an empowering or mild disposing as opposed to a determining that threatens our responsibility. Yet the difference is largely one of emphasis. 'Concurrence, or the cooperation of God, is the act of Divine Providence whereby God, by a general and immediate influence, proportional to the need and capacity of every creature, graciously takes part with second causes in their actions and effects.'[72] The account of divine determination in the *concursus*

---

[70] See Heppe, *Reformed Dogmatics*, p. 274. The distinction is made for example by Wollebius: 'Bad things are ruled by *actuosa permissio* and so by permission, determining and direction' (cited in ibid., p. 274).

[71] Ibid.

[72] David Hollaz (1707) as cited in Heinrich Schmid, *The Doctrinal Theology of the Evangelical Lutheran Church*, trans. Charles E. Hay and Henry E. Jacobs (Philadelphia: United Lutheran Publication House, 1889), p. 172.

seems equally strong in Quenstedt's famous image of the hand that moves the pen to produce a single simultaneous action through a first and a second cause.[73]

A clear and comprehensive Reformed exposition of God's providence is offered by Francis Turretin in his *Institutes of Elenctic Theology*.[74] Writing in the latter part of the seventeenth century, he is confronted by revisions to the classical doctrine among Lutherans, Arminians, Socinians and Molinists. While not departing from the mainstream position of the church, these seek in different ways to allow greater scope to human autonomy, often by distinguishing between divine willing and permitting. Here God's concurring with human action takes the form of a simultaneous permission rather than an act of prior determination.

Turretin's account is replete with references to classical philosophy and Scripture. He employs a range of arguments in defence of the standard Reformed account, while also making common cause with Thomists in his own day. Providence is largely understood as the temporary government and execution of all things according to the eternal decree of predestination. This tends to undercut all attempts to concede a measure of independence to creaturely causes. Turretin insists everywhere that God is not listless, idle or indifferent to what happens; the divine will is actively engaged in each event. With respect to the troubling case of sin, God's providence ordains permissively and directs efficaciously.[75] So even here some distinction needs to be espoused between the active and permissive wills of God, although these are aspects of a single providential action. The divine concursus is both prior and simultaneous for Turretin. Recognising the difficulty in maintaining this, he appeals

---

[73] See for example Adolf Hoenecke, *Evangelical Lutheran Dogmatics*, vol. 11, trans. Richard A. Krause and James Langebartels (Milwaukee: Northwestern Publishing House, 2009), pp. 253–4.

[74] Francis Turretin, *Institutes of Elenctic Theology*, vol. 1, trans. George Musgrave Giger (Phillipsburg, NJ: P&R Publishing, 1992).

[75] Ibid., p. 493.

both to Scripture and to philosophical argument.[76] God is the first and necessary cause of everything, apart from which no secondary causal power can be effective. Without the divine will as the self-sufficient first cause of all that happens, we are unable to adequately explain events in the cosmos. Furthermore, bare permitting of some possibilities would disrupt the divine economy of creation and salvation. Scripture teaches clearly that God unerringly directs events in accordance with the divine purpose: 'The human mind directs the way, but the Lord directs the steps' (Proverbs 16:9). Without this purposive ordaining of contingent events, God might have been frustrated in the selling of Joseph into Egypt or in the providentially ordained crucifixion of Christ.[77] Divine permission is not passive for Turretin but is 'active physically' (though not ethically), so that God is never distant or disengaged.[78] In ordaining sin, God's will is effective through a testing, correcting or punishing of creatures. In working through voluntary and self-determining agents, God's providence guarantees our free actions by willing them. Again a compatibilist account of freedom is generated, but it is clear that Turretin and others are firmly committed to maintaining voluntary action. And while admitting the misuses of providence, Turretin claims that its practical benefits are apparent in promoting trust, gratitude, patience, repentance and tranquillity.

The Reformed orthodox defence of divine providence may represent the high point of the Latin providentialist tradition. Carefully formulated and rigorously argued, it provides an account that has a richness, consistency and beauty. Here a place is found for freedom, contingency and chance, yet these creaturely phenomena are circumscribed and overruled by the purposes of God, which will always be served by whatever happens. Resisting the charge of fatalism levelled by Lutheran dogmaticians, the

---

[76] Ibid., pp. 506–11.

[77] Ibid., p. 512.

[78] Ibid., p. 516.

Reformed theologians of the seventeenth century offered quite sophisticated and developed accounts of human freedom as spontaneous rather than indifferent, as ordered by God rather than as random acts.[79]

These arguments also make extensive appeal to Scripture and offer a detailed philosophical rebuttal of the claims of Arminian and Molinist thinkers. The objection to each is structurally similar. The Arminian foregrounding of divine foreknowledge as a condition upon which divine determination reposes places God in a position that is too dependent upon the outcome of contingent creaturely processes. The objects of divine foreknowledge do not sit apart from God as the primal cause of the world; these must themselves be constituted by an act of divine will in any creation that arises from out of nothing by the Word of God. Similarly, the Molinist account of creation as in some sense dependent upon God's middle knowledge (*scientia media*) attributes a quasi-independent status to the actions of possible beings which makes little sense apart from their having been created. Hence counterfactual future conditionals are not knowable by God. These refer to nothing willed by God and hence are without substance or truth value. It is not so much that God's foreknowledge is hereby restricted; rather, there is nothing to be known. To account for creation as in part determined by this divine middle knowledge is to make God beholden to entities that God can know but may not actually will. Yet what God discerns in future conditionals must be the result of the decree rather than a factor that determines it. Van Asselt likens God in this Molinist scenario to a Homeric Jupiter consulting the Fates.[80] The sovereignty of God, a root conviction of the Reformed tradition, is here

---

[79] See Willem J. van Asselt, J. Martin Bac and Roelf T. te Velde, *Reformed Thought on Freedom: The Concept of Free Choice in Early Modern Reformed Theology* (Grand Rapids: Baker, 2010).

[80] Willem J. van Asselt, The *Federal Theology of Johannes Cocceius (1603–1669)* (Leiden: Brill, 2001), p. 167.

compromised.[81] And yet these theologians were also careful to guard against an unequivocal claim that God is the author of evil and sin. Here the distinction between divine permitting and willing had to be accommodated, though in a more monergist context. The permissive will of God (*voluntas permittens*) is evident in the decision whereby God 'permits evil or sin by not impeding their accomplishment and by not withdrawing the divine concursus required for the existence of things.'[82] The animating impulse in this commitment to a maximalist account of providence is a conviction about the sovereignty of God. Any attempt to qualify, abridge or soften the classical view must compromise the power of God to overrule every event and bend it to an appointed end.

One cannot fail to be impressed by the intellectual rigour and spiritual force of this account. And, like its sixteenth-century predecessor account, this high doctrine of providence had the capacity to sustain its exponents and their communities at times of political uncertainty and persecution. Similarly, it also ensured that a moral and spiritual seriousness would characterise the faithful as they traced the hand of God in the fluctuating circumstances of their life stories. This lived context of providentialist theology deserves further exploration. Reformed theologians were conscious of the wider pastoral hinterland to their teaching. And, aware of possible distortions, they often directed their readership to the proper reception of the theology of providence. Hence Pictet in his 1696 compendium of doctrine warns against a murmuring at God, an ignoring of the secondary causes provided for our benefit, of excusing ourselves by attributing undue responsibility to God for our sin, and a misplaced anxiety about temporal affairs.[83]

---

[81] See for example the discussion in Richard A. Muller, *Post-Reformation Reformed Dogmatics, Volume Three: The Divine Essence and Attributes* (Grand Rapids: Baker, 2003), pp. 411–32.

[82] Ibid., p. 471.

[83] Benedict Pictet, *Christian Theology*, trans. Frederick Reyroux (London: Seeley and Burnside, 1834).

Although eschewing both Stoic and Epicurean accounts of providence, the Reformed tradition has tended to view the latter as its primary target. The result has been a theology of providence that is much closer to the determinism of the Stoics than the indeterminism of the Epicureans. This is evident for example in the ways in which Reformed orthodox theologians stressed God's concurrent activity in secondary causation. Allied to the doctrine of double predestination, this heavily deterministic theory of providence elicited much anxiety and even outright rejection among later Reformed thinkers. The Scottish moderates of the eighteenth century tended merely to maintain a silence on those doctrines that they had mentally discarded. They spoke instead of a general providentialism without reference to the doctrine of election and in ways that allowed greater scope for creaturely causes. Some of them were charged with deism. Others of more evangelical persuasion – Thomas Chalmers in Scotland and Charles Hodge in Princeton – maintained the tradition but in ways that treated predestination and providence as mysteries that required very careful handling. They were well aware of the Enlightenment preoccupation with freedom and attempted to reconcile this divine determinism, usually by invoking a compatibilist account of human action.

In early nineteenth-century Berlin, Schleiermacher adopted a different strategy while maintaining the same commitment to divine sovereignty. This is worth registering as a universalist inflection of this position. The determinism of the Reformed tradition impressed him in many ways. The world is dependent upon God for its being at each instant and in every particular. We cannot think of anything as not determined by this relationship to the divine. In this respect, the whole system of natural causes must be seen as providentially ordered. Nevertheless, he could not accept the final eschatological separation of the elect and the reprobate. At best, the double aspect of predestination refers to the manner in which some people believe the gospel while others appear to reject it. Schleiermacher concluded that the Christian faith is destined to take hold on people only gradually and by a long historical process. In the end, divine grace will gather everyone, but for the moment we find a division between the church and the world. The distinction between elect and non-elect is therefore a vanishing distinction. There are believers and there are those who are not yet believers. Upon reinterpretation, therefore, the doctrine of double predestination expresses this distinction but it is superseded by a universalism in which God draws everyone into fellowship with Christ. Thus we have in Schleiermacher a benign determinism. And in much of this, the doctrine of providence gets squeezed. It is a doctrine that expresses the ways in which the total system of causes is ordained by God. Indeed, Schleiermacher tends to dismiss it as a pagan import into Christian theology which did more harm than good.[84] In particular, the distinction between a general and a special providence is of little use to him, as is the category of miracle. Particular divine interpositions would only compromise the manner in which the world is already approved, as it were, in its entirety, from the perspective of divine eternity. Schleiermacher's theology of predestination (a term he prefers to 'providence') both sits closely to Calvin in its more deterministic phase but also departs quite radically from him with its commitment to universalism. It illustrates the acuteness of Brian Gerrish's remark that Calvin's 'place in the history of Christian theology is partly given by his ability to set an agenda and incite dissent'.[85]

Yet notwithstanding its formidable intellectual weight, architectural beauty and baroque appeal, the Reformed orthodox account of providence faces a range of modern anxieties, rendering it neither persuasive nor attractive to most Christian audiences today. The reasons for this have already been noted: they include its adequacy to the diverse materials of Scripture, a prioritising of divine control

---

[84] F. D. E. Schleiermacher, *The Christian Faith*, trans. H. R. Mackintosh and J. S. Stewart (Edinburgh: T&T Clark, 1928), p. 727.

[85] Brian Gerrish, 'The place of Calvin in Christian theology', p. 302.

over love, a determinism that problematises human freedom, and a heavy stress on the will of God in relation to everything that happens. The inability sufficiently to articulate themes of divine struggle, the present imperfections of the world, the theodicy problem, the contingency of our vast cosmos, the full range of the teachings of Jesus and the promise of an eschatological resolution have placed contemporary audiences in a different social, intellectual and spiritual space. The caveats introduced by exponents of Reformed orthodoxy have done little to allay the cogency of these criticisms which, taken together, have generated something approaching a modern consensus against this position. We shall return to these points in later discussion, but some of the practical outcomes of early modern Protestant providentialism are worth consideration at this juncture.

2.5 Providentialism Among the Protestant Faithful

The theology of providence, particularly as it developed in the Reformed tradition, was not merely the construct of a theological elite. It informed the confessions, catechisms and liturgical life of the churches, particularly through their psalms, paraphrases and hymns. Early modern historians have recently drawn attention to the ways in which individuals understood their lives in providential terms. This is especially evident from a range of printed materials, especially the diaries that have survived; these provide further valuable evidence of the widespread empirical impact of providentialist theology within Protestantism.

In sermons touching on the subject of providence, Richard Sibbes, theologian and preacher at Gray's Inn in London, illustrates the strong connection between Reformed doctrine and piety. Always exhorting acceptance and trust in his hearers, he grounds these dispositions in a conviction concerning God's providence as this unfolds in Scripture. Since everything comes from the hand of God, whose steady and wise will governs events both great and small, we should live patiently, gratefully and resolutely. 'None feel more sweet experience of God's providence than those that are most resolute in their obedience.'[86] Sibbes insists that this obedience is demanded by a divine ruling and ordaining of all that comes to pass: 'God's providence extends to every particular thing.'[87] In a striking manner, his preaching offers a sense of security and assurance, yet this demands everywhere an acceptance that is both passive and active in its outcomes. If we cannot see the reason or sense in what happens, this is only because God's ways are mysterious and for much of the time beyond our reach. Yet they work for our good, if only we will trust and follow obediently.

> If a skilful physician doth us no good, it is because it pleaseth God to hide the right of curing at that time from him. Which should move us to see God in all that befalls us, who hath sufficient reason, as to do what he doth, so not to do what he doth not, to hinder as well as to give way.[88]

A vital feature of this account is the construction placed upon the divine *concursus*. God not only wills everything that happens but intends it as an integral feature of an overall plan. Each detail of our lives and all eventualities are intended, not merely conceded, for the sake of their contribution to an ordained scheme. Every event, however trivial or random, is meant and sent by virtue of a single immutable design. This aspect of the Reformed teaching on providence was apparent in countless sermons and pamphlets until quite recently. Although it persists in some quarters, its teaching has become a stumbling block.

The constitutive role of providence in the Christian life is a hallmark of much early modern Protestantism. Notwithstanding its medieval antecedents, this has generated the sense that providence

---

[86] Richard Sibbes, 'The soul's conflict with itself, and victory over itself by faith' in *Complete Works*, ed. Alexander B. Grosart, 7 vols. (Edinburgh: James Nichol, 1862–4), vol. I, pp. 119–214 at p. 208.

[87] Sibbes, 'Of the providence of God' in *Complete Works*, vol. v, p. 85.

[88] Sibbes, 'The soul's conflict', p. 206.

is a doctrine largely owned by the Reformed churches. The linkage with predestination, another Augustinian doctrine commandeered by Reformed theologians, has undoubtedly contributed to such an impression. As people examined their lives meticulously for signs of their election, so the conviction took hold that each happenstance must serve in some way, however inscrutable, the eternal will of God. If providence was the means, predestination was its origin and end.

Alexandra Walsham has contested the earlier thesis of Keith Thomas that providentialism was the preserve of a ruling elite who did not engage the wider populace. In a magisterial study, she has sought to demonstrate the ways in which providential piety gradually took hold upon whole societies. Contingent events, whether public or private, were widely interpreted as signs of divine favour or displeasure.[89] The people of God had a duty to discern the divine will from the events around them. They had to 'sanctify' and 'improve' the messages sent by God in whatever befell them. Finding contemporary parallels with scriptural history was one standard way to do so. In the case of calamities, this was particularly important. These could variously be interpreted as forewarnings of an everlasting punishment by the eternal Judge, or the parental chastisement of the saints by their heavenly Father. 'History was the canvas on which the Lord etched His purposes and intentions; nature a textbook and a laboratory in which He taught, demonstrated and tested His providence.'[90] The providence taught by the church was pitted against a range of rival ideologies and practices, including fortune, nature worship, astrological fatalism, witchcraft and other supernatural agencies such as Bunyan's 'hobgoblins and foul fiends'. These had to be resisted and overcome by a clearer recognition of God's good and all-sovereign power. Elsewhere, Walsham writes,

---

[89] Alexandra Walsham, *Providence in Early Modern England* (Oxford: Oxford University Press, 1998). In what follows, I have borrowed from her fascinating study.

[90] Ibid., p. 2.

Nowhere is the puritan propensity for detecting the finger of God in the most mundane events more vividly exhibited that in their journals and diaries, letters, autobiographies, and private memorabilia ... Saturated with references to the special blessings and judgements which the Lord had graciously bestowed upon the writer such texts record the perennial inner struggle of the godly for assurance of their elect status on paper.[91]

Portents of God's providence could also be public and political in significance. In the summer of 1558, it was reported that a fire reached Scotland from the North Sea and that a dragon was seen upon the ramparts of Edinburgh Castle. Shortly afterwards the Reformation took hold. The scattering of the Spanish Armada in 1589 was attributed by James VI to a wind that was directly sent by God. The search for a benevolent providence is understandable amid circumstances that were often precarious, testing and uncontrollable. The plaque in the late sixteenth-century Reformed church in Burntisland illustrates the extent to which local fisherman lived in need of divine protection from a climate that was frequently hostile and always unpredictable. Inscribed is the Puritan motto 'God's providence is our inheritance.'

Susan Hardman Moore has made similar observations in her study of New England pilgrims, particularly those who returned to the home country. Before departing for America, emigrants wanted to be sure that they were following the steer given them by the hand of providence. And in their time in the new world they constantly sought assurance that they remained under God's protection and blessing. This was done again by seeking to discern the signs of favour or displeasure in the fluctuating circumstances of their lives. Attention is given to the memoirs of Susanna Bell. These were dictated from her deathbed and provide a graphic and moving account of how she sought to serve God and her family, by

[91] Ibid., p. 20.

discerning the tokens of providence in her life. She recalls how the presence of one small child and the anticipated arrival of another were signs that God did not wish her emigrate. But the subsequent death of her child then led her instead to interpret this as a further sign from God that she should now sail for New England.[92] And so as an expectant mother she crossed the Atlantic in 1634, only later to return again.

Hardman Moore recalls many other instances of providential signs anxiously discerned by settlers. Some of these are less worthy than those of Susanna Bell. John Winthrop's son had a room full of books, which included in one volume the Greek New Testament, the Psalms and the Prayer Book. He noticed that a mouse had eaten the Prayer Book while leaving the other two intact, a sure sign of divine displeasure at this text. Yet, as Hardman Moore notes, Winthrop appeared to overload the episode with theological significance. The same Prayer Book actually survives in the holdings of the Massachusetts Historical Society – less than half its pages are nibbled and these 'only at the tips of the lower-right hand corners'.[93]

One feature of this popular piety was that it reinforced the role of texts in mediating the divine Word. If the *digita Dei* was to be discerned in the unfolding of historical events, this required a narrative. It was not so much places, relics or artefacts that were enchanted by the divine presence. God was now discerned in a sequence of natural or historical circumstances. These had to be interpreted rightly and this required a story to be told. So the work of God was narrated. Indeed believers were encouraged to maintain journals and diaries which recorded faithfully how the divine was at work in their own lives. These could be passed on to one's relatives and descendants. In particular, the dramatic tales of how divine vengeance had been wreaked upon malefactors were to be

[92] Susan Hardman Moore, Pilgrims: *New World Settlers and the Call of Home* (New Haven: Yale University Press, 2007), pp. 1ff.

[93] Ibid., p. 219.

105

circulated *pour encourager les autres*. Walsham records the case of the Essex rector John Beadle who insisted that it was the spiritual duty of every 'thankful Christian' to recount the punishments visited upon notorious offenders. Best known among such anthologies was Thomas Beard's *The Theatre of God's Judgements*. First published in 1597, this recounted wondrous tales of God's appropriate punishing of wrongdoers. These included the case of the nobleman who regularly broke the Sabbath by riding out with his horse and hounds. The Lord caused his wife to bear him a child with a dog's head, 'that seeing hee preferred his dogges before the service of God, he might have one of his owne getting to make much of'.[94] Although the piety represented here is a popular form of Protestant providentialism, it also reflects earlier Catholic stories of the saints and the miraculous deeds attending their life and influence.[95]

Reading the diaries and other testimonies of those who sought to discern the hand of providence in the microscopic details of their lives, we become aware of the effect that doctrine can have in the lives of those who receive it in good faith. Much of this is moving and occasionally profound, although at times we are left feeling that it could readily become oppressive, self-serving, indulgent and superstitious. There is a popular downside here to the Reformed doctrine of providence which might enable us to see why the subsequent emergence of more deistic patterns of thought was liberating for some. If the work of God was perceived in setting only the general conditions of natural and moral life, then we could get on with the business of life without anxiously attempting to interpret each chance outcome as a coded message from the Almighty. If the order of secondary causes was itself part of God's dispensation, then these could be trusted to yield providential outcomes without seeking a direct divine interposition in everything that happened, as if each

---

[94] Cited by Walsham, *Providence in Early Modern England*, p. 1.

[95] This is discussed in ibid., pp. 328ff.

natural occurrence had to be deciphered to provide a singular theological meaning.

Providentialist piety did not disappear during the seventeenth
century but it underwent some significant changes that were carried
forward into the Enlightenment. Within England, the more extravagant speculations surrounding divine providence were subjected to
two forms of criticism, particularly after the civil wars and inter-
regnum.[96] On the one side, the forces of established religion regarded
the unregulated interpretation of signs and wonders as the marks
of an unseemly religious enthusiasm or, even worse, a dangerous
fanaticism that threatened social stability. An over-determination
of natural events with theological significance by individuals and
splinter groups was disruptive of organised religion and its teaching
authorities. For political reasons, this had to be resisted. On the other
side, the emergence of Newtonian science and early modern philosophy had the effect of largely confining divine providence to secondary causes. In their regularity and consistency, these expressed
a divine wisdom and purpose. Though God could suspend natural
laws and act directly without the intermediate agency of secondary
causes, such miracles were rare. For some, they were confined to
the apostolic age, since when they had ceased. A Fellow of Corpus
Christi in Cambridge, John Spencer wrote a *Discourse Concerning
Prodigies* (1663) which restricted divine action to the natural and
the miraculous. The middle ground of the 'preternatural' – which
attributed religious significance to strange signs, portents and prodigies – was excluded. These involved interpretations of events that
were so 'hugely perplex'd, doubtful and uncertain' that no reliable
inference about the future could be made.[97] At most, the preternatural could denote only events the causes of which were largely
unknown and hitherto unexplained. Such wondrous events should

[96] I am indebted here to William Burns, *An Age of Wonders: Prodigies, Politics and
Providence in England 1657–1727* (Manchester: Manchester University Press, 2002).

[97] John Spencer, *Discourse Concerning Prodigies* (London, 1663), p. 12.

direct us towards the power and goodness of God as in Psalm 29, rather than exciting fevered speculations about the future.[98] As a category that merely signified the limitations of our knowledge, the preternatural could not be loaded with prognostic meanings.

As these counter-arguments gained ground, providence tended to be more closely associated with regular patterns of behaviour in the natural and social world, at least among an educated elite who liked to distinguish themselves from the credulous masses and their susceptibility to unlikely tales.[99] This may mark the beginning of processes of refraction and displacement which resulted in significant shifts in providential thinking.

2.6 Conclusion

The standardised account of providence in the western church has Augustinian and Boethian roots. With its systematic location either in the doctrine of God or in the doctrine of creation, it was generally articulated in close proximity to philosophical considerations. The resemblances between Aquinas and Calvin are sometimes overlooked at least in this domain, perhaps as a result of the later Catholic condemnation of Jansenism. But the similarity of their accounts is striking and suggests something like a doctrinal default setting that persisted, like much else, through the Reformation. With a careful distinction between primary and secondary causation, the leading challenges to divine providence could be met. Although sovereign, God was not the author of evil. While willing everything that happens, God guarantees our freedom and responsibility. Though not dependent upon us, God can use our prayers as instruments of the divine will.

[98] Ibid., p. 406.

[99] Burns points to the ways in which gender functioned as a criterion of credulity. Tales of wondrous signs of divine providence could be dismissed as 'old women's fables'. *An Age of Wonders*, pp. 125–48. Cf. John Spencer's reference to 'little, weak, feminine instances of devotion'. *Discourse Concerning Prodigies*, p. 22.

In all these ways, a maximalist and meticulous theology of divine providence emerged. Yet, in the formulation of this impressive account, scriptural narratives of divine interaction, redemption and spiritual inspiration were often left in the background. Themes of struggle and improvisation were difficult to accommodate. The virtues of gratitude and patience tended to exclude other dispositions such as lament and resistance. And with the foregrounding of providence in Protestant theology, we witness an over-spiritualising of the mundane. Contingent events are coded messages; these carry information about the intentions of God's wise providence for each of us. With insight and sound doctrine, these can be properly interpreted. As this theology was developed and applied in shifting contexts, other intellectual and practical problems emerged. In the next two chapters, we shall further explore the difficulties facing this default position.

3 | Dispersals of Providence in Modernity

Religion cannot disappear from the world; it can only change its form.[1]

This chapter tracks the different ways in which providentialist thinking developed from the early modern period onwards. Rather than disappearing under the impact of Enlightenment forces, ideas about providence underwent a steady process of reformulation and refraction. Instead of a demise, we find the emergence of providential notions in more secular contexts. These owe a debt, even when undeclared, to the earlier traditions of the church, though in important respects they became increasingly detached from scriptural roots. Yet, in other ways, the finely grained providentialism of the Reformed tradition in which everything is willed by God to some purpose is stubbornly persistent. Throughout this process of dispersion, the language of providence becomes even more pronounced in the literature of the eighteenth and nineteenth centuries. To a contemporary reader, its prevalence throughout this period is startling. I shall argue that these alterations to the theology of providence are instructive, not least for exposing some of the inherent flaws in earlier formulations as they are manifested in a variety of practices and ideological positions.

3.1 Shifts of Focus

Two related shifts of emphasis are apparent during the seventeenth century; already noted in the discussion of prodigies in early

[1] St Simon, as reported in William Chambers and Robert Chambers, *Chambers's Journal*, 6th series, 1 (1897–8), 584.

modern England, these adumbrate wider developments in thinking about divine providence. First, we begin to see a preoccupation with the general providentialist ordering of the world in its natural and moral conditions. The wisdom of God is evident in the law-governed behaviour of the natural world and in the moral order of societies where divinely ordained laws are respected. This was often accompanied by a belief in miracles and acts of special divine revelation, though these were regarded as rare and mainly confined to the apostolic age. A second shift of emphasis tended to displace the Puritan conviction that a divine plan governed every single event. In its place, there emerged a sense of a purpose being fulfilled through the overall direction of nature and history, even though not every event could be assigned a distinctive role in contributing to this *telos*. This assumption characterised much rationalist thinking, notwithstanding the evident theological differences between Descartes, Malebranche, Leibniz and Spinoza.[2]

Despite being a frequent object of caricature and mockery, Leibniz's theodicy should be seen in this context. The bold assertion that this was the best of all possible worlds could certainly appear naïvely optimistic and vulnerable to sceptical challenge. But Leibniz's claim was not that everything was perfect, only that it was as good as it could be given the intentions of the Creator and the necessary conditions of a created order. A presupposition of this theodicy was that God had ordered the world as Creator without the need for constant miraculous interposition.

In thinking about providence, the rationalists begin to move the focus from the particular to the general. In the order of the natural world, God's will and purpose are to be discerned. And since this is the mark of divine providence in nature, we should expect a similar order in matters of revelation. The hand of God works through the

---

[2] See for example Stephen Nadler, 'Conceptions of God' in Desmond M. Clarke and Catherine Wilson (eds.), *Oxford Handbook of Philosophy in Early Modern Europe* (Oxford: Oxford University Press, 2011), pp. 525–47.

regular, the consistent and the rational. Although this does not negate the possibility of revelation, the emphasis upon order tends to set the terms in which it is conceived.[3] Descartes maintained that the world comprises particles that are initially equal in size and motion and governed by simple laws; in its proportions and order, the created world reflects the perfections of God. Whereas for Malebranche miracles must be viewed as instances of an order that we do not yet fully grasp, for Spinoza they are rationally offensive and theologically misguided. Indeed, there can be no particular acts of providence since the attribution of a personal will to God is an anthropomorphic error. We should not conceive God as a supernatural potentate with intentions and purposes. This is the result of human projection, which attributes an intentionality to natural events where there is none. If the whole of nature is identical with the divine being, as Spinoza maintained, then no sense can be attached to God acting in particular ways upon the world. This criticism of traditional religion is apparent in his *Ethics* (Appendix to Part One), where the human propensity to attribute a divine intention to earthquakes, storms and diseases is falsified by the indiscriminate outcomes of these catastrophes. Yet in our fear and ignorance, we still cling to such superstitious patterns of thought. Spinoza describes this recourse to the will of God as 'the sanctuary of ignorance.'[4]

Descartes had tended to see a providence in the overall course of nature to which we must subdue our passions through the exercise of will. Here his thinking leans in a Stoic direction, though it remains committed to more Christian notions of immortality and the afterlife.[5] By contrast, Spinoza strives for an understanding of a

[3] See Stuart Brown, 'The regularization of providence in post-Cartesian philosophy' in Robert Crocker (ed.), *Religion, Reason and Nature in Early Modern Europe* (Dordrecht: Kluwer, 2001), pp. 1–16, and Mark W. Elliott, *Providence Perceived: Divine Action from a Human Point of View* (Berlin: de Gruyter, 2015), pp. 189–93.

[4] Benedict de Spinoza, *Ethics*, trans. Edwin Curley (London: Penguin, 1994), p. 29.

[5] See Genevieve Lloyd, *Providence Lost* (Cambridge, MA: Harvard University Press, 2008), pp. 160–91.

world that is devoid of providence as traditionally conceived in the Abrahamic faiths. At most, divine providence should be understood in terms of nature's conservation.

> [W]hen Scripture says that God did this or that, or that this or that happened by the will of God, what it really means is just that it happened according to the laws and order of nature, and not, as the common people think, that for some period nature ceased to act, or that for some time its order was interrupted.[6]

For Spinoza, the virtuous person will seek the fullest possible understanding of the workings of nature (or God). To this extent, a special providence may be possible along Stoic lines, not dissimilar to those advocated by Descartes to Princess Elizabeth of Bohemia. Our conflicted passions can be subdued and regulated by our rational will. But this possibility cannot be construed in terms of the grace of a transcendent God; it is the result of human effort.[7] We can comport ourselves to live in a particular way so that we can contemplate the world *sub specie aeternitatis*. In all its austerity and beauty, this vision of Spinoza is intentionally far removed from any traditional understanding of divine providence,[8] though Stephen Nadler views this as a legitimate development of the medieval Jewish rationalist positions formulated by Maimonides and Gersonides.[9]

These intellectual shifts were accompanied by other changes in perspective, method and mode of operation as far as providence was concerned, while also driving arguments for greater religious

---

[6] Benedict de Spinoza, 'The theological-political treatise', 111/89, in Edwin Curley (ed.), *Collected Works of Spinoza*, vol. 11 (Princeton: Princeton University Press, 2016), pp. 160–1.

[7] For further discussion of Descartes's Neo-Stoicism, see Charles Taylor, *A Secular Age* (Cambridge, MA: Belknap Press of Harvard University Press, 2007), pp. 130–6. See also John Cottingham, *Descartes* (Oxford: Blackwell, 1986), pp. 152–6.

[8] See Lloyd, *Providence Lost*, pp. 192–234.

[9] Stephen Nadler, *Spinoza's Theory of Divine Providence: Rationalist Solutions, Jewish Sources* (Budel, The Netherlands: Damon, 2005), pp. 21–9.

toleration. Appeals to Scripture continued to be advanced but greater weight was gradually accorded to science, philosophy and natural religion. In early Enlightenment thinkers, the need for revelation was reduced if not obviated by a confidence in human reason to discern theological and ethical truth. Similarly, the commitment to general providence is foregrounded in theological debates; this is apparent from the eighteenth-century preoccupation with the design argument. God's action tended to be restricted to miracles, for which apologetic arguments were advanced.[10] But this delimiting of divine agency resulted in a tendency to identify providence with the general ordering and sustaining of the world. Living in a well-regulated cosmos, human beings could discern and enjoy the blessings of the Creator. A true piety would be displayed in adhering gratefully to the moral precepts of the Christian faith, which confirmed and extended the insights of our natural instincts. The wisdom of God was discerned in the particular but largely as an instance of the general, rather than in more direct ways. All of this of course was contested, especially by thinkers such as Jonathan Edwards who remained deeply committed to the theology of their Reformed orthodox predecessors. And among others, as we shall see, hybrid positions emerged which reflected post-Reformation and Enlightenment influences.

Charles Taylor has also noted an 'anthropocentric' turn in providentialist thinking.[11] Calvin had seen the function of providence as leading us into a truer obedience and a glorifying of God in the Christian life. He believed that we are called primarily to glorify God rather than to secure our personal salvation. In this

---

[10] For Locke, miracles had to occur but rarely, in order that they might fulfil their divinely appointed function of attesting revelation. 'Yet his Wisdom is not usually at the expense of Miracles but only in cases that require them, for the evidencing of some Revelation or Mission to be from him.' John Locke, *The Reasonableness of Christianity As Delivered in the Scriptures*, ed. John C. Higgins-Biddle (Oxford: Oxford University Press, 1999), p. 91.

[11] See Taylor, *The Secular Age*, p. 221. In some of what follows, I am indebted to his argument.

sense, his thought is theocentric rather than anthropocentric. But now it is assumed that what providence offers us is simply our own happiness, if only we abide by the dictates of our moral sense. John Toland seems to have believed that God could do without our servile glorification, being content merely that we should follow the laws of morality for our own welfare. Indeed, it was the adoption of this view in his moral philosophy that led the eighteenth-century philosopher Francis Hutcheson into difficulties with the Presbytery of Glasgow.

3.2 The Shape of Providential Deism

Deism is sometimes used rhetorically as a debased term to dismiss positions that threaten to make divine existence otiose. After an initial act of origination, God (as a placeholder for First Cause or Designer) is altogether absent, remote and irrelevant to the subsequent direction of the world. In the border country between deism and atheism, there may have been some who held this position, including Voltaire and Hume. Yet, not all were so minimalist. An elusive term, deism could take many different forms. Representing more a family of views than one single established position defined by a *locus classicus*, the deists included many who evidently believed themselves to be part of a Christian mainstream but wished to establish their faith on a stronger and more consensual basis by appeal to reason.[12]

---

[12] E. C. Mossner once wrote that, 'The deists were long subjected to the *odium theologicum*, and the historians of the movement have almost without exception downgraded or slandered them socially as well as intellectually ... No really satisfactory, complete, impartial, and scholarly account of the significance of the movement has as yet appeared.' See 'Deism' in Paul Edwards (ed.), *Encyclopaedia of Philosophy*, 8 vols. (New York: Macmillan, 1967), vol. II, p. 335. But see Peter Byrne, *Natural Religion and the Nature of Religion* (London: Routledge, 1989), and Robert E. Sullivan, *John Toland and the Deist Controversy* (Cambridge, MA: Harvard University Press, 1982).

In the second series of his Boyle Lectures (1705), Samuel Clarke distinguished four kinds of deist, all of whom rely on the powers of reason rather than the deliverances of revelation.[13]

i) There is a minimalist theism in which God is understood as the origin of the world but without concern or involvement in its course. Clarke compares this with ancient Epicureanism.

ii) A variant on this position is the view that God creates the world and controls its natural operations but without establishing a moral order of any form. This is left up to us.

iii) Beyond this, some deists, although affirming a providential God with moral perfections, are unwilling to commit to the notion of an afterlife.

iv) And finally there are more orthodox deists who affirm a God with moral attributes, a providential order and an afterlife in which virtue is rewarded and vice punished.

Clarke argues that the first three forms of deism amount to a practical atheism since the idea of God ceases to be of any real moral significance in terms of motivation or ultimate ends. Each lies on a slippery slope to a more fulsome form of atheism. Only the last form deserves the designation 'deist' but it is caught in a contradiction. If such a God existed, we should reasonably expect a revelation to reinforce our faith and advance our welfare. Hence, according to Clarke's analysis, the true deist ought to become a Christian theist. In this way, deism must collapse into outright atheism or return to a more orthodox theological form. The only consistent scheme of deism identified by Clarke is found in the pre-Christian works of the pagan philosophers. But the necessary complement to their philosophical thought is now available through Scripture and the church.

---

[13] 'A discourse concerning the unchangeable obligations of truth and certainty of the Christian revelation', *The Works of Samuel Clarke*, ed. Benjamin Hoadly, 4 vols. (Bristol: Thoemmes, 2002), vol. 11, pp. 595–733.

Although Clarke's schema is designed to serve an apologetic argument that is not altogether fair in its characterisations, it does reflect the variety of positions held by deists at the beginning of the eighteenth century. The last type identified by Clarke retains a lively belief in providence and immortality. William Wollaston's *The Religion of Nature Delineated* (1722) provides a good example of this – he remains committed to both general and particular providence but defends these as tenets of a natural or philosophical religion.[14] Indeed the lack of stress on other key loci ensured that providentialist notions came to the fore, though with less attachment to Scripture or tradition. Hence providentialism remained central to the self-understanding and confidence of individuals and societies. Yet the result of this transposition is a significant alteration in the forms taken by providence. In particular, it was manifested in human happiness, secular progress, political stability and a religion without the enthusiasm, intolerance and episodic violence that had characterised much of the previous century. The success of Newtonian science also played its part in this context through reinforcing and foregrounding a sense of a pervasive natural order, characterised everywhere by mathematical precision.

These patterns of thought characterised much Enlightenment thinking of the eighteenth century. Its exponents believed that they had history on their side. The wars of religion had hindered the progress of civilised life in the previous century. Fanaticism had led to a disproportionate significance being attached to minor doctrinal differences between groups of believers, sometimes at the cost of violence. Historical study of the Bible demanded a more discerning approach to its contents – the critical challenge posed by Spinoza and others could not be ignored. There was much in Scripture that seemed a declension from the purer moral religion of the deists. Yet the relegation of revealed theology was not merely the result of

---

[14] See William Wollaston, *The Religion of Nature Delineated* ([London], 1722), section v, chapter XVIII.

scruples about the Bible. General providence had bestowed a natural religion and ethics upon the human race as a whole. Divine revelation could not therefore be confined to a single historical episode that made sense of everything else, access to which was limited to a few. This egregious favouritism was unworthy of providence.[15] The scientific and economic benefits of the age suggested that a better way had been found and one that could unite people of different confessional allegiance in common political pursuits. Provided some commitment to the church and to the teaching of Jesus could be elicited, this might be sufficient for social cohesion, moral order and the advance of Christian society.

A providentialism of this ilk dominated the thinking of the Scottish Enlightenment, some of whose leading figures were suspected of deism. The standard theology of the moderate intellectuals at this time tended to follow lines already apparent in thinkers such as Francis Hutcheson. The role of God as creator and sustainer of the world is emphasised. The signs of the divine presence are evident in the natural world; in this respect, the design argument is widely assumed to be valid. The beneficial function of religion in civil society is stressed. Religion contributes to social order and harmony. When purged of irrational fanaticism and intolerance, faith exercises a cohesive function through the moral direction and focus that it offers human life. As benevolent and wise, God has ordered the world so that its moral and scientific laws contribute to human welfare. The prospect of an eschatological state, in which virtue and felicity coincide, provides further moral motivation.

The moderates had little interest in revisiting the doctrinal controversies of the previous century. Concentrating on creation and providence, their theology was less specific on the tenets of revealed theology. A pragmatic religion emerged that was preoccupied with the business of living well here and now. The Stoics were

---

[15] This point is elucidated by frequent examples from deist literature in Byrne, *Natural Religion and the Nature of Religion.*

more important than early Christian writers in providing useful source material. Indeed, as Alexander Broadie has shown, many moderates argued that it may have been part of God's providential purpose that, for the sake of the practical concerns of life, human beings are given only such knowledge as is sufficient to that end. This appears to have been the position of thinkers such as Thomas Reid (1710–96) and Hugh Blair (1718–1800), both ministers of the Kirk. Reid's philosophy is remarkable in that he says so little about theology, yet in his epistemology and moral theory the providential purposes of God are everywhere assumed. In his study of Reid, Nicholas Wolterstorff has pointed to the ways in which he stresses the epistemological restrictedness of our human condition.[16] This awareness of the limits of knowledge produces a distinctive form of piety. By attending to what we can know, we are able to live 'wisely in the darkness'. For Reid, this is divinely ordered. We are enabled by the Creator to act in ways that lead fulfilled and useful lives. Blair's famous sermon on 'seeing through a glass darkly' makes a practical virtue out of an epistemological necessity. Although 'we are strangers in the universe of God', this is fitting. Had God equipped us with too keen a vision of transcendent realities, we would likely have been incapacitated for the tasks to which we are called here and now.[17] While functioning as a characteristic moderate theme, this also resonates with the earlier Reformed stress on the limitations of human reason before the mystery of God.[18]

Blair's sermons ran to numerous editions and were translated into German by Schleiermacher. His instructions on providence are still

---

[16] Nicholas Wolterstorff, *Thomas Reid and The Story of Epistemology* (Cambridge: Cambridge University Press, 2001), pp. 250ff. See also Nicholas Wolterstorff, 'God and darkness in Reid' in Joseph Houston (ed.) *Thomas Reid: Context, Influence, Significance* (Edinburgh: Dunedin Academic Press, 2004), pp. 77–102.

[17] Blair's argument is examined by Alexander Broadie, *The Scottish Enlightenment* (Edinburgh: Birlinn, 2001), pp. 146ff.

[18] This connection is noted by Broadie: ibid.

moving to read. These combine cautionary Enlightenment notes on the limits of knowledge with an earlier Reformed confidence in the hand of God in everything that befalls us. Every difficulty and disaster must serve some benevolent divine purpose.

> Why this man was prematurely carried away from the world in the beginning of a promising course; why that deserving family were left overwhelmed with grief and despair, by the loss of one who was their sole benefactor and support; why friendships cemented by tender ties were suddenly torn asunder by death; these are inquiries to which we can now make no reply, and which throw a dark gloom over the conduct of the Almighty. But the spirits of the just above, who are admitted to a larger view of the ways of God, see the reasons of such counsels. They see that one man was seasonably taken away from dangers and evils to come, which, unknown to him, were hovering over his head. They see that Providence was in secret preparing unexpected blessings for the family who appeared to be left disconsolate and hopeless. They see that it was time for friendships to be dissolved, when their longer continuance would, to some of the parties, have proved a snare. Where we behold nothing but the rod of power stretched forth, they discern an interposition of the hand of mercy.[19]

Blair argues that the world is already wisely ordered and well adjusted by divine benevolence. God's great project is on track – we should never doubt this. And God wills everything that happens, though its purpose may not be presently apparent. For the moment, we are given sufficient light and knowledge to trust in the hand of providence. As the beauty of the world is eloquent testimony to its Maker despite the presence of seeming deformities, so we should conclude that there is a moral government of the world. For Blair,

---

[19] Hugh Blair, 'Of our present ignorance of the ways of God' in David Fergusson (ed.), *Scottish Philosophical Theology* (Exeter: Imprint Press, 2007), pp. 79–86 at p. 84.

our present lack of knowledge is itself a sign of divine providence. Epistemological limitations serve a purpose. For the moment, we see only as through a glass darkly but this is for the best. A fuller knowledge of the future would overwhelm us and distract us both from truths that are accessible and useful and also from duties that lie at hand. Our eyes thus remain on the road that lies immediately ahead and not in contemplation of distant scenes.

There is much of the Reformed tradition in this – its abhorrence of speculation, the practical focus and the sense that God's ways are often hidden. The commitment to a meticulous providence strangely persists, though its goal of human happiness is more pronounced – everything that happens is ordained by God to our ultimate benefit. I confess to finding this material moving and persuasive, and not merely on account of its rhetorical beauty. Blair's is a theology that is quite serviceable for one's mid-life, for those who are in for the long haul and who need enough but not more to keep them moving along. Significantly, one of his most striking sermons is about the opportunities afforded by middle age. Yet, despite its undoubted appeal, there is also something missing and other elements that seem out of place.

One problem is that it suggests too readily that everything must work out for the best. In some future estate, there will be a perspective by which these seeming misfortunes are rendered blessings. There is some practical wisdom here. But at least three problems attach to Blair's formulation.

i) While the future may enable us to overcome or even forget the past, it cannot on these terms be said to justify it, as if what once cursed us was merely a blessing in disguise. In this context, it is worth noting how many familiar platitudes are overloaded with notions of a divine providence: 'These things are sent to try us'; 'It was meant to be'; 'What's for you, will not go by you'.

ii) This epistemological perspective is not ours, at least not yet. We have to assume it in order to offer this type of response, and this we cannot do simply as an interpretation of what is presently accessible. The surd element in human existence is not adequately acknowledged here. The extent to which our lives are torn apart by accident or sheer bad luck or horrendous mistakes seems missing. The dysteleological nature of much suffering is not properly registered in these reflections. For all its elegance and genuine sensitivity, Blair's pastoral exhortation seems out of place after the traumas of the twentieth century. We should not assume that the agonies of human existence are seemingly dissonant sounds in a perfect harmony that we will eventually learn. Too much of the Leibnizian theodicy persists in Blair's conviction that everything is ordained to serve our eventual felicity.

iii) Finally, from a Christological perspective, we have to regard this world not as perfectly ordered but in need of redemption. The doctrine of providence must also take a cruciform shape rather than appear as a theology of glory in which everything is already perfectly in place. In deism, Jesus is an instructor who informs us how life is ordered, rather than a Saviour whose work is to re-order and remake it. The death and resurrection of Christ merely exemplify an immanent teleological pattern, rather than a new configuration into which we are to be drawn by the Spirit. The virtue of hope is directed in deism to God's settling of unfinished business whereby we each receive our just deserts. But this is not the hope that Paul describes in Romans 8 when speaking of the love of God in Christ from which nothing can separate us. One symptom of the practical difficulty with Blair's account is that it offers little scope for lament. If everything is ordered by God for our well-being, then lament or complaint seems misplaced. At best, it is a natural reaction that must be suppressed by faith or better resolved by contemplation of the bigger picture. Yet this is at odds with much of our human experience, especially when young lives are cut short, as well as the significant place assigned to lament in the Psalter.[20]

What we are witnessing here is a further drift away from scriptural sources in the more rationalist type of religion that emerges after the early modern period. The providentialism that is presented seems more self-confident and complacent than anything we find in the Bible, where a greater measure of patience and struggle are found alongside elements of surprise and grace. The clearest example of this philosophical trend can be found in Leibniz's theodicy, with its claim that everything is properly ordered in a universe that must be the best of all possible worlds. In creating this world, the divine intellect is constrained by considerations of simplicity and variety. The highest simplicity yields the greatest variety with the maximum degree of order. So God must choose to actualise this world as the best possible.[21] David Blumenfeld points out that the austerity of this vision leads to a diminution of the earlier sense in Leibniz of God's parental care for creatures: 'In the *Discourse* Leibniz describes God as a father who is infinitely solicitous of the needs of his children, but in the *Theodicy* he warns us not to view God as a "mother ... whose almost only care concerns ... the happiness of [her child]".'[22] The rational demand that God create such a world imposes a necessity upon everything that happens and requires that we see each particular as making a unique contribution to the perfection of the whole. Thus mistakes, calamities and crimes contribute in some way to the overall harmony of the cosmos. In its variety and order, the

---

[20] Nicholas Wolterstorff argues that this suppression of lament has been a regular failing of theologians. See 'If God is good and sovereign, why lament?', *Calvin Theological Journal*, 36 (2001), 42–52.

[21] G. W. Leibniz, *Theodicy*, ed. Austin Farrer (London: Routledge & Kegan Paul, 1951).

[22] David Blumenfeld, 'Perfection and happiness in the best possible world' in Nicholas Jolley (ed.), *Cambridge Companion to Leibniz* (Cambridge: Cambridge University Press, 1995), pp. 382–410 at p. 410.

history of the world is held to express the divine will in every detail. Here biblical themes of struggle, resistance and covenant partnership are increasingly disconnected from the aesthetic or instrumental justification of evil.

3.3 The Lisbon Earthquake

Yet already within the eighteenth century much of this was being challenged. The Lisbon disaster was a hinge event for many thinkers, particularly Voltaire, who attacked the optimism of Leibniz and Pope's insistence that 'all is well'.[23] An earthquake, followed by a raging fire and tidal waves, struck the people of Lisbon and surrounding areas on 1 November 1755. Its geological effects were registered in disturbances far across Europe. Though estimates vary, thousands died, many of them while celebrating All Saints' Day in churches built on soft sediment. Lasting for a week, the fires destroyed libraries, churches, art collections and the Royal Palace, though, it is claimed, the local brothels and their occupants survived largely unscathed. The sudden receding of the sea attracted crowds of mystified onlookers to the shoreline. Many of them perished when the tidal waves arrived. These events fascinated and shocked an entire continent, occasioning a widespread debate which reflected conflicting views of divine providence. Voltaire's poem on the Lisbon disaster satirised the arguments of Leibniz. Rejecting claims that the death of mothers and their little children could be construed as divine punishment – surely the people of Lisbon were no worse than those in Paris and London – Voltaire also mocked the notion that this could contribute to some greater good or to the achievement of a collective whole: '*Tout est bien aujourd'hui, voilà*

---

[23] See the discussion in Jonathan Israel, *The Democratic Enlightenment: Philosophy, Revolution and Human Rights 1750-1790* (Oxford: Oxford University Press, 2011), pp. 41–55.

l'illusion.[24] His poem precipitated the publication of hundreds of pamphlets across the continent, many of them in agreement with Voltaire's scepticism.[25]

In his well known *Essay on Man* (1733/4), parts of which the young Kant is said to have recited, Alexander Pope claimed that the world was providentially ordered. The seeming imperfections of life, including those of our own nature, belong to a greater whole that eludes our gaze.

> All nature is but art, unknown to thee;
> All chance, direction, which thou canst not see;
> All discord, harmony, not understood;
> And partial evil, universal good:
> And, spite of pride, in erring reason's spite,
> One truth is clear, Whatever is, is right.[26]

Pope's point seems to be that the harmony of the world requires the admission of some discordant notes; evils contribute to the greater good in which we participate. Whether Voltaire's *tout est bien* fairly captures Pope's actual dictum – whatever is, is right – is a moot point,[27] yet it is clear that his contemplation of the Lisbon earthquake casts serious doubt on the optimism of Pope. For many after Lisbon, it seemed impossible to assign the appearance of evil to the

---

[24] 'All now is well, that's the illusion.' See Voltaire, 'Poem on the Lisbon disaster; or an examination of the axiom, "All is well"' in Joseph McCabe (ed.), *Toleration and Other Essays by Voltaire* (New York: Putnam's, 1912), pp. 255–63. For a useful exploration of the range of religious reactions to the Lisbon earthquake, see E. S. Brightman, 'The Lisbon earthquake: a study in religious valuation', *American Journal of Theology*, 23.4 (1919), 500–18.

[25] See Theodore Besterman, *Voltaire* (London: Longmans, Green & Co, 1969), pp. 351–9. The best known satirisation of the Leibnizian theodicy is of course Voltaire's classic novel *Candide* (1759).

[26] Alexander Pope, *An Essay on Man* (Edinburgh, 1797), Epistle 1, lines 289–94.

[27] See Jean-Paul Poirier, 'The 1755 Lisbon disaster, the earthquake that shook Europe', *European Review*, 14.2 (2006), 169–80.

category of an unsolved mystery that was not permitted to disrupt a positive judgement about the world and our place in it.

Yet other reactions were less sceptical. In a letter to Voltaire, Rousseau maintained a commitment to providence as vital to his own personal experience and to his belief in the order of the world. Blame for the Lisbon disaster should not be placed upon God. The primary causes were of human origin. For example, if the buildings had not been so high and more dispersed, many would have survived. If people had fled quickly instead of assembling their possessions, they could have saved themselves. Notwithstanding the inadequacy of this response, it possesses the advantage over some rival accounts by not promoting a sense of passivity or resignation in the face of disaster. If a disaster is viewed as a divine visitation intended to inflict suffering and death, then acceptance appears to be the most appropriate response. For Rousseau, at least, the postulated element of human responsibility can induce acts of relief and resistance in the short term, and counter-active measures in the longer term.

Rousseau continued to maintain that the benefits of this life far outweigh its disadvantages. In any case, a swift and premature death may not be the worst that can befall us. So a commitment to providence is maintained, partly because he cannot endure the prospect of living without such faith. But he recognises that our individual lives can only make sense when seen in terms of some greater good – this is God's real concern. By contrast, the particular details are less important. Consequently, Rousseau's account of providence is of a general rather than a special oversight. 'It would seem that in the eyes of the Lord of the universe particular events here below are nothing, that his Providence is exclusively universal, that he leaves it at preserving the genera and the species, and at presiding over the whole, without worrying about how each individual spends his short life.'[28]

---

[28] Jean-Jacques Rousseau, 'Letter to Voltaire', Section 25, in *The Discourse and Other Early Political Writings*, ed. Victor Gourevitch (Cambridge: Cambridge University

More traditional theological responses abounded in sermons and pamphlets. John Wesley offered some thoughts on the earthquake set in the wider context of other seismic events and the anticipated reappearance of Halley's comet in 1758.[29] Two features of his account require comment. First, he understands the earthquake in judicial terms. This was God's judgement on Lisbon – a city 'where so much blood has been poured on the ground like water'.[30] This should not be viewed as an isolated event since others have been observed in England – he alludes to recent seismic events at Whitson cliffs – and more terrible catastrophes may strike nearer home. Who knows indeed whether Halley's comet may devastate the earth? Viewing this as an opportunity for repentance, Wesley exhorts his readers to make 'this wise, this powerful, this gracious God our friend' by devoting our lives to true piety and service of one another.[31] Second, Wesley seems clear that earthquakes do not have a sufficient natural explanation. As such, these are peculiar events wrought by God without intermediate secondary causes. Natural explanations for such upheavals of the earth and sea are unavailable – this appears to be a clear example of a 'God of the gaps' theory. Wesley seems to reckon that we should not propose blind, random or material causes for events of this magnitude. The action of God directly assails us in the earthquake, not through the regular powers of nature, though Wesley acknowledges that God can also work through the agency of created forces.

While Wesley here sides with much mid-eighteenth-century opinion in attributing earthquakes to divine retribution, this was by no means a unanimous position among theologians at that

Press, 1997), p. 241. For further discussion, see Victor Gourevitch, 'Rousseau on providence', *Review of Metaphysics*, 53.3 (2000), 565–611.

[29] John Wesley, 'Serious thoughts occasioned by the late earthquake at Lisbon' in John Emory (ed.), *The Works of the Rev John Wesley*, 7 vols. (New York: Carlton and Porter, 1856), vol. VI, pp. 238–47.

[30] Ibid., p. 238.

[31] Ibid., p. 245.

time. Writers in the ancient world had pondered possible natural explanations. Aristotle favoured the idea that earthquakes are the result of trapped wind in the earth's cavities – when released, the pressure generated causes a major disturbance. This continues in a series of aftershocks. The earthquake can also cause tidal waves by driving back the sea winds which, lacking any vent, return in a single mass.[32] This explanation was accommodated by Albert the Great, Thomas Aquinas and later Jesuit theologians, who implicitly reject the idea that earthquakes are the result of special divine action.[33] Although these events are governed by the primary will of God, they cannot be attributed to divine wrath through a bypassing of regular natural processes. According to Aquinas, Psalm 17 should not be read literally in its attribution to the movement of the earth to God's anger, though earthquakes may indeed provide an opportunity for repentance.[34]

One feature of the discussion is the different ways in which primary and secondary causality can be constructed. In the case of earthquakes (as with portents and prodigies), many writers assumed that these were the result of divine intervention rather

[32] Aristotle, *Meteorologica*, 2.6–8, translated by H. D. P. Lee (London: Heinemann, 1952), pp. 199–223.

[33] Rival scientific accounts were offered in the seventeenth century, partly to explain more adequately the simultaneous tremors that could be identified over long distances. A Benedictine monk and pioneer of Enlightenment ideas in Spain, Jerónimo Feijóo, argued for an electrical explanation in which currents led to the explosion of combustible gases – yet such theories had to be cautiously presented for fear of slighting theological explanation and hence provoking ecclesiastical censure. See Israel, *The Democratic Enlightenment*, pp. 47–8.

[34] Aquinas offered a commentary on Aristotle's work in his *Meteriologicorum*, in *Opera Omnia*, 25 vols. (Parma, 1852–73), vol. XVIII. Commenting on Psalm 17, he repeats this naturalised explanation for earthquakes: '*Causa terrae motus est impulsio unius venti ab alio.*' *Opera Omnia*, vol. XIV, p. 197. For further discussion, see Agustín Udías, 'Earthquakes as God's punishment in 17th- and 18th-century Spain' in M. Kölbl-Ebert (ed.), *Geology and Religion: A History of Harmony and Hostility* (London: Geological Society, 2009), pp. 41–8.

than events which were susceptible to natural explanations. One obvious weakness of such an assumption is that it is vulnerable to subsequent scientific advance. As and when seismologists offer a scientifically plausible account of the phenomenon, the appeal to divine causality fails. Other writers, by contrast, could concede secondary causality to earthquakes, whether or not this was fully understood, while also arguing that the primal will of God is served in and through these intermediate agencies. Immune to scientific falsification, this approach views divine action as consistent with natural causation. But, here again, at least two possible views can be adopted. Working with a tighter fit between divine intention and creaturely occurrence, a Thomist or Calvinist can view each event as expressive of the positive will of God and foreordained to make a unique contribution to the whole economy of creation and salvation. Earthquakes might then serve a divine purpose, whether of judgement or warning or trial, even though these can also be considered natural phenomena. By contrast, a revisionist approach might see the divine will as more loosely connected to the order of secondary causes. The will of God concedes the total series of finite causes to the created order, and works constantly in and through these to bring about a predetermined set of purposes. But this permissive will of God does not determine each and every event as making a unique and indispensable contribution to a single blueprint for creation. On this account, the Lisbon earthquake would be regarded as a natural phenomenon in which God remained present and active, but not as an event that was purposefully intended as a divine visitation. The division between these two viewpoints then is set not by the scheme of double agency itself, but by the ways in which primary and secondary causality are to be configured.[35]

---

[35] Molinism could be seen as occupying the middle ground between these two possibilities. A particular scheme is ordained in every single detail by God, though some of the parts therein are the objects of a divine foreknowledge (generated by God's impeccable middle knowledge) rather than the divine will.

There is some evidence to suggest that theological explanations for the Lisbon earthquake and predictions of worse to come may actually have hindered the long-term relief operation. If God had visited this retribution upon the people of the city, then the first response should be repentance rather than mitigation of its effects. The Jesuit preacher Malagrida declared, 'It is scandalous to pretend the earthquake was just a natural event, for if that be true, there is no need to repent and to try to avert the wrath of God.'[36] Yet Malagrida was an isolated figure who was eventually banished and then executed. The secular hero of the hour was the Portuguese prime minister, the Marquês Pombal (a title conferred in 1770). In response to the earthquake, he ensured that the dead were buried, refugees fed, fires extinguished and injured tended. Food supplies were maintained, looters were executed and the city was defended from piracy. The weekly newspaper continued without interruption. In all this, Pombal was supported by the work of the churches on the ground.[37] A better theology of providence would surely view Pombal and his relief workers as the agents of God, rather than the earthquake itself. Despite the dominant theological reception of the time, intellectual opinion gradually shifted. Lisbon proved a hinge event in uncoupling moral and natural evil. Catastrophes could no longer be viewed as divine acts expressing a moral intention such as retribution.[38]

These sombre reflections on the Lisbon disaster cast doubt on a providence that actively wills each event. To some extent, it strengthened the hand of deists, who argued for a God remote from mundane concerns. This drift towards deist accounts of providence was viewed by the more orthodox as a declension from earlier and more robust views. Signalling a largely absentee God, the deists

[36] Quoted by T. D. Kendrick, *The Lisbon Earthquake* (Philadelphia: Lippincott, 1955), p. 138.

[37] See ibid., pp. 73–84.

[38] This is vividly explored by Susan Neiman, *Evil in Modern Thought: An Alternative History of Philosophy* (Princeton: Princeton University Press, 2002), pp. 240–50.

were regarded as paving the way towards a practical atheism. Devoid of divine action and involvement, the world could run its course without significant reference to its Maker, whose ethical and religious value was not much greater than Aristotle's prime mover. In some respects, these criticisms are valid. The shift from revelation to reason ensures an inevitable detachment from scriptural themes, particularly with respect to the work of Christ (often viewed with Socinian scepticism) and the action of the Holy Spirit (associated with fanatic and enthusiast fringe groups). At its best, as Matthew Tindal argued, Scripture merely re-publishes the truths of natural religion. And, now confined to the task of conserving the natural order, God's action is largely remote from particular events. Somewhat ironically, this was reinforced by the stout defence of miracles on the part of the more orthodox. Their typical strategy tended to restrict special providence to occasional interpositions which may themselves have been largely or wholly confined to the apostolic age. On the basis of the reliability of historical testimony (nothing here was said about the persuasion of the Spirit), we can assent to the miracles attested by Scripture and so to the truth of revelation contained in the same set of texts. But, in any case, the deist confidence in natural reason and natural religion now seemed misplaced. Subsequent historical study militated against the proposed convergence of the world religions upon a common core (e.g. creation, providence and ethics) which could be discerned by philosophical reflection.

Nevertheless, the deists' revision of earlier positions often displayed a measure of political courage as they endured opprobrium for their dangerous heterodox tendencies. And their conviction that God's providence should be discerned primarily in the regularities of the natural world is not without force or scriptural precedent. There is at least a grain of truth in deism which requires acknowledgement. Instead of viewing every single event as if it were a work of particular providence intended for a specified end, they insisted upon a providence that worked in and through the regularities and contingencies of the world, even when this resulted in accident, mishap and tragedy. In loosening the fit between divine intention and created particularities, deism offered greater scope for freedom and contingency within the created order. Without committing wholesale to deism, we might recognise this. The action of the Holy Spirit can be construed in terms of an enablement of providential possibilities rather than a single decree that actualises each particular, ranging from the intensely trivial to the grotesquely genocidal. Within this shift of perspective, the configuration of primary and secondary causality is modified from its classical expression in its Thomist and Calvinist inflections. While not immune from criticism or challenge, the deist modification tends to represent the position of a majority today, or at least one with which many of us are more instinctively comfortable.[39] To that extent, as inhabitants of the contemporary world with its reliance on medicine, technology and scientific expertise, we share a central deist intuition, when measured against our Puritan ancestors.[40]

With the slippage from earlier scriptural and doctrinal themes, it is not surprising that ideas of providence underwent a secular replacement. The ideas persisted but were now located in altered contexts and put to different work. The following two examples illustrate this.

3.4 Imperial Expansion and Slavery

William Robertson (1721–93) was the Principal of the University of Edinburgh and the leader of the moderate party in the Church of Scotland. As an Enlightenment scholar, he ranks alongside Hume,

---

[39] One significant shift today surrounds the 'anthropocene'. The world is not simply a given for us; its ordering is in part the result of human activity, thus creating a causal loop between nature and culture.

[40] One could substitute here several other important religious traditions which once shared much the same set of assumptions.

Gibbon and Voltaire as among the leading European historians of the eighteenth century. His first published work already reveals a strong providential narrative of history, a theme that is later developed in detail in his acclaimed *History of America* (1777). Writing at the outset of his scholarly career, he repeats the ancient argument of Augustine and others that the Christian revelation was given to the world at a providential time. Under the conditions of the Roman empire, the new faith was able to spread rapidly and to counteract negative aspects of Judaism and paganism. 'Favoured by the union and tranquillity of the Roman empire, the disciples of Christ executed their commission to great advantage.'[41] Robertson describes the Christian commitment to marriage as mutual friendship rather than patriarchal ownership, and he criticises the brutality of slavery in the Roman empire. This is mitigated and counteracted by the equality of personhood and mildness of spirit which are the genius of Christianity. And in that part of the world where Christianity has been adopted most fully, we can see the benefits it brings to the sciences, as well as other improvements of power and reputation. This is Europe, and Robertson believes that the spread of its commerce, customs and political power is a further mark of divine providence, not least as this will also be accompanied by the wider transmission of the Christian faith. 'And tho' hitherto subservient to the designs of interest or ambition, may we not flatter ourselves, that, at last, they should become noble instruments in the hand of God, for preparing the world to receive the gospel?'[42]

Robertson reflects the spirit of the age. British imperial expansion is seen as an expression of divine providence, continuous with the rise and spread of Christianity in the ancient world. Nevertheless, his vision is measured and subtle in places. He abhors slavery and offers an account of marriage which stresses the equality of women and

---

[41] William Robertson, *The Situation of the World at the Time of Christ's Appearance, and Its Connexion with the Success of His Religion Considered* (Edinburgh, 1755), p. 14.

[42] Ibid., p. 43.

men. In writing of the American Indians in his *History of America*, he deplores the cruelty and greed of the Spanish conquistadores. The humanity and suffering of the native population are defended. Meanwhile, he continues to judge in favour of the benefits that are brought to the Americas by European agriculture and commerce.[43]

The theological views harboured by Robertson are notoriously elusive. Although the leading Presbyterian clergyman of his day, he was suspected by some of harbouring deist leanings. There is less about original sin, predestination, the atoning work of Christ and the order of salvation in the life of the believer than one finds in the Reformed orthodoxy of the previous century. Yet, he remains in touch with many important features of that tradition. The church persists as a powerful institution that is vital to the moral fabric of society. Without its influence and restraining powers, civil society would quickly degenerate. Nevertheless, there may also be a revisionary quality to Robertson's work that adumbrates later theological developments. At the end of his life, he was working on a history of India. Its ancient civilisation fascinated him and he expresses admiration for the scholarship and thought of the Brahmins, comparing them to the Stoics.[44] The capacity of Hindu polytheism and Islam to coexist likewise impressed him. He quotes a letter advocating an accommodation of Hindus, Christians and Muslims as necessary to the future prosperity of India. Perhaps for this reason, his critics suspected that he was not fully committed to the evangelising of that region. Discussing the reception of Robertson's history of India, Nicholas Phillipson has suggested that there may be 'hints here of the seeds of a new religion, pluralistic, united by a common stoic

[43] William Robertson, *History of America* (Edinburgh, 1777). For further discussion, see Stewart J. Brown, 'William Robertson (1721–1793) and the Scottish Enlightenment' in Stewart J. Brown (ed.), *William Robertson and the Expansion of Empire* (Cambridge: Cambridge University Press, 1997), pp. 7–35.

[44] In what follows, I am indebted to Nicholas Phillipson, 'Providence and progress: an introduction to the historical thought of William Robertson' in Brown, *William Robertson and the Expansion of Empire*, pp. 55–73.

ethics and a belief in toleration, a religion absorbing all creeds and denominations.'[45]

All this shows the subtlety and complexity of the leading Christian thinkers of the Enlightenment. Their work pulls in different directions and cannot easily be enlisted without some distortion to any one ideological perspective. Nevertheless, shorn of key classical elements, the theology of providential history in Robertson informs and constructs a narrative of progress that is very much to the advantage of the project of European expansion. It is neither unequivocally supportive nor lacking in moral discrimination, yet it invests European culture with a value by comparison with which other parts of the world are seen as backward, savage and primitive, albeit with some qualification. In need of the enlightenment that has emerged in Europe, their societies will inevitably benefit from a process of colonisation. Robertson of course remains connected to the older theological traditions and practices that he is self-consciously revising. Affirming the moral and social cohesion created by religion, he is a strong supporter of the establishment of the Church of Scotland while also in favour of extending greater toleration to Roman Catholics. The moral texture of society is given close attention (as it is in Adam Smith). And, like other moderate thinkers, Robertson is committed to a programme of national virtue that is advanced not only by scholars and politicians but also by preachers. Richard Sher has pointed to the way in which the rhetorical device of the 'jeremiad' is brilliantly adapted by moderate preachers such as Blair and Carlyle.[46] With echoes of the covenanting sermons of the seventeenth century, they castigate their congregations for moral laxity, greed and selfishness. Fast days are called at times of national crisis, especially during the American War of Independence. Their sermons urge repentance and a return

---

[45] Ibid., p. 73.

[46] Richard Sher, *Church and University in the Scottish Enlightenment: The Moderate Literati of Edinburgh* (Edinburgh: Edinburgh University Press, 1985), pp. 207–12.

to the ways of true religion. Within this preaching, the discourse of 'providence' is again marked. There is a sense in which God has particularly blessed the people of Scotland (and Britain), although this is combined with a lament about backsliding and a call for acts of penance and reform. In all this, the secular and anthropocentric turn in the doctrine of providence remains allied to a strong Reformed theology.[47]

This is also apparent on the other side of the Atlantic, where John Witherspoon, drawing upon the same theology of providence, could identify the will of God with the political cause of the colonies. Appointed President of the College of New Jersey, Witherspoon had arrived in Princeton in 1768, following years of ministry in Scotland, where he was regarded as a leading evangelical churchman. The only clergyman to sign the Declaration of Independence, he aroused support for the confederate cause in his popular sermons. Several features of his political theology of providence are apparent.[48] A sovereign divine will governs the fluctuating circumstances of human history. Everything is perfectly subject to the purpose and glory of

---

[47] This is evident, for example, in Blair's fast-day sermon at the outbreak of war in 1793. '[W]e have much reason to respect those rulers, under whose administration the empire, though engaged in a hazardous and expensive war, has all along continued to hold a high rank among the nations of Europe, and has attained to that flourishing state of commerce, opulence, and safety, in which we behold it at this day.' Hugh Blair, 'On the love of our country' in *Sermons*, vol. v (London,1808), pp. 114–39 at p. 138.

[48] In what follows, I am paraphrasing material from Witherspoon's sermon in Princeton on 17 May 1776. See John Witherspoon, 'The dominion of providence over the passions of men' in *Collected Works*, vol. v (Harrisonburg, VA: Sprinkle, 2005), pp. 17–42. Richard Sher has shown the ways in which this theology has roots in the Scottish Reformed traditions of the previous century rather than in New England Puritanism. See 'Witherspoon's *Dominion of Providence* and the Scottish jeremiad tradition' in Richard B. Sher and Jeffrey R. Smitten (eds.), *Scotland and America in the Age of the Enlightenment* (Edinburgh: Edinburgh University Press, 1990), pp. 46–64. For a fuller treatment of the shifts in providentialist discourse in American public life, see Nicholas Guyatt, *Providence and the Invention of the United States 1607–1876* (Cambridge: Cambridge University Press, 2007).

God, even the wrath of human beings as they wage war and commit acts of violence upon one another. Yet providence works through all of this in three ways – in exposing sin, in providing an inducement to repentance and in setting boundaries and constraints upon human wickedness. Witherspoon is confident that he can detect the just cause of God in world affairs. Despite its purported invincibility, the Armada was destroyed in part by the wind. In Oliver Cromwell, God raised up a strong leader to maintain the cause of religious liberty at a time of severe threat. The flight of persecuted Christians to American settlements advanced the gospel in that part of the world. And now in their surprising success against veteran British soldiers, the colonies are being vindicated by God in their struggle for civil and religious freedoms. Witherspoon defends the American cause against the misplaced attempts of the British government to trample on their rights. And in claiming their independence, the colonies can reasonably expect success to be granted by God if they combine godliness with their search for justice. Among those of piety and principle, 'we may expect to find the uncorrupted patriot, the useful citizen, and the invincible soldier'.[49]

Witherspoon's address is almost the mirror image of fast-day sermons that were preached simultaneously in Scotland by Hugh Blair and George Campbell. The same theology of providence is apparent, though enlisted for the opposing political position. Three features merit attention at this juncture. The traditional Reformed view that God works through the events of history in a comprehensive and seemingly determinist manner is maintained. While this mode of operation is not clearly specified, there is an overriding sense that all of history is shaped according to a single divine purpose. Accordingly, wars, famines and other evils must be interpreted as either punishments, warnings or occasions for repentance. Although Witherspoon is careful to avoid any simple equation between individual sin and suffering, there remains a

---

[49] Witherspoon, 'The dominion of providence', p. 42.

general correlation in his preaching. Second, the will of God tends to work through secondary, intermediate causes. Although this is not explored in much depth, there appears to be an assumption of compatibility between the primal will of God and the ordinary causes of events, as these can be discerned by the historian. This complementarity of explanations is consistent with what is claimed, though how it avoids a certain arbitrariness of theological judgement is unresolved. Finally, the Reformed jeremiads of the period appear to move in the direction of a political exceptionalism. God has singled out a people for a pivotal function in world history. For this purpose, they are to be judged and blessed in ways that resonate with Israel in the Old Testament. The transfer of the language used of Israel to Scotland or America (or elsewhere) is a standard feature of sermons from the time. Witherspoon's jeremiad recalls the appeal to providentialism in John Winthrop's image of the Puritan colony in Massachusetts as a 'city set on a hill'. These early ideals served the dual purpose of providing reassurance to the community at a time of threat and warning of the dangers of moral and religious declension. In Witherspoon, we can see some of the significant adjustments that this idea is undergoing. Whereas it once signified the godly ideal of a Puritan society, now it is gradually being pressed into the service of forging a new national identity.[50]

As this providentialism morphed into a warrant for a distinctive nationalism, it carried the attendant risk of over-determining the religious significance of one nation over others. Generating a perception of a distinctive national vocation, preachers could too easily lend support to the notion that one people was uniquely destined in world affairs for prosperity, leadership, imperial expansion and missionary endeavour. Not all of this is harmful, but its dangers are obvious, at least with the benefit of hindsight. As we shall see, much

---

[50] See Mark A. Noll, ' "Wee shall be as a citty upon a hill": John Winthrop's non-American exceptionalism', *Review of Faith and International Affairs*, 10:2 (2012), 5–11.

of this mind-set can be discerned in the nineteenth century, when the discourse of providence reached its apogee.

In her study of the use of the jeremiad in political discourse, Cathleen Kaveny notes the different ways in which it functions from the rhetoric of moral deliberation.[51] Using the language of moral indictment, the jeremiad questions the status of the opponent in relation to core commitments. In asserting a radical lapse from fundamental standards, its advocates use the language of denouncement to challenge and confront, rather than to offer a reasonable and civil argument (in Rawlsian mode) for an alternative position. And noting the flexible political uses of this rhetorical form, Kaveny analyses its more contemporary adaptation in disputes in the USA over abortion and torture. Notwithstanding its perils, she recommends a constrained use of the jeremiad in contemporary public debate. To work effectively, its exponents need to be aware of its risks – the demonising of opponents and outsiders, the appearance of moral arrogance and national exceptionalism, and the tendency towards a 'moral balkanisation' of a pluralist society. Kaveny argues that these can be offset by ensuring that the jeremiad is truly radical in recovering the roots of our deepest moral convictions in dealing with fresh crises, by reserving it for the most fundamental and threatening of issues, and by ensuring elements of self-criticism, intellectual humility and hope. In appealing to the ironic and universal themes of the Book of Jonah, as opposed to other Old Testament prophetic denunciations of the nations, she identifies scriptural resources for this contemporary task. The heroic cases of Lincoln's Second Inaugural Address and Martin Luther King's 'I have a dream' Memphis speech (delivered at the Lincoln memorial) provide exemplars of this constructive use of the jeremiad. In the end, these perorations united rather than divided people, despite the presence of formidable opposition.

---

[51] See Cathleen Kaveny, *Prophecy Without Contempt: Religious Discourse in the Public Square* (Cambridge, MA: Harvard University Press, 2016).

And the willingness of their exponents to stand in difficult and uncomfortable places contributed in part to the success they achieved.

Kaveny's work deserves close attention, not least because of the possibilities it offers for a contemporary use of religious discourse in the political domain. One obvious challenge surrounds its effectiveness for societies that are religiously divided and increasingly indifferent to faith claims. The early modern use of the jeremiad was predicated upon a society that was religiously unitary, at least in its commitment to the precepts of the Christian faith, if not in its adherence to a single confessional body. In the case of Martin Luther King, the more recent deployment of this rhetorical form succeeded in part through a fusion with other forms of moral discourse, including the language of civil rights and the American constitution.[52] But, in the present context, it is worth asking whether the jeremiad can survive without some commitment to the providential possibilities of politics. A strong Reformed theology of providence pervaded the fast-day sermons of the eighteenth century. The divine will was variously discernible in the events of world history as judgement, summons and blessing. By understanding the Word of God in this context, the community could be restored, galvanised and directed towards a better future. Much of the confidence in this political theology has now dissipated for reasons already outlined. And the assurance with which earlier generations detected the hand of providence in historical events has been shaken by counter-narratives. The flourishing of the Reformation produced religious fragmentation rather than the reform of the one catholic church. The colonising of the new world was disastrous for its indigenous peoples and their way of life. The exporting of Christianity to India and China did not result in the supersession of other world religions and ethical systems. A single plausible narrative was just too difficult

---

[52] See David L. Chappell, *A Stone of Hope: Prophetic Religion and the Death of Jim Crow* (Chapel Hill: University of North Carolina Press, 2005).

to construct from the myriad and seemingly haphazard fluctuations of multiple peoples, civilisations and histories.

Yet the question remains whether there can be a faith-based contribution to public life without a robust sense of the providential possibilities of politics. Can there be a Christian involvement in the political process, if the public domain no longer offers some prospect for a measure of peace and the amelioration of injustice? Here a contemporary theology of providence has a responsibility to recover some key elements of the tradition in the service of prophetic witness and social engagement. History can be over-determined in relation to providence, but there is also a danger of under-determination to which we shall return. The maintenance of hope requires some prospect of success through the (admittedly dangerous) recognition that the grace and inspiration of the Holy Spirit can motivate and empower people to succeed in their collective endeavours. This requires all the critical conditions set by Kaveny. In addition, the maintenance of this rhetorical tradition, even in modified form, as a religious discourse also reposes upon some residual commitment to divine providence as a political force. The extent to which similar notions recur in secular form – for example, in notions of vocation, destiny and timeliness – suggests its pervasiveness and necessity, perhaps more than is readily admitted.

Immanuel Kant's political writings provide an important illustration of this more secular refraction of providential themes. The 'Idea for a universal history with a cosmopolitan aim' (1784) offers a philosophical account of history in which the base and selfish aims of human beings in society bring about a rational political constitution in which these are overruled. In this essay, he makes his famous remark about the 'crooked wood' of humanity from which nothing entirely straight can be made.[53] Yet the exhausting and destructive

[53] Immanuel Kant, 'Idea for a universal history with a cosmopolitan aim' in *Anthropology, History and Education*, ed. Robert B. Louden and Guenther Zoeller (Cambridge: Cambridge University Press, 2007), pp. 108–20.

effects of conflict eventually persuade human persons of the worth of a better political order. Through suffering and the ill effects of our 'unsociable sociability', we are constrained to acknowledge and to assent to the rule of law. Similarly, even the just political state will find itself in conflict with rival states in the international arena. Although the selfish drives of individuals are writ large in competition and wars, in the course of time these will yield to the establishment of a more just cosmopolitan order. The exhaustion and economic drain of repeated warfare contrasts unfavourably with the benefits of trade and cooperation. Hence there are strong drivers which will 'prepare the way for a future large state body' which lacks any historical precedent.[54]

Kant's hope for a rational cosmopolitan order is based on a conviction that, despite the unsociable and selfish tendencies of human beings, there is a capacity latent within nature to produce a greater good to which we will assent. The traumas of war and the benefits of trade will ensure that, through selfish means, a greater common good can emerge. With its sense of organic development, Kant's account appears indebted to Stoic notions of a natural law unfolding everywhere in the cosmos. This order manifests itself through the actions of individual agents which from a more local perspective appear base and irrational. Yet, in describing how this occurs in world history, Kant seems to distance himself from Rousseau's account, in which individual goals have to be deliberately suppressed to achieve a common good.

Genevieve Lloyd regards Kant's vision of world history as a secularised version of Augustine's providential account of the city of God.[55] The principal difference is that the earthly city is the exclusive focus of Kant's attention – it is the only arena in which providence

---

[54] Ibid., pp. 117–18.

[55] Genevieve Lloyd, 'Providence as progress: Kant's variations on a tale of origins' in Amélie Oksenberg Rorty and James Schmidt (eds.), *Kant's Idea for a Universal History with a Cosmopolitan Aim: A Critical Guide* (Cambridge: Cambridge University Press, 2009), pp. 200–15.

is now manifested. This providence, moreover, is the result of the outworking of natural laws rather than a future fashioned by the redeeming work of Christ. There are echoes of Leibniz and Rousseau in much of Kant's essay, although he seems more focussed than either of his predecessors on the actual outcomes of world history. Whether Kant intended the cosmopolitan vision as an imminent historical probability or a more regulative ideal is not entirely clear, but the redirection of the idea of providence to international relations governed by organic processes of development is evident.

The natural forces of human history lend themselves to the eventual establishment of a cosmopolitan world order. Under such a regime, our more rational and moral capacities will be developed. This is not to be equated so much with happiness as with the cultivation of what makes us distinctly personal. There are threads in Kant's writing which are also discernible in Robertson. The narrative of progress may be qualified in important respects – in particular, given the genuine openness of our free choices, the exact course of history appears to be indeterminate and unpredictable – but in general it seems to support some form of European expansionism. Again, Kant's position is ambivalent. He deplores conquest by force – the ends of civilisation cannot justify the means of coercion – while his stress on the respect to be accorded each human person provides a powerful argument against enslavement. However, he maintains a troubling silence on the matter of chattel slavery, despite having the resources to attack it. In his writings on race, Kant assumes that in some racial groups the development of human potential has been greater than in others.[56] This results in a privileging of white Europeans which is narrowed to further developments within Europe itself. Much of this is typical of Enlightenment thinkers, although no less objectionable for that

---

[56] For an exploration of Kant's writings on race, see Robert Bernasconi, 'Kant as an unfamiliar source of racism' in Julie K. Ward and Tommy L. Lott (eds.), *Philosophers on Race: Critical Essays* (Oxford: Blackwell, 2002), pp. 145–66.

reason. What is significant in this context is the implicit notion that providence seems to have ordained the hegemony of a particular type of civilisation in which distinctive human capacities have been developed. This is most evident in the notorious claim that there is a hierarchy of racial characteristics with the greatest perfections being confined to 'the white race'.[57]

Examples of pro-slavery theology further confirm the ways in which providentialism could readily be pressed into the service of conservative ideological forces.[58] Drawing on an array of scriptural examples, writers could argue that enslavement had been ordained by God. To disrupt the institution is to threaten the fabric and order of Christian society. James Thornwell's address on 'The Christian doctrine of slavery' is suffused with providential imagery. In defending the institution, moreover, he is adamant that this represents a wider contest in which social order (including the obligation to labour for another without the provisions of a contract) must be preserved from the assault of atheists, socialists, communists, red republicans and Jacobins.

When we consider the diversities in moral position, which sin has been the means of entailing upon the race, we may be justified in affirming, that, relatively to some persons and to some times, Slavery

---

[57] 'Humanity is at its greatest perfection in the race of the whites. The yellow Indians do have a meagre talent. The Negroes are far below them and at the lowest point are a part of the American peoples.' This remark is found in Kant's lectures on physical geography. The translation is from E. C. Eze (ed.), *Race and the Enlightenment: A Reader* (Oxford: Blackwell, 1997), p. 63. The range of interpretations of Kant's views on race is summarised by Robert B. Louden, *Kant's Human Being: Essays on His Theory of Human Nature* (New York: Oxford University Press, 2011), pp. 131–5. J. Kameron Carter has discussed ways in which the racialised subject of Kantian philosophy becomes a theological construct as well. See *Race: A Theological Account* (New York: Oxford University Press, 2008), pp. 80ff.

[58] For a survey of the established tenets of slavery theology, see Paul Harvey, *Christianity and Race in the American South: A History* (Chicago: University of Chicago Press, 2016), pp. 73–82.

may be a good, or, to speak more accurately, a condition, from which, though founded in a curse, the Providence of God extracts a blessing.[59]

The dangers in this providential construction of political events and systems are manifold. The exceptionalism that often accompanies forms of civil religion (and not only in large nations and empires) can have the effect of overriding the competing claims of other nations and political groups when these clash. There is no New Testament warrant for concluding that the gospel might be advanced by the peculiar singling out of one nation-state, race or empire as its vehicle. Yet many of the arguments advanced in favour of imperial expansion from the sixteenth century revolve around the notion that Europeans served a divinely ordained purpose by colonising other parts of the world. In particular, two arguments recur in variant forms, particularly in the Americas. Appeal is made to (bogus) notions of the empty and the promised land. In the case of the former, the ancient Roman legal principle of *res nullius* was cited. Empty things may be considered common property. If a land is largely vacant or only sparsely populated, settlers from other parts have a right of occupation and a duty of development.[60] This was reinforced by the further claim that if native inhabitants came into conflict with such occupation then they could be assimilated or improved. Since it would be in their interests to do so, one could even assume tacit assent on the (spurious) ground that if they were able to make an informed choice then they would surely choose to do so. This reasoning was buttressed by the thought that, in the event of outright opposition, enforced conquest might be justified

---

[59] James Henley Thornwell, 'The Christian doctrine of slavery' in John B. Adger and John L. Girardeau (eds.), *Collected Writings of James Henley Thornwell*, vol. IV (New York: Carter, 1873), pp. 398–436 at p. 421.

[60] See the discussion in Anthony Pagden, *Lords of All the World: Ideologies of Empire in Spain, Britain and France c1500–c1800* (New Haven: Yale University Press, 1995), pp. 76ff.

by the precedent of the Israelite occupation of Canaan. While not forming a systematic corpus, these arguments recur in haphazard ways over several centuries and provide something like a Christian ideology for imperial expansion. At the same time, dissenting voices were also raised, most notably Bartholomé de las Casas, who argued on theological grounds against the subjugation and slaughter of American Indians. But the drift of political ideologies drawing upon theological claims is clear, as are their deleterious consequences.[61] This is exposed ironically in a letter of Columbus, who, in his search for wealth, princes and great cities, sent two men further into the country: 'They trawled for three days and found an infinite number of small villages and people without number, but nothing of importance.'[62]

In assessing the ways in which providential thinking was absorbed into political discourse, we should note that it could equally well be identified with judgement as with blessing. This is already apparent in the preaching of Witherspoon, which combines elements of promise and threat. In the United States, the abolitionists could argue that the division and demise of the nation was the likely consequence of its crimes against Native Americans and African slaves. Divine punishment was an alternative manifestation of divine providence, thus complexifying the narrative of a favoured exceptionalism. In his study of the different appropriations of providential theology in the Unites States, Nicholas Guyatt has

---

[61] The fusion of empty land and promised land motifs in relation to the American Indians is expertly documented by Alfred A. Cave, 'Canaanites in a promised land: the American Indian and the providential theory of empire', *American Indian Quarterly*, 12.4 (1988), 277–97. Estimates suggest that around 95 per cent of the indigenous populations of the western hemisphere were rapidly destroyed through the violence and disease that attended European colonialism. This has been described as 'the most massive act of genocide in the history of the world'. David E. Stannard, *American Holocaust: The Conquest of the New World* (New York: Oxford University Press, 1992), p. x.

[62] Quoted in ibid., p. 258.

pointed to this persistent ambivalence, particularly where slavery is concerned.[63] This was reflected in the preaching of Henry Ward Beecher, in the writing of Harriet Beecher Stowe and in Lincoln's political addresses. Guyatt writes,

> Those people who had better prepared for secession and civil war, on the abolitionist or proslavery side, had tailored providential interpretations to suit the breakup of the United States. For the abolitionists, this meant a wrathful version of judicial providentialism that would destroy the Union or ravage the South, and a willingness to sacrifice a shared history that was contaminated by concessions to the slave power. For proslavery southerners, God had entrusted the South with the mission of conserving and perpetuating slavery until the mists that surrounded the purpose and prospects of this baffling institution finally cleared.[64]

One might seek to overcome the partiality and myopia of providential exceptionalism by viewing the whole of history with its gains and tragic losses as moving forward under some divine influence. But this would be done in such a way that each of its constituent parts makes a contribution to the whole, so that none is selected at the expense of the other. The weak and the strong, the righteous and the unrighteous, the successful and the unlucky would all be gathered into a single movement that collectively leads to the realisation of some overarching scheme, though its many details are not apparent. Divine providence would here overrule all nations and empires in working out a single purpose. This might represent a historicised version of Leibniz's theodicy in which each particular

[63] Guyatt, *Providence and the Invention of the United States*. Mark Noll also points to the ways in which the same providentialist concepts were deployed by both sides in the civil war. The eventual outcome was interpreted not only as divine vindication of abolitionism but as judgement upon a troubled nation. See Mark Noll, *The Civil War as a Theological Crisis* (Chapel Hill: University of North Carolina Press, 2006), pp. 81–6.

[64] Guyatt, *Providence and the Invention of the United States*, p. 256.

makes its distinctive contribution to an overall harmony and in which its identity is realised only in relation to everything else.

In Hegel's philosophy of world history something resembling this scenario appears. Here it is the global function of providence that is set out. Protesting against a view which reduces providence to the 'petty commerce' of isolated cases,[65] Hegel argues that God must have a providence that works comprehensively, even if we cannot everywhere specify its effects. Spirit directs the particular events and actors of history with an 'absolute cunning'. Each contributes in some way to an emergent whole which cannot be understood except, if at all, with the benefit of hindsight. It is not that this is a meaning imposed deterministically in a top-down manner. By contrast, it is a pattern that emerges on the 'slaughter bench of history' through the evils, self-interest and violence of human affairs. Hegel employs a fabric metaphor by which the interweaving of the idea of God within the passions of history brings about a realisation of divine consciousness in human freedom.[66]

Although there are similarities with Kant's providentialism, Hegel is more cautious in several important respects. The idea of progress does not appear to have the same regulative function in his philosophy precisely because this is discernible only with the benefit of hindsight. It is backward and fragmentary rather than forward-looking. An instant reading of meaning into history, whether of individuals or nations, is generally disparaged by Hegel. Only in retrospect can we discern a meaning amid the historical processes we inhabit. Progress is neither smooth nor unilateral nor inevitable.[67] While Hegel's position has unfairly been castigated for

---

[65] G. H. F. Hegel, *Lectures on the Philosophy of World History*, ed. Robert E. Brown and Peter C. Hodgson, 2 vols. (Oxford: Clarendon Press, 2011), vol. 1, p. 84. See also Peter C. Hodgson, *Shapes of Freedom: Hegel's Philosophy of World History in Theological Perspective* (Oxford: Oxford University Press, 2012), p. 162.

[66] For a discussion of how this works in Hegel, see Peter Hodgson, *God in History: Shapes of Freedom* (Nashville: Abingdon, 1989), pp. 118ff.

[67] 'When philosophy paints its grey on grey, then has a shape of life grown old. By philosophy's grey on grey it cannot be rejuvenated but only understood. The owl of

the promotion of a bland optimism, nevertheless there remains the same sense of an immanent purpose of an all-encompassing spirit within world history which closely resembles this secularising or raising to a speculative register of older ideas of divine providence. All history must be unified, its disparate parts contributing through an inexorable logic to a single whole in which Spirit realises itself in and through the world. This appears again in materialist mode in the work of Marx and his followers with the belief in the eventual revolution of the proletariat and the end of economic alienation.[68] Hegel, however, is restrained in salutary ways. Although we cannot see everything as 'for the best', we should seek some advances in what are otherwise tragic and irredeemably awful events.[69] In the end, Hegel seeks reconciliation rather than a speculative explanation for the slaughter bench of history. To this extent also, he remains indebted to his theological roots.[70]

The writings of great historians and philosophers are nuanced and qualified, offering different strands of thought, each of which can lead in a particular direction. To claim that Robertson, Kant and Hegel simply offered a *carte blanche* for European imperial expansion and the imposition of Enlightenment values

Minerva spreads its wings only with the falling of the dusk.' G. W. F. Hegel, *Philosophy of Right*, trans. T. M. Knox (Oxford: Clarendon, 1952), p. 13.

[68] Recent scholarship has questioned the extent to which Marx himself was committed to the inevitability of capitalism's demise. Historical progressivism was a feature of Engels's thought and Marxist thinkers more generally from about 1880 to 1920. Yet Marx maintained a more nuanced position, perhaps complicated by his family's increasing economic dependence on Engels. See Gareth Stedman Jones, *Karl Marx: Greatness and Illusion* (London: Allen Lane, 2016), pp. 565–8.

[69] 'The point, for (Hegel), is not to present a bland, idealized view of history, but to consider where in all this historical confusion and bloodshed progress does actually show itself, and to what extent massive historical upheavals – such as the Thirty Years War … or the French revolution – were the tragic result of *advances* in human religious or political self-understanding.' Stephen Houlgate, *An Introduction to Hegel: Freedom, Truth and History*, 2nd edn (Oxford: Blackwell, 2005), p. 19.

[70] See Hodgson, *Shapes of Freedom*, pp. 167–75.

would be to distort the subtlety of their thought, its capacity for self-criticism and the challenging of regnant assumptions. Nevertheless, there does seem to be a clear link between the providential historicism of Enlightenment thinkers and the imperial projects of the eighteenth and nineteenth centuries. These often employed the questionable language of a theological exceptionalism to justify their ventures both at home and abroad. Given its frequency, it seems apt to describe the myth of exceptionalism as itself unexceptional.[71]

In addition, much of the providentialism aligned with imperial projects tends towards the view that history must display a single trajectory and destination. To this extent, it has some difficulty in accommodating a pluralism of ends and forms of life. Over the long run, the parts all contribute to a comprehensive evolution of the whole. This seems inimical to a more variegated and kaleidoscopic account in which there can be different projects, civilisations and life forms, each of value and purpose to their practitioners without reference to a single unifying trajectory. The unconscious prejudice that in the long run the rest of the world will come around to one (i.e. our) way of thinking and living ought to be challenged. There are risks of oppression when groups of people are condemned to be the means to a greater end or coerced into adopting the position of the few or the many. In his discussion of Alexander Herzen, a Russian political writer of the nineteenth century, Isaiah Berlin writes of the absence of a libretto in human history:

> The end of each generation is itself – each life has its own unique experience; the fulfilment of its wants creates new needs, claims, new forms of life ... Has history a plan, a libretto? If it did, 'it would lose all interest, become ... boring, ludicrous'. There are no

---

[71] 'Among great powers, thinking you're special is the norm, not the exception.' Stephen M. Walt, 'The myth of American exceptionalism', *Foreign Policy*, 189 (2011), 72-5 at 75.

literary

timetables, no cosmic patterns; there is only the 'flow of life', passion, will, improvisation.[72]

Christian theology of course gives some credence to the notion that all history is set in one direction, culminating in a single outcome for all. 'At the name of Jesus, every knee shall bend, in heaven and on earth' (Philippians 2:10). Yet other scriptural resources, particularly the wisdom literature, suggest that this idea requires some nuancing. There is a diversity of language, custom, religion and culture which can display a divine wisdom. The final outcome, moreover, is the result of an eschatological transformation rather than the yield of an organic cosmic process. The remaking of the world is consistent with a variety of patterns which arise spontaneously in the contingent creation with their own value, irrespective of any contribution to a wider whole. These should not be forced onto a Procrustean bed devised by political agencies.

Much of the British imperial drive through the nineteenth century was fuelled by the conviction that this was a divinely appointed mission and one which rendered an important service to other parts of the world. Religion not only promoted internal civic life but legitimised imperial expansion. William Wilberforce, the evangelical reformer and leading abolitionist, argued that the opening of India to the imperial venture was itself providentially organised. The renewal of the East India Company charter in 1813 enabled Wilberforce and the Clapham sect to campaign for the insertion of the so-called 'pious clause' in the parliamentary act, which required formal support for Christian mission in the subcontinent. Petitions were submitted to parliament. These amassed almost half a million signatures, much of the supporting campaign drawing heavily upon notions of divine providence. Robert Hall, a Baptist minister, claimed that 'Our acquisition of power has been so rapid, so extensive, and so disproportionate to the limits of our native empire,

---

[72] Isaiah Berlin, *Russian Thinkers* (London: Penguin, 1978), p. 195. I owe this reference to Jay Brown.

that there are few events in which the interposition of Providence may be more distinctly traced.'[73] The *Evangelical Magazine* of May 1813 could even claim that 'in the course of Providence, Britain is become mistress of the East'.[74]

This confidence in divine providence as authorising imperial success is still evident in theological work at the end of the nineteenth century. In his Gifford Lectures (1896–98), A. B. Bruce argued that providence works in several ways, one of which is the election of nations and individuals to serve a purpose for the world.[75] Called to be a light to the nations, Israel was not alone in this vocation. Others were elected to perform similar service to the world in a variety of spheres. Bruce notes that divine election is predicated upon racial differences which render some peoples peculiarly suited to serve a particular purpose. He also suggests that small nations seem to be preferred by providence – the examples of Israel, Greece, Rome and the British Isles are cited. And he argues that, for a time at least, interracial mixing is to be avoided to allow these distinctive features to manifest themselves and serve their intended purpose. Representative of the time, Bruce's intentions were evidently benign. He stressed that election serves the good of all, and pride and arrogance are to be shunned, while warnings are sounded about despising 'the little and the obscure'.[76] And in a successive chapter, human solidarity is stressed as a further method of God's providence. Yet, a century later, the tendentiousness of these views strikes us forcibly. Claims for racial superiority, the failure to calculate the negative effects of imperialism, and the tendency to diminish other cultures are all deeply problematic. Any serviceable account of providence must avoid these defects. Ways of

---

[73] Quoted in Stewart J. Brown, *Providence and Empire 1815–1914* (Harlow: Longman, 2008), p. 37.

[74] Ibid.

[75] A. B. Bruce, *The Providential Order of the World* (New York: Scribner's, 1905), pp. 256–79.

[76] Ibid., p. 275.

affirming the prospect of historical advances need to be combined with a greater self-criticism, a recognition of the ambivalence of the past and an awareness of the ways in which the wisdom and spirit of God can work across peoples and societies.

3.5 Free Trade

Alongside arguments for imperial expansion, we can discern related but different claims for the value of trading under free market conditions. Here considerations were advanced that appealed to a similar 'cunning of reason'. By engaging for private ends in commercial transactions, individuals contributed unwittingly to a wider public good. This was already recognised by thinkers such as Mandeville and Butler but its classical expression is found in Adam Smith's notion of the 'invisible hand', an image evocative of providential themes once again transposed into a secular context.

Writing in *the Wealth of Nations* (1776), Smith notes the ways in which the pursuit of private commercial ends by a variety of individual agents can result in an overall benefit to the common good. Human acquisitiveness is thus turned to the advantage of all by the working of laws of economic generation. This is a sign of the operation of an 'invisible hand'.

By preferring the support of domestic to that of foreign industry he intends only his own security; and by directing that industry in such a manner as its produce may be of greatest value, he intends only his own gain, and he is in this, as in many other cases, led by an invisible hand to promote an end which was no part of his intention … by pursuing his own interest he frequently promotes that of the society more effectually than when he really intends to promote it. I have never known much good to be done by those who affected to trade for the public good.[77]

[77] Adam Smith, *An Enquiry into the Nature and Causes of the Wealth of Nations*, ed. R. H. Campbell, A. S. Skinner and W. B. Todd (Oxford: Clarendon Press, 1979), p. 456. For an extended discussion of the ways in which providentialist concepts were

Critics are divided over the extent to which Smith implies a theological context for this invisible hand. Secular commentators have tended to insist that it is merely a metaphor for the natural mechanism of equilibrium in competitive markets. All we have are efficient causes that happen to function in an orderly manner. In this way, Smith is closely aligned to the naturalism of Hume. Other critics read this as a modern eisegesis that fails to take sufficient account of the implicit theology of his *Theory of Moral Sentiments*. The removal of any hidden superintendence of economic processes is itself ideologically driven by the belief that the economy does best without external management.[78]

Yet it is clear that the image of the invisible hand is redolent of theories of divine providence. This is entirely consistent with understanding superintendence to work through the medium of natural economic forces. The philosophers of the Enlightenment typically saw the hand of providence in the arrangement of the natural world. In promoting our prosperity, the constitution of human nature and society could be seen as benevolently designed by God. Moreover, in deploying this Smithian notion, later thinkers were inclined to attribute to market forces a quasi-sacral function.[79] Given free rein, these could be relied upon to bring about beneficial outcomes. To interfere with them is to violate a natural order. In the writings of early nineteenth-century political economists, as we shall see, these Smithian arguments were aligned with

transposed from theology to early modern economics see Joost Hengstmengel, 'Divine Oeconomy: The Role of Providence in Earl-Modern Economic Thought Before Adam Smith', PhD thesis, Erasmus University Rotterdam (2015).

[78] See David Martin, 'Economics as ideology: on making "the invisible hand" visible', *Review of Social Economy*, 48.1 (1990), 272–87. For a summary of the different lines of interpretation, see Craig Smith, *Adam Smith's Political Philosophy: The Invisible Hand and Spontaneous Order* (London: Routledge, 2006), pp. 82–4. Emma Rothschild, for example, dismisses Smith's image as a mildly ironic joke.

[79] In what follows, I am indebted to Alastair Macleod, 'Invisible hand arguments: Milton Friedman and Adam Smith', *Journal of Scottish Philosophy*, 5.2 (2007), 103–17.

more distinctively theological commitments than we find in Smith himself.[80]

This argument may be most cogent when directed against the inefficiencies and harmfulness of excessive state planning and control over the market. As it stands, however, it raises several problems about what is intended by self-interest and the good of society. Does it assume that economic agents will always narrowly pursue their selfish interests? How are these to be understood? And is the good of society to be measured in terms of total economic output, average incomes or levels of poverty? Aside from these questions, there are also important issues around the social, legal and moral conditions which are required for such transactions to take place in a transparent and equitable manner that commands the confidence of both parties.

In any case, a commitment to equal trading partnerships can be presented as a plausible argument against the aforementioned project of imperial conquest. This is apparent from Hume's criticism of empires which overreach themselves, resulting in a multitude of deleterious consequences. A supporter of American independence, he deplores the conquest and colonial rule of overseas territories, perceiving these to contain the seeds of their own downfall. By contrast, he argues for free trade among peoples as the means to promote material prosperity and forms of peaceful interaction.[81]

Smith's own position on these questions is not always clear. For example, in *The Theory of Moral Sentiments*, his use of the invisible hand image appears to be directed to the observation that human

---

[80] 'The physiocrats, Adam Smith, and later Kant, but not on the whole the major English classical economists, in effect demanded that there be added to the Decalogue a condemnation of governmental interference with the economic freedom of individuals going beyond the enforcement of commutative justice.' Jacob Viner, *The Role of Providence in the Social Order* (Philadelphia: American Philosophical Society, 1972), p. 85.

[81] See for example David Hume, 'The idea of a perfect commonwealth' in *Essays Moral, Political, and Literary* (Edinburgh, 1742), Part II, essay XVI.

acquisitiveness and ambition lead naturally to greater wealth for the poorest in society. It is a means for the improvement of the whole social order. Why is this? The generation of wealth by the most industrious and ambitious persons in society is unlikely to satisfy their appetites. But, rather than condemn the pursuit of luxury as early civic humanists had done, Smith (with Hume) celebrates it as contributing to the benefit of all sectors of society, including the poorest.

> [The rich] consume little more than the poor, and in spite of their natural selfishness and rapacity, though they mean only their own conveniency, though the sole end which they propose from the labours of all the thousands whom they employ, be the gratification of their own vain and insatiable desires, they divide with the poor the produce of their achievements. They are led by an invisible hand to make nearly the same distribution of the necessaries of life, which would have been made, had the earth been divided into equal portions among all its inhabitants, and thus without intending it, without knowing it, advance in the interest of the society, and afford means to the multiplication of the species. When Providence divided the earth among a few lordly masters, it neither forgot nor abandoned those who seemed to have been left out of the partition.[82]

Smith's religious commitments seem minimal – biographers have struggled to discern where his true allegiance lies. Despite his early lectures on natural theology, he is reticent in his two principal publications about the resting place of his theological views. In contrast, the Stoic influences upon his thought are unquestionable and much that appears in the *Theory of Moral Sentiments* has clear deist antecedents.[83] What we are offered is something like a

---

[82] Adam Smith, *Theory of Moral Sentiments*, ed. R. P. Hawley (London: Penguin, 2009), Part IV, chapter I, p. 215.

[83] Paul Oslington has recently argued for a much greater theological influence upon Smith than has hitherto been recognised. See 'Divine action, providence and

description of a world that is providentially ordered but without any sense of particular divine interpositions. Hence the onwards movement of human civilisation is the outcome of laws of development that produce rising levels of prosperity and happiness, as well as the increase of populations. This arises from many successful adaptations of nature in which particular actions or tendencies are harnessed in ways that serve the purpose of the whole. The division of labour produces not just greater degrees of wealth but also contributes to technological development. At the same time, our natural disposition of sympathy moderates human interaction and yields beneficial levels of cooperation. 'The uncoordinated, self-regarding acts of individuals, ultimately form part of a wider beneficent pattern orchestrated by Providence and geared towards human happiness and material prosperity.'[84] What Smith shows by reference to this ordered pattern is that human moral and economic exchanges do not constitute a 'zero-sum' game. The result of increased trading, manufacturing and the division of labour was not the wealth of a few but the wealth of nations. All the boats in the water will rise when the tide flows. How far Smith actually perceived his theories to require a theology as their necessary condition is, for the moment, beside the point. And whether he was as sanguine about the universally positive effects of market forces, as his later followers were, is doubtful. What we see at work here is the socialisation of a theory of general providence. There is an order to the moral and economic world that is beneficial. The intellectual antecedents of this view are in Reformed theology and its transposition to deism. Again, this generates a further movement in which providentialist notions do not disappear but are increasingly refracted in a range of other disciplines.

Smith's argument for the invisible hand is but one strand in his overall understanding of how society functions. What is sometimes

Adam Smith's invisible hand' in Paul Oslington (ed.), *Adam Smith as Theologian* (London: Routledge, 2011), pp. 61–76.

[84] Lisa Hill, 'The hidden theology of Adam Smith', *European Journal of the History of Economic Thought*, 8:1 (2001), 1–29 at 14.

missed is his recognition that economic transactions require relatively stable social and moral frameworks. These provide conditions of trust, honesty and equity that ensure the regulation of economic relations. Our trading is facilitated by a social order than cannot be understand solely in terms of market relations between autonomous agents with acquisitive desires. Many exponents of Smith's economics in the nineteenth century recognised the importance of this wider context, particularly in relation to religious institutions and ends. The clearest example of this is in the slogan 'commerce and Christianity' that was prominent between about 1840 and 1860.[85] It denoted the alliance between the interests of free trade and Christian mission that was justified in heavily providentialist language by exponents such as David Livingstone and Samuel Wilberforce. While the interests of free trade and Christian mission did not always coincide – these were presented for a time as convergent – the latter was capable of correcting the excesses of the former and investing it with spiritual purpose. To justify this, the language of divine providence was once again powerfully invoked.

> Commerce ... is a mighty machinery laid in the wants of man by the Almighty Creator of all things, to promote the intercourse and communion of one race with another, and especially of the more civilised races of the earth with the less civilised ... As this commerce must exist for the supply of the wants of man, it follows, I think, that Christian nations are bound to seek to impregnate commerce with their Christianity, and so to carry to the ends of the earth those blessings of religion which are the chiefest of all possessions.[86]

Several claims are embedded in passages such as this. God has not blessed the British empire with success for material ends alone.

---

[85] See Brian Stanley, ' "Commerce and Christianity": providence theory, the missionary movement, and the imperialism of free trade, 1842–1860', *Historical Journal*, 26.1 (1983), 71–94.

[86] Samuel Wilberforce, *Speeches on Missions* (London, 1874), pp. 176–7.

There is some greater purpose at work here. Christianity can most readily be communicated through the medium of other civilising forces such as law, education, government and free trade. Hence the promotion of free trade around the world will work in tandem with the spread of the gospel to other lands. These alliances may have proved temporary and not without their strains.[87] Sometimes the interests of commerce and Christianity could diverge, resulting in the former being viewed with suspicion by the latter. Yet the extension of a classical doctrine of providence to a secular context is again apparent as a key element of the ideological justification for spreading both commerce and Christianity at a time when these were seen as convergent ends. John Bowring, Governor of Hong Kong, could make the startling equation that 'Jesus Christ is Free Trade and Free Trade is Jesus Christ'.[88]

More recently, however, we have witnessed the isolation of 'invisible hand' arguments in which a surfeit of faith has been placed too exclusively on market forces, as if these possessed some quasi-magical function in producing widespread benefits for an entire society or international order. Furthermore, this pattern is extended from economics to other areas of human culture as part of a wider argument to restrict the role of government in interfering with these beneficial processes. 'A society's values, its culture, its social convention – all these develop in the same ways, through voluntary exchange, spontaneous cooperation, the evolution of a complex structure through trial and error, acceptance and rejection.'[89]

The link between providence and secular ideology should not be overstated, though theologians have succumbed to the temptation. There will always be counter-examples to consider amid the historical complexities. Other considerations intrude, with the

---

[87] See also Andrew Porter, ' "Commerce and Christianity": the rise and fall of a nineteenth-century missionary slogan', *Historical Journal*, 28.3 (1985), 597–621.

[88] Quoted in Stewart J. Brown, *Providence and Empire 1815–1914*, p. 145.

[89] Milton and Rose Friedman, *Free to Choose* (London: Secker and Warburg, 1980), p. 26.

result that theology is neither a necessary nor a sufficient condition for adhering to a political creed. Mono-causal explanations are best avoided. Yet some resonance of providential beliefs with social attitudes can undoubtedly be detected in the case of *laissez-faire* economics in the first half of the nineteenth century. Throughout much of this period, the operation of market forces was identified with the workings of a wise and benevolent general providence. As with the laws of nature, the divine will works in and through economic laws.[90] This generated some significant correlations between understandings of providence and social attitudes. For some, a belief in the divinely ordained status of economic laws justified a commitment to *laissez-faire* economics and politics. Any adjustment of social laws and their outcomes implied interference with an order ordained by God. Here the fit between a perceived natural order and the divine will was again too tight. In some quarters, evangelical opinion in the early nineteenth century was at odds with Tory paternalism on precisely this ground. With his Christianised brand of free trade economics, Thomas Chalmers provides an influential example. In his *Bridgewater Lectures*, he summarises his position elegantly.

> The philosophy of free trade is grounded on the principle, that society is most enriched or best served, when commerce is left to its own spontaneous evolutions: and is neither fostered by the artificial encouragements, nor fettered by the artificial restraints of human policy ... a more prosperous result is obtained by the spontaneous play and busy competition of many thousand wills, each bent on the prosecution of its own selfishness, than by the anxious

[90] In what follows, I am indebted to Boyd Hilton, *The Age of Atonement: The Influence of Evangelicalism on Social and Economic Thought, 1795–1865* (Oxford: Clarendon, 1988). For some criticism of Hilton's over-statement of this correlation and his unduly negative characterisation of the social theology of pre-millennialism, see Martin Spence, *Heaven on Earth: Reimagining Time and Eternity in Nineteenth-Century British Evangelicalism* (Eugene, OR: Wipf and Stock, 2015), pp. 211–16.

superintendence of a government, vainly attempting to medicate the fancied imperfections of nature.[91]

Chalmers insisted that this economic order was ordained by divine providence; if respected it would prove benevolent in its outcome. Moral discipline was required, for example through sexual restraint in not over-populating the land and in the moderation of excessively selfish desires. Episodes of bankruptcy were nature's way of self-correcting the system and so regulating avaricious behaviour. The internal order of the system constrains us to develop Christian virtues, thus demonstrating its providential worth. Other considerations were also advanced by evangelical economists, including the thought that a population surfeit amid scarce resources would encourage emigration and so the spread of the gospel to distant places.[92] State intervention through the Poor Laws was correspondingly criticised as destructive *inter alia* of personal initiative, philanthropic endeavour and family ties.

Though ranged against state amelioration of poverty as unnatural, this outlook could also advocate abolitionism on the grounds that slavery was itself an institution that offended against our divinely ordained freedom.[93] Providence was identified with general laws rather than special interpositions. Partly for this reason, the tradition of fast days had become marginalised by the 1830s, while natural disasters were viewed less as particular divine judgements and more as collateral damage from natural processes that were generally benign. The Irish famine played an important role in shaking confidence in natural processes and even Chalmers, otherwise a

---

[91] Thomas Chalmers, *On the Power, Wisdom and Goodness of God as Manifested in the Adaptation of External Nature to the Moral and Intellectual Constitution of Man* (London: Pickering, 1833), pp. 33–4.

[92] See also Boyd Hilton, 'Chalmers as political economist' in A. C. Cheyne (ed.), *The Practical and the Pious: Essays on Thomas Chalmers (1780–1847)* (Edinburgh: St Andrew Press, 1985), pp. 141–56.

[93] See Hilton, *The Age of Atonement*, pp. 209–11.

strong advocate of *laissez-faire* economics, advocated government action to provide relief.[94]

The tendency to attribute natural disasters to divine judgment continued, though only fitfully and in the face of growing public scepticism. In one of his sermons, Dr James Begg attributed the Tay Bridge disaster of 1879 to a divine verdict on the running of trains on the Sabbath, the presence of ungodly people on board, and the failure of the Free Church of Scotland to deal with Professor Robertson Smith (who was considered to hold profane opinions about Scripture). Begg's views had little traction, however. These were even treated with derision by the editor of the *Scotsman*, a newspaper with little sympathy for Sabbatarian movements: 'Apparently the Directors of the North British Railway may rebuild their bridge, as strong as they please, but unless they and others adopt certain views of Dr Begg and his associates, the re-erected structure may again be hurled into ruin by an angry Providence as suddenly and terribly as was done nine days ago.'[95] Despite some popular characterisations that persisted in the pulpit, it seems that natural disasters were no longer regarded by the cultural and political mainstream as exercises in divine retribution.

Before concluding this survey of nineteenth-century evocations of divine providence, one important qualification is required; this is central to the case for a more constructive approach and will be developed later. At least some of those whose theology reflected the optimistic and progressive spirit of modernity were strong advocates of political reform.[96] Attempts to improve education, health care, working conditions and prison life were carried out by

---

[94] Ibid., p. 112.

[95] *Scotsman*, 6 January 1880, p. 4. I am grateful to William Johnstone for this reference. For discussion of the wider Sabbatarian context, see R. Douglas Brackenridge, 'The "Sabbath War" of 1865–66: the shaking of the foundations', *Records of the Scottish Church History Society*, 16 (1969), 143–67.

[96] For a survey of these different forms of social Christianity in their nineteenth- and early twentieth-century contexts, see Paul T. Phillips, *A Kingdom on*

exponents of a social Christianity. They believed that they had history on their side, and were living at the outset of a new age in which social conditions could be greatly improved. This was represented variously by the incarnational theology of F. D. Maurice, the welfare politics of idealist philosophers closely aligned with the church, the rediscovery of Jesus' message of the kingdom of God, the emergence of a Christian socialist movement, and pre-millennial visions of social renewal that energised evangelical campaigners on both sides of the Atlantic.[97] Into the twentieth century, Walter Rauschenbusch's social theology continued to exercise a strong influence. Writing in 1917, he could describe the pronounced importance of the social gospel for the times:

> The social gospel registers the fact that for the first time in history the spirit of Christianity has had a chance to form a working partnership with real social and psychological science ... It seeks to put the democratic spirit, which the Church inherited from Jesus and the prophets, once more in control of the institutions and teachings of the Church.[98]

These movements shared not only a commitment to prophetic criticism of the existing social order, but also a belief that this could soon be transformed through structural changes. Christian action now extended beyond private philanthropic work to a redesign of the fabric of society. The significance of this critical approach is enduring. These nineteenth-century reforming theologies deserve greater attention, not least for their conviction that divine providence can work through forms of democratic government and social improvement. The political arena was not without its possibilities. Christian social action should not be confined to charitable

---

Earth: Anglo-American Social Christianity 1880–1940 (University Park, PA: Pennsylvania State University Press, 1996), pp. 1–47.

[97] See for example Spence, *Heaven on Earth*.

[98] Walter Rauschenbusch, *A Theology for the Social Gospel* (Nashville: Parthenon Press, 1978), p. 5.

initiatives, thus ignoring the wider structural causes of injustice and poverty. Into the present century, this has left an indelible effect upon the ecumenical movement. Yet these forces may also have been allied to the spirit of nineteenth-century providentialism, with its confidence in progress and its sense of a divine vocation being fulfilled in the realisation of Christian social witness. And, like other forms of providentialism, it suffered similarly from the collapse of confidence in historical progress occasioned through the First World War.

3.6 Conclusion

In terms of lending ideological support for imperialism and free market economics, the theology of providence was transposed to more secular contexts in problematic ways. Might the root of the problem already be latent within classical formulations of the theology of providence? These attribute a divine control and wisdom to every single event in the cosmos, each lending itself indispensably to the outworking of a set of purposes. Every entity, force and event has its purpose, combining to achieve an overall *telos*. As scholars turned their attention to historiography and the social sciences, it is hardly surprising that providential notions would feature in more secular contexts. In seeking to understand progress in history and the laws governing social forces, writers were as equally apt to discern divine foresight and design as they had done in the natural world. Arguments from providential design, which were so pervasive in the natural philosophy of the eighteenth and nineteenth centuries, had their inevitable counterparts in the fields of history and economics. These were easily popularised and pressed into political service.

In his study *Politics as Religion*, Emilio Gentile has pointed to the ways in which various neo-pagan and atheist ideologies have borrowed – one might say hijacked – the discourse of providence in disturbing ways. He distinguishes this from civil religion, which reinforces the political culture of democratic societies. This misappropriation of religious themes takes place through various means. These include the placing of a secular collective entity at the centre of a set of beliefs and myths surrounding its origin and purpose, the formalisation of commands that prescribe the loyalty and devotion of citizens, and the creation of a 'political liturgy' usually around the personality cult of an individual leader.[99] Gentile argues that traditional expressions of religion are typically usurped rather than annihilated by new forms of politics. By deploying myths, symbols and rituals, a sacral politics can succeed, at least for a time.[100] What Gentile's work powerfully reveals is how dangerous religion becomes, when the critical standards that have been exercised by traditions of theological debate are lost or occluded by sudden changes in sociopolitical culture. Swept of the traditional demons that inhabit the house, the empty spaces become vulnerable to ever more harmful ones. Merely to ignore or suppress conventional expressions of religion is to risk clearing a space that will be inhabited by dangerous appropriations of its typical forms.

Several elements of this analysis need to be taken forward in any reconstruction of the theology of providence. The fascination with scientific order in the eighteenth and nineteenth centuries resulted in a tendency to equate natural and social processes too closely with the will of God. This resulted in some detachment from scriptural themes of resistance, struggle and redemption. With the drift towards natural theology, disciplines such as philosophy, economics and history seemed capable of discovering the intentions and actions of God. This was accompanied by a degree of cultural self-confidence that, with the benefit of hindsight, now seems misplaced

---

[99] Emilio Gentile, *Politics as Religion* (Princeton: Princeton University Press, 2006), pp. 138–9.

[100] Ibid., p. 30.

and lacking an appropriate measure of criticism and reserve. Yet a retreat from the wider public domain may itself signify a loss of faith and confidence in the scope of divine providence, as Hegel had already noted. Worse still, it may result in the co-opting of religious themes for a totalitarian politics. The presence and activity of God are not to be confined to a private domain; this ought to be impossible for a faith with roots in the Hebrew prophets. Political and economic life should not be viewed as a godless arena which has been abandoned to base forces. This will produce an equally damaging attitude of contempt and cynicism, if not indifference, to public life, a problem that increasingly besets western democracies today.

4 | Providence in Nature

I cannot think that the world, as we see it, is the result of chance; and yet I cannot look at each separate thing as the result of Design.[1]

Published in 1859, Charles Darwin's *Origin of Species* is often represented as a watershed in the history of relations between science and religion. With the explanatory mechanism of natural selection much that had previously been attributed to the operation of divine design could now be explained by purely natural causes. Almost overnight, God had become redundant. Although not advanced by Darwin himself, this view was encouraged by some of his followers, most notably T. H. Huxley, Darwin's bulldog. For Huxley, the teleological theory favoured by William Paley could now be given natural explanation. The adaptation of means to ends throughout creation no longer needed to be attributed to design. Organs had evolved with greater complexity, species had adapted to the environment, and changes had taken place in life forms under the pressure of natural selection rather than divine design. What theology called providence, science perceived only as natural order.[2] This fundamental opposition was affirmed also by voices on the theological side. John Duns, who taught natural science at New College in Edinburgh from 1864, scornfully dismissed the idea that one species could evolve from another. The evidence of geology as well as Genesis, he insisted, pointed to species having

---

[1] Charles Darwin, 'Letter to Asa Gray, 26 November, 1860' in Francis Darwin (ed.), *Life and Letters of Charles Darwin: Vol. II* (London: John Murray, 1888), p. 353.
[2] Cited by David N. Livingstone, *Darwin's Forgotten Defenders: The Encounter Between Evangelical Theology and Evolutionary Thought* (Grand Rapids: Eerdmans, 1987), p. 49.

existed from the beginning of the world as distinct and separate.[3] In Princeton, Charles Hodge pronounced Darwinism to be practically atheism, on the ground that it excluded teleological explanation from nature. He regarded this as a defining feature of Darwinism, and the one that rendered it in principle opposed to religious explanation.[4]

Hodge's criticism was not directed at the consistency of Darwinian evolution with the idea of creation. The theist could readily claim that the entire process had been devised and initiated by God as First Cause. The problem with evolution by natural selection was its replacement of providential order by a worldview marked by randomness and absence of purpose. No longer exhibiting evidence of a detailed design, the natural world now appeared as a haphazard and wasteful process devoid of direction or superintendence.

Darwin's ideas occasioned widespread discussion and much of the religious reception in the late Victorian period was favourable. Indeed, as we shall see, some leading commentators perceived evolution to hold theological advantages over earlier conceptions of a more static natural world punctuated by occasional moments of divine intervention. In any case, the term 'Darwinism' itself was never a univocal notion that described a single coherent set of ideas. As James Moore has noted, several versions of Darwinism can be

---

[3] 'The existence of specific character, as something fixed in the creative act, is clearly and most emphatically recognised in the Bible. The Scriptures thus decide the question of the *origin* of species.' John Duns, *Science and Christian Thought* (London, 1866), 205. For a discussion of the reception of Darwin in Scotland see David N. Livingstone, 'Public spectacle and scientific theory: William Robertson Smith and the reading of evolution in Victorian Scotland', *Studies in History and Philosophy of Biological and Biomedical Sciences*, 35 (2004), 1–29.

[4] Charles Hodge, *What is Darwinism?* (London: Nelson, 1874). For a detailed exploration of the controversy in Princeton, see Bradley J. Grundlach, *Process and Providence: The Evolution Question at Princeton, 1845–1929* (Grand Rapids: Eerdmans, 2013).

detected in the late nineteenth century – these reflect a range of wider philosophical and ethical assumptions.[5]

4.1 Conceptual Concerns

4.1.1 Determinism

In much of the literature surrounding the theological reception of Darwin, we encounter notions of contingency, randomness, chance, determinism and teleology. These require careful handling since equivocal meanings can be attached in different contexts, particularly across discussions that focus on selected issues in physics and biology.

The philosophical notion of determinism (or causal determinism) typically involves the claim that an event is fully determined by a set of antecedent conditions. Hence if someone (e.g. God or a Laplacean super-intelligence) has a comprehensive knowledge of the total set of such antecedent conditions at the time prior to t, then what happens at t can be predicted with certainty. Though related, these notions of determinism and predictability are separate. For example, the location of a super-intelligence outside time might prevent such an entity from obtaining the comprehensive knowledge required to predict the future. Theistic notions of omniscience and divine timelessness are often intended to overcome such difficulties, but these illustrate the conceptual gap between determinism and predictability. One major difficulty with the determinism of each event is that the causal conditions need to be specified with an almost endless set of *ceteris paribus* conditions. It may be a safe prediction that I will attend a meeting today at 3 pm, given my diary commitments and plans for the afternoon. These are the antecedent conditions that will determine the

[5] James Moore, 'Deconstructing Darwinism: the politics of Evolution in the 1860s', *Journal of the History of Biology*, 24 (1991), 353–408.

outcome of my movement in mid-afternoon. But we would need to add to these the rider 'other things being equal', which quickly becomes an almost limitless set of ancillary conditions about not breaking a leg, not receiving an urgent summons elsewhere, avoiding an unexpected outbreak of war or earthquake or asteroid collision, and so on. Quite rapidly, the specified set of conditions needed to guarantee strict determinism over against high probability spirals out of control as these extend across vast regions of space–time. In response to this difficulty in isolating the conditions that determine each event, the description of determinism is better cast in terms of the entire world as a system of causes in which antecedent conditions fully determine successive effects. These in turn become part of the subsequent causal determination of future events. With the possible exception of God as the outlier, predictability and determinism inevitably drift apart at this point, especially when we consider the behaviour of complex chaotic systems. Exhaustive description is unrealistic since complete knowledge of the total set of conditions is impossible to attain, even for a computer with almost limitless powers.

Universal determinism is generally accompanied by a strong account of the laws of nature. These describe the regularities that govern events across the universe in terms of explanatory conditions.[6] The current absence of full description is accounted for in terms of our limited capacity to describe them adequately. Whether a theory of everything will eventually be achieved is a

---

[6] Less realist accounts of the laws of nature have also been proposed. These may further weaken the case for determinism. For example, Nancy Cartwright argues that, while within confined, controlled and specified conditions the laws of nature work well, these lack similar predictive force in wider contexts. And this is not merely on account of our limited knowledge. She cites Neurath's example of the one-thousand-dollar bill that floats down from the leaning tower – its exact resting place in St Stephen's Square cannot be predicted by a physicist. *The Dappled Universe: A Study of the Boundaries of Science* (Cambridge: Cambridge University Press, 1999), p. 27.

question that can be left open – its possibility in principle seems all that is required for determinism to be expressed coherently.

But there are two principal challenges facing determinism. The first concerns physical processes. Do these always behave deterministically or are there some events which lack a full causal explanation in terms of antecedent conditions? Candidates for undetermined events can be found in quantum physics and chaos theory. Both are employed in recent accounts of divine action which attempt to show how this may occur in the natural world without any suspension of normal physical processes. Since these suggest gaps which cannot be filled by scientific explanation, there may be scope for a mode of divine action that is consistent with natural description. But for the purpose of evaluating determinism, divine action may be left aside. If there are events at the quantum level or chaotic systems behaving non-deterministically, then not everything that happens is fully determined by antecedent conditions. This entails the conclusion that not everything is fully predictable. Given the current state of physics, it seems more likely that quantum events offer the most likely instance of indeterminacy. According to the standard Copenhagen interpretation, the momentum and location of a subatomic particle are not both fully predictable; we must assume a degree of indeterminacy in its behaviour. *Pace* Einstein, who famously remarked that 'God does not play dice', this is often interpreted in a realist manner as an inherent feature of the physical universe rather than a function of our lack of understanding. Other interpretations, most notably that of David Bohm, postulate a hidden variable that can generate full determinism. Yet the majority view continues to hold this as somewhat contrived, favouring instead the standard indeterminacy account. Hence, while conceding that one should not hitch one's theology too closely to a scientific theory that may become outdated, we should acknowledge a substantial body of opinion among contemporary physicists in favour of quantum indeterminacy. In the case of chaos theory, there is no such consensus, though some continue to suggest that chaotic systems are not merely unpredictable in practice but inherently undetermined.[7]

In admitting to physical indeterminacy, nevertheless, the theist may seek to combine this with some form of theological determinism, though here the theories strain to accommodate the facts. One approach that is available is the Molinist account of God's deployment of middle knowledge. In selecting this universe, from among all those possible, God ensures that one and only one set of total causal outcomes is actualised. Although from a scientific perspective there is no complete causal explanation of physical behaviour, each quantum outcome is guaranteed *ab initio* in this scenario. The only requirement here is that God has complete foreknowledge of all quantum events (and chaotic systems) prior to deciding which universe to create. How this is possible would require explanation. Alternatively, in a Thomist or Calvinist account one might aspire to maintain determinism not by reference to middle knowledge but by a divine concursus that ensures the success of primary causality through intermediate agencies. In the case of undetermined quantum events, one could view these as determined (in some empirically hidden way) by divine action. Elements of occasionalism or of the miraculous might need to be annexed here, in order to hold together physical indeterminacy with a traditional commitment to the comprehensiveness of God's primal causality. Though these accounts are somewhat forced, one can reasonably concede that any configuration of foreknowledge, eternity, temporality and indeterminacy is likely to prove elusive or baffling in some respect.

4.1.2 *Divine Temporality*

Closely allied to this combination of creaturely contingency with divine determinism is the claim that divine eternity should be

---

[7] For example, John Polkinghorne, *Science and Religion in Quest of Truth* (London: SPCK, 2011), pp. 34–42.

conceived as a timelessness in which distinctions between past, present and future collapse.[8] Since God is unbounded by temporal predicates, an atemporal knowledge of every world occurrence is possible. Each event is then the object of an eternal divine gaze, saturated in every detail. Considered in relation to one another, events may not be causally determined, but in relation to the knowledge of God there is a completeness that does not permit an indeterminate future. The 'block universe' has a long theological pedigree, and it has received some added support from recent considerations deriving from special relativity theory showing that the passage of time varies according to motion. Together with the observation that simultaneous events are measured differently by observers in different parts of the universe, this consideration appears to deconstruct the notion of the present as a psychological illusion that has no place in processes of physical description. Allied to theological considerations about divine time-lessness, these arguments support a block universe which is complete in every respect – no entity or event awaits future causal determination. In viewing the universe *sub specie aeternitatis*, therefore, we need to dispense with notions of past, present and future.

The block universe needs to be rejected for the sake of the argument that is being developed in this theology of providence. There are several considerations that support this. Its inadequate account of time threatens to undermine our projects as these relate to a determinate past unalterably fixed, a present moment in which our agency is being exercised, and an indeterminate future which is the object of hopes as yet unfulfilled.[9] The cosmos itself seems to have

---

[8] This has been the preferred option of classical theology since Augustine and Boethius. Nevertheless, one could still commit to determinism while affirming a universe whose future is still unrealised. Hence Laplace believed that a knowledge of initial conditions would be all that a super-powerful intelligence would require in order to compute every future outcome. In this way, a commitment to determinism could be combined with divine sempiternity.

[9] Here I follow the claims of J. R. Lucas. 'The block universe gives a deeply inadequate view of time. It fails to account for the passage of time, the pre-eminence of the

something like a single temporal axis from the big bang onwards, while human agents require temporal notions to make sense of their plans, activities, relationships and prayers. In any case, if the Copenhagen interpretation of quantum behaviour is correct, then the block universe is in some difficulty. Attempts to resolve this tend quite quickly to become contrived. Hence, unless there are very strong theological considerations for accepting a block universe, I tend to the view that it should be rejected in favour of an unfolding and not fully determined world.

As this suggests, a second area of chronic anxiety surrounding determinism concerns the free actions of voluntary agents. Libertarian freedom is typically characterised in terms of the capacity of an agent to choose otherwise at time t, despite the obtaining of exactly the same set of antecedent conditions at t-1. This notion is at odds with the earlier description of determinism in terms of the causal completeness of antecedent conditions. Given these conditions, only one outcome is possible. Hence, freedom cannot be construed in terms of a capacity to do otherwise in the presence of the same set of conditions which will include reference to the agent's physical and mental states at t-1. This may be the most telling consideration against determinism, although compatibilist theories have found many advocates in both the theological and secular literature. For the compatibilist, free action is typically characterised in terms of internal causes referring to the agent's desires, character, dispositions and inclinations. As these are fixed at t-1, then there is a fully determined choice at t. This choice is compatible with soft or hard determinism. Yet the counter-intuitive nature of

present, the directedness of time and the difference between future and past, and has to make out that these fundamental features of our experience and thought are merely psychological and linguistic aberrations. It also fails to accommodate our sense of agency, the belief that we can make up our minds for ourselves, and that it is up to us what we decide and what we do. And it runs counter to the thrust of quantum mechanics, the most fundamental physical theory we have, which portrays a universe that is not determinist but only probabilistic.' *The Future: An Essay on God, Temporality and Truth* (Oxford: Blackwell, 1989), p. 8.

compatibilist accounts, particularly in relation to our sense of choice, deliberation, responsibility and patterns of praise and blame, provides a case for *prima facie* resistance. And if voluntary agents can exercise libertarian freedom, then we have good grounds for resisting determinism as described above.[10]

An adjacent concern surrounds divine temporality, a further illustration of the ways in which the theology of providence is bound up with an extensive range of philosophical commitments. A full discussion of the relationship of God to time is impossible in this context, but several points should be registered.[11] The traditional Boethian view of divine atemporality – a view found in Augustine, Anselm, Aquinas and Calvin – is committed to the notion that God is outside time and therefore not to be essentially characterised by the use of temporal predicates.[12] Each event is known as eternally present from God's perspective rather than experienced within a temporal flux. Strictly speaking, there is no before, during or after in God's awareness of creaturely events. For this reason, our own experience of a passing from present to future betokens a transitory awareness that does not characterise the divine life. The fluctuating moods, anxieties and anticipations that mark temporal existence have no place within the perfections of God. The best known image of God's non-temporal awareness of creaturely events is in Aquinas's analogy of the spectator on the hilltop who can follow the movements of a succession of travellers along a pathway from one single position.[13] Although employing a spatial metaphor, Aquinas suggests here an eternal perspective that comprehends all events

---

[10] Here I leave open the question of whether there could be divine foreknowledge of libertarian choices. This is taken up in the following chapter.

[11] For an overview of several competing positions, see Gregory E. Gannsle (ed.), *God and Time: Four Views* (Downer's Grove, IL: IVP, 2001).

[12] See Boethius, *The Consolation of Philosophy*, Book v.

[13] 'Just as he who goes along the road, does not see those who come after him; whereas he who sees the whole road from a height, sees at once all travelling by the way.' Thomas Aquinas, *Summa Theologiae*, 1a.14.13, cited from the Blackfriars edition.

in their temporal sequence. Yet God's perspective cannot itself be temporally located since tensed relations belong only to creaturely causal series. In terms of McTaggart's distinction between an A-series (a description of events as past or present or future that assumes a temporal location with words such as 'now' or 'yesterday') and a B-series (a description of events as ordered in a before and after sequence, but without any indexical reference to the temporal observer's own location), only the B-series is real for God.[14] The A-series will appear different, in accordance with the temporally moving position of the observer. By contrast, the B-series remains constantly in view, irrespective of one's temporal location. For the exponent of divine atemporality, God will have an eternal awareness of all events as ordered in a B-series, whereas the A-series will not represent anything of which God can be conscious. Hence the A-series is at most a limited creaturely awareness that is illusory where the eternal perspective is concerned.

Arguments for divine atemporality typically focus on two related sets of consideration. First, the divine life appears as incomplete and lacking in fullness if God inhabits (in some sense) the flow of time. In experiencing an event as present or as future, some things would be added temporally to the life of God so that the divine life increases and flows relative to the passage of time. This would be unfitting for the perfect and complete being of God as one who transcends the creaturely realm. The most perfect being is one who must possess everything simultaneously, thus excluding any loss or lack of existence. A second type of consideration points to the messy tensions and possible incoherence generated by assuming that God is set within time. These include a worry about confusing creator with creatures, as well as fears surrounding the possible loss of divine sovereignty, if God is subject to temporal fluctuations. For these reasons, divine atemporality provides a more hygienic

---

[14] See J. M. E. McTaggart, 'The unreality of time' in *Philosophical Studies* (London: Arnold, 1934), pp. 110–31.

position, it is claimed, and one that befits the most perfect being of God. Despite widespread opposition in recent philosophy of religion, this can rightly be regarded as a standard and well-established account in the church's theological traditions.[15]

Against this, critics of divine atemporality can also draw upon two sets of powerful considerations.[16] The first attends to the difficulty in offering a coherent account of the divine life. While it may make sense to ascribe a non-temporal ontological status to mathematical objects such as numbers, this becomes much harder in the case of God, whose perfections include love, knowledge, freedom and will. These conceptual problems become particularly acute with reference to divine agency, which requires closely related notions of intentionality, movement and accomplishment. Within a timeless mode of existence, these make little sense. Can a timeless being create, sustain and interact with the world? One suggestion here is that God eternally wills the creation in every respect, including God's own sustaining and involvement in each outcome. All this takes place by virtue of a single timeless divine action which guarantees all temporal events. This indicates that divine atemporality and the block universe have close conceptual ties. But the strangeness of this view, which seems to place God simultaneously outside (in eternity), alongside (in perpetually sustaining) and inside (in salvation history) creation, is baffling for many. Hence, according to its critics, the actions of a timeless being are beset with conceptual confusion. This is coupled with the claim that, since the God of

---

[15] Recent attempts to defend divine timelessness have argued not only that it is consistent with classical theological convictions but also that it can uniquely safeguard these. Only a timeless God can be immutable, omniscient and fully provident. See for example Brian Leftow, *Time and Eternity* (Ithaca: Cornell University Press, 1991), and Paul Helm, *The Eternal God*, 2nd edn (New York: Oxford University Press, 2010).

[16] A third and more technical argument is that the atemporality view cannot make any sense of God knowing what time it is now. The present, it is claimed, must appear quite opaque from this theological perspective.

the Bible is characterised as possessing life, intentions, agency and involvement in creaturely processes, we cannot uphold divine atemporality without seriously compromising the scriptural rendition of God. The account of divine agency in Scripture cannot readily be dismissed as metaphorical, anthropomorphic or a concession to creaturely modes of comprehension. While the stories of the Bible may contain such elements, we need to think of God's activities as temporally extended and located. Since the works of God require narration – here we should note the temporal spread of the classical creeds – we cannot think coherently of God as outside time, or of temporal distinctions (as in McTaggart's A-series) as unreal. For God, there is a set of actions that are tensed – notions of succession, completion, simultaneity and anticipation apply to these.

Despite the problems of stating clearly the relationship of God to time, we must depart from the standard account of divine timelessness in favour of something more like a divine everlastingness. At the very least, the burden of proof must lie with those who affirm the seemingly counter-scriptural and counter-intuitive account of God's atemporality.[17] A better construal of God's life is in terms of everlasting life – a temporally extended mode of being that can accommodate past, present and future with all that is required for agency. This need not confine God to a creaturely frame of reference, as may be entailed by some forms of process theology, but it does require us to ascribe temporal predicates to God while rejecting the classical view of timelessness. Brian Leftow suggests that a temporal God must be bounded by time, since temporality cannot strictly be an aspect of creation.[18] To this extent, God's providential control is compromised by the limitations that time will place upon the divine being. But the best response to this is to argue that God,

---

[17] Here I largely follow the account offered in two essays of Nicholas Wolterstorff in *Inquiring about God* (Cambridge: Cambridge University Press, 2010), pp. 133–81. For a recent and robust defence of divine temporality, see Ryan Mullins, *The End of the Timeless God* (Oxford: Oxford University Press, 2016).

[18] Leftow, *Time and Eternity*, pp. 277–8.

though temporal, is Lord over all creaturely history.[19] By virtue of
God's wisdom, patience and duration, there are no restrictions on
what can be accomplished. As everlasting and infinite, God is not
diminished or threatened, as we are, by the prospect of death or the
limitations of time and space. As Lucas remarks, 'God is the master
of events, not their prisoner: time passes, but does not press.'[20]

4.1.3 Chance

Following this brief sketch of indeterminism and divine temporality, we are now in a position to consider the different ways in
which concepts such as 'chance' and 'randomness' can be appropri-
ately deployed. Since these terms are often used quite loosely and
incommensurately in the literature, some further clarification may be
useful. In referring to evolutionary processes as chance happenings
or random events, biologists often instance genetic mutation and
the intersection of seemingly unrelated causal systems. For example,
an accidental exposure to UV rays may result in a genetic mutation that is then transmitted to a subsequent generation. This may
prove beneficial, detrimental or inconsequential in relation to the
survival and prosperity of one's progeny. Alternatively, a change that
occurs in the ecological environment may have consequences for
the physiology and behaviour of some members of the species. The
beak size of finches in one of the Galapagos Islands is recorded by
Peter Grant and Rosemary Grant as having increased by 10 per cent
in 1976 owing to a prolonged drought.[21] Since only larger plants with
bigger seeds survived, these conditions favoured larger beaks with

[19] Here I follow Alan G. Padgett, *God, Eternity and the Necessity of Time* (Basingstoke:
Macmillan, 1992), pp. 123–5.
[20] J. R. Lucas, *Treatise on Time and Space* (London: Methuen, 1973), p. 306, cited in
Padgett, *God, Eternity and the Necessity of Time*, p. 124.
[21] '[T]he birds were not simply magnified by the drought: they were reformed
and revised. They were changed by their dead. Their beaks were carved by their

the capacity to crack them open. The selection of this feature was the result of changes in the weather system. This might be viewed as a random occurrence insofar as it involves the intersection of two different causal systems. Evolutionists can also point to changes in the cultural behaviour of animals as a result of alterations to their environment. To cite one familiar example, from the 1920s great tits became adept at piercing the caps of milk bottles to consume the cream at the top (they are able to digest cream rather than milk owing to the lack of lactose). Recent study suggests that this behaviour was transmitted very quickly among the great tit population.[22] Although the changes are more cultural than genetic, these also took place on account of causally independent processes. In these contexts, chance and random-like occurrences do not designate events that lack a natural explanation or are held to be uncaused. The focus is on contingency (what might have been otherwise), chance (unpredictable occurrences) and randomness (accidental intersection of seemingly unconnected processes). The best-known example of this appeal to chance is Stephen Jay Gould's claim that the entire process of evolutionary history is a one-off phenomenon. If the tape of life were run a million times over from a Burgess beginning, it would never produce *Homo sapiens* a second time.[23] Yet this does not imply that events within the process lack a causal explanation. Indeed, most of Gould's writings were intended to explain the working of these causal processes to wider public audiences.

losses.' Jonathan Weiner, *The Beak of the Finch: The Story of Evolution in Our Time* (New York: Random, 1994), p. 82.

[22] See Lucy M. Aplin, Damien R. Farine, Julie Morand-Ferron, Andrew Cockburn, Alex Thornton and Ben. C. Sheldon, 'Experimentally induced innovations lead to persistent culture via conformity in wild birds', *Nature* 518 (26 February 2015), 538–41.

[23] Stephen Jay Gould, *Wonderful Life: The Burgess Shale and the Nature of History* (New York: Norton, 1989), p. 289. Michael Ruse points out, however, that Gould's position is sufficiently nuanced to suggest that natural selection would probably stumble upon intelligence as advantageous in some ecological niche. See *Charles Darwin* (Oxford: Blackwell, 2008), pp. 251–2.

This scenario of evolutionary uniqueness is, however, compatible with the full causal determinism outlined earlier. If one assumes a universe in which every occurrence is determined by previous states and laws of nature, then we can envisage a tape of life in which each microscopic detail is necessarily and sufficiently conditioned by whatever obtains at the preceding moment. Hence a natural world with a Gould-like random appearance could turn out to be as causally determined and predictable as Laplace imagined, though it could equally well cohere with assumptions about indeterminacy.[24]

The use of terms like 'chance' and 'random' may also be intended as covert criticisms of earlier teleological accounts, which viewed each and every change as guided by an overarching purpose. Reflecting an intentionality, the evolutionary process could be viewed as directed and shaped according to a set of envisioned goals. As described by William Paley, nature is providentially designed in the arrangement and order of each species and its adaptation to the created environment. This vision exercised a strong hold over the young Darwin, but gave way to a more messy and disorganised picture when evolution by natural selection was understood as the better explanation for change and variety in species.

4.2 The Problem of Teleology

There is little doubt that Darwinism, however constructed, sounded the death knell for the precise form of teleology advocated in Paley's *Natural Theology*. In this immensely influential work, Paley reworks the eighteenth-century design argument according to the famous metaphor of the watch found on the heath.[25] Our intuition is to ascribe its origin to the design of a watchmaker; this seems

---

[24] See Brendan Sweetman, *Evolution, Chance and God: Understanding the Relationship Between Evolution and Religion* (London: Continuum, 2015), pp. 130–5.

[25] William Paley, *Natural Theology* (New York: American Tract Society, 1881). The work was first published in 1802.

rationally unassailable. In analogous manner, we can similarly infer that the contrivance in biological organisms of parts to whole for the sake of some beneficial function is the work of an intelligent designer, namely God. The complexity of the eye is the result of its different components interlocking to enable clear vision. How else could this have arisen except by design? Paley's work multiplies these examples from the natural world, while also noting the ways in which species are well equipped to flourish in their various ecological niches. Such arrangements are providentially organised by God to produce a harmonious and flourishing world.

Although Paley's argument was rhetorically effective, it proved inadequate to the changing scientific and philosophical mood of the nineteenth century.[26] In proposing a God who meticulously organised parts to whole throughout nature, Paley likened the world to a machine that was designed and manufactured through a succession of divine actions. This failed to accommodate the growing recognition of the mobility in life forms and of changes to topography that palaeontologists and geologists were recognising throughout the first half of the nineteenth century. Paley, moreover, believed the role of chance events to be insignificant compared to the process of design that was everywhere apparent. The prospect of chance contributing a formative role in shaping the constitutive features of the natural world was too readily dismissed. With the benefit of hindsight, we can see why these characteristics of Paleyan teleology could not survive Darwinism. A static world of animal complexity was attributed to the work of a celestial watchmaker who had created and arranged the parts according to a purpose.

---

[26] 'Paley's genius was to so organize his material around a controlling analogy that its imaginative power more than adequately compensated for its argumentative weaknesses.' Alister McGrath, *Darwin and the Divine: Evolutionary Thought and Natural Theology* (Oxford: Wiley-Blackwell, 2011), p. 88. In his analysis of Paley, McGrath points out that the changing standards for assessing evidence and competing explanatory hypotheses in both natural science and law courts were to render Paley's approach suspect.

Combined with an incomprehension of the creative role of 'chance', Paley's accumulation of examples of organised complexity seemed to provide an overwhelming testimony to the hand of God in the constitution of complex life forms. Yet Darwin could explain what had hitherto seemed inexplicable. A process of natural selection that conferred an advantage on small physiological variations could generate change, adaptation and diversity across vast stretches of time and space. Moreover, this high-level hypothesis could accommodate those shifts and quirks in biogeography that seemed puzzling to the Paleyan observer.

The development of multi-cellular organisms and the adaptation of species to environment do not need to be explained by the providential action of God in the absence of any known scientific mechanism. Genetic mutation and natural selection can do much of the work (even though a fuller story will surely unfold in the biological sciences[27]) without appeal to supernatural teleology. This point is admirably captured in Daniel Dennett's metaphor of cranes and sky hooks.[28] As the power of nature's cranes becomes better understood with the march of science, so the need to appeal to a sky hook recedes. Here the assumption is that science and religion occupy common ground in their explanatory accounts of nature. At earlier stages in the history of ideas, large and incomprehensible gaps in our understanding of nature were filled by recourse to a divine sky hook. But, as these gaps diminish, so the cranes take over the heavy lifting, with the result that, according to some forms of atheist criticism, religion becomes ever further marginalised. The story, however, is more complex.

Given the ways in which Darwin's theory of evolution built upon a significant body of scientific discovery in the first half of the nineteenth century, we should not be surprised to discover that

---

[27] In any case, the term 'Neo-Darwinism' no longer features prominently in the scientific literature.

[28] Daniel Dennett, *Darwin's Dangerous Idea* (New York: Touchstone, 1995), p. 136.

theologians were already somewhat prepared for the subsequent debate. Charles Lyell's work in geology had persuaded many that the earth must be millions of years older than the traditional dating of 4004 BCE proposed by Archbishop Ussher on the basis of the biblical record. Although nowadays the custom is to lampoon Ussher, in terms of the body of evidence available in the early seventeenth century his was quite a good calculation. Yet by the early nineteenth century, geologists could show that through 'uniformitarian' processes the formation of rocks and changes to the earth's surface could be explained by natural causes such as volcanoes, glaciers, sedimentation and erosion by water. These processes, however, required a great deal of time and only a much older universe than the one posited by Ussher would fit the bill. From about 1820, therefore, we find many theological writers denying a young universe that had been decisively shaped by a catastrophic event such as the flood. The capacity to interpret Genesis 1–11 in non-literal ways was already apparent.[29] As always, the intellectual causes for a sudden shift in perspective were complex and multiple.

While the teleology defended by Paley in his blending of natural theology and science may seem rather quaint to later audiences, there were ways in which Darwinian recognition of chance and randomness could coexist with a belief in divine providential intention. Three considerations can be offered in defence of this position. The metaphors used to characterise the evolutionary process are generally suffused with aesthetical, moral and religious interpretations of material events. This explains why competing versions of Darwinism were already in play in the late nineteenth century, these tending to reflect wider cultural assumptions. Moreover, the capacity of late Victorian theology to assimilate and even welcome the process of evolutionary change and descent from primates confirms the loose fit between divine teleology and Darwinian science. There

---

[29] Symbolic readings of the Genesis story were commonplace in the early church, as is evident in Augustine's *Confessions*.

is no relationship of strict entailment or dependence between these intellectual commitments. Whether one sees evolution as a pointless struggle for survival marked by suffering and waste, or a grand process of kaleidoscopic beauty in which successive species flourish, will not be determined exclusively by one's scientific understanding. Questions of fit between science and theology must be negotiated at the disciplinary interface. Science may raise wider metaphysical questions, but these will not be resolved merely by reference to the best empirical theory currently available.

Teleology in terms of a divine intention or a single programme betokening design cannot be derived either deductively or inductively from scientific observation and theory. To that extent, Darwin represents a watershed for the biological sciences. Some theorists wish to retain teleological notions for the purpose of understanding the causes of goal-driven activity in the biological world. Such uses of teleological language neither assume nor imply an overriding intention or superimposed purpose, but are judged to be consistent with naturalism. Denis Walsh speaks of 'teleology' only in the sense of an 'irreducible explanatory role for goal-directedness'.[30] As a heuristic device for scientific enquiry in biology, though not physics, this can prove necessary and useful. But it comes untainted by connotations of a supervening intentionality or evolutionary purpose requiring a non-natural description.

A further feature of recent debate reveals a significant post-Paleyan shift from biology to physics as the most promising site for rehearsing some version of the design argument. The point here is to accept that Darwinian description can adequately account for animal evolution while at the same time pointing to the wider physical parameters of a universe that enables such evolution to take place at least once in the history of the cosmos. That the universe is endowed with the matter and laws that facilitate the evolution of life

[30] See Denis Walsh, 'Teleology' in Michael Ruse (ed.), *Oxford Handbook of Philosophy of Biology* (Oxford: Oxford University Press, 2008), pp. 113–37 at p. 122.

forms can itself be explained by a supervening teleological intention. This is often reinforced by claims about fine-tuning, which point to the very delicate structure of the cosmos in the first milliseconds after the big bang. What happens thereafter is only possible by virtue of the conditions that obtain at the outset, together with scientific laws that generate a constancy and regularity across the universe. Hence what appears from one perspective as biological chance can be viewed from another in terms of a wider cosmic intentionality. One may doubt that any single knockdown argument will resolve these metaphysical questions any time soon. But these philosophical and theological claims illustrate at least the possibility of combining concepts of 'chance' and 'randomness' with divine teleology in ways that do not infringe the integrity of the biological sciences.

In addition, the development of work in the biological sciences currently appears to offer some support for constructive forms of interaction between evolutionary theory and theology. Simon Conway Morris's research on convergence argues against Gould's thesis that human evolution is a one-off accident that could seldom or never be repeated by hitting the reset button. The constraints within the physical universe tend towards the emergence of organs and capacities (including the eye, the forelimb and large mammalian brains), so that some of these can and do actually recur in the history of evolution. Given the geographical space within which evolution occurs, biological organisms will tend to find ways of adapting to take maximal advantage of evolutionary possibilities. This directionality is suggested by the manner in which similar capacities have emerged down different biological trajectories. Birds display intelligence, parental care, social play and self-recognition independently of the same processes in mammals. Conway Morris also points to recent research indicating that these directional tendencies may be evident at the level of molecular evolution, genetic mutation and adaptive radiation, thus further providing a different set of parameters from those that suggest sheer randomness and unpredictability. More speculatively, he muses over the possibility that such directionality represents the allurement of life forms towards the consciousness of a supra-mundane source and ideal goal.[31] While such metaphysical suggestions will inevitably raise hackles, his convergent model of evolution at least has the important function of checking assumptions that biological randomness lends credence to a materialist atheism. Here again we see that Darwinism is consistent with more than one set of metaphysical commitments. A constrained and convergent model of evolution may be better placed to enter into constructive conversation with forms of theological explanation, though once again there is no simple fit or direct route from science to theology or vice versa.

In a different context, the role of cooperation has also received greater attention as a significant element in the behaviour and adaptation of species to their environment. Counteracting the more popular image of a genetically driven individual selfishness, this approach suggests a continuity between evolutionary cooperation and altruism, as well as focussing on the wider social elements that shape evolution. Martin Nowak claims that cooperation should be regarded as the third explanatory principle of evolution after genetic mutation and natural selection.[32] In bearing a cost in order to benefit another member of the species, an individual may be enhancing the

---

[31] Noting that song may have preceded speech in hominid life forms, he asks whether we are being drawn towards a recognition of a 'cosmic music' and 'language' which we reflect but do not create. See Simon Conway Morris, 'Evolution and convergence: some wider considerations' in Simon Conway Morris (ed.), *The Deep Structure of Biology: Is Convergence Sufficiently Ubiquitous to Give a Directional Signal?* (West Conshohocken, PA: Templeton Press, 2008), pp. 46–67 at pp. 61–2.

[32] 'New levels of organization evolve when the competing units on the lower level begin to cooperate ... Cooperation is the secret behind the open-endedness of the evolutionary process. Perhaps the most remarkable aspect of evolution is its ability to generate cooperation in a competitive world. Thus, we might add "natural cooperation" as a third fundamental principle of evolution besides mutation and natural selection.' Martin A. Nowak, 'Five rules for the evolution of cooperation' in Martin A. Nowak and Sarah Coakley (eds.), *Evolution, Games and God: The Principle of Cooperation* (Cambridge, MA: Harvard University Press, 2013), pp. 99–114 at p. 110.

survival and welfare of the group as a whole. This is demonstrated by mathematical formulae for calculating several principles at work, such as kin selection and network reciprocity. These tend to overcome any tendency of defectors to outlast and outbreed cooperators, over whom they may otherwise gain a decisive advantage. Such behaviour may enable the group to prosper over other groups or species where cooperation is less marked. This raises important issues about the relationship of such behaviour to moral altruism and the source of its value. Is there a naturally inclined continuum between the cooperation facilitated by evolutionary processes and the sociality, friendship and sympathy that characterise a fulfilled human life? The virtue of altruism does not reduce to evolutionary cooperation, but there may be ways in which our naturally evolved capacities enable us providentially to develop and realise virtues which cannot be entirely explained 'downwards' in terms of evolutionary pressures. While alternative accounts can also be offered, the salience of this question at least raises the possibility of a constructive conversation across evolutionary biology, anthropology, ethics and theology.[33]

Christian theology seems heavily invested in the notion of an evolutionary directionality. The appearance of *Homo sapiens* (or something like us) is often read as the inevitable culmination of a long history of increasing complexity in which language, culture, art, science, ethics and religion must emerge. In an important sense, we must have been intended; hence we are inevitable in the course of evolution. Both creation stories in Genesis reinforce this anthropocentric assumption, as does the doctrine of the incarnation. According to the cosmic Christology of the New Testament, the human appearance of the Word of God was intended from the outset to bring creation to its appointed goal. This suggests an inherent direction in the course of evolution. Yet biologists remain

---

[33] For further discussion, see the forthcoming publication of Sarah Coakley's 2012 Aberdeen Gifford Lectures, *Sacrifice Regained: Evolution, Cooperation and God* (Oxford: Oxford University Press, in press 2018).

divided on this matter. Somewhat ironically, Richard Dawkins suggests that intellectual development and complexity are an almost inevitable outcome of the struggle for survival among species. On the assumption that greater brain power will confer an advantage in this arms race, we can understand why intelligent primates would emerge. Against this, other biologists want to insist upon the impact of myriad contingent and random factors on a process that may just as well favour unicellular organisms. The view adopted here is the more minimalist one that theology requires only the recognition that the cosmos (not merely our own planet) has a built-in tendency towards the emergence of intelligent life forms at some time and place. This potentiality need not specify *Homo sapiens* on planet earth as the point of arrival for all created life in the universe. It is sufficient that the possibilities and constraints that establish planetary conditions can produce conscious life forms. This may require some contestation of Gould's radical thesis about randomness, along the lines of Conway Morris's claims for evolutionary convergence. And in any case, it is possible that the biological sciences may soon generate fresh material on this matter as research continues on convergence, cooperation and epigenetics.

Furthermore, a theological virtue can be made out of the necessary recognition of the proliferation and diversity of creatures over long periods of time. The anthropocentrism that has characterised earlier theologies has tended to diminish the significance of creaturely diversity, particularly through the over-determination of the *imago Dei* as a divine similitude held uniquely by human beings. In acknowledging the relatively late arrival of *Homo sapiens* on the scene, we can better accommodate the value of different life forms in the kaleidoscopic patterns of creation. This confirms the argument of Thomas Aquinas that a diverse world with many creatures is a more fitting testimony to the creativity and love of God than one that contains only a solitary life form.[34]

[34] Thomas Aquinas, *Summa Theologiae*, 1a.47.1.

4.3 Reconciling Darwin with Divine Providence

Darwin's theory of evolution is believed to have created a crisis for religious belief. For the most part, this narrative of conflict is largely a myth.[35] Many leading theologians were quickly able and willing to absorb evolutionary science into their worldview, even though pockets of resistance can be identified. More troubling for the churches in the late nineteenth century were some of the controversies generated by the application of methods of historical criticism to the Bible. By contrast, the engagement with Darwinism was more of a skirmish. And yet evolutionary science did raise some important questions for theologians as they absorbed its findings in relation to the transience of life forms, common descent and the role of natural selection. Four sets of question can be identified, each of which has a decisive bearing on the theology of providence.

4.3.1 Does the Affirmation of Theistic Evolution Lead to Deism?

The effect of William Paley's natural theology on Darwin has often been noted.[36] Darwin was deeply influenced by Paley, once remarking that he was so familiar with his work that he could recite passages by heart. As already noted, Paley had been struck by the phenomena of organised complexity that he observed throughout the natural world. The analogy with human artefacts was so impressive that the argument for a designer seemed unassailable. The

---

[35] The literature on this is now extensive. But for a popular account see Jon H. Roberts, 'That Darwin destroyed natural theology' in Ronald Numbers (ed.), *Galileo Goes to Jail: And Other Myths about Science and Religion* (Cambridge, MA: Harvard University Press, 2009), pp. 161–9.

[36] See the discussion in John Hedley Brooke, 'The relations between Darwin's science and his religion' in John Durant (ed.), *Darwinism and Divinity: Essays on Evolution and Religious Belief* (Oxford: Blackwell, 1985), pp. 40–75. Brooke notes the ways in which Paley gestures towards the possibility of alternative explanations only to dismiss these as implausible. The following comment is remarkably prescient: 'There may be particular intelligent beings guiding these motions in each case; or they may

evidence of design was too compelling to sustain such scepticism. Successive contributions to the Bridgewater Treatises confirmed this confidence in the design argument by extending Paley's reasoning to other fields of enquiry including chemistry and the human mind. Though later mocked for their dullness and credulity, these treatises were immensely popular in the 1830s and did much to maintain public confidence in design and the order of creation, particularly in the face of political radicalism.[37] Given that so much of the natural world appeared inexplicable in its complexity and successful functioning without appeal to the God-hypothesis, scientists and theologians assumed that a greater understanding of its workings would only confirm the intuitive impression of design. Authorised by the Archbishop of Canterbury and the President of the Royal Society, these forms of popular scientific reflection were regarded as spiritually uplifting and reassuring in the conviction they afforded of God's providence. They resonate strongly with the historical forms of providentialism explored in the previous chapter. Benevolently ordered towards the economic benefits of free trade or imperial progress, the world could also be viewed as naturally shaped by similar forces of design. In displaying an optimism, self-confidence and sense of divinely ordained progress, these historical and natural forms of providence fitted together very well.

By contrast, Darwin's *Origin of Species* absorbed fresh evidence and insights from the first half of the nineteenth century, including claims concerning the age of the earth, the mobility of life forms as revealed in the fossil record and the way in which chance

---

be the result of trains of mechanical dispositions, fixed beforehand by an intelligent appointment, and kept in action by a power at the centre.' Paley, *Natural Theology*, p. 272.

[37] See Jonathan Topham, 'Science and popular education in the 1830s: the role of the Bridgewater Treatises', *British Journal for the History of Science*, 25 (1992), pp. 397–430. For a wider contextualising of this material within nineteenth-century natural theology, see John Brooke and Geoffrey Cantor, *Reconstructing Nature: Engagement of Science and Religion* (Edinburgh: T&T Clark, 1998), pp. 156–9.

forces (minor physiological variations and ecological diversity) contributed to change in the natural world.[38] In key respects, Paley's work was superseded. Yet the order and balance that he attributed to God's design of nature persisted in Darwin. The principal difference was that divine design was now supplanted by the principle of natural selection to explain the extraordinary complexity and harmony of life forms. With this paradigm shift, several popular forms of the design argument disappear. The matching of species to environment does not need to be explained by divine wisdom – natural selection can do the work instead. And the emergence of organised complexity in organs such as the eye can be explained by incremental changes which over long periods of time generate significant physiological developments.

In the face of these claims, theologians could readily offer the following rejoinder. The evolutionary process, with its capacity to generate diverse and highly complex life forms across the world, is itself a wonderful phenomenon. The vast array of species that rise and fall in the history of life display a concerted beauty, diversity and flourishing that is no less striking than the Paleyan worldview. Nature's endowment with such evolutionary potential can be given a theistic explanation. If order and complexity are produced by evolutionary force, then the theologian can simply posit divine design at one remove. Instead of postulating a sequence of divine actions that produces complex order and harmony, the theologian can appeal to a creation invested with an aboriginal potential to evolve.

This theological appropriation of Darwinian science requires only a shift of emphasis from special to general providence.[39] God

---

[38] Alister McGrath has usefully charted the ways in which natural theology progressed beyond Paley in the first half of the nineteenth century. In particular, the importance attached by Whewell to the role of interpretation, as opposed to intuition, prepared the way for Darwin's long argument. McGrath, *Darwinism and the Divine*, pp. 108–42.

[39] See the argument of John Hedley Brooke, 'Natural law in the natural sciences: the origins of modern atheism?', *Science and Christian Belief*, 4:2 (1992), 83–103.

is no longer required occasionally or frequently to intervene in the cosmic process in order to achieve the intended results. The manner in which the world was established under the general working of evolutionary laws is itself sufficient to realise those creaturely states and entities desired by God. Evolution comes wholesale, rather than by retail.[40] Not surprisingly, this move remains the stock response to Darwinian theory. If evolution is how states of greater complexity emerge in the history of the cosmos, then it is open to the theologian to claim that this is how God does it. We find Frederick Temple adopting this strategy in his 1884 Bampton Lectures. In an oft-quoted passage, he writes that God 'did not make the things, we may say: no, but He made them make themselves'.[41] This was teleology at one distance removed and it offered a different account of design from that of Paley. And, in one important respect, Temple sees his view as improving upon Paley. Instead of an Artificer who has to interject at regular intervals to bring about the intended effects in the production of life forms, we now have a Creator who has from the very beginning endowed the creation with sufficient natural powers to evolve as intended. A cosmic process that does not require divine tinkering along the way to produce the intended results is a more fitting testimony to the wisdom of the Creator. God may be no worse for now appearing less like a watchmaker.

This argument was already employed by Principal Robert Rainy in his inaugural address at New College, Edinburgh, in 1874.[42] According to Rainy, the patterns of evolution require explanation by reference to divine design. All that has changed is our conception

---

[40] See David Livingstone, *Dealing with Darwin: Place, Politics and Rhetoric in Religious Engagements with Evolution* (Baltimore: Johns Hopkins University Press, 2014), p. 109.

[41] Frederick Temple, *The Relations Between Religion and Science* (London: Macmillan, 1884), p. 115.

[42] Robert Rainy, *Evolution and Theology* (Edinburgh: Maclaren and Macniven, 1874). For a discussion of the context in which this accommodation with Darwin became possible, see Livingstone, *Dealing with Darwin*, pp. 27–57.

of a world that is originally endowed with sufficient fruitfulness to yield these emergent patterns. Rainy notes that there may be some loss 'of the argumentative benefit of pleading earlier interpositions as analogical instances' of divine revelation in history. A God who regularly intervenes to direct the course of history might be expected to do the same in the natural world. However, this assumption can be yielded in favour of an evolutionary worldview. While expressing some reservations about Darwinism, Rainy seeks to distinguish the approach of the natural scientist from that of the theologian. These different forms of understanding occupy separate domains, allowing a relative independence within each but a complementarity when viewed in conjunction. One upshot of all this was a growing recognition of the disciplinary boundaries between theology, philosophy and the natural sciences. Furthermore, this division of labour was accentuated by the increasing professionalisation of science as its practitioners staked out their territory free from ecclesiastical interference.[43]

Providential design is thus formally consistent with evolution. Theistic evolution can be presented as a strategy for accommodating Darwinian science. But one difficulty is that this line of response leaves the theologian more exposed to the charge of deism. While a role is assigned to divine providential design, it is a singular action that belongs to the creation of the world. The action of God is thus reduced to an originating impulse with no further interaction or ordering required, since the world is endowed with fructive, self-evolving properties. God is confined to the far end of the cosmos with little subsequent input apparent – a position that is reminiscent of the attenuated deism with which Hume concludes his *Dialogues Concerning Natural Religion*. The action of God is here singular, original, remote and discharged. Any interest we may have in this initial impulse is purely speculative and antiquarian, according to this criticism.

---

[43] See Frank M. Turner, 'The Victorian conflict between science and religion: a professional dimension', *Isis*, 69 (1978), 356–76.

In response, several comments might be offered. First, the mere fact that this accommodation of Darwinism happens to be consistent with deism does not in itself commit the theologian to that position. It is compatible with many types of theism, of which deism is but one. Furthermore, a theology of an originating providence is not exhaustive. There will be other forms of divine sustaining, interaction and involvement with the cosmos that are compatible with the claim that God makes a world that makes itself. We should avoid accounts of divine agency which suggest that this can only take one form. As already stated, the Trinitarian shape of Christian theology might assist in important ways here. Those actions such as creation and preservation that are appropriated to the Father do not exclude the assignation of other works such as incarnation, remaking and indwelling to the Son and the Spirit, the 'two hands of God'.[44] In any case, there may be a need for a 'deist moment' in a contemporary theology of providence which challenges the tight fit between contingent occurrence and the divine will. The good creation is not ordained in every single respect to reflect God's will and purpose, except on some very minimalist construction around the notion of concession. The world has its relative autonomy in relation to the forces of nature and history. The production of a universe in which chance and randomness are assigned a creative role may indicate some divine restraint with respect to what takes place in space and time. Inevitably, this generates further questions.

4.3.2 Are Chance and Providential Control Compatible?

Some theological anxiety can be detected around the role assigned to 'chance' by Darwinian science. As already noted, for Charles Hodge in Princeton, the random course of evolution was the most troubling aspect of the argument of *The Origin of Species*. He regarded

---

[44] This is a point stressed repeatedly by Colin Gunton. See for example *The Triune Creator* (Edinburgh: Edinburgh University Press, 1998).

this as practically atheistic since there could be no governing purpose or overriding control exercised over the direction of nature. Creation was not the problem since God might have originated such a world, but it would be one without providential government. Hodge could concede that a process of evolution was consistent with theism. But the particular account offered by Darwin, with its stress on natural selection, led him to believe that it was metaphysically inconsistent with the teleological principle that belonged to both revealed and natural theology. If God were no longer in control of the course of life on earth, then it could not be perceived as directed towards an appointed end. Many passages from Darwin were cited to demonstrate that the appearance of design and intentionality in nature was in fact only a veneer. The salient causal processes were basically material; these could be characterised without any reference to divine intention or interposition. Apart from his scruples about the details of Darwinian theory – and Hodge was here very well informed – he seems to have concluded that the creative role assigned to natural causes effectively renders God otiose: 'This banishing God from the world is simply intolerable and, blessed be his name, impossible. An absent God who does nothing is, to us, no God. Christ brings God constantly near to us.'[45] Hodge seems to have assumed that the appearance of organs such as the eye could not be explained by a natural, incremental process. To suggest such was simply incredulous – in raising this possibility, Darwin himself pointed to its impossibility. It is 'the most credulous men in the world (who) are unbelievers. The great Napoleon could not believe in Providence, but he believed in his star and in lucky and unlucky days.'[46] In any case, Hodge was fully persuaded that the teaching of Genesis effectively falsifies theories of evolution which postulate

---

[45] Charles Hodge, *What is Darwinism? And Other Writings on Science & Religion*, ed. Mark N. Noll and David A. Livingstone (Grand Rapids: Baker, 1994), p. 88. Hodge's essay was first published in 1874.

[46] Ibid.

the emergence of mind from matter as opposed to a special divine creation.[47]

Despite his erudition and force, Hodge could be challenged on two counts. First, the incremental emergence of organs such as the eye can be neatly explained by an evolutionary story about the advantage obtained by images, even very partial ones. And, second, it is entirely open to a theist to perceive 'chance' as a set of enabling processes that generate a diversity of life forms. Within a macro-context, this can be perceived as providentially ordered. Asa Gray, the Harvard botanist, replied to Hodge in those terms. Gray claimed that Hodge's difficulty with Darwin arose out of an unduly restricted account of how divine teleology works. The Creator can endow nature and organisms with the powers of evolution into states of greater complexity. Hodge simply begs the question against this type of teleology with his commitment to an older, Paleyan strategy. This was also the line take by Robert Flint in his Baird lectures on *Theism*, which went through numerous editions during the late nineteenth century. Here his interaction with Darwinism offers a set of responses that have become standard in theological appropriations of evolutionary science. The development from lower to higher organisms can be explained as a mark of design. The tendency towards improvement and progression requires explanation. Evolutionary process can be envisioned as a vast scheme of order and beauty, rather than a grim arena of conflict and waste. This more positive vision of evolutionary complexity would be later developed by writers such as J. Arthur Thomson and Patrick Geddes in their 1912 study.[48]

That Darwinism perceived an order, regularity and lawfulness governing the seemingly haphazard history of life enabled

---

[47] See Charles Hodge, *Systematic Theology*, 3 vols.(Grand Rapids: Eerdmans, 1989), vol. II, p. 18.

[48] J. Arthur Thomson and Patrick Geddes, *Evolution* (London: Williams & Norgate, 1912). What much of this shows is that there was no clear consensus about

theologians quite quickly to reach an accommodation and to maintain patterns of teleological explanation. This was the apologetic move against Huxley and Haeckel favoured by writers such as Flint, Drummond and George Campbell, the Duke of Argyll. Darwin himself, they noted, had used the language of purpose in his descriptions of how natural selection operated. Although this may have been intended metaphorically, it showed how easy the reconciliation of evolution and theism could be. Aubrey Moore, Canon at Christ Church, Oxford, expressed it succinctly in his claim that the 'belief in the universality of law and order is the scientific analogue of the Christian's belief in Providence'.[49]

Along with other Anglican writers, Moore offered a more immanent account of divine involvement in the evolutionary process with his famous remark about Darwinism. In banishing the notion of God as an occasional visitor, it performed the work of the friend though under the disguise of a foe.[50] This model of divine engagement resonated with the kenotic theologies that flourished in the late nineteenth century and exercised a particularly strong hold over Anglican thinkers, with their stress on divine passibility. The model here is of God's 'letting the world become itself', not in such a way as to abandon it, but in the interests of a patient accompanying that seeks to work within and alongside creative processes. A model of providence is thus suggested that avoids both the perceived determinism of much of the Augustinian tradition and also the deism that persisted from the early modern period.

Darwinism at that time. It was interpreted in a wide variety of ways so that even to talk of Darwinism, as if it meant one thing to everyone, is quite misleading. James Moore, biographer of Darwin, has argued that in the 1860s there were as many as five different types of Darwinism, each contending with one other. See Moore, 'Deconstructing Darwinism'.

49 Aubrey Moore, *Science and the Faith* (London: Kegan Paul, 1889), p. 197.
50 Aubrey Moore, 'The Christian doctrine of God' in Charles Gore (ed.), *Lux Mundi* (London: J. Murray, 1889), pp. 57–109 at p. 99.

More than most, Moore was able to see clearly some positive theological gains. The occasional interventions of a remote deity could now be replaced by the constant sustaining and creative activity of the divine spirit. This has the significant benefit of correlating the Christian understanding of how God acts in nature and history. The God of the Bible is portrayed as deeply involved in the stories of Israel, Christ and the church, an ongoing personal drama that takes narrative shape in the successive books of Scripture. After Darwin, theologians could see the world of nature as having a history, as being constantly in the process of making. The universe too had a narrative shape that could increasingly be discerned by advances in the natural sciences. Like history, therefore, nature was a work in progress, a construction site in which God could be seen as a sustaining, creative, guiding presence. And this appearance of the natural world as undergoing significant change across time was further confirmed by the emergence of big-bang cosmology in the following century.[51]

The tendency of this response confirms the earlier conceptual discussion of chance. Set within a wider context of convergence and direction, it can combine elements of contingency and unpredictability with notions of order and constraint. While this may be consistent with different models of providence – no one theory is demanded – room is available for an account that conjoins divine foresight with a measure of creaturely indeterminism. The openness of an evolving world may not express the will of God in every detail, as in occasionalist accounts of divine action, but evolution may prove capable of exhibiting signs of a general providence by virtue of a shape and direction, alongside forms of special providence

---

[51] Peter Harrison notes the ways in which a providential reading of history might enable a similar account of nature, despite appearances of randomness. '[T]he full implications of natural history's transformation into a temporal enterprise were not fully recognized at the time.' 'Evolution, providence and the nature of chance' in Karl W. Giberson (ed.), *Abraham's Dice: Chance and Providence in the Monotheistic Traditions* (New York: Oxford University Press, 2016), pp. 260–90 at p. 278.

that facilitate divine presence and interaction within those given parameters. Directionality rather than determinism is required to maintain such a position, but this is consistent with assigning some scope to chance and unpredictability in the history of evolution. The kinds of constraint alluded to earlier with reference to Conway Morris are sufficient to check the counter-claim that the history of life is entirely random.[52]

Where Aubrey Moore's late nineteenth-century proposal falters is in its lack of specification of divine involvement in evolution. This is mooted as a positive gain over the periodic interpositions of the Paleyan deity, but too little is said about the mode and efficacy of God's action. Elements of divine sustaining and accompanying can readily be affirmed but does God actually make a difference beyond this? In terms of evolutionary direction, this remains opaque in his account. Descriptions of God as the 'eternal Energy of the natural world' are highly elusive and run the risk of drifting into a pantheism which Moore otherwise eschews.[53] And, in any case, if God is required along the way to provide some causal additive to natural forces then we simply reprise the worldview of Paley and commit to some variant of intelligent design theory. To register this point is not to embrace uncritically current versions of Darwinism as adequate and finalised explanations. Our understanding of the full range of physical causes is presumably incomplete, particularly with respect to the origin of life, causes of genetic mutation, principles of cooperation, and epigenetic factors; the scientific story may look rather different fifty years from now. Yet it would be a mistake to seek scientific gaps in order to keep God on the employment register. Divine action needs to be characterised in complementary ways as working in, through and against the grain of nature but not so as to

---

[52] For a similar set of arguments employing both evolutionary constraints and cosmic fine-tuning, see Stephen J. Pope, *Human Evolution and Christian Ethics* (Cambridge: Cambridge University Press, 2007), pp. 111–28.

[53] Moore, 'The Christian doctrine of God', p. 102.

disrupt scientific explanation or to render it incomplete within its own domain.

4.3.3 Does the Principle of Natural Selection Compound the Problem of Evil?

In speaking about Darwin, I have often encountered the criticism that any accommodation of his theory of evolution must make the problem of suffering far more difficult. In relation to the integral and pervasive role assigned to pain and death, evolution by natural selection magnifies the age-old problem with which Job and his friends wrestled. Although the phenomena of disease, suffering and death were manifestly visible to earlier generations, Darwin pointed to the ways in which these were integral to the evolutionary process. As part of the 'design', these aspects of biological existence enabled the emergence of species, including human beings. Instead of Paley's notion of creatures living in a state of equilibrium, their prosperity secured by a single divine blueprint, theologians now faced a bleaker scenario in which earlier species were driven to extinction in a perpetual warfare of life forms. How could this betoken a divine providence?

One set of responses argued confidently that the end justified the means. Since evolution produced fitter and more advanced species, particularly *Homo sapiens*, we could conclude that the laws of evolution were all part of a benevolent divine plan. Such theodicies were already in vogue in the early nineteenth century and could be adapted by Christian exponents of Darwinism. Here Paley's reflections remain salutary. In the closing stages of his *Natural Theology*, he considers the possible benefits and compensations of pain, suffering and moral evil.[54] The argument commences by observing that incidences of acute pain are generally infrequent and

---

[54] Paley, *Natural Theology*, pp. 320–43.

of short duration. These highlight for us longer periods of health and contentment. On the basis of evidence supplied by a local apothecary, he notes that most people are cured of their ailments. The body has natural recuperative powers and can often successfully combat disease and infection. Paley also observes that physical pain has the useful function of promoting vigilance and caution. Without it, we are less likely to engage in those endeavours which may be necessary to our preservation. Frostbite is so perilous, he observes, precisely because it is reported to be pain-free, as if the affected limbs were anaesthetised. Even mortal disease, Paley speculates, can have a positive function in enabling us to face death with equanimity, when otherwise its prospect might overwhelm us. And death itself, despite the sorrow of parting, is necessary for the generations to rise and fall. He judges that we would have it no other way. 'It is better that we should possess affections, the sources of so many virtues and so many joys, although they be exposed to the incidents of life as well as the interruptions of mortality, than, by the want of them, be reduced to a state of selfishness, apathy and quietism.'[55]

In judging of moral evils, Paley is similarly upbeat. Social inequalities are considered to be less injurious to human comfort than is sometimes supposed. Wealth and rank may be overrated by comparison with more natural comforts. Provided their deleterious effects are counteracted by public laws, these need not be disadvantageous to the majority. Against Hume, he observes that the peacefulness of a human community is often the result of a large class of its members preferring a quiet life of relative ease and contentment; in this respect, idleness may be considered a useful corrective. We would not wish for society to be comprised entirely of high achievers. Human agency can of course lead to serious abuses, but freedom of the will is a necessary condition for our rational and moral character – we cannot be human without it. Above all, we

---

[55] Ibid., p. 323.

should regard our present state as one of probation. Our lives are not filled with either unalloyed happiness or simple misery. Given the overwhelming evidence for design, we must assume that a purpose is here unfolding. Our 'condition is calculated for the production, exercise, and improvement of moral qualities, with a view to a future state, in which these ... receive their reward'.[56]

In contemplating divine providence, Paley argues that its appearance is often hidden. We cannot live well on the assumption that God will persistently interfere to remedy the troubles we face each day, as if we were protected by a divine safety net. This may be our condition hereafter but it does not serve us well now. There is an intentional reserve in God's interception of our lives which itself is part of a providential plan. By permitting natural laws to run their course, God fulfils the work of creation. In this respect, there is an imperceptible providence constantly in our midst. This does not directly impact our conduct since we must look to nature rather than to the expectation of divine miracles in order to live well. Yet the doctrine of providence remains important for 'sentiment and piety'. This article is of much benefit for it 'applies to the consolation of men's minds, to their devotions, to the excitement of gratitude, the support of patience, the keeping alive and the strengthening of every motive for endeavouring to please our Maker'.[57]

Before we enter upon criticism of Paley's theodicy, its merits should be acknowledged. Despite its seemingly detached and patrician air, his work expresses a practical wisdom that resonates with much of the Enlightenment preaching noted earlier. His arguments for a theological reserve on matters of providence resonate with Thomas Reid's insistence that we are ordained to live wisely in the darkness. Paley had evidently thought deeply about these issues. With the early death of his wife and afflictions of ill health, his own

---

[56] Ibid., p. 338.
[57] Ibid., p. 337.

days were not devoid of personal trials.[58] He has much to say about a beneficial modicum of pain and illness, the rhythms of life and death, the need for spiritual and moral growth, the underrated value of health and times of ease by comparison with the excesses of power and money – all this makes for sound Christian pedagogy. Under the right conditions, these insights will preach well. But the difficulty is less that of validity as of adequacy. The extensive and intensive features of evil are not fully registered in the Paleyan worldview. There is a lack of protest at the excess of *dysteleological* suffering – the relentless misery endured by some, the death of children, grim episodes of war and pestilence that destroy the life of millions, the obscenities of the slave trade (which Paley publicly opposed) and the egregious injustice visited by tyrants upon their populations. Here appeals to the general good or national progress or the success of future generations do not have the full measure of the problem, unless we make the fatal mistake of arguing that the end justifies the means.

These objections might be met by appeal to the consolations of a future life. This is an important component of Paley's theodicy. The prospect of a transformed creation provides a resolution of present evils by remedying injustice, compensating those who have suffered unfairly, and rewarding the righteous. It can reasonably be argued that, without this eschatological dimension, any theodicy will struggle to provide a satisfactory justification. Again this rejoinder has some merit. But, in the present context, it faces two difficulties. The first is that a resolution of evils does not necessarily constitute a justification for their origin. Overcoming evil is not equivalent to explaining it, in the sense intended by the Paleyan theodicy with its stress on divine design. The question why God ordains a world that requires redemption is left hanging, and this is not readily answered unless we can minimise the extent and force of natural and moral

---

[58] Recent secondary literature on Paley is limited. But see M. L. Clarke, *Paley: Evidences for the Man* (London: SPCK, 1974).

evil. A second consequence of the eschatological addendum is that we now appear to be moving beyond the province of natural theology in drawing upon some key elements of the Christian tradition. Admittedly, there is a deist argument for eschatological compensation that can function as an element of a wider design hypothesis. Since the world is ordered towards our moral and spiritual improvement, we can reasonably assume that this process is perfected in some future estate. This had some traction in the eighteenth century but it now appears highly implausible for the sorts of reasons that Hume advanced. There is a circularity in arguing that the world is well designed, only to explain its evident flaws through the hypothesis of a future world in which these flaws are remedied. There may be reasons for affirming a transformed creation, but not in terms of a design argument that postulates this as a solution to the counter-evidence. The theologian must here repose upon more contextual claims that will reflect the particularities of a faith-based tradition. And at this point the fit between natural and revealed theology is far from exact, owing to those intensive and extensive aspects of the problem of evil noted above. The foolishness of the cross and the wisdom of the world remain in some dialectical tension.

Yet the Paleyan theodicy flourished through much of the nineteenth century. Several of the writers of the Bridgewater Treatises also assumed that suffering contributed to the greater good of the human race. This justification of the means by the end was appropriated in responses to Darwin. The production of better-adapted forms of life was viewed as an outworking of an overall teleology. This was the strategy pursued by the Duke of Argyll and Henry Drummond in Scotland, and also by Temple in his aforementioned Bampton Lectures.[59] The steady progress achieved by evolution offers a ready justification for the suffering that is its necessary means. To this extent, Paleyan theodicy could be reinvigorated by

---

[59] See the discussion in James C. Livingston, *Religious Thought in the Victorian Age* (London: T&T Clark International, 2006), pp. 69–105.

Darwinism.[60] In this endeavour, a different set of metaphors was introduced to overcome the prevailing sense of waste and random, meaningless suffering. Attention was drawn to the interdependence of species, the unity of the natural world, the long periods of relative equilibrium characterised in large measure by the enjoyment of life, and the beautiful harmony of flowers and insects. '[T]he doctrine of Evolution binds all existing things on earth into one ... All things are embraced in one great design beginning with the very creation.'[61]

Others would point to patterns of self-sacrifice in nature that adumbrated later Christian moral ideals. In his study *Christianity and Evolution*, James Iverach noted that individuals often sacrifice themselves for the wellbeing of the species to the extent that something like a virtuous family life emerges naturally.[62] But once again the danger inherent in this kind of teleology is that it employs the principle of the end justifying the means. If nature discards the weak and the unsuccessful, then this is so that fitter and better-adapted species may emerge. The ends of evolution enable us to explain why the system is one in which much is discarded as unfit, superfluous and disposable. This could tilt in dangerous directions, particularly as human evolution came into focus. Should social policies be developed that artificially selected the fittest for reproduction? We are not very far here from the principles of social Darwinism and

---

[60] 'To the many partial designs which Paley's Natural Theology points out, and which still remain what they were, the doctrine of Evolution adds the design of a perpetual progress. Things are so arranged that animals are perpetually better adapted to the life they live.' Temple, *The Relations Between Religion and Science*, p. 117.

[61] Ibid., p. 122. Given the stress in modern environmentalism of preserving the world, including places of wilderness where animals can live in their natural habitat, this metaphor has some traction against more Manichean constructions of nature. See William Hasker, 'Response to David Ray Griffin' in John B. Cobb Jr and Clark H. Pinnock (eds.), *Searching for An Adequate God: A Dialogue Between Process and Free Will Theists* (Grand Rapids: Eerdmans, 2000), pp. 39–52, esp. pp. 42–3.

[62] James Iverach, *Evolution and Christianity* (London: Hodder & Stoughton, 1894), p. 184.

the eugenic theories and practices that were evident and surprisingly widespread in the early twentieth century.[63]

Did the insights of evolutionary science render the problem of evil more intractable for Darwin? Beset with ill health and filled with grief following the death of Annie, his beloved daughter, he struggled with the problem of suffering in his scattered remarks on religion.[64] Writing on 22 May 1860 to Asa Gray, he states, 'I cannot persuade myself that a beneficent and omnipotent God would have designedly created the Ichneumonidae with the express intention of their feeding within the living bodies of Caterpillars, or that a cat should play with mice.'[65] It is not difficult to multiply such examples, though Darwin goes on to concede that he cannot rest content with the idea that this wonderful universe, and especially the human race, is merely the result of brute force. In these and other reflections his position seems to oscillate between deism and agnosticism. While remaining open to some sense of general providence, he bridles at the notion of a special providence. The laws of nature, though inexorable, may be expressive of some purpose, but particular events cannot be attributed to divine interposition.

The problem of evil was already on the agenda before the nineteenth century – as a counter-argument to theistic belief, it had become an important theme in early modern and Enlightenment philosophy.[66] Previous generations were no less aware of nature 'red in tooth and claw', particularly as fewer people were sheltered from

---

[63] For further discussion, see Diane B. Paul, 'Darwinism, social Darwinism and eugenics' in Jonathan Hodge and Gregory Radick (eds.), *Cambridge Companion to Darwin* (Cambridge: Cambridge University Press, 2003), pp. 214–39.

[64] 'Darwin's inner sensitivity to pain, no doubt intensified by his own celebrated illness, resonated with an image of nature in which pain and suffering were concomitants of evolution.' John Hedley Brooke, 'The relations between Darwin's science and his religion', p. 66.

[65] Charles Darwin, 'Letter to Asa Gray, 22 May, 1860' in Darwin, *Life and Letters of Charles Darwin: Vol. II*, p. 312.

[66] This raises the question as to why the evidentialist case against God was not more acutely felt at earlier periods. Before modernity, conditions were generally harsher

the animal world in urban environments. Familiarity with animal predation was hardly new. But Darwin's theory of evolution drew attention to the ways in which all living things were engaged in a struggle for survival, long before the emergence of human beings.[67] The scope of suffering was enlarged, thus generating a heightened sense of its pervasiveness to the created order. As we have seen, one typical response was to point to the evolutionary advantages arising from suffering and death. To this extent, the presence of pain exercises a creative function in an evolving universe. Predation, death and extinction were integral to the entire process of evolution, rather than extraneous by-products. As far as we can tell, biological change and diversity would be impossible in our world without the losses incurred by the process of natural selection. Darwinism can offer some explanation of the point of suffering, though it cannot suppress further questions about justification (is it worth it?) or instrumentality (does the end justify the means?). In his popular 1850 poem *In Memoriam*, Tennyson had already protested against those robust theodicies that sought too readily to justify the ways of God.

> Are God and Nature then at strife,
> That Nature lends such evil dreams?
> So careful of the type she seems,
> So careless of the single life;
> I stretch lame hands of faith, and grope,
> And gather dust and chaff, and call
> To what I feel is Lord of all,
> And faintly trust the larger hope.

for most Europeans, yet concerns around theodicy played out very differently. Karen Kilby has suggested to me that Julian of Norwich may have been an exception to this rule.

[67] See McGrath, *Darwinism and the Divine*, pp. 202–7, and Michael J. Murray, *Nature Red in Tooth and Claw: Theism and the Problem of Animal Suffering* (Oxford: Oxford University Press, 2008), pp. 2–9.

Despite this legitimate protest, one possible gain of Darwinism on this point is the way in which it underlines the solidarity of creatures in the evolutionary process. The problem is spread to embrace all forms of life. This too may assist in offsetting anthropocentric suggestions that the suffering of animals is of little consequence or can be justified on purely instrumental grounds. Significantly, recent writers on animal suffering have tended towards the view that every creature must be accommodated in any adequate eschatological resolution of the problem.[68]

By the late nineteenth century, self-confident styles of theodicy were being replaced by more reserved approaches to the problem of evil which tended to stress our lack of knowledge, the suffering of God and eschatological hope. J. R. Illingworth's essay in *Lux Mundi* represents something of a transitional exercise. Acknowledging the probative, punitive and pedagogical benefits of suffering, he muses over the problem of undeserved suffering in the course of evolutionary history. The sacrificial contribution of one generation to the next is recognised, but this is set under the shadow of the cross as the paradigm of redemptive suffering. With the self-giving life of God, all creaturely life yearns to be united.

> The simplest Christian 'knows that, in his present state, the unitive way, the way to union with both God and man, is the 'via dolorosa', the way of the cross: – a serious and solemn belief that is very far from leading to complacency, in presence of the awful spectacle of animal and human pain; but still is based on sufficient experience to justify the hope that all its mystery will be one day solved.[69]

For Illingworth, even while admitting a surd element, we can make enough progress in dealing with the problem of pain to uphold a rational Christian faith.

---

[68] See Murray, *Nature Red in Tooth and Claw*, pp. 122–9; T. G. Mawson, *Belief in God* (Oxford: Oxford University Press, 2005), pp. 207–8; Christopher Southgate, *The Groaning of Creation* (Louisville: Westminster John Knox, 2008), pp. 78–91.

[69] J. R. Illingworth, 'The problem of pain' in Gore, *Lux Mundi*, pp. 113–26 at p. 126.

The subsequent traumas of the First World War destroyed much of the self-confidence evident in earlier writings in theodicy. Many nineteenth-century preoccupations suddenly felt strangely irrelevant in this context. Instead of discussing miracles, biblical criticism and science, a generation scarred by the experience of war became more preoccupied with the suffering of God and the mission of the church in the world. Speculating on what a chaplain or a layperson in the trenches would have made of *Lux Mundi*, Alan Wilkinson suggests that its evolutionary optimism and lack of fresh engagement with ethical questions would have jarred.[70] Along with the decline in traditionalism and deferential social habits, a shift towards divine passibility, the cross of Christ, the amelioration of social conditions, and the eschatological kingdom belonged to a theological mindset that now had to adapt to new circumstances. Earlier patterns of thought suddenly seemed ill-equipped to serve this context.

These changes also coincided with a decline in providentialism. E. R. Wickham comments that 'the First World War raised the question of Providence ... in perhaps the most acute way that has ever happened, and certainly in the most public way'.[71] Much of this questioning arose through the loss of a narrative of progress, which had been shattered by the experience of war. And, as the twentieth century unfolded, theologians and church leaders found it increasingly impossible to set out a story of steady cultural improvement or a gradual spread of Christian civilisation or the export of peaceful democratic government. The Whiggish stories that had energised nineteenth-century thinkers and activists now seemed implausible. This was at least as true of secular narratives of progress, especially Marxist-Leninism, as of their religious precursors. Twentieth-century attempts at recovering a theology of providence

---

[70] Alan Wilkinson, *The Church of England and the First World War* (London: SPCK, 1978), 240.

[71] E. R. Wickham, *Church and People in an Industrial City* (London: Lutterworth, 1957), p. 204.

were required to offer more modest and tentative proposals, generally conscious of the failure of earlier theodicies and the acute difficulties generated by industrial-scale violence.

A neglected symptom of this shift in cultural attitudes was the reaction to the Spanish flu of 1918. With estimates of up to 100 million deaths worldwide, this surpassed any other natural disaster in recorded history. The death toll, moreover, exceeded that of the two world wars combined. Yet, unlike the Lisbon earthquake of 1755 or the cholera outbreak in 1832 (when a National Fast Day for repentance was organised in the UK), attributions of the influenza to divine causality were evident only at the margins of organised religion. More attention was devoted to containing and combatting the disease, with some churches perceiving this as an opportunity to advance their medical services overseas. But few seemed inclined to view the pandemic as an act of special providence. Elements of taboo or sin did not feature significantly in public responses to the catastrophe.[72]

A key lesson to be learned here is that the theology of providence must survive in the absence of an adequate theodicy. Attempts to resolve the problems, in either a pre- or post-Darwinian world will prove inadequate to the immensity of the problem of widespread, intense, destructive and undeserved suffering. The theology of providence should not assume the burden of explaining evil and suffering.

4.3.4 Does Evolutionary Science Reduce Human Significance?

This brings us to another hotly debated topic emerging from Darwinism, namely the significance of human beings in creation.[73]

---

[72] These comparisons are drawn by Niall Johnson, *Britain and the 1918–19 Influenza Pandemic: A Dark Epilogue* (London: Routledge, 2006), pp. 150–1.

[73] For recent discussion, see Wentzel van Huyssteen, *Alone in the World? Human Uniqueness in Science and Theology* (Grand Rapids: Eerdmans, 2006).

Above all else, the anxiety around evolutionary theory concerned its apparent threat to the intellectual, moral and spiritual distinctiveness of being human. But again the initial type of response was quite simple. A process of descent from other higher primates could produce a distinctive species just as effectively as a creation *de novo*. A gradual appearance may be part of the design plan, assuming that it yields the same set of intellectual, spiritual and moral characteristics that are judged to be constitutive of a uniquely human existence. The *how* of human existence may require a revision of early scientific opinion, without detriment to the fuller exploration of *what* it is that has emerged over several million years of hominid evolution. These questions are not entirely separate – pursuit of the *how* question has led to a heightened awareness of the continuities between human and other forms of animal life – but a recognition of evolutionary descent does not in itself negate a distinctive phenomenology of the human.

Much of the late nineteenth- and early twentieth-century literature was dominated by discussion of the faculty of conscience, which seemed to require a non-natural transcendent explanation. In this domain, a careful distinction needs to be made between competitive and complementary forms of understanding. It is too tempting for the theologian to seek out a major lacuna in scientific explanation and then immediately postulate God. If we cannot explain the evolution of mind, then God must be invoked. If we cannot discern obvious analogues of conscience in animal life, then there must be a transcendent cause. Yet these types of argument evidently give hostages to fortune. When science advances and starts to fill in the gaps, then religious explanation is squeezed to the margins. A better type of argument will insist upon complementarity. Even after science has done all its work, there will be ways of understanding and describing the phenomena that draw upon different conceptual resources. There are questions, commitments and insights that by their nature require description in terms that are not reducible to the methods of the natural sciences. No single discipline has an exhaustive or totalising role to play. If the engagement with Darwinism has taught theologians one thing it might be this. The sciences must be given their place freely to investigate and hypothesise according to their methods and findings. A clearer delineation of the differences with theology will result in a recognition of complementarity rather than a misplaced anxiety about the directions in which science might lead us. The converse of this is that 'scientific' description will itself need to be challenged when it steps beyond its boundaries by seeking to 'explain away' other types of description. This does not exclude conversation and useful interaction of discourses, but its delineation of types of description may prevent a 'zero-sum' game in which either science or religion must succeed at the expense of the other.

In more recent philosophical theology, attention has shifted from conscience to the more general phenomenon of consciousness. In particular, claims around the adequacy of forms of materialism and physicalism to explain consciousness are regularly challenged. The spread of Darwinian explanation to consciousness is contested, primarily on account of the qualitatively different phenomena that need to be explained. On a standard emergentist scenario, combinations of matter (e.g. in the evolution of nerve cells) produce a conscious activity which needs to be described in a different set of terms from material events or properties. The development of matter is thus accompanied by a new set of activities and qualities that can only be understood from the perspective of first-person awareness. To understand what it is to experience a sunset requires something quite different from the language of the natural sciences. While various brain states may constitute the necessary and sufficient conditions for such experiences, these do not seem to be identical with the latter. This is the rock on which eliminative materialism and more sophisticated forms of physicalism founder. The emergentist can plausibly explain the ways in which consciousness arises from material processes, but here critics question whether this correlation constitutes a full 'explanation'.[74] Unlike the relationship of dependence between biology, chemistry and physics, we are dealing here with entirely different and non-material sets of descriptors. Why should matter give rise to mind in this way? There is no scientific answer to this question beyond the response that this is simply a brute fact about the cosmos. At this juncture, there is further scope for philosophical or theological explanation, whether in terms of a more pan-psychist account of matter and/or in terms of an account of the creation of the world by the mind of God. These options require much fuller exploration, but their possibility is worth registering here, if only to show that Darwinian evolution in itself entails neither materialism nor atheism nor a brute randomness with respect to the particularity of scientific laws. And, for this reason also, evolution does not exclude the possibility of a providential characterisation of the natural world.[75]

In any case, contemporary discussion, with its heightened ecological awareness, may be less exercised by strong claims for human distinctiveness. If Darwinism points to our deep connections with the animal world, then this may provide an opportunity to examine and adjust some of the anthropocentric assumptions that have

---

[74] This seems to me the most plausible element of Thomas Nagel's otherwise over-extended argument in *Mind and Cosmos: Why the Materialist Neo-Darwinian Conception of Nature Is Almost Entirely False* (New York: Oxford University Press, 2012). Critics have pointed to the possibility that 'explanation' may not extend beyond the description of the ways in which neural states correlate with mental ones. See Elliott Sober, 'Remarkable facts: ending science as we know it' [review of Thomas Nagel's *Mind and Cosmos*], *Boston Review* (November/December 2012), pp. 50–5.

[75] Kevin Kimble and Timothy O'Connor hold that an argument from consciousness can contribute to a cumulative case for theism by reinforcing claims for fine-tuning. This thesis turns on the key consideration that the existence of God as creator can explain what otherwise remains somewhat mysterious, namely the emergence of mind from matter. Theism can thus provide a 'maximally unified' account that must elude both physicalism and emergentism. See Kevin Kimble and Timothy O'Connor, 'The argument from consciousness revisited' in Jonathan Kvanvig (ed.), *Oxford Studies in the Philosophy of Religion*, vol. III (Oxford: Oxford University Press, 2011), pp. 110–41.

governed many of our theological traditions. The isolating of human beings as ends in themselves, apart from the rest of creation, distorts both our own identity and the value of other creatures. Drawing on resources in Maximus the Confessor and other Orthodox theologians, recent scholarship has tended to stress the importance of more holistic approaches to the world and its redemption by the Word of God incarnate.[76] In an important respect, this has the capacity to draw together general and special (or particular) concepts of providence. Where the scope of these special acts of providence is not confined to human beings but is recognised as having a wider cosmic significance, then it becomes co-extensive with the reach of a general providence that governs the entire created order. For example, when viewed in terms of its widest cosmic significance, the incarnation has a reach that is not less than the totality of creation. Its intent is thus identical to the scope of general providence. Similar remarks could be made *mutatis mutandis* with respect to eschatology. In its particularity, it does not exclude but comprehends the entire span of the created world, the new heavens and new earth matching though transforming the old.[77]

4.4 Conclusion

The encounter with Darwinism took place in a nineteenth-century context in which shifts were already apparent in natural theology, theodicy and the politics of providentialism. The tendency to equate natural and historical processes with the will of God was increasingly problematic whether it was with respect to science, economics or politics. In particular, the robust efforts to offer a teleological

---

[76] See for example Ian A. McFarland, *From Nothing: A Theology of Creation* (Louisville: Westminster John Knox Press, 2014), pp. 57–84.

[77] Notwithstanding this point, the eastern Orthodox idea of humans as 'priests of creation' remains anthropocentric in problematic ways. I discuss this in *Creation* (Grand Rapids: Eerdmans, 2014), pp. 102–3.

justification of evil in the wake of Paley's *Natural Theology* had to be abandoned in favour of more tentative and aporetic responses.

For the theology of providence, three types of outcomes can be registered. First, the providence of God cannot be established by natural theology alone. Though the hypothesis is not self-evident or unassailable, we cannot exclude the possibility of interpreting nature as an amoral brute fact. The problem of suffering places a question mark against inductive and deductive arguments from natural law to divine providence. To assert this is not to deny the possibility of a more limited exercise that shows the compossibility of scientific and theological claims, nor the value of a fruitful conversation across disciplinary boundaries, nor the necessity of exploring and adapting important philosophical notions. But earlier attempts to derive an entire theology of providence from observation of the natural world must now be eschewed.

A second outcome is the increased recognition of the complementarity of scientific and theological work. The practice of science was liberated from theological concerns, while the work of theology could take place in relative freedom, if not isolation, from the findings of modern science. Following Kant, German Protestant theology had already tended to set its face against natural theology. For the Ritschlian school, the providence of God was primarily a church doctrine that emerged from an encounter with Jesus. The outcome of the engagement with Darwinism confirmed this clearer differentiation of theology from the natural sciences. In his *Idea of a University* (1852), John Henry Newman had already pointed the way.[78]

A third outcome is the need to distinguish the theology of providence from the task of theodicy. The growing recognition that the

[78] 'Catholic Theology has nothing to fear from the progress of Physical Science, even independently of the divinity of its doctrines. It speaks of things supernatural; and these, by the very force of the words, research into nature cannot touch.' John Henry Newman, *The Idea of a University* (London: Longman, Green & Co, 1907), p. 438.

problem of evil has no adequate resolution has led in some quarters to the abandonment of the task altogether, even to the point of moral denunciation. The Paleyan theodicies were not merely inadequate but counter-productive in their characterisation of God and its concomitant pastoral outcomes. The positing of a God who directly intended the violence, pain and slow death of creatures seemed incommensurate with the God of Jesus characterised in terms of parental care and abundant provision. By allowing the construction of providence to be driven by the apologetic demands of theodicy, scholars took a wrong turning. This temptation has to be resisted for the sake of a providential theology that is ethically and pastorally adequate. It was a mistake to construct providence as if it were merely the answer to an apologetic question about the problem of evil. Theological reactions to suffering and evil remain central to any worthwhile account of providence, but these should not become sidetracked by the attempt to resolve satisfactorily the intractable *why* questions surrounding the prevalence of evil.

Finally, the extent to which strategies of retrieval can also be discerned is worth a passing note. In moving away from an undue anthropocentrism, theologians could return to those more theocentric approaches to creation found in Scripture and the theological traditions of the church. When modern theodicies were found wanting, the theology of the cross might be recovered. If God's agency can no longer be characterised in terms of occasional visitations, then an account of the presence and perpetual activity of the Holy Spirit may again be advanced.

4.5 Excursus: Divine Action

4.5.1 The Problem

The theology of providence everywhere encounters two problems – suffering and divine action. The first is preoccupied with attempts to understand the compossibility of a God of providence with the

evils that we discern in the cosmos. This becomes acute in the face
of what Marilyn McCord Adams describes as 'horrendous evils',
those outrageous circumstances and events which strike us as egre-
giously unfair, cruel and destructive of a fulfilled human life.[79] To
these must be added the persistent suffering of animals, not least at
the hands of human creatures. By contrast, describing the mode of
divine action in the world presents a very different type of problem,
though also intractable. This has become a central preoccupation
of the science–religion dialogue, especially through the project on
special action in the 1990s which has yielded a series of proposals by
several of the leading figures in the field.[80]

Divine action has become a hot topic at this phase in the history
of theology for several reasons. These might be divided into scientific, theological and philosophical considerations.

i) One feature of modernity is the way in which the natural
    sciences have successfully filled many gaps in our understanding
    of the world. This has generated a sense of 'disenchantment', at
    least among many western intellectuals. What was formerly
    attributed to divine agency can now be explained in natural
    terms, for example, epilepsy, infertility and drought. Hence
    the space (gaps) within which divine action can take place
    amid creaturely causes has shrunk, almost to vanishing point.
    This is somewhat exaggeratedly spoken of in terms of modern
    assumptions about nature as a closed causal continuum.

ii) A more positive theological reason for doubting specific forms
    of divine action derives from the sense that God has created and

[79] Marilyn McCord Adams, *Horrendous Evils and the Goodness of God* (Ithaca: Cornell
    University Press, 2000).

[80] See, for example, Robert John Russell, Nancey Murphy and Arthur R. Peacocke
    (eds.), *Chaos and Complexity: Scientific Perspectives on Divine Action* (Vatican
    City: Vatican Observatory Publications, and Berkeley: Center for Theology and the
    Natural Sciences, 1997). For a summary, see Wesley Wildman, 'The Divine Action
    Project 1988–2003', *Theology and Science*, 2.1 (2004), 31–75.

constantly preserves (general divine action) a natural order to which God remains faithful. Hence the eschewal of particular divine action can be defended on religious grounds through appeal to the sufficiency of general providence. Although intended as a criticism of quantum indeterminacy, Einstein's remark that 'God does not play dice' could be adapted here.

iii) A more philosophical doubt about divine action surrounds the problem of the 'causal joint'. We have no decisive criterion for determining which events are acts of God and which are not. Hence, if God acts in the world, we cannot know this. The possibility of an exhaustive natural causality cannot easily be excluded. On account of this epistemological difficulty, we must remain sceptical about special divine action. Although this does not *a priori* exclude its possibility, we are unable to offer any positive confession. For some, therefore, the declaration of God's particular acts in nature and history will have to be translated into affirmations about general providence.

The exponents of the divine action project typically resist all these considerations. They eschew deism – that is, the view that divine action is confined to the origination and preservation of the cosmos. Although not incompatible (as we have seen) with a theology of providence, deism requires an exclusive 'front-loading' of creation with a structure, fruitfulness and order by which the divine rule is exercised. No subsequent intervention is necessary. This view tends to be rejected on account of its religious inadequacy. The Abrahamic faiths, for example, appear committed to assumptions about a repeated divine agency in creation. The economy of salvation requires that more be attributed to God than creation and preservation. A second presupposition of the project is that God does not suspend the processes of creaturely causality since this would amount to an arbitrary sequence of interventions that destabilised the intended patterns of life. An occasional series of miracles that halted ordinary processes would be theologically baffling. Why there and then, but not here and now? Why spare my child but not yours? The attraction of a God who eschews such modes of action is sometimes represented in terms of a divine restraint. The world is allowed to run its course without suspension, interruption or sudden interposition of a paternal agency. Much of this thinking is driven not by convictions about scientific law or philosophical scepticism surrounding miracles,[81] but by a consideration of the problem of suffering. George Ellis, for example, claims that if we adopt an account of 'miraculous intervention' then the question of infrequency will arise with respect to 'my toothache as well as the evils of Auschwitz'.[82] Here the challenge becomes one of theological adequacy as much as philosophical or scientific coherence.

In view of these constraints, the divine action project attempts to steer a path between God's inactivity (deism) and God's hyper-activity (interventionism). God must act, but only within the interstices of natural processes so that divine action is consistent, scientifically undetectable and effective in bringing about changes that would not otherwise have occurred. These modalities of agency – divine and creaturely – must work together. Two prime candidates for explaining this form of special divine action are quantum mechanics and chaotic systems. In the former, as expounded by Robert Russell and Nancey Murphy, the indeterminacy of events at a sub-atomic level provides scope for divine action in ways that can be neither detected nor disruptive of physical explanation. In the latter, as developed by John Polkinghorne, a divine input of information results in some top-down influence upon finely balanced and inherently unpredictable chaotic systems.[83] Such divine action

---

[81] These considerations are subjected to some rigorous deconstruction by Alvin Plantinga in 'What is "intervention"?', *Theology and Science*, 6.4 (2008), 369–401. Plantinga rightly doubts whether the concept of 'intervention' is quite as problematic and dispensable as suggested.

[82] George Ellis, 'Ordinary and extraordinary divine action' in Russell, Murphy and Peacocke, *Chaos and Complexity*, pp. 359–95 at p. 383.

[83] See, for example, the essays in Russell, Murphy and Peacocke, *Chaos and Complexity*.

is empirically undetectable but can still make a difference to what happens in the natural world.

The literature is extensive, much of it requiring a technical acquaintance with quantum physics that few theologians command – the present author is not one of them. But several features are apparent. The first is the propriety of this sort of enquiry. If our physical world is characterised at the quantum level by a degree of indeterminacy, then it is incumbent on the theologian to reflect upon the ways in which this may or may not be consistent with an account of divine action. How can we situate quantum theory with other understandings of the purpose and nature of the physical world? This seems a legitimate question to pursue and it is one which arises in related contexts, particularly our understanding of the human person as an embodied agent with non-material properties. Much of this literature aims at greater specification and conceptual precision in describing divine involvement in the world. Many post-Darwinian theologians argued that God was engaged in the evolutionary process, yet without really specifying how or in what ways that actually made a difference to outcomes. In referencing quantum theory, the special divine action project has worked hard at offering a more intellectually satisfying account of such notions.

Similarly, in the case of chaos theory, the way in which minor fluctuations cause widespread exponential change across interrelated systems renders predictability impossible. If these are genuinely open systems, then there is scope for divine involvement without violating physical description. This yields a theologically attractive account of divine agency in Polkinghorne. God works constantly with the grain of the universe to realise divine intentions. In this mode of activity, God is constrained by the terms and conditions of the physical universe. Evil and suffering may thus be perceived as by-products of creation, against which divine activity must wrestle. These proposals are carefully formulated and offer several attractions. If sustained, they may provide a way of thinking about how the world is constantly susceptible to divine action, even though this is empirically concealed and self-limiting. Hence the problems identified above can be minimised by such approaches, which remain religiously adequate in their commitment to regular forms of divine interaction with the creaturely world.

One common criticism of this type of manoeuvre is to claim that it invokes a 'God of the gaps'. This is typically associated with attempts by theologians to find a role for God by pointing to gaps in scientific explanation. Since Darwin's confirmation of the principle of natural selection, this approach has looked increasingly dubious. In any case, Laplace had already argued in relation to Newtonian physics that he could manage very well without the hypothesis of God. With the expansion of scientific knowledge, the gaps for divine action start to close. Hence, to set theology in competition with the natural sciences in their explanatory functions is to risk redundancy. This seems an obvious problem with intelligent design theory. Yet it is doubtful whether recent exponents of special divine action are committed to such strategies. Their claim is that there are natural gaps which have been exposed by scientific developments as fundamental to the way the world is. These are not gaps in our knowledge, so much as genuinely open features of the world as described by contemporary physics.

Nevertheless there are some downsides to this pursuit of a scientifically coherent account of particular divine action. One obvious problem is the commitment to indeterminacy readings of quantum behaviour and chaotic systems.[84] On the Copenhagen theory, indeterminacy is an inherent feature of quantum mechanics. Yet this is contested by other models which revert to more determinist interpretations. According to the de Broglie–Bohm reformulation, the apparent indeterminacy is only a function of our lack of complete knowledge of the workings of the system as opposed to being one of its inherent features. In the many-worlds proposal, the act of

---

[84] In what follows, I am indebted to the discussion in Nicholas Saunders, 'Does God cheat at dice? Divine action and quantum possibilities', *Zygon*, 35.3 (2000), 517–44.

measurement does not presuppose a prior indeterminacy so much as select in which of the many worlds arising from the act of measurement we find ourselves. Although this seems highly extravagant, with its putative breach of Ockham's razor, it retains determinacy within all its possible universes. By contrast, the 'orthodox' view favoured by exponents of special divine action argues that the measurement of the observer 'collapses the wave function'. On this account, a genuinely indeterminate and unrealised set of possibilities collapses into only one of the modalities. In the case of Schrödinger's cat, which was neither dead nor alive until the point of measurement, an act of observation brings about the disappearance of one branch of the wave function. Until this happens, however, we cannot know what outcome will be selected. On this basis, we might conclude that the system contains sufficient openness to allow for a hidden divine action that will make a difference to which of the possible outcomes is selected.

This approach has some potential, yet it faces formidable problems. The specification of how God brings about quantum effects that subsequently shape changes in the macroscopic world is problematic. If God collapses the wave function does this happen often or only infrequently? And, in doing so, does God assume the position of the observer or determine in some hidden way the effects that an observer will then perceive? These questions can lead to some strange answers, for example the notion that quantum indeterminacy everywhere is secretly resolved by divine action. A further difficulty concerns the ways in which quantum involvement on God's part can actually bring about the intended effects in the macroscopic world of embodied persons. God's quantum adjustments may have to precede their intended consequences by many millions of years to be successful. This might restrict divine action in ways that render God largely incapable as an effective agent.

Owing to this difficulty, Polkinghorne is more inclined to see chaotic systems as having greater potential for understanding divine action.[85] Yet his adoption of chaos theory has not been widely accepted, principally because of the widely held view that chaotic systems can be adequately described by deterministic equations. If so, they lack the inherent openness necessary to the account of divine action. Our inability to predict outcomes is a function of epistemic limitation rather than an ontic ingredient of the physical processes. Polkinghorne's proposal is that God is able to exert an influence on the world by the input of 'information' rather than 'energy' into chaotic systems, and that deterministic equations are only an approximation to a 'more subtle and supple physical reality'.[86] While this has the attraction of suggesting ways in which a consistent and restricted set of divine actions might be possible, the proposal is also elusive in specifying how and in what ways this informational input can make a difference. In his response to criticism of this use of chaos theory, Polkinghorne describes it more tentatively as a thought experiment which may or may not prove useful in the long run.[87] This seems legitimate. If we are to postulate a form of divine action in the world, then it is worth reflecting on how this might mesh with contemporary physics. But this intellectual exercise should not be given a controlling function in what modes of divine activity can be affirmed, nor should it be allowed to constrain God's action according to one very provisional account of a possible causal joint. In any case, whether chaos theory describes an ontically (as opposed to epistemically) indeterminate system seems questionable on many readings of the subject today.

Polkinghorne's commitment to identifying a restrained or kenotic account of divine action is largely driven by the problem of

---

[85] See for example John Polkinghorne, *Belief in God in an Age of Science* (New Haven: Yale University Press, 1998), pp. 48–75.

[86] John Polkinghorne, 'Divine action: some comments', *Science and Christian Belief*, 24.1 (2012), 31–2.

[87] 'The fact of the matter is that we are not in a position to give a fully accurate account of the details of agency, either human or divine. What we can say is that appeal to the models of causal joint explanation show that these possibilities are not excluded

evil. This is worth noting. The departure from popular notions of occasional intervention or the Thomist account of primary causality arises from the perceived need to admit a degree of autonomy, contingency and even chance into the created order. This is determined by a divine kenosis in which creation is allowed to be and to evolve according to its own structure. Here permission is pulled apart from divine willing. God concedes, as it were, a set of physical processes which shape us non-deterministically. These have a shadow-side which constantly threatens and sometimes overwhelms us. Within these parameters we live and act, but so too does God, who works persistently (somehow) in and through these creaturely processes. Hence, Polkinghorne frequently characterises his account of providence as mediating, if not always comfortably, between deism and determinism.

4.5.2 Double Agency: The Classical View

One way of cutting the Gordian knot of divine action is to return to the default account of double agency that we identified in Aquinas, Calvin et al. This has undoubted attractions and it has regained some momentum in recent literature.[88] By setting God's action on a different causal plane from creaturely causes, one can preserve the integrity of the latter while making sense of God's involvement in everything that happens. Much is made here of a 'zero-sum' game in which God and creatures do not compete on the same causal territory. Divine agency is entirely different from secondary agency,

---

by what an honest science can actually tell about physical processes.' Ibid., p. 32. For an overview of the different phases of Polkinghorne's approach, see Ignacio Silva, 'John Polkinghorne on divine action: a coherent theological evolution', *Science and Christian Belief*, 24.1 (2012), 19–30.

[88] See for example Ignacio Silva, 'Thomas Aquinas holds fast: objections to Aquinas within today's debate on divine action', *Heythrop Journal*, 54 (2013), 658–67, and Alexander S. Jensen, *Divine Providence and Human Agency: Trinity, Creation and Freedom* (Aldershot: Ashgate, 2014).

functioning as both originating condition and overall *telos*. Despite my earlier criticism of this approach, two features of this account are retained in the position outlined below. First, its recognition that divine agency does not exclude a natural causality seems valid. The conviction that God works in and through the processes of nature and history is central to most accounts of the religious life. Divine action is not restricted to those fleeting moments when the natural or social sciences fall silent. We can offer complementary descriptions of the same event – one set will invoke natural causes and the other may offer a theological account. But the latter does not depend upon either a breakdown of or errors in the former. These types of description are complementary; each is important in its own way and addresses a different form of understanding. Second, accounts of double agency depict God as involved in everything that happens – in keeping Israel, God neither slumbers nor sleeps but is ever vigilant. This sense of divine constancy is also captured by the rendition of providence in Aquinas and Calvin. There is no secondary cause that is not in some way ruled or accompanied by the primal will of God. This sense of divine involvement in natural causality needs to be captured in any adequate account.

What are the objections to double agency? Three types have been identified. The first is its determinism. In setting too tightly the fit between primary and secondary orders of causality, the theory does not allow for any slack or movement. Each secondary event, presumably down to the quantum level, is governed by the primal act of God. This is described not simply in terms of a setting of initial conditions or fixing of parameters, but as a strong willing of everything that happens. Typically in the Latin tradition, this prevented the earlier distinction between willing and permission from gaining much traction, even though it had to be reintroduced somewhat belatedly. The result was a drift towards fatalism, with all its deleterious consequences.

A second anxiety is somewhat ironic. The theory tends towards a rather monistic and undifferentiated rendering of divine action which makes God remote to the point of disappearance. This is encapsulated in Clayton's remark that a God who does everything is a God who does nothing.[89] If God's work is restricted to a single and immutable divine will, then particular forms of interaction within the created order become harder to accommodate. Exponents of the theory were of course aware of this difficulty and they sought to explain how, for example, the incarnation and the answering of prayer might be located within a world that had been ordained to include such phenomena. Yet this stance appears either to superimpose new models of divine action on the standard one, or else to intensify the anxiety that the world is merely the instantiation of a single divine vision that is immutable in every detail. The performance of free action and the occurrence of contingent events are in accordance with a single script from which there can be no temporal deviation. One stock response to this problem is to insist upon the difference between divine and creaturely causality. God's transcendence is such that we cannot think of God's action alongside creaturely causes. By a process of negation, we can remove it from the domain of the world and view it as a pure act of the transcendent and timeless God. But here divine action starts to recede from view and to lose its sense of taking place in and alongside creaturely agencies. The absence of a common field of action makes it difficult to see how there can be a genuine interplay between God and creatures whereby God acts with, through and sometimes against people.[90]

A third related concern surrounds the scriptural adequacy of the model. The interaction of God and creatures which dominates the

---

[89] Philip Clayton, *God and Contemporary Science* (Edinburgh: Edinburgh University Press, 1997), p. 196.

[90] Frank Kirkpatrick makes the point that 'a commonality of a field of agency' is required to demarcate the space within which we can talk meaningfully of interaction between God and creatures. *The Mystery and Agency of God: Divine Being and Action in the World* (Minneapolis: Fortress, 2014), p. xiv. While this notion is frequently charged with anthropomorphism, it seems necessary for articulating the view of God implicit in the Abrahamic faiths.

biblical narratives seems remote from these two planes of causality that move in tandem without criss-crossing or covenanting. The senses in which God assails, directs, prompts, promises and even threatens human agents seem strangely lacking. To this extent, primary causality ironically does too little. In short, double agency, on the classical construction, offers either too much or not enough or not the sorts of things that Scripture and the life of faith attest.

4.5.3 The Analogy with Human Agency

How then might double agency be reconstructed in recognition of its more desirable features? The approach I adopt is borrowed from a body of philosophical work on human agency. According to this perspective, human action should not be located via a causal joint or a gap in physical explanation. Intentionality is distributed across the entire range of bodily movements. A holistic account is required which views the behaviour of the embodied self as constituting intentional personal activity. This requires a set of descriptors that are complementary to those of physiological and neurological description. To this extent, we have two types of causal explanation (double agency) which are complete in their own terms but which are both required to achieve a more comprehensive understanding. As human persons, we are agents. This is a basic set of categories for living in the world and understanding it, including notions of intentionality, purpose, relationality, freedom and love. Our agency cannot be read as an epiphenomenon of a scientific worldview, though persons emerge and are situated in a material and organic world. We might think analogously of God as an agent with intention, goals, freedom of action and a capacity for interaction. The Bible is more concerned with what God does than in specifying God's being, though these in the end must be related. To enable a sufficiently adequate account of divine action, we should begin here and allow other notions to be organised around this centre. Although the model of agency, when applied to God, carries disanalogical elements around divine embodiment and transcendence, the other conceptual categories can still be deployed in faithfulness to Scripture, tradition and the liturgy of the church. One advantage of this is that it affords a richer and more differentiated account of divine action, thus accommodating the two hands of God – Word and Spirit.

Frank Kirkpatrick has recently developed this approach in conversation with three philosophers – John Macmurray, Edward Pols and Raymond Tallis.[91] The agent is to be understood not in terms of occasional intervention in the cause–effect nexus but as one whose activity utilises and is spread upon the world.[92] While some bodily movements such as blinking and breathing are not actions, much of what we do and think as embodied persons can only be understood through a personal discourse of reason, intention and social relations. These terms are not to be fitted into gaps in a scientific description of the world as in forms of materialism, where they become at worst delusional and at best epiphenomenal. In acting, we are not under the sway of causal relations in the material world so much as ordering, embracing and disposing these to bring about an intended effect. The action takes place in, with and through the causal processes of the material world.

Undoubtedly, there is an *aporia* here, when it comes to explaining both how divine action is effective in a material and spiritual world and how these two complementary forms of description fit together. Some of the thought experiments of the scientist-theologians might point to ways in which this is possible, or at least allow us to 'defeat the defeaters'. Thomas Tracy has worked this out with theological dexterity in a succession of publications.[93] Yet we should not introduce

---

[91] See Kirkpatrick, *The Mystery and Agency of God*, pp. 79–96.

[92] Nancey Murphy speaks of the body as the 'substrate' for personal characteristics. See *Bodies and Souls, or Spirited Bodies* (Cambridge: Cambridge University Press, 2006), p. 141.

[93] See for example Thomas Tracy, 'Scientific vetoes and the hands-off God: can we say that God acts in history?', *Theology and Science*, 10.1 (2012), 55–80.

wholesale changes into our theology simply because of difficulties around the causal joint connecting the finite and the infinite, or current thinking on quantum mechanics or chaos theory. As Keith Ward suggests, if we cannot provide a complete account of human action, perhaps we ought not to be troubled if we encounter similar problems with divine action, at least not to the point of abandoning the project.[94]

If we think of God in terms of an absolute agency that supervenes upon the world, then we can correlate transcendence and immanence in accordance with divine action. As an agent who is not reducible to creaturely processes, God transcends the world yet in ways that enable forms of interaction. Here divine presence can itself be understood as a mode of agency when understood as God's making Godself present in and through creation. And an account of omnipresence can elucidate the notion that there is no situation or event from which God can be absent. In contradistinction to human forms of agency, God's action is not confined in its scope, though its mediation by creaturely processes through which God acts may generate both some restriction and an enabling condition. The complexities of creation thus produce both restraints and possibilities. Here the entire created realm can be viewed as the arena of divine action without reducing this to God's body or drifting into a panentheism in which divine transcendence and otherness cannot be properly expressed. Multiple forms of description are here deployed to give an adequate account of the world without seeking to privilege one model, whether physical or mental, to which all others are reduced.

---

[94] Keith Ward, *Divine Action: Examining God's Role in an Open and Emergent Universe* (West Conshohocken, PA: Templeton Foundation Press, 2007), pp. 76–7. Thomas Tracy similarly claims that if we can show that there are ways in which God could act within the physical universe, then we should not feel over-burdened by the requirement of specifying the causal joint. See 'Divine action, created causes, and human freedom' in Thomas Tracy (ed.), *The God Who Acts: Philosophical and Theological Explorations* (University Park, PA: Pennsylvania State University Press, 1994), pp. 77–102.

In his Gifford Lectures, Roger Scruton pleads for a similarly personalist approach both to the human agent and to God. The person will disappear from the world as a significant category if we confine ourselves to material processes and forms of explanation. When discussing the brain and its intricacies we cannot suddenly introduce 'why?' questions in relation to actions and outcomes. Similarly, if we seek to explain the world downwards by appeal to Neo-Darwinian principles working upon matter, we are unlikely to find any space for religious description. This results in a narrowing of scope and the loss of important ways in which we understand the world and ourselves.[95]

What remains then of the traditional notion of double agency? The insight that God and creatures do not compete on the same causal plane needs to be retained. In part, this reflects the 'onto-logical size gap' between finite and infinite. God is not to be located as one element in a set of empirical events that constitute the necessary and sufficient conditions for a causal explanation, whether in terms of scientific or social forces. Divine action does not exclude or annihilate creaturely causes but works in, with and through these, according to this model. In relation to specific Christian convictions, this entails recognition of the divine commitment to work graciously in each and every circumstance. This may be frequently frustrated, ignored or resisted, yet the presence and persistence of God neither cease nor withdraw when thwarted by creaturely processes. This is an implication of some core claims for divine constancy in both Scripture and tradition. At the same time, it does not commit us in classical fashion to claiming that the will of God is the primary cause that guarantees each and every effect through the medium of secondary causality. Divine double agency is more about

---

[95] 'Take away religion, however; take away philosophy, take away the higher aims of art, and you deprive ordinary people of the ways in which they can represent their apartness. Human nature, once something to live up to, becomes something to live down to instead.' Roger Scruton, *The Face of God* (London: Continuum, 2012), p. 72.

the universality and faithfulness of God than the determination of everything that happens. At its minimum, it entails a commitment to the concessionary will of God as ordaining this world and accompanying it along the way. More maximally, it perceives the presence of the Spirit as everywhere moving and striving to fashion the world and its creatures according to a divine purpose that is discerned in a series of focal events to which the church returns again and again. The 'two hands of God' thus give a multi-dimensional meaning to the concept of double agency, even if this does not play out according to the classical distinction between primary and secondary causality. The fit is looser to accommodate the contingency of creation, the freedom of creatures and the striving of God to fashion a future for us. By invoking the divine will, the Lord's Prayer has a forward trajectory which seeks to change the way the world is. Living for the future reign of God, we acknowledge a present that is not in accordance with God's will. Not everything now is as God intends.

4.5.4 Double Agency: Austin Farrer

Austin Farrer's work is dense, elusive and highly stylised. While he has a happy turn of phrase, this can be maddening in its obscurity. One feels that clarity and simple communication are being sacrificed to standards of cleverness or felicity, allied to a determination to avoid footnoting. Yet on several re-readings his material is rewarding and perceptive, as perhaps the most important reworking of the concept of double agency in recent literature.[96] Farrer is a writer who sees the bigger picture and draws out connections that can often be missed by a more narrowly focussed enquiry. This applies also to

---

[96] For helpful accounts of Farrer on double agency, see Edward Henderson, 'Double agency and the relation of persons to God' in Douglas Hedley and Brian Hebblethwaite (eds.), *The Human Person in God's Word: Studies to Commemorate the Austin Farrer Centenary* (London: SCM, 2006), pp. 38–64, and Brian Hebblethwaite, *The Philosophical Theology of Austin Farrer* (Leuven: Peeters, 2007), pp. 41–52.

his sermons and popular work, which continue to stand the test of time – they require slow and careful reading, so that one wonders what his congregations must have made of them.[97]

The banal example of Mr Jones's rheumatism illustrates a popular account of divine providence that sees God playing a constant game of adjusting natural processes.[98] His rheumatism was reckoned a test of patience sent by God but actually proved a blessing from the hand of providence when it excused him from a pensioners' bus outing which crashed. It is more tempting to think in such ways than we care to admit; we are intuitively attracted to the idea that God (or the gods) have made some special arrangement for us. But this is empirically implausible – it is not how we experience the world, with both its regularity and its randomness. Accidents happen – an insurance company must calculate what the probabilities are – as part and parcel of a natural world populated with fallible agents. And it is theologically deficient since we celebrate the order and regularity of the natural world in ways that largely exclude the need for continual divine interference. This would create a God of 'shove halfpenny'. Farrer firmly resists this approach.

What is striking is how the two intractable problems of the theology of providence constantly coincide in Farrer – the problem of evil and the problem of divine action. The world is a complex kaleidoscope of interlocking systems, each of which emerges through a process of evolving parts. Despite their natural order, these patterns of growth and interaction exhibit a randomness and unpredictability which can damage creatures. Farrer wants to maintain that God works both through natural process and through personal agents. This involvement is constant and universal, neither occasional nor episodic. Yet the causal joint is undetectable because we are dealing

---

[97] Basil Mitchell describes Farrer as an 'epidiascopic' rather than a 'searchlight' thinker. See 'Introduction' in Hedley and Hebblethwaite, *The Human Person in God's Word*, pp. 1–13 at p. 8.

[98] Austin Farrer, *Faith and Speculation: An Essay in Philosophical Theology* (Edinburgh: T&T Clark, 1988), p. 68.

here with the interaction of finite and infinite. The paradigm for divine action is not miracle, though this category is not excluded, but a form of immanent inspiration of creaturely processes, and an enablement of divine possibilities through them.

If the causal joint is undetectable, then why affirm it? For some of his critics, Farrer's position too easily capitulates to a lazy fideism or a Thomistic determinism.[99] Yet this is a misinterpretation of his position. He seems to have three types of response to this challenge. The first is philosophical: the natural world raises reflexive questions about its origin and constitution which lie beyond the sciences. The 'why something' and 'why order' questions are unavoidable. These can be given a variety of answers, though the possibility of a theological metaphysics cannot be excluded. The Christian theist, Farrer suggests, will be inclined in this direction. Is the world merely a disorderly wilderness or a garden that someone is struggling to cultivate?[100] Second, there are strong pragmatic reasons ('contextual encouragements') for believing in a divine order.[101] This is a quasi-Kantian insight about the practical efficacy of believing in a providence that orders our human lives towards love of God, love of self and love of one's neighbour. We can live well by holding to providential convictions about the grain of the natural world and the possibilities for collective action. These provide a regulative benefit that stands us in good stead, in both good and bad times. This, however, is insufficient, even if useful. The Christian lives by the conviction that these claims are in some sense true and have been disclosed. They are not merely useful regulative claims which we hold while recognising our epistemological darkness. In acknowledging this,

---

[99] See Maurice Wiles, *God's Action in the World*, (London: SCM, 1986), pp. 33–4.

[100] The allusions to the evidence for a gardener presumably echo John Wisdom's parable that was much discussed by analytical philosophers of religion in Oxbridge at that time. See John Wisdom, 'Gods', *Proceedings of the Aristotelian Society*, 45 (1944–5), 185–206.

[101] Farrer, *Faith and Speculation*, p. 74.

we are led to the fundamental religious claim that this is the way that the world is ordered. Here Farrer's third appeal is to divine grace enacted in Christ and discerned through prayer and practice. This provides a reliable perspective by which divine action can be discerned and characterised.[102] God works in and through us in grace-filled ways, in an 'agency [that] envelopes and pervades our own'.[103] But this only makes sense through participation rather than detached speculation. Faith is a pre-requisite for the discernment of divine action in the world. There is no neutral space from which this coincidence of finite and infinite can make sense.[104] Within the Christian life, we cannot apportion some of what we do to God and the rest to ourselves. These are inextricably bound together, so that we must affirm the integrity of human agency and the sufficiency of divine grace: 'I, yet not I, but the grace of God within me' (1 Corinthians 15:10). This identity of divine and human is most perfectly expressed in Christ. And this is refracted in the Christian life and attested by the cumulative experience (or much of it) of faith.[105]

4.5.5 Multiple Forms of Divine Action

While Farrer appears not to map his position onto the classical three-fold classification of providence, there are ways in which we might do this for the sake of greater clarity. As with the concept of double

---

[102] On this point, Vincent Brümmer's account appears as a constructive clarification rather than a criticism of Farrer's position. See 'Farrer, Wiles and the causal joint', *Modern Theology*, 8 (1992), 1–14.

[103] Tracy, 'Divine action, created causes, and human freedom', p. 100.

[104] This is developed in Diogenes Allen, 'Faith and the recognition of God's activity' in Brian Hebblethwaite and Edward Henderson (eds.), *Divine Action: Studies Inspired by the Philosophical Theology of Austin Farrer* (Edinburgh: T&T Clark, 1990), pp. 197–210.

[105] Although Farrer attempts to see the differences in these forms of divine action as only scalar, one might question the adequacy of this account with reference, for

agency, the threefold form of God's providence is not to be jettisoned but requires some restatement in order to capture the rich and differentiated ways in which divine action should be characterised.

First, God's work involves a creating and sustaining of the world. This is established through the endowment of nature with a potentiality enabling the evolution of complex forms and systems, together with God's determination to hold it in being. The conservation of the world is not by a mere and remote divine fiat – it can be read as a sustained act of divine constancy. God sticks with us and the rest of creation. To invert Hume's image, we might say that our universe is not abandoned or terminated as a failed experiment in the art of world-making. Its constant, regular and pervasive features are attestation of God's constancy. In the practical manifestation of providence, this suggests a divine patience, a willingness to stay the course, a faithfulness that endures. In this respect, the providence of God has a capacity to outlast us, returning to view only after prolonged periods of confusion and turbulence. Consider the following passage from John Updike, in which President James Buchanan contemplates his imminent failure to prevent the outbreak of the civil war.

> Having long been troubled by the silence into which his prayers seemed to sink without an echo, Buchanan in his majestic fatigue appreciated that this silence *was* an answer, the only answer whose mercy was lasting, impartial and omnipresent. Just so, Lincoln's silence from Springfield was an answer of a certain grandeur, after all the clamour of the Cabinet meeting. As if through the gimlet eye of an eagle soaring in God's silent wind Buchanan saw the nation beneath him, a colourful small mountain meadow scurrying with frantic life; its life would perish but infallibly recover itself in the turning of seasons, in the great and impervious planetary motions.[106]

example, to Christ's resurrection. Brian Hebblethwaite suggests a loss of nerve at this juncture. See *The Philosophical Theology of Austin Farrer*, p. 47.

[106] John Updike, *Memories of the Ford Administration* (New York: Alfred Knopf, 1992), pp. 346–7.

A Christian theology of providence has more to opine on the subject, particularly in relation to grace, redemption and resurrection. But this element of divine patience remains important. The outcomes of providence are not immediately achieved by a divine quick-fix. God takes time to reach a place of resolution. Such a deferral of intended outcomes remains a perpetual feature of creaturely occurrence. But, rather than signalling divine abandonment or neglect, we can interpret an infinite patience and constancy. One token of this is the rhythms of nature and the mores of societies which can reassert themselves after periods of disruption, violence and upheaval. At most, this is a sign discerned by a providential faith, rather than a proof that can sway the sceptic or an argument that can silence criticism and doubt.

Second, there is a divine concurrence throughout this process. This does not result in each event being predetermined and eternally willed in God. Nowhere does this appear to be a tenet of Farrer. But the notion of concurrence as permission or concession does yield an account of divine action in which God is present in and through each creaturely event. Living and active, God strives to generate intended outcomes within material and social processes. This mode of divine activity is not reducible to a mere sustaining and accompanying, though it assumes these. At this juncture, the doctrine of the Holy Spirit requires greater emphasis in a fuller account of providence. God's work is to be characterised pneumatically to convey a sense of its ceaseless and universal scope. Confined neither to an initial setting of created conditions nor to an occasional historical interposition, divine action is spread across space and time. Here, again, we recall the two hands. God is always active but in ways that have a specificity characterised by the Word and universalised in the Spirit. The impulse of the Spirit has a strong present aspect and is confined neither to the church nor to the Christian life, though its description is shaped by these. Yet concurrence should not be elucidated in terms of a stamp of divine approval upon everything that happens. Although this may befit a theological metaphysics that cannot allow anything to escape the determination of God's primal will, we should resist such a move. For the most part, it does not adequately represent the direction of Scripture nor the sense of God seeking to overcome what is contrary to the divine will. A return to divine determinism is not required by concurrence recast in this way. With its ordering under the third article of the faith, it can be released from the more monergistic formulations that have dominated its historical expression, especially in the western churches.

Third, there is a divine succeeding in which God is particularly present and engaged in creation through the events *inter alia* of the incarnation and the church. These point towards an eschatological transformation of creation at some future end point. In this respect, there is an in-breaking or irruption of divine activity within specified temporal episodes and historical traditions, though these also are embedded and graduated in their appearance. Performed by God, they are pointers to a more universal success that remains in the future tense. Jesus is the Son of God incarnate, but he does not appear from nowhere. He is born a Jew in Israel in the reign of Caesar Augustus. 'When the fullness of time had come' (Galatians 4:4), Christ was sent. Here divine action can be better characterised by images of intervention and transcendence than by indwelling and immanence, though these need to be accommodated to a wider historical context governed by complex processes of interpretation. It is hard to see how Christian faith can manage without this account of divine activity, given its pattern of constant return to one name and one historical life.

Divine overruling is a repeated theme of the prophetic literature. The Word of God confronts the prophet, who in turn is required to assail the people with its message. Divine agency is often surprising and works against the grain of history. Those who seem least fitted to the office are often the ones who are called. God acts not because of who we are, but in spite of our manifest deficiencies. The most striking instances of divine initiative are in the birth and resurrection of Jesus, as narrated in the gospels. These are historical manifestations of divine love and victory, though in ways that disrupt conventional standards of wisdom and power. Significantly, these events also take the form of promise, as tokens and guarantees of a future inauguration of God's will – hence the Pauline image of 'first fruits' in relation to what is signified by the raising of Jesus from the dead. Divine providence has a dual dimension expressed by its perfect and future tenses.

> I got me flowers to straw thy way
> I got me boughs off many a tree
> But thou wast up by break of day
> And brought'st thy sweets along with thee.[107]

Here we note the 'once for all' character of events that do not merely evolve out of earlier historical possibilities. Their *novum* is to be attributed to a divine action of particular intent. Though disruptive, they cast light on everything else, thus connecting with other modes of divine action. But, in doing so, these revelatory events also sound a promissory note, without which they cannot be fully understood. By their light, everything else is illumined, including the end of our own lives.

In the time between the perfected action of Christ and the end of life, the church witnesses to the previous form of divine action, namely the indwelling of the Spirit. This will be explored further in Chapter 6, but suffice it to say here that it offers a more synergistic set of possibilities alongside the other types. Through influence and persuasion, the second hand of God is continually at work in ways that the New Testament identifies closely with the work of Christ. Since there is no time in which the Spirit is not active, we are committed to framing divine action in the present tense, as well as past and future. These different accounts of God's activity correspond to the plurality of forms described in Scripture. Though differentiated strands, these can be interwoven in complex ways.

---

[107] George Herbert, 'Easter' in *The Complete English Poems* (Harmondsworth: Penguin, 1991), p. 37.

There are questions and problems generated by this account, especially in relation to the loss of simplicity engendered by a plurality of modes of divine agency.[108] But it has some theological attractions in relation to how we might think of providence, evil and divine action. God works paradigmatically in and through the events of nature and history. These are neither semi-detached from God's purposes nor subject only to occasional interference. Farrer's work may also help us to understand that we can discern God's action and intention in our world and our own lives only with the eye of faith. Theology should admit its epistemic limitations – our pathway is often dim without the light of the noonday sun.

---

[108] Some theologians would prefer to reduce these forms of providential action to exclude the performative, or at least to subsume it under pneumatological influence. Jesus would thus be understood as an exemplary instance of a general type of spiritual inspiration. Though I choose a more complex pattern, the account of double agency which I have defended could accommodate this revision.

5 | Twentieth-Century Reactions

Providence is the forgotten stepchild of contemporary theology.[1]

5.1 The Legacy of the Nineteenth Century

The theology of providence reached its modern zenith in the latter part of the nineteenth century with the affirmation of an evolutionary and historical progressivism. While the subsequent loss of confidence in this project may have resulted in a decline in providentialist ideas, particularly after the First World War, some scattered efforts at recovery are evident. These may have resulted from a belated recognition that an adequate account of the God–world relationship cannot function without a description of providence.

In a perceptive analysis, Langdon Gilkey highlighted several problems and reactions which had become apparent by the early 1960s.[2] Unlike other doctrines – for example, revelation, incarnation, sin and eschatology – providence had not been the subject of reinvigoration. Whether from neglect or outright repudiation as a pagan import, it had fared badly. Gilkey's primary reasons for the loss of confidence in providentialism resonate with much of the preceding historical analysis. First, the enormity of evil has occasioned the collapse of the optimistic theodicies of the nineteenth century, which tended to buttress claims for divine providence. We can no

---

[1] Langdon B. Gilkey, 'The concept of providence in contemporary theology', *Journal of Religion*, 43.3 (1963), 171–92 at 174.

[2] Ibid. His analysis is reproduced more clearly in *Reaping the Whirlwind: A Christian Interpretation of History* (New York: Seabury, 1976), pp. 222–6.

longer regard suffering in merely probative terms, as if it imposes a discipline resulting in moral and spiritual improvement, analogous to a vigorous work-out in the gym. After the experience of trench warfare such responses seemed not merely inadequate but entirely out of place. And, following the Shoah, theologians became even more allergic to the standard moves of theodicy. The enterprise itself was denounced as morally dubious. Second, the stress on freedom has resulted in greater explanatory force being attached to creaturely autonomy in relative independence of divine action. Here the condition of the world is the result of the misuse of human freedom, rather than an inscrutable divine will. And third, the stronger commitment to natural explanation, whether in science or history, has made us more reluctant to identify the providential will of God with natural events. Apart from the legal terminology of insurance companies, earthquakes, avalanches, plagues and droughts could in no sense be described as 'acts of God'. This has been reinforced by the first factor noted above, namely our reluctance to identify suffering with the will of God.

In the face of these anxieties, twentieth-century theology has tended either to shun the theology of providence or else to treat it only briefly and episodically. The classical tradition sought to identify everything that happened with the will of God, while maintaining that God was not to be characterised as the author of evil. Within this paradox, there was no disputing the sovereignty of God. By contrast, modern theology is inclined to deny that everything is willed by God, since evils are to be attributed to creaturely forces. The paradox is thus repositioned. God remains sovereign but without willing much of what actually happens; how this sovereignty is then exercised remains something of a mystery. Gilkey also notes that much providentialism was viewed with suspicion as the incursion of philosophical and cosmological theories into theology. At a time when natural theology was treated with disdain, the idea of providence was diminished. And its seeming absence as a key semantic term in Scripture only compounded this alienation.

In the existential theologies of the twentieth century, especially that of Bultmann, providence was sidelined in favour of a divine–human encounter characterised by judgement, grace and deliverance. There was little sense here of the historical realm (let alone nature) as ruled by God, except in terms of judgement or some eschatological resolution of its plight. The dialectical tension between the transcendent God and the world did not readily facilitate a description of the threefold form of providence in everything that happens. 'Although we make a great deal of the sovereignty of God over history, we have intense difficulty in spelling this out convincingly to ourselves in any but inward terms.'[3]

While Gilkey's analysis remains magisterial, there are some additional considerations that have become increasingly apparent since the 1960s.[4] Through an intensified hermeneutics of suspicion, we have an ineluctable sense that theologies of providence were often politically misplaced in identifying God too readily with the national interest or imperialist expansion or *laissez-faire* economics. Their effects tended to reinforce a prevailing political cause, as opposed to expressing some solidarity with those at the receiving end. Winners rather than losers were vindicated by divine providence. Although important counter-examples can be cited, this tendency of modern providentialism has resulted in some nervousness today in any strong linkage with a political cause. The converse problem arises when providence is then restricted merely to denunciation or negation, as if the public domain has become a godless arena. The political theologies from the 1960s onwards have tended to speak in a much more critical register, sometimes to the point where deconstruction has become the default setting of western academics. A further chastening is evident from the recognition that previous approaches were vitiated by an overreaching anthropocentrism. God's primary concern was human beings, so

---

[3] Gilkey, 'The concept of providence in contemporary theology', p. 179.

[4] Gilkey's own subsequent work reacts to these. See *Reaping the Whirlwind*.

that the rest of the creation featured only as a stage or at most a set of minor characters. The scope accorded the natural world, apart from its human significance, was thus diminished, with the result that other creatures were not accorded a proper place in a wider scheme of creation and providence. Although evolutionary science pointed the way, theologians have only recently become alert to this deficit within the tradition. A corrective is evident in questions about how the providence of God was manifested prior to the appearance of *Homo sapiens*, and how it may even now function in distant galaxies inhabited by unknown life forms.

Finally, there is the wider question of the adequacy of theological descriptions of providence with respect to the practices of lived religion. As in other areas, there has long been a mismatch between what theologians felt able to affirm and what was actually assumed in the habitual actions of the faithful. This problem is especially acute with respect to the practice of petitionary prayer and the pastoral counsel that everything is wisely willed by God and should be faced with an admixture of patience and gratitude. There may be a wide array of assumptions and misconceptions on display here. But systematic theologians have sometimes circumvented these more practical problems for fear of exposing themselves to easy criticism on the intractable issue of divine action, or else to charges of reductionism by their ecclesial critics. In a fine passage, Charles Wood offers this diagnosis of the reception of the traditional account.

> For all of its learned consistency and ecclesial support, this official line of teaching has always been received with something short of universal approbation. To be sure, many have found it profoundly consoling. Others have done their best to accept it, believing that any difficulties they may have with it are difficulties in them (the believers) and not difficulties in it (the doctrine). But others have found it impossible to accept. Some – as their circumstances permit – have left the church on this account. Others, have followed

the time-honored practice, of 'defecting in place' – a new name perhaps, for a very old phenomenon.[5]

In the face of these challenges, recent theologies of providence
have tended to react in several different ways. These are identified
in what follows as:

i) repristinations of the traditional view, often grounded in
Scripture but with increasing accentuation of our epistemological limitations;
ii) the espousal of a variety of forms of open and relational theism;
iii) a return to a single general providence, reminiscent of the
deism of the eighteenth century; and
iv) a more exclusively Christological determination of providence.

We can measure each of these approaches against the aforementioned problems identified by Gilkey and supplemented above.
While each model offers something of value under each of the three
articles of the faith, none is successful as an exhaustive account.
Although this may seem a piecemeal strategy, my claim is that a
dispersed approach will serve the theology of providence better
than an account constrained by a single model or dominant theme.
Consequently, I shall argue for a view that seeks to appropriate
insights from each to advance a more differentiated and diffuse
account. This represents a wider strategy that distributes providence
across all three articles. To that extent, the concept of providence
attaches to different theological trajectories rather than constituting
a single constitutive principle around which all thinking about God
and the world must be organised. This 'de-systematising' of providence is intended as a strategic move. The theology of providence
today should be viewed as an *ad hoc* or tracking manoeuvre that

---

[5] Charles Wood, *The Question of Providence* (Louisville: Westminster John Knox Press,
2008), p. 65. A similar diagnosis is suggested by Douglas T. Ottati in his moving
discussion of the tragedy that engulfed Jonathan Edwards and his family. See *Theology
for Liberal Protestants: God the Creator* (Grand Rapids: Eerdmans, 2012), pp. 245–9.

summarises and connects several forms of divine action rather than itself constituting a *Grundprinzip*. In following, rather than leading, providentialism might then cease to be a driver of inflated claims and bad practice.

5.2 The Tradition Defended

Although the theology of providence has remained a greater preoccupation among Protestant theologians, several Catholic theologians have endeavoured to rehabilitate elements of their own tradition. Along predictably Thomist lines, Garrigou-Lagrange devoted an entire study to the theology of providence in 1932.[6] The affirmation of a perfect divine sovereignty is maintained, with a steady sense of the will of God ruling and overruling over events. While conscious of some departure from the classical teaching on providence, Garrigou-Lagrange seems untroubled by contemporary criticisms of historical formulations. The providence of God can be philosophically demonstrated, though its finer details and practical outcomes require attention to the teaching of Scripture. Several cosmological considerations are employed to show that the cause of the universe can be no less great than the effects. The prime mover must be spiritual, omnipresent, simple and unique. As such, God cannot lack a providential wisdom that rules over all things. This is confirmed by a rehearsal of the design argument. The order and finality that we discern throughout the natural world require an intelligent cause who is no less perfect than the effects. Following Aquinas, providence is located here in the doctrine of God primarily, and in creation secondarily.

---

[6] Reginald Garrigou-Lagrange, *La Providence et la confiance en Dieu: fidélité et abandon* (Paris: Desclée, 1932) was translated by Dom Bede Rose as *Providence* (London: Herder, 1937). A more recent example of Catholic engagement with the theology of providence is Thomas P. Flint, *Divine Providence: The Molinist Account* (Ithaca: Cornell University Press, 1998).

'Providence is the conception in the divine intellect of the order of all things to their end.'[7]

For Garrigou-Lagrange, this is confirmed by Scripture, which offers further insight into divine providence and directs us towards the efficacy of prayer. The teaching of the Old Testament discloses the universality and infallibility of God's providence and its ordering towards a divine mercy and justice. In times of suffering and misfortune, God's wisdom becomes inscrutable, yet the Book of Job reveals that this is sent to test us, as gold is proved in the furnace. Such evils are permitted by God for the sake of some deeper purpose. With some assurance, Garrigou-Lagrange declares that this conclusion of Job is 'obvious'.[8] And the New Testament confirms all this, since Job is a type of Christ. While pointing us towards our heavenly end, its teaching remains mysterious, with respect both to the redemption of the world through the passion of Christ and also to the light and shade of divine election.

There is a strong practical slant in this study, as the original French title suggests. Garrigou-Lagrange's characteristic conjoining of Thomas and St John of the Cross is powerfully attested. We are to apply ourselves to a contemplation of God's being when rising in the morning, through the course of the day and at our nightly rest. And, by attending to God's will in the small duties of quotidian life, we will be overtaken by divine guidance in times of darkness and incomprehension. The more God 'seems to blind their eyes, the saints tell us, the more surely does He lead them, urging them on in their upward course into a land where, as St John of the Cross says, the beaten track has disappeared'.[9] With respect to prayer, providence is to be understood as 'the primary cause of efficacy'.[10] It is not so much that we bend God's will to our own, as that God

---

[7] Garrigou-Lagrange, *Providence*, p. 27.

[8] Ibid., p. 184.

[9] Ibid., p. 203.

[10] Ibid., p. 204.

has ordained that our prayers shall be the intermediary means to some good. This is the guarantee of their validity. Though we often talk as if prayer had its primary source in ourselves, this is only a metaphorical expression, a human way of speaking. Prayer is first ordained by God to some end – our uttering the prayer is only the instrumental cause. In some ways, this solution looks neat. But we might ask whether this makes much sense in relation to how we approach prayer and focus on our own needs and those of others. The spontaneity and responsibility of daily devotion is not much assisted by the thought that God has from eternity determined what ends should be accomplished by our own prayers. Again, the official theology of the church may have to be forgotten or cast to the side in the immediate practice of the faith.

Despite its undoubted spiritual force, particularly in the moving section on praying each day for those who will die, Garrigou-Lagrange's treatment seems strangely detached from any historical context. His reassertion of the Thomist position is clear and incisive, but for the most part there is no full registering of the theodicy problem, nor the difficulties of earlier treatments of providence, nor the humanisation of God with respect to catastrophic and tragic occurrences. Garrigou-Lagrange is confident that the problems are largely resolved in the Book of Job, whereas for many modern commentators the lack of any resolution to Job's questioning is precisely part of its meaning. Similarly, he is sanguine about the extent to which classical philosophy can be seamlessly conjoined to the teaching of Scripture. Reason and faith are aligned; from different starting points, they lead in the same direction, with Scripture confirming and extending what is already knowable from a right use of reason. Providence thus provides a paradigmatic instance of an *articulus mixtus*, one that is shared in part with other schools of thought and religions, while also displaying distinctively Christian traits. This 'strict observance' Thomism has a timeless quality that reflects Garrigou-Lagrange's confidence in the stability of church teaching over against new and modernist trends.[11] Elements of dialectic tension are assigned to the category of a lived mystery into which we are drawn. Yet, to his credit, practical concerns are foregrounded in this work, saving it from an exclusively speculative air, even if these are largely confined to the spiritual life of the individual Christian, as opposed to the church in the world.

Within the Reformed tradition, C. G. Berkouwer offers a similarly robust defence of the tradition in a study first published in Dutch in 1950. By contrast with Garrigou-Lagrange, he claims that providence is not a mixed article comprising philosophical and theological arguments. Rather its proper derivation is only scriptural and it must be affirmed on grounds of faith. Here there is a steady insistence on the rule of God as largely hidden. We cannot see it clearly or speculate on the rationale within each event. To this extent, he is cautioned by the problem of evil and earlier attempts to theorise too glibly about manifestations of God's will. Although the theology of providence is substantially similar to that found in Herman Bavinck's *Reformed Dogmatics*, Berkouwer is less inclined to establish any links with philosophy. In responding to the existential crises of two world wars, he locates providence in Scripture and the doxology of the church. Displaying an embattled quality and situated alongside those 'in storm and night, in distress and fear', faith in providence is asserted in defiance of much counter-evidence.[12]

---

[11] For further discussion of the contours of Garrigou-Lagrange's theology, see Richard Peddicord OP, *The Sacred Monster of Thomism: An Introduction to the Life and Legacy of Reginald Garrigou-Lagrange* (South Bend, IN: St Augustine's Press, 2005), esp. pp. 114–35.

[12] C. G. Berkouwer, *The Providence of God* (Grand Rapids: Eerdmans, 1962), p. 17. Noting its prevalence in philosophy and the history of religions, Bavinck describes providence as a mixed article, though stressing its distinctive intellectual and practical orientation for Christians. 'In Scripture belief in God's providence is absolutely not based solely on God's revelation in nature but much more on his covenant and promises.' *Reformed Dogmatics, Volume 2: God and Creation* (Grand Rapids: Eerdmans, 2009), p. 594.

Despite its awareness of the shifts in historical context, Berkouwer's treatment reflects his preference for much of the earlier Reformed confessional tradition. He reacts critically to what he perceives as the universalist and overly speculative nature of Barth's revisionism (for which, see section 5.4). His defence of the threefold form of providence includes a nuanced treatment of the *concursus Dei*. The ways in which God concurs with every creaturely action avoid a pantheism in which the divine and human are confused, a deism in which they are disjoined and the deplorable position that makes God responsible for evil. Within a constrained setting, the distinction between God's active willing and permitting can be employed, although there is never a bare permitting that does not see God fully engaged with each particular. Yet, in exploring the various formulations of Bavinck, Kuyper and Berkhof, he struggles to come to an adequate account of what is involved in concurrence without lapsing into either a baleful determinism or a mere enabling. Berkouwer concludes that, in the end, this remains a mysterious relation to be apprehended by faith. 'This inscrutability need not shock us nor fill us with a panic which might haunt our entire lives. The problem is resolved, though not rationally, in the confession of guilt and in faith.'[13] Yet, it is not clear how this achieves much more than restating the problem identified at the outset, rather than resolving it. The altered context in which the theology of providence has to be pursued is noted, yet the content remains largely that of the seventeenth-century Reformed tradition. For Berkouwer, the reassertion of this tradition remains paramount. 'To persist in unconverted thinking is, in the end, to shove our own guilt and responsibility aside.'[14] This declaration looks like a conversation stopper.

In fairness to Berkouwer, there comes a point when an appeal to incomprehensibility and mystery will need to be made by the

---

[13] Berkouwer, *The Providence of God*, 133.
[14] Ibid.

theologian. The dialectical tension between the way the world appears to us and the way God intends it to be is pronounced. We walk not by sight but by faith. But this seems to be his only concession to the problems identified above. Where explanations are lacking, we must abandon reason and commit to faith, confessing our guilt and trusting in the mercy of God.[15] In this vein, we can affirm the divine providence that constantly rules the world and each human life. While Berkouwer retrieves the classical Reformed view, his affirmation of providence is sombre and beleaguered. And, despite his commitment to Scripture, one consequence of this slant is a failure fully to register those elements in Scripture which attest God's providence in the regular patterns of the natural and social worlds. The Noahic covenant is treated primarily in terms of God's forbearance, rather than as affording possibilities for order, wisdom and blessing.[16]

Though both Garrigou-Lagrange and Berkouwer mount rearguard actions in defence of their ecclesial traditions, the latter displays a keener awareness of the modern crisis surrounding the theology of providence. For Garrigou-Lagrange, by contrast, attention to the contextuality of knowledge claims merely represents a slippery slope to modernism. Berkouwer's work has a sombre post-war character which places him firmly alongside other mid-century Protestant theologians. Yet, in other respects, Garrigou-Lagrange's treatise fares better at registering the different aspects of divine providence in creation, redemption and eschatological fulfilment. His commitments to Thomist philosophy serve him well in respect of articulating a richer theology of creation and redemption within which providence can be situated. Multiple dimensions

[15] 'The problem of theodicy is insoluble outside of a faith that knows the limits of human reason. According to revelation, the confidence of faith in God's holy direction of the world is possible only in the recognition of his guilt.' Ibid., p. 266.

[16] 'Only as He is seen, as He reveals Himself to be the longsuffering God in the redemption of the world in Christ, can we understand and confess Providence as sustenance.' Ibid., p. 80.

are incorporated, if rather timelessly. To that extent, his greater interest in philosophy may avoid a constriction of his providential thinking. Berkouwer's work suffers from a disproportionate focus on one problem alone, with a resultant tendency to provide only one type of response in terms of faith, confession of guilt and trust in divine mercy.

The efforts of Garrigou-Lagrange and Berkouwer are not lacking in intellectual rigour either. In their different ways, each is instructive. But these hardly take us beyond the impasse registered by Gilkey, which has determined other twentieth-century reconstructions of the theology of providence. To assess more revisionist treatments of the subject, we turn to writers prepared to break out in quite different directions.

5.3 Revisionism Type One: God As Persuasive

A plethora of revisionist proposals has emerged which offer a modified account of providence in response to the difficulties that have beset earlier approaches. We can detect several recurrent anxieties, including the following: the prevalence of evil in quantitative and qualitative degrees that defy all traditional theodicies; the unevenly distributed fortunes of human beings; the comprehensiveness of natural explanation; and the offensiveness of a God who seemingly chooses to intervene occasionally, but not often or always, to mitigate particular sufferings. In the face of these difficulties, some writers have suggested that the classical idea of divine providence should be abandoned altogether in favour of a less determinist account which promises intellectual and practical advantages.[17] This

---

[17] Within Jewish theology, Richard L. Rubinstein has argued that the God of providence is no longer believable after Auschwitz. His claim appears to have been driven by the Christian proposal that the Shoah was a judgement upon the people of Israel under divine providence. This is explained in the second edition of *After Auschwitz: History, Theology and Contemporary Judaism* (Baltimore: Johns Hopkins University Press,

is evidently the case in those approaches that might be labelled as open or relational theism. Each converges on the notion of God as persuasive rather than controlling.

5.3.1 Process Theology

Originating with the work of A. N. Whitehead in the 1920s, process theology offers a radical re-description of the being of God in relation to the world. Divine openness is not the result of a voluntary act of self-renunciation occasioned by the act of creation. The process of persuasion is part of the ontological constitution of the God–world relationship governed by an eternal interdependence. Whitehead eschews the metaphors of God as monarch, law-giver and prime mover in favour of a persuasive love that is in greater accord with the teaching and example of Jesus. 'God is the poet of the world, with tender patience leading it by his vision of truth, beauty and goodness.'[18] For process thought, all entities embody two (dipolar) aspects of creativity, albeit in significantly varying degrees – the power of self-determination and the power to influence others. This creative action is expressed both by God, who eternally accompanies all non-divine occasions, and by individuals. As such, God 'is the only primordial, omnipresent, all-inclusive embodiment of creativity'.[19] Characterised primarily in terms of love, God's power is both active and receptive, with the result that the divine mode of action is consistently evocative, rather than coercive. By nature, rather than by choice, God lacks any unilateral power to produce *ex nihilo* or to coerce individuals. Power is shared essentially and not by divine fiat.

1992), pp. 168–79. In the first edition (1966), he had written, 'We stand in a cold, silent, unfeeling cosmos, unaided by any purposeful power beyond our own resources. After Auschwitz, what else can a Jew say about God.' Ibid., p. 172.

[18] Alfred North Whitehead, *Process and Reality* (New York: Free Press, 1978), p. 347.

[19] David Ray Griffin, *Evil Revisited: Responses and Reconsiderations* (Albany, NY: State University of New York, 1991), p. 23.

In relation to providence, this account has some obvious attractions. God does not cease to be active after creating the world, as in some forms of deism. Nor does God have a power which is unexercised – this avoids questions about the lack of divine action. The doctrine of God enunciated by process thinkers results in a model of divine action that is persuasive but limited by the conditions of material existence. This suggests some providential directionality in the history of the cosmos, for example in the realisation of conscious individuals with a capacity for love of God and neighbour, knowledge of the world, and aesthetic pleasures. Patterns and tendencies can be discerned which attest the influence of God, though these are often frustrated and arrested with an admixture of pain, suffering and evil. Given the freedom of non-divine individuals, this is an inevitable consequence of a world continually in development. 'God's creative activity is exercised as an influence which seeks to "lure" or "persuade" each concrescing occasion to actualize that form which will result eventually in the greatest aesthetic satisfaction overall.'[20]

Process theology has the advantage of facilitating a concept of divine action as constant and effective, but limited in a manner commensurate with creaturely freedom and material recalcitrance. God can attract but not coerce, influence but not override, evoke but not control. Theologians have drawn upon the resources of process thought to rearticulate notions of creation through struggle and to describe the manner in which divine influence can be exerted in a panpsychist universe.[21] With respect to this latter point, its account of spiritual influence has some potential to characterise at

---

[20] David A. Pailin, *God and the Processes of Reality: Foundations of a Credible Theism* (London: Routledge, 1989), pp. 139–40.

[21] In what follows, I am grateful to Joanna Leidenhag for drawing my attention to the pneumatological possibilities of panpsychism outside the parameters of process thought. Now receiving renewed philosophical attention, panpsychism may also be able to accommodate patterns of emergence and to provide a suitable aid to thinking further about divine action.

least one mode of divine action.[22] Where each entity has a subjective or mental pole, it has some capacity, however minimal, by virtue of its awareness (prehension) of the surrounding environment, to respond to the lure and presence of the divine. This spiritual interaction can be effective for the development and realisation of finite individuals, particularly (though not exclusively) self-conscious human agents. And the wider scope of process thought on this matter may also have some important ecological gains which counteract the anthropocentrism noted at the outset of this chapter. In this way, an omnipresent divine spirit might be communicative and influential in facilitating outcomes that would not otherwise be likely. Such spiritual interaction would be the result of the divine presence acting not coercively but through something akin to a steady pressure. In some circumstances, this may result in sudden breakthroughs which in retrospect have the legitimate appearance of unexpected interruptions of God's grace. An understanding of petitionary prayer may emerge here in terms of its contributing to an overall spiritual environment in which the energy of God can become more effective.[23] And, beyond the framework of process metaphysics, a description of divine omnipresence may enable clearer specification of one mode of divine activity, perhaps to be appropriated to the third person of the Trinity.[24]

Several theologians have drawn upon the insights of process theology, partly in order to find a conceptuality that offers a radical

---

[22] See Pailin, *God and the Processes of Reality*, pp. 141–2.

[23] See for example Marjorie Hewitt Suchocki, *In God's Presence: Theological Reflections on Prayer* (St Louis: Chalice Press, 1996). This material is developed in the following chapter.

[24] Writers who otherwise have little affinity with process metaphysics generate statements of divine action which display some striking similarities. For example, Rowan Williams writes of God's power as a 'steady swell of loving presence'. See *Tokens of Trust: An Introduction to Christian Belief* (Norwich: Canterbury Press, 2007), p. 44.

alternative to traditional patterns of thought. In his later work, Gilkey himself moved in this direction, though there are few traces of it in his 1963 diagnosis. In *Reaping the Whirlwind*, divine action is reduced to the ground and enablement of the freedom that we realise in history. To articulate this, Gilkey draws increasingly upon the work of Whitehead and Tillich. From the mid-1970s onwards, he appears to have found this to be more intellectually defensible, while also more adequate to the spiritual life and the requirements of religious pluralism. His mature account of providence seems far removed from the neighbourhood of neo-orthodoxy occupied in his earlier work. 'God is being as the source and continuing ground of the flux and becoming of the actuality that we are and that forms our destiny.'[25] Gary Dorrien perceptively describes this as a rendition of providence that retains the elements of divine preservation and *concursus* but without governance.[26]

Despite its possibilities, process theology, as a systematic project, faces formidable criticism from more traditional quarters. Dan Migliore has remarked that 'process theodicy is arguably the most comprehensive and consistent of modern theodicies, but at the same time it may also be the one most distant from the biblical witness.'[27] Given the losses incurred by process metaphysics in relation to some core theological commitments, this seems a fair judgement. At least three vital elements of Christian theology are sacrificed or muted through this approach. The first of these is the concept of creation out of nothing, which expresses the ontological priority and independence of God in relation to the world. This notion is discarded in favour of an ontology in which God and the world are eternally united as two necessary aspects of the process of creativity. Consequently, the notion of a general providence

[25] Gilkey, *Reaping the Whirlwind*, p. 253.

[26] Gary Dorrien, 'Modernism as a theological problem: the theological legacy of Langdon Gilkey', *American Journal of Theology & Philosophy*, 28.2 (2007), 64–94 at 88.

[27] Daniel Migliore, *Faith Seeking Understanding* (Grand Rapids: Eerdmans, 1991), p. 112.

discerned in the laws of nature and the regularity of the physical world is difficult to attribute to divine intentionality. If we cannot conceive of God bringing the material world into being *ex nihilo*, then the endowment of nature with a creative potential can only in part be attributed to God's presence. While process thinkers have attempted (somewhat obscurely) to view the direction of evolution in terms of divine allurement at critical junctures, it is much harder to see how the laws which govern material processes can themselves be the result of a divine endowment of nature.[28] A second and parallel difficulty in this account of divine persuasion is that eschatological outcomes seem far from guaranteed. On this description of God's relationship to the world, a divine overruling that brings about a new creation does not appear to be a possibility. One might hope for the emergence of a better world than the one we presently experience, but a general resurrection for all non-divine creatures is excluded.[29] And, thirdly, the performative actions of God which typify Christian faith, particularly the person and work of Christ, are further problematised. These might be handled in terms of influence and inspiration, yet this only further illustrates the way in which, for process theology, divine action is reduced everywhere to one single mode and possibility. Instead of a Trinitarian differentiation of agency types, we have one exclusive form characterised along pneumatological lines.[30]

---

[28] In this respect, there are some surprising similarities between the process approach to evolution and intelligent design theory. This is recognised by Catherine Keller, *On the Mystery: Discerning God in Process* (Philadelphia: Fortress, 2008), pp. 61–2.

[29] In fairness, David Ray Griffin argues that process theology can accommodate a commitment to the immortality of the soul, a view to which Whitehead remained open. See David Ray Griffin, 'Process theology and the Christian good news: a response to classical free will theism' in John B. Cobb Jr and Clark H. Pinnock (eds.), *Searching for an Adequate God: A Dialogue Between Process and Free Will Theists* (Grand Rapids: Eerdmans, 2000), pp. 1–38 at p. 3. One might also posit some attenuated form of immortality through a divine prehension of all past life forms.

[30] Gunton's memorable description of the God of process theology as 'the moved unmover' may not be entirely accurate, given the effects of allurement. But in relation

Given its metaphysical terms of reference, process theology cannot easily qualify or augment its understanding of divine limitation. This is built into the fabric of the God–world relationship and must remain an integral feature of the divine being, which cannot act in ways postulated by more traditional forms of Christian theism. God's limits are not the result of a voluntary self-imposition; the constraints are not willed, so much as ontically necessitated. In this respect, the process model derives its support from moral and psychological considerations. Like a good parent or friend, God will always 'let be'. This is a condition of love which cannot admit coercion or control, except perhaps as a last resort accompanied by regret.[31] The divine does not act at all except by patience and persuasion. God's perfection is adjudged to take this form – a view that is confirmed owing to its coherence, applicability and consonance with our best ethical and religious insights.[32]

Yet even here process thought is exposed to challenge. If we follow the model of parenthood, then we may have to acknowledge that there are boundary situations in which intervention is entirely appropriate, as well as decisions about whether, when and how often to have children. The parent may aim at some restraint and recognise the importance of 'letting be', even when mistakes will ensue. But this does not exhaust the range of available and

---

to much that has been constitutive of credal Christianity, it seems apposite. See Colin E. Gunton, *Becoming and Being: The Doctrines of God in Charles Hartshorne and Karl Barth* (Oxford: Oxford University Press, 1978), p. 41.

[31] See John B. Cobb Jr and David Ray Griffin, *Process Theology: An Introductory Exposition* (Philadelphia: Westminster, 1976), pp. 53–4, and Keller, *On the Mystery*, p. 88.

[32] See Lewis S. Ford, *The Lure of God: A Biblical Background for Process Theism* (Philadelphia: Fortress, 1978), p. 27. More recently, G. Michael Zbaraschuk has argued that the Whiteheadian God affords a 'wider, stronger and more adequate view'. *The Purposes of God: Providence as Process-Historical Liberation* (Eugene, OR: Pickwick, 2015), pp. 93–8.

appropriate actions, especially given the asymmetry of a relationship that includes some elements of direction, control and dependence. Of course, to admit this will only reintroduce the theodicy problem that process theologians are generally resolved to avoid. But, as a comment on an argument that surfaces in defence of process thought, this requires consideration. The salient point here is that a God whose relationship to the world includes elements of initiation (creation), performative interaction (revelation) and resolution (eschatology) may be morally and spiritually more effective than the God of process thought. And this consideration cuts across the claim that process thought is more consonant with our best ethical and religious insights.[33] To put it crudely, a God who can and will eventually coerce in order to realise moral goals is of greater utility than a God who could never do this.

Somewhat ironically, process theodicy tends also to eliminate those elements of complaint, *aporia* and divine silence that are registered in the face of intense and persistent evils. These feature in the Psalms, Job and (arguably) Jesus' cry of dereliction. Times and places where God is silent and unresponsive can be readily explained by process thought – God is present but unable to do more – but the hurling of such questions at a God who is largely a helpless bystander seems pointless. The validity of anger and indignation in some situations requires a God with sufficient capacity to do something, if not now, then in the future. The protest and impatience that characterises human distress *coram Deo* reposes upon an understanding of divine sovereignty that is generally unavailable in process metaphysics. This argument is not intended as a cheap dialectical trick – its scope is very restricted. But it may point to the way in which emotions of anger and expressions of complaint, like those

---

[33] This is argued by David Basinger, *Divine Power in Process Theism: A Philosophical Critique* (Albany, NY: State University of New York, 1988). Process theists, he concludes, should concede 'that divine noncoercion is an unfortunate metaphysical limitation' (p. 52).

of gratitude and praise, require an appropriate focus of address and so make sense only in a specific context.

A striking example of this absence of divine speech is found in Shūsaku Endō's novel *Silence* (1966). In the face of intense and almost unbearable persecution at the hands of the authorities, Rodrigues, the Jesuit priest, is overpowered by the silence of God. No sign is given to relieve the unremitting misery and horror of what his Japanese companions suffer. There is no resolution for him in a quick and glorious martyrdom. Haunted by doubt and the complexity of his position, he finally apostatises to relieve the suffering of others. As he does so, he finds the presence of Christ in his humiliation. But the silence of God is real. In eschewing speech, God seems to lead him another way. Or at least this is one reading that is held open by the text. The intensity of the silence, however, seems to require the possibility of speech.[34]

5.3.2 *Open Theism*

Since the 1970s, a further range of models for divine providence has been developed, mainly through concerted attempts to develop an account that avoids both an overbearing determinism and a deist standoff. These models can be grouped under the rubric of open or relational theism. Other traditions reflect similar tendencies, including several Anglican writers who have anticipated some elements of open theism.[35] Allied to the stress on a continual asymmetric divine–human partnership, there is often an appropriation of the concept of kenosis to the first article of the faith. Formerly deployed as a Christological notion to describe God's self-accommodation to an incarnate condition, kenosis has more recently featured in

---

[34] Shūsaku Endō, *Silence*, trans. William Johnston (New York: Picador, 2016), p. 147.

[35] John Polkinghorne explicitly presents this notion as a *via media* which avoids both deism and determinism. See *Science and Providence: God's Interaction with the World* (London: SCM, 1989), pp. 36–44.

theologies of creation. In willing a world that is granted a contingent shape and order, God allows the cosmos to proceed according to natural laws and evolving processes. This condition is conceded, as it were, so that God's relationship with the cosmos respects the integrity of its original endowment.[36] Hence a kenotic creation is constrained by the forms of human autonomy and divine action. God works in, with and through causal agencies while continuing to respect their ways of working. At least four models are worth mention as explications of this theme.[37]

William James first introduced the idea of the celestial chessmaster in an essay suggesting the possibility of divine interaction without determinism.[38] This has been developed by Peter Geach in his study *Providence and Evil* (1977). God is likened to a grand chessmaster with a capacity to compute all the possible moves of an opponent while also possessing a strategy of responding to each one of these in order to secure a complete victory. Although God does not control the moves of the opponent, nevertheless God can respond to any move of the opponent's with an appropriate counter-strategy. Hence there is a genuine interaction of players in a game that is bound by its own set of rules, though in this contest

---

[36] Jürgen Moltmann employs the kabbalistic notion of 'zimzum' to articulate this sense of a kenotic creation. But his suggestion that an act of divine self-retraction generates a space, i.e. nothingness, in which the world can be situated seems overly speculative. See *God in Creation* (London: SCM, 1985), pp. 86–93.

[37] Other possible models could be derived from musical performance, particularly with respect to the improvisational elements of jazz. This is the preferred image in Ann Pederson, *God, Creation and All that Jazz: A Process of Composition and Improvisation* (St Louis: Chalice Press, 2001). One difficulty, however, is whether jazz is as unstructured or classical music as rigid as Pederson suggests. See for example Bruce Ellis Benson, 'Improvising texts, Improvising communities: jazz, interpretation, heterophony, and the *ekklesia*' in Jeremy S. Begbie and Steven R. Guthrie (eds.), *Resonant Witness: Conversations Between Music and Theology* (Grand Rapids: Eerdmans, 2011), pp. 295–322.

[38] William James, *The Will to Believe and Other Essays in Popular Philosophy* (New York: Longmans, Green & Co., 1897), pp. 180–3.

the general direction and eventual outcomes are always established by God.[39]

In the model of improvised theatre, we have a setting, a director and a given set of characters.[40] Yet these are able to develop their identities, as the actors judge fit. As the play unfolds, the *dramatis personae* exercise a degree of freedom and creativity, while the director seeks to instil some direction and meaning within the proceedings. Drawing on the work of Peter Brook, theatre and film director, Gorringe notes that the worst director of all may be 'the honourable unassuming one' who develops a habit of non-intervention by conceding too much to the players.[41] In this interplay of forces, both the director and the actors have creative roles. One might also include the audience here – their interactions with the cast can significantly shape the performance. In this 'rough theatre', the audience joins the cast and answers back in ways that absorb and haunt all the participants. The final production is the result of a complex set of interactions. Each party is constrained by an initial identification, but the overall outcomes reflect the initiatives, tensions and reactions between the characters and the director.

In the example of the Persian carpet-maker, one which I first heard in John Lucas's philosophy of religion seminar in Oxford in the early 1980s, the expert engages an apprentice child in the business. They sit at either end of the rug and together weave a single design into the fabric. The apprentice child makes many mistakes and departs from the initial plans, but so skilful is the parent that each mistake can be accommodated into a revised version of the original

---

[39] Peter Geach, *Providence and Evil* (Cambridge: Cambridge University Press, 1977), p. 58.

[40] The best example is T. J. Gorringe, *God's Theatre: A Theology of Providence* (London: SCM, 1991), esp. pp. 69–87. The example of improvised theatre is developed by Sam Wells in the context of Christian practice. See *Improvisation: The Drama of Christian Ethics* (Grand Rapids: Brazos, 2004), pp. 59–70. Wells makes the telling point that originality is a sin in improvised theatre.

[41] Gorringe, *God's Theatre*, p. 79.

design to produce a final product displaying its own overall pattern and unity. 'The children fail to carry out their father's instructions exactly, but so great is their father's skill, that he adapts his design at his end to take in each error at his children's end, and work it into a new, constantly adapted, pattern.'[42] Lucas goes on to argue that God has no single 'best possible' plan for each of us. There is an infinity of plans, at least one of which can be providentially adapted to shifting circumstances. This point is not without pastoral significance in situations of major disruption and turmoil.

Finally, there is the image of a family life in which the accommodation of members of a household to one another's habits and life stories takes a direction that is neither completely random nor set along a common and preconceived trajectory. This is illustrated in a celebrated passage from W. H. Vanstone.

> A happy family life is neither a static situation nor a smooth and direct progression: it is an angular process, the endless improvisation of love to correct that which it has itself created. Parents will testify that their equal love for two children must express itself in quite different ways; and that what they have learned in bringing up the elder can be no programme for bringing up the younger. The care of children teaches us that the resolute and unfailing will of love becomes active in improvised and ever-precarious endeavour.[43]

Each model has something to commend it, although inevitably all are limited. The chessmaster and the carpet-maker analogies perhaps render providence too individualised – God does much more than act one on one with human persons, although this may be part of it. Perhaps the more social analogy of family life comes closest to the intimacy and relationality of a covenant partnership, although it too does not wholly capture the wider nexus of relationships

---

[42] J. R. Lucas, *Freedom and Grace* (London: SPCK, 1976), p. 39.

[43] W. H. Vanstone, *Love's Endeavour, Love's Expense* (London: Darton, Longman and Todd, 1977), p. 47.

and events which shape our identities. But the notion of divine overruling which informs Christian eschatology seems to be absent in this model, unlike the chessmaster analogy. Yet it does provide an insight into how parental love might be adapted and improvised to provide the least misleading of creaturely analogies to divine providence. The image of God as theatre director captures best the ontological asymmetry of the divine–human partnership and the different modes of divine action – the director's position transcends that of the actors and can both circumscribe it while also working more laterally with the human resources available. But, as with all aesthetic images, including the carpet-maker, it risks suggesting that every detail contributes to an overall harmony. Without some surd or discordant elements, the wider whole to which these contribute would be diminished; here lies one of the besetting temptations of theodicy.[44]

What these models achieve is their expression of divine providence as involving an assymetric partnership and a measure of improvisation. God's work is adapted or accommodated to the constraints of creaturely materials. Both notions – partnership and improvisation – are inherent in scriptural accounts of covenant. In directing our thinking, each image strains towards an alternative to the classical idea of God willing everything, with its accompanying diminution of any divine interaction within nature and history.

My principal criticism is not with the validity of these models, which have much pneumatological potential. But, as systematic accounts of divine providence, they have a tendency to funnel all thinking about divine action, as if it must take only one form or mode. If instead we have a differentiated account of the forms of divine providence then a multiplicity of models may be required

---

[44] Rowan Williams points out that this temptation has long been present in the Christian tradition. 'Reply [to Marilyn McCord Adams]: redeeming sorrows' in D. Z. Phillips (ed.), *Religion and Morality* (New York: St Martin's Press, 1996), pp. 132–48 at p. 135.

to characterise its several manifestations. To reduce these to one modality alone is to inhibit the full range of actions that the distribution of providence across the various articles of faith requires. Again, we see the importance of avoiding the construction of providence as a single doctrine or a piece within a theological jigsaw which accounts for one problem or offers a single construction of divine agency.

This difficulty can be highlighted by attending to the relational construction of providence in one important recent version of open or free-will theism. This represents a body of philosophical literature – described as 'open theism' but representing one variant of the position described in this section – that converges on several revisionist claims challenging traditional notions of divine foreknowledge, determinism and providential control.[45] A dissatisfaction with Calvinist and Molinist accounts of divine omniscience is typically expressed on the grounds that these are intellectually incoherent, scripturally inadequate and theologically unhelpful. A universe that is perfectly foreknown by God is not one in which human freedom or divine improvisation can be exercised. Hence, attempts to reconcile theological determinism and human freedom must fail, with the result that vital notions of responsibility are lost. A scriptural account of divine interaction with human agents requires an openness in the created order that facilitates both divine initiative and human response. And this, it is further argued, has the added theological advantage that evil outcomes can be viewed as consequences of a general order that is sustained by God but not willed 'meticulously' in every particular outcome. To this extent,

---

[45] For a theological overview of open theism thus construed, see Clark Pinnock, Richard Rice, John Sanders, William Hasker and David Basinger, *The Openness of God: A Biblical Challenge to the Traditional Understanding of God* (Downer's Grove, IL: IVP, 1994). For two subsequent and impressive defences of its key tenets, see William Hasker, *Providence, Evil and the Openness of God* (London: Routledge, 2004), and John Sanders, *The God Who Risks: A Theology of Divine Providence*, 2nd edn (Downer's Grove, IL: IVP, 2007).

there is a kenotic element within much open theism. As a philosophical position, this resonates with the models of providence described above, and its key tenets may be necessary conditions for these notions of partnership and improvisation.[46]

The doctrinal loyalties of open theism tend to lie with Arminianism, although its goes beyond strict adherence to the position of the Remonstrants by either denying or abridging full divine foreknowledge. To this extent, it has some historical affinities with Socinianism.[47] For Arminius and his followers, divine election reposed upon God's foreknowledge of our free choice. For open theism typically, there is no comprehensive foreknowledge. Our final eschatological destiny is in part a function of our eventual choices. This has given rise to the hypothesis of post-mortem evangelism in elements of the literature.[48]

The opposition that open theism has attracted is largely owing to its abandonment of divine foreknowledge and the embracing of a 'risk-filled' world in which God must relinquish control of events and outcomes. While attempts to resolve this by appealing to God's resourcefulness have some purchase, one is left unsure whether final outcomes can really be secured by divine action. Indeed, some exponents of open theism have pushed further in this direction.

Tom Oord's bold and impressive defence of a risk-taking, kenotic God leads him to affirm that God does not merely permit evil effects, but that God is essentially incapable of doing otherwise. What on one account is deemed a voluntary permission or withholding of power becomes here an essential incapacity. Given the nature of God's being, which must concede autonomy to

---

[46] Earlier philosophical exponents of open theism such as Keith Ward and John Lucas have also been advocates of this sort of providentialism.

[47] John M. Frame claims that Socinianism is the 'missing link in open theism's genealogy'. See *No Other God: A Response to Open Theism* (Phillipsburg, NJ: P&R Publishing, 2001), pp. 32–6.

[48] See for example Clark Pinnock, *A Wideness in God's Mercy: Jesus Christ in a World of Religions* (Grand Rapids: Zondervan, 1992), pp. 168–72.

creatures in a law-governed world, God cannot intervene to prevent evils. Oord indeed regards this commitment as necessary 'to solve the problem of evil'.[49] This then raises issues of what capacities God actually possesses and how these can be exercised. At this point, the position seems to slide towards that of process theology with its affirmation of the potential for divine persuasion. The limits of this persuasion are set by the need to respect human free choice, with the result that divine action cannot guarantee any definite future state.[50] Oord attempts to offset this by reframing the concept of a miracle along the lines of divine influence having some exceptionally beneficial results in individual cases. This works largely through God's suggesting or prompting, but never coercing, particular events. Oord maintains that the miracle stories documented in Scripture do not have recourse to divine compulsion, but represent dramatic accounts of God's spirit working in and through creaturely agencies, particularly human ones. This view has some traction, though it is not without its difficulties. Special divine action is presumably required via the firing of some relevant neurons in the human brain for God's suggestions to be communicated, which implies that God has power to intervene in causal processes. Oord might legitimately reply that this mode of divine activity is possible for God, because it does not break the non-coercion principle by which God is essentially bound. But, if this is the only possible mode of divine action, then other possibilities seem to be excluded, especially the raising of Jesus from the dead and the eschatological consummation of which this is an anticipatory sign. These present as performative acts of God rather than unusual instances of a more universal spiritual influence at work in human lives.[51]

---

[49] Thomas Jay Oord, *The Uncontrolling Love of God: An Open and Relational Account of Providence* (Downer's Grove, IL: IVP, 2015), 169.

[50] With this significant modification of any eschatological prospect, there is an accompanying adjustment of the doctrine of creation out of nothing.

[51] In response, John Sanders argues that Oord can either resolve the problem of evil through his theory of essential kenosis or else offer an adequate account of miracles,

One of the programmatic weaknesses of open theism as a total worldview is that its exponents tend to construct it as the solution to a compatibility problem – either the antinomy of divine fore-knowledge and human freedom, or that of divine love and manifest suffering.[52] Yet the theology of providence will be misrepresented or unduly restricted when it appears as the solution to a philosophical problem. This is not to deny either that these problems are genuine or that theologians should not be able to offer some response. But the richness of a theology of providence should not be lost on account of its functioning solely or primarily as the answer to a single intractable question. Here is an instance of the requirements of epistemological simplicity (coherence) and metaphysical richness (adequacy) pulling in different directions. A tendency to over-simplify scriptural material or to over-determine human freedom may result in a disproportionate emphasis upon risk. To this extent, anxieties around risk theories are not wholly misplaced. Some narrowing of focus, moreover, is also evident in the preoccupation with the vertical relationship of God and the individual person. While this again represents one important form of divine–human interaction, it does not exhaust the multiple ways in which the creation is governed by God's providence. Attention to the wider fields of nature and history as determined by divine governance is largely

---

but that he cannot do both consistently. 'Why Oord's essential kenosis model fails to solve the problem of evil while retaining miracles', *Wesleyan Theological Journal*, 51.2 (2016), 174–87.

[52] In fairness, this is generally regarded as the necessary setting for some wider theological claims and scriptural interpretation. See Clark Pinnock, 'Systematic theology' in Pinnock et al., *The Openness of God*, pp. 101–25. Yet, as Bruce McCormack has strikingly observed, the scheme is generally established without sufficient reference to central Christological claims and so displays a rather abstract philosophical cast. A consequence is that the Christological determining of the world, as attested in several key New Testament passages, is never fully registered. See 'The actuality of God: Karl Barth in conversation with open theism' in Bruce L. McCormack (ed.), *Engaging the Doctrine of God: Contemporary Protestant Perspectives* (Grand Rapids: Baker, 2008), pp. 185–242, esp. pp. 199–201.

absent. This lacuna may again be the result of a restricted attention to one set of problems of a more philosophical cast.

Leaving aside questions of scriptural interpretation, which are seldom resolved by appeals to isolated texts, we should note that the principal objection to open theism appears to be its loss of divine sovereignty.[53] While in some respects it has an 'existential fit'[54], the pastoral nervousness generated by such a scenario is a legitimate anxiety. To introduce this risky element into the creation threatens to frustrate God, it is claimed, and so to introduce a sinister uncertainty and loss of confidence in the Christian life.[55] Whatever pastoral gains it achieves in accommodating a sense of divine love and pathos will be lost as the world spirals out of control and the objects of Christian hope cease to be 'sure and certain'. What responses might one then offer which enable the harnessing of the best insights of open theism without abandoning a commitment to divine sovereignty?

Two comments may be ventured. The first is that the loss of an exhaustive divine foreknowledge does not exclude the possibility of a highly extensive set of well-grounded beliefs about agents and their decisions on the part of God. These might come close to equating, in content if not epistemic status, with divine foreknowledge, which may in turn give God more than is needed to exercise the forms of providence that are attested in Scripture. As an open theist, John Sanders argues for a 'dynamic omniscience' that may characterise God's comprehensive knowledge without requiring the inclusion

---

[53] This explains the force of the conservative counterblast literature. For a robust example of such, see Frame, *No Other God*.

[54] See Clark Pinnock, *Most Moved Mover: A Theology of God's Openness* (Grand Rapids: Baker, 2001), pp. 153–78.

[55] 'While claiming to offer meaningfulness to Christian living, open theism strips the believer of the one thing needed most for a meaningful and vibrant life of faith: absolute confidence in God's character, wisdom, word, promise, and the sure fulfilment of his will.' Bruce A. Ware, *God's Lesser Glory: The Diminished God of Open Theism* (Wheaton, IL: Crossway, 2000), p. 21.

of all future-tense and, therefore open contingent, statements.[56] In any case, the form that divine perfection takes in an open world may be rather different from that of a closed world. The God of an open theism does not reflect a reduced or diminished creator, only one who is committed to working in ways that involve cooperation, partnership and self-abasement. It may reasonably be argued that, without a world that includes a measure of openness, divine perfection cannot take the form in which it is expressed in Scripture. 'If we insist that everything God tries to bring about must surely happen, we restrict the operation of the Holy Spirit, which works through human agents, and depends essentially on human co-operation.'[57] While this claim does not exhaust the forms of divine action, it expresses one important instance.

This seems to me the contribution of open theism: while it does not offer a comprehensive account of providence, it successfully identifies a vital function of the Holy Spirit that is central to the Christian life, but one which has hitherto been conceptually squeezed by systematic formulations. And it can be argued that it emerges not via an independent philosophical argument about maximally perfect divine attributes but as the conceptual scheme most appropriate to religious insights regarding God's ways with the world. The creator of an open universe is not diminished in perfection for failing to deliver a deterministic product.

[56] Sanders, *The God Who Risks*, pp. 206–9. It is possible for exponents of open theism either to deny the principle of bivalence (i.e. that every statement must be true or false) or to assert that the truth value of future-tense statements is essentially unknowable, even for God. Against this, Bruce R. Reichenbach has argued that a complete divine omniscience is compatible with libertarian freedom, thus avoiding any need for its abridgement to protect the openness of the future. See *Divine Providence: God's Love and Human Freedom* (Eugene, OR: Cascade, 2016), pp. 151–70.

[57] J. R. Lucas, 'Foreknowledge and vulnerability of God' in Godfrey Vesey (ed.), *The Philosophy in Christianity*, Royal Institute of Philosophy Lecture Series 25 (Cambridge: Cambridge University Press, 1989), pp. 119–28 at pp. 121–2.

Second, a world that is open with respect to some of its causal effects may also be (happily) limited at the beginning and end by divine grace. If we find our powers of freedom overtaken by the mercy of God, then this may be an occasion not for grumbling about loss of autonomy but for celebrating the limits of its damage excess. To this end, the stress on 'risk' may need to be heavily qualified and restricted in ways that significantly qualify what is 'open'. Although a full account of divine providence should capture elements integral to an open theism, a witness to its closure and boundedness is also demanded. That the world is finally determined in the ways announced by Jesus – the kingdom of God is at hand – is neither negotiable nor defeasible. With Jesus' resurrection from the dead, the victory of God is already promised, anticipated and guaranteed for the whole cosmos. In the end, God still loves us anyway. This claim can be juxtaposed alongside recognition of elements of interim openness in the creation. Our freedom is bounded by grace and so cannot finally frustrate the promises of God. A necessary component of Christian hope is that elements of risk are thus constrained and eventually overcome.

5.4 Revisionism Type Two: Christological Determinism in Karl Barth

In the theology of Karl Barth, one of the most sustained twentieth-century readings of providence can be located. Although it may not be the high point of his *Church Dogmatics*, his work on providence merits sustained attention. Seeking an integrated account in close conversation with the Reformed tradition, Barth nevertheless registers criticisms of its determinism, overly speculative tenor and psychological leanings. The concept of providence requires a much more robust Christological inflection, though this takes places through a revitalising of its threefold form in Reformed orthodoxy. In this account, the sovereignty of God remains paramount, though its material content derives more fully from the person and work of Jesus.[58]

Based on lectures delivered in 1948, Barth's treatment of providence in *Church Dogmatics* III/3 reposes upon the doctrine of election outlined in *Church Dogmatics* II/2. The divine rule over creation serves the eternal election of human beings in Christ. This has both ontic and noetic consequences for the theology of providence. The works of God *ad extra* make sense only by reference to this eternal decision before the foundation of the world. And this is known exclusively on the basis of faith in Jesus Christ, the basis of our election. Hence, the knowledge of divine providence is not shared, even in part, with Stoic philosophy. Given its Christian character, it stands apart from all speculative worldviews. Not to be construed as an *articulus mixtus*, providence cannot be derived from arguments for cosmic order or preservation. For this reason, Barth is reluctant to press the distinction between general and special providence, as if these might denote two separate spheres of divine activity or two different ways in which God can be known.[59]

In his preference for a maximalist account of providence, Barth follows Calvin. The constant involvement of God in the life of the world entails that we cannot think of God as absent, passive or idle.[60] This appears to rule out notions of kenosis or partial withdrawal,

---

[58] In what follows, I have condensed the exposition from my essay on providence in Paul Dafydd Jones and Paul T. Nimmo (eds.), *The Oxford Handbook to Karl Barth* (Oxford: Oxford University Press, in press).

[59] On this point, as well as many others, Barth stands close to Schleiermacher. '[T]he world of nature is not to be considered as going its own ways on the strength of the divine preservation, the divine government only exerting influence on it through special isolated acts, so as to bring it into harmony with the kingdom of grace. To us, rather, the two things are absolutely one, and we have the certainty that from the beginning the whole disposition of nature would have been different had it not been that, after sin, redemption through Christ was determined on for the human race.' F. D. Schleiermacher, *The Christian Faith*, trans. H. R. Mackintosh and J. S. Stewart (Edinburgh: T&T Clark, 1928), p. 723.

[60] Karl Barth, *Church Dogmatics* III/3 (Edinburgh: T&T Clark, 1960), p. 13.

as noted above, though we shall find ways in which Barth characteristically qualifies himself. Yet Barth's repeated insistence that providence is known only through faith, and so tentatively, partially and existentially, sets him apart from Zwingli, Calvin and the older Reformed tradition. Divine providence cannot be read off the pages of history or deduced from natural order or political forces. Here Barth is alert to over-inflated and triumphalist accounts that mistakenly attribute providence to historical figures and movements, not least in Europe in the 1930s. Although this does not exclude our perceiving 'hints and signs' of God's justice and mercy at work in our midst, the Christian should exercise a freedom and caution in affirming these.[61] The fatherly rule of God is known only through the Son. Hence the nature and purpose of divine providence are Christologically determined.

Despite the revisionary elements in his approach, Barth follows a standard pattern of exposition in his treatment of providence. This is governed by two sets of tripartite distinctions. The first views providence under the three headings of divine preservation (*conservatio*), accompanying (*concursus*) and ruling (*gubernatio*). The second set of distinctions is found within the treatment of accompanying and follows a sequence of *praecursus* (preceding), *concursus* (concurring) and *succursus* (succeeding or overruling).[62]

Our affirmation of divine preservation is not the outcome of a cosmological argument regarding the dependence of contingent beings upon a necessary God. A convenient alliance with philosophy is shunned. Preservation is the result of God's mercy to be with us in Christ. 'It is the love of God which preserves the creature.'[63] And we

---

[61] Ibid., p. 23.

[62] Here Barth follows the order of exposition in Heinrich Heppe, *Reformed Dogmatics*, trans. G. T. Thomson (London: Allen and Unwin, 1950), pp. 251–80. This appears to derive in particular from the Leiden Synopsis (1625). For further discussion, see Rinse H. Reeling Brouwer, *Karl Barth and Post-Reformation Orthodoxy* (Farnham: Ashgate, 2015), pp. 91–5.

[63] Barth, *Church Dogmatics* III/3, p. 59.

must think of ourselves as existing not by right, but for the appointed task of being heralds of good news. Hence our preservation is good cause for praise and thanksgiving. The act of conservation also signifies divine opposition to evil. Creation is threatened by nothingness (*das Nichtige*) but the reality of this threat is demonstrated by God's decision to defeat it. Here Barth anticipates the discussion of *das Nichtige* later in *Church Dogmatics* III/3. Jesus has entered upon the dark places of our existence to defeat the 'sinister neighbour'. This finally is why the world is preserved.[64] We are given a time and a place in which to live in accordance with God's great work, and as creatures we are eternally memorialised within the life of God.[65]

When he moves to the divine accompanying of creation, Barth revisits the language of primary and secondary causality and the three aspects of the divine *concursus*. Though noting that the language of causality is not itself biblical, he argues for its usefulness subject to several qualifications.[66] Provided this does not reduce God and creatures to mechanical 'things' or set both under a common genus, the language of causality can be employed. Yet God and creatures must be considered active *subjects* (though quite unlike each other) and not objects.

Where the older theology really falls down, in Barth's estimation, is not in its deployment of causal language but in the material content with which this was invested. The God who was characterised as the primal cause was conceived in too abstract and philosophical a manner. As a result, the first article of the creed became detached from the second – the *prima causa* was insufficiently designated as the Father of Jesus Christ, with the further consequence that the *causae secundae* were not properly viewed as the

---

[64] Ibid., p. 77.

[65] Ibid., p. 90.

[66] For further discussion, see McCormack, 'The actuality of God', pp. 225–31, and Darren Kennedy, *Providence and Personalism: Karl Barth in Conversation with Austin Farrer, John Macmurray and Vincent Brümmer* (New York: Peter Lang, 2011), pp. 229–34.

objects and recipients of divine mercy.[67] To do its proper work, the *concursus divinus* must be filled with Christian content. The sovereign and almighty will that accompanies all creaturely activity is that of a fatherly disposition to have mercy upon us and to bring us into fellowship with God's own self. Barth's decision to retain the traditional language of the *concursus* is not without its problems, as we shall see, but it resides in his commitment to uphold the being of God in freedom and love as this is enacted in Jesus. The divine priority, universality and efficacy are best safeguarded, he believes, by the traditional schema. Throughout his exposition, Barth insists upon Christ as the material content of the *concursus* and its enablement of human freedom. With its dual failure, Reformed orthodoxy too often veered towards a Stoic or Islamic fatalism, with disastrous consequences. (For Barth, Islam is merely a cypher for fatalism and determinism – there is no evidence of any familiarity with Muslim writers on this subject.) With this now established, Barth proceeds to expound the divine accompanying in terms of its traditional tripartite structure.

1. The activity of God precedes (*praecurrit*) that of the creature. This is a function of the sufficiency of God's own being, which is prior to the world. Barth expresses this both in terms of the election of grace, which precedes the creation of the world, and in terms of the eternity of God's being as Father, Son and Spirit, which precedes all time. God's *prius* is not merely a foreknowledge (as in Arminianism) but involves an active bringing to pass of what God wills. The precedence of God's activity is not reducible to the formation of laws and processes by which creaturely events are governed, even though it may include these. By themselves alone, these are not the causes of events. In any case, Barth reckons that such 'laws' are our own imperfect assertions by which we seek to grasp the reliability and regularity of the world as ordered by God.

---

[67] Barth, *Church Dogmatics* III/3, p. 105.

Here he offers some brief comment on the possibility of miracles (*Wundern*). While somewhat densely expressed, Barth's views appear to converge on three thoughts. First, we should not think of miracles as transgressions of an otherwise unbroken order. This would place God at odds with the world as it is providentially ordered. Second, we should not limit divine action to our knowledge of what constitutes natural order. Our own fallible perception of such order may be 'ruthlessly ignored' by God in the enactment of an ordained order.[68] And third, we should not be surprised to discover in the witness to covenant history a mention of miracles, especially as we approach the coming of the Son of God in fulfilment of Old Testament prophecy. But what is revealed here, just as in creation out of nothing and the final revelation of Christ, is not a miraculous exception but a comprehensive divine rule to which our concepts of law can only approximate. Affirming miracles in this sense, Barth stands in the premodern tradition of Augustine and Aquinas, who view these as an integral part of God's providential order. Miracles are not construed in the contrasting Enlightenment sense of mere transgressions or ruptures of the natural realm.

Though delivered *en passant*, this account of miracles seems about right in neither exaggerating nor dismissing the significance of 'signs' and 'wonders' at crucial stages in the history of revelation or the life of Christians. A 'miracle' may stand out as an unusual testimony or confirmation of what is received in faith, but it belongs to some wider context with which it coheres. This can be maintained without commitment to miracles as occasional suspensions of nature, or as evidential proof of divine revelation. In general, the evidential significance of miracles has been overstated since the early modern period, particularly in the philosophy of religion.[69]

---

[68] Barth, *Church Dogmatics* III/3, p. 129.

[69] From a different starting point, John Polkinghorne reaches a similar conclusion in *Science and Providence*, pp. 45–58.

2. A second element is the concurrence of divine activity, though we are really dealing with a single divine action under different headings. (Somewhat confusingly, this element is also the name under which the entire tripartite division falls.) A pattern of simultaneity is advanced. In and with creaturely actions, we have also to do with the divine action. These do not run along separate parallel lines. Each event is to be viewed as displaying both a creaturely and a divine agency. This is the witness of Scripture, Barth insists. 'He would not be God at all if He were not the living God, if there were a single point where He was absent or inactive, or only partly active, or restricted in His action.'[70]

Barth has little interest in seeking a philosophy of divine action or a theory of the causal joint which attempts to show the compatibility of scientific and theological explanation. Such apologetic manoeuvres are avoided. The *concursus* is based on confession rather than explanation – the confessing of Jesus Christ as the act of God as this reaches us through the Word and the Spirit. Apart from this, the 'how?' of God's action is incomprehensible. Yet, on the basis of this one conviction, we must also acknowledge every event as accompanied and ruled by God. Here, one suspects, lies the fundamental problem of Barth's account. In following the Reformed orthodox tradition into this affirmation of a meticulous causing of everything that happens, not in a sense of general permission but through willing each and every event, Barth merely returns to the root problem. While the Christological determinism of his position offers a happier construction of God's intentions, the affirmation of a comprehensive set of divine volitions merely revives the anxieties that accompanied the older position. New wine is poured into old wineskins, with predictable consequences.

Barth's rendition of the *concursus* follows the maximal account of the classical Reformed tradition. He speaks of 'adhering so decidedly to the older doctrine of the Reformed Church.'[71] We must really

---

[70] Barth, *Church Dogmatics* III/3, p. 133.
[71] Ibid., p. 148.

confess that each and every event is willed by God. Anything less threatens the divine sovereignty and grace that assail us in Christ. For this reason, he has little use for the distinction between divine permitting and willing that has been deployed by scholars in other traditions (for example, Lutheran, Orthodox, Jesuit and Methodist theologians) to offset the threat of divine determinism. For Barth, this compromises the lordship of God over all things. He concludes with the dubious claim that those who cannot subscribe to this reading of providence are in the grip of fear and sin, especially the fear of God's sovereignty as this confronts us in Christ and his resurrection. The only remedy for such deep-seated affliction is prayer and fasting.[72] We may wonder at this point whether he 'protesteth too much'.

3. The rule of God completes a sequence that has begun with preservation and continued through divine accompaniment. Under divine government, our world is neither chaotic nor gripped by mechanistic forces. There is scope for God to work through both lawful activity and also more occasional and unexpected events. Barth speaks of the victories of common sense as expressions of divine wisdom. God 'loves the law-abiding bourgeois as well as the nomad', while also delighting in the fact that two plus two equal four, not five![73] In governing the whole world, God's providence does not obliterate the life of the individual as if it were too inconsequential or only the means to an end. Here lies 'the political or economic totalitarianism which has caused us so much anxiety today both in its Western and also in its Eastern forms'.[74]

The coordination of the spiritual and the temporal, the sacred and the secular, and the religious and the civil are marked out largely along Old Testament lines. Hence we cannot think of God's rule as

---

[72] Ibid.

[73] Ibid., p. 161.

[74] Ibid., p. 173.

extending only to the province of religion, the faith community or our private lifestyle choices. This must mean that the divine reign extends over all world history. There is a movement of perception from inside to outside, but it is always extensive rather than restrictive. In the order of understanding, we may begin with Israel, Christ and church, but we cannot confine God's rule to any one demarcated domain. To this extent, there is no such thing as a 'secular' history in which God is an uninvolved bystander. For this reason also, Barth is nervous around the classical distinction between a general and a special providence, as if the work of God had two separate compartments with the special alone reserved for miracles, revelation and the incarnation of Christ. This distinction, if it is maintained, will have to be adapted to register the ontic and noetic basis of God's rule of the world according to a single purpose.[75]

Barth frequently stresses the limitations of our knowledge. Yet, despite eschewing a God's eye perspective on the course of history, he affirms those elements that in their own way constitute 'signs and witnesses' for us of divine government. As partly hidden and needing to be understood from a particular perspective, these do not become a second Bible for us. Yet Barth feels able to list four such signs, to which he then adds another. These are significant for their narrow concentration.

i) The history of the Bible. In terms of its origin, transmission and interpretation, the Bible itself bears witness to God's rule over world occurrence. Its writings are admittedly conditioned by the time and place in which they were produced and redacted – to this extent, the interpretation of Scripture has been beset by error and mixed motive, and the history of its effects has suffered from distortion and misuse. Yet the Bible has endured as a trustworthy and indispensable witness.

ii) The history of the church. As another special element in world occurrence, the church is a sign of the rule of God, particularly

75 Ibid., p. 185.

in its capacity to endure persecution, to survive hostility and indifference, and to display patterns of renewal in its life. Though situated within world history, its life and work need to be described in theological terms. These are not to be specified through dogmas, institutional forms or individual personalities, even when these can be viewed positively. The most salient reason is that the divine call in the living Word of Scripture 'does actually win through in the Church'.[76]

iii) The history of the Jews. The survival of the Jewish people in world history after 70 CE is also, for Barth, a sign of divine providence. Here he echoes an ancient Talmudic saying.[77] Jewish identity is not to be explained on ethnic, cultural, linguistic or even religious grounds for Jews display diversity in all these respects. The fact that 'they are still there' is itself testimony to the Jews as those who continue post-Christum to be the people of God. Barth insists that the covenant has not been abrogated. The continued existence of Jewish people serves a dual purpose for the church – they are a living testimony to the books of the Hebrew Bible and also to the Jewish identity of Jesus. Writing shortly after the foundation of the modern state of Israel in 1948, Barth sees here a further confirmation of providence.[78] Although concerns about the displacement and dispossession of the Palestinian people now need to be more clearly registered by the church, we should recognise that Barth wrote at a time when the horror of the Shoah was only beginning to be addressed by his contemporaries. As a pioneer of

---

[76] Ibid., p. 209.

[77] This Talmudic saying states that 'Israel is immune from planetary influence', thus suggesting that the continuation of Israel reposes upon an act of special rather than general providence. See Yosef Achituv, 'Theology and the Holocaust: the presence of God and divine providence in history from the perspective of the Holocaust' in Steven T. Katz (ed.), *The Impact of the Holocaust on Jewish Theology* (New York: New York University Press, 2005), pp. 275–86 at p. 277.

[78] Barth, *Church Dogmatics* III/3, p. 212.

anti-supersessionism, his work merits attention, though we need to acknowledge that it suffers from a tendency to view the Jewish people (considered rather monolithically) as the negative counterpart of the church. Yet Barth's claims for the persistence of Judaism as an instance of divine providence can still hold.[79]

iv) The limitation of human life. This fourth mark stands apart from the preceding three in that it is primarily a biological phenomenon rather than a particular feature of world history. Barth's account is quite elusive. But he seems to envisage the bracketing of each human life by birth and death as positioning it within world history. Each person is unique in their allotted time and place, as situated for encounter with the Lord of history. This fourth sign appears important yet strangely undeveloped. In some later ruminations, Barth suggests that other creaturely patterns and constants can attest the providential rule of God throughout the creation. He speaks of music, birdsong, the laughter of children, the scent of flowers and poetry.[80] Further use of the wisdom literature of the Old Testament might have enabled him to extend this within his doctrine of providence without lapsing into a prohibited natural theology. Yet Barth's theology of providence remains uneven and lacking development in this context, though the theme of the limits and possibilities of each human life is again taken up in *Church Dogmatics* III/4. Here there is a stronger sense of a constrained freedom afforded each of us in the time and place in which we are set. The parameters of our lives are determined, but within these we have the opportunity of accepting our God-given vocation. This theme expresses Barth's overriding sense of the goodness of creation, his commitment to affirming important elements of

---

[79] For further discussion, see Mark R. Lindsay, *Barth, Israel and Jesus: Karl Barth's Theology of Israel* (Farnham: Aldershot, 2007).

[80] Karl Barth, *Church Dogmatics* IV/3 (Edinburgh: T&T Clark, 1962), p. 698.

the secular world, and his robust theological account of human freedom. In stressing these possibilities, Barth's theology seems relatively uninterested in the afterlife as compensation for present evils or as fulfilment for lives cut short by death.[81] Instead, he accentuates the glories of this life even amid tribulation. Indicative of a key ingredient in his thought, the reference to Mozart provides more than a passing illustration.

He died in misery like an 'unknown soldier', and in company with Calvin, and Moses in the Bible, he has no known grave. But what does that matter? What does a grave matter when a life is permitted simply and unpretentiously, and therefore serenely, authentically and impressively, to express the good creation of God, which also includes the limitation and end of man.[82]

This sense of fittingness is very powerful in Barth and points to ways in which his doctrines of redemption and creation are integrated. In all this material, however, there appears to be a distinct absence of any pneumatological reflection. The limited time in which we live under the call of God and our gracious election in Christ is a time between birth and death in which our circumscribed freedom is exercised. But the accompanying presence and contemporaneous influence of the Spirit do not really feature in these reflections. This neglect of the Spirit is not total, but it tends to pervade much of what Barth says about worship, prayer and vocation.[83] Whether it results from a fear of synergism or a pietistic psychologism, or a desire not to attribute

---

[81] 'The fact remains, however, that it is both important in itself and for universal history, that, even though he may die as a child only one day old, he should still exist in his time and not the contrary.' *Church Dogmatics* III/4 (Edinburgh: T&T Clark, 1961), p. 574.

[82] Barth, *Church Dogmatics* III/3, p. 298–9.

[83] For example, there is a brief exposition of key Pauline texts on the enabling power of the Spirit in the small print at ibid., p. 94. But here arguably Barth's tendency is to conflate the Spirit and Christ in their action.

too much to the action of the church, or a wish never to dero-
gate from the sufficiency of Christ's work can be debated. But
Barth's approach tends in a binitarian direction, at least at this
juncture. The constant accompanying of God which requires
the 'inward' language of spiritual indwelling and influence is
generally muted. In the section on prayer, for example, the primary component is that this is permitted and commanded of
free agents, rather than prompted.[84] The dominant movement
is external rather than internal. As such, it is primarily a human
act on our part, rather than one of God within us. As a form of
petition, our prayers have a strong ethical cast – yet much less
is said here of the capacity of prayer to evoke within us a sense
of divine presence, or of the significance of regularly attending
to God.[85]

v) The sign and testimony of the angels. Although Barth does not
list this as a fifth mark, he appends what he regards as the most
important of these creaturely witnesses to the rule of God in
world history. The appearance of angels at crucial moments in
the gospel story – at Advent, Christmas and Easter – reveals that
the great work of God is of cosmic significance. They belong to
a 'luminous border' beyond which we cannot clearly see,[86] but
in light of which the significance of history is revealed in its
relation to God's Word. His angelology is developed at much
greater length later in *Church Dogmatics* 111/3, though it has
been somewhat neglected on the part of later commentators,
perhaps through embarrassment or a concern around its speculative tenor.[87]

---

[84] Barth, *Church Dogmatics* 111/4, pp. 87–115.

[85] '[P]rayer is not a state but an act.' Ibid., p. 111.

[86] Barth, *Church Dogmatics* 111/3, p. 238.

[87] More might be made by Barth of angelic appearances as disruptive in Scripture
and hence consonant with God's wrestling with creaturely materials. For further
discussion, see Christopher Green, *Doxological Theology: Karl Barth on Divine
Providence, Evil, and the Angels* (London: T&T Clark, 2012), pp. 187–209.

Barth's doctrine of providence concludes with some further practical observations which recapitulate earlier themes. Faith must take the form of obedience, its primary impulse being petitionary prayer. Situated within the Christian community, our prayers move outwards in requests for others 'who do not so far pray, or who no longer pray'.[88] In this way, we can cooperate in doing the will of God. Prayer is not primarily about our self-edification or spiritual growth – it is our participation by grace in the divine government of the world. In this way, the 'friends of God' are permitted to cooperate in God's *succursus*.

An old Swiss motto (in abridged form) is often cited by Barth – *Hominum confusione et Dei providentia* ('by human confusion and the providence of God'). The confusion of human effort does not reveal the hand of God in any obvious way. But in the long run it is overruled by divine providence. This confusion is ambiguous with its admixture of motives and outcomes. 'It does not describe world history as a night in which everything is black, as an utter madhouse or den of criminals, as a graveyard, let alone an inferno.'[89] Here Barth speaks of the importance of being resolute *(entschlossen)*. Combining notions of sobriety, confidence and modesty, such resolution proceeds from faith in Jesus and is animated by hope for the wider world. Acknowledging the seeming insignificance of the church in world affairs, Barth notes how little interest the World Council of Churches attracts compared to the Winter Olympics or international football.[90] But if the endeavours of the church appear to belong to the margins of world history, this may itself be a cause for confidence. Its success is largely hidden in the secular domain because it is grounded in Christ and inspired by the Holy Spirit. This should spare us from unnecessary anxiety or scepticism about outcomes measured in other terms.

[88] Barth, *Church Dogmatics* III/3, p. 282.
[89] Barth, *Church Dogmatics*, IV/3, p. 695.
[90] Ibid., p. 247.

Barth's discussion of providence has not received as much scholarly attention as other elements of the *Church Dogmatics*. Although
it may not scale the heights of his doctrine of God or reconciliation, the *Vorsehungslehre* still ranks as one of the most important
renditions of providence in modern theology. Admittedly, the
material suffers from presentational difficulties, as it makes the tran-
sition from lecture theatre to text.[91] At times, the discussion becomes
prolix, even rambling, as it loops back to earlier arguments while
failing to engage with other issues that appear pressing. The reiter-
ation of the rule of God in world occurrence at *Church Dogmatics*
IV/3 suggests further possibilities that were not yet fully appreciated
by Barth in III/3. And, as elsewhere, Barth's rhetoric has the capacity to bludgeon the reader into reluctant submission, even as it
reaches soaring heights along the way. The discussion is replete with
powerful spiritual insight. Reviewing the material, Brian Gerrish
once observed that some of the most interesting features are the
incidental details.[92]

Several significant advances are made in Barth's theology of
providence. These include: a Christocentrism which resists abstract
descriptions of divine power and sovereignty through a refocussing
on the person and work of Jesus; a deflation of earlier triumphalist
accounts which stresses our lack of speculative knowledge about the
evidences for providence; and a recognition of the practical dimension of providence in relation to prayer and Christian action, particularly in hard times. On this last point, Barth remains alert to
the importance of aligning the church's high theology with the ways
in which the faith is actually practised on the ground. The deepest
attraction of Barth's approach is that providence is focussed on
Jesus. The Christian life is lived in the vicinity of Golgotha. 'For all
we can tell, may not we ourselves praise God more purely on bad

---

[91] W. A. Whitehouse, *Creation, Science and Theology: Essays in Response to Karl Barth*
(Edinburgh: T&T Clark, 1981), p. 34.
[92] Brian Gerrish, 'Creation and covenant', *Interpretation*, 16 (1962), 216–20.

days than on good, more surely in sorrow than in rejoicing, more truly in adversity than in progress?'[93] He notes that many of the great hymns of providence were written in times of crisis. (Martin Rinkart's *Nun Danket Alle Gott* may be the finest providential hymn in the history of the church. Written in 1637 during a time of plague and heartbreaking loss, it celebrates the goodness of God, preceding and succeeding our lives.) And from this perspective, we can make some sense of the truth that this is God's good creation. Because we experience it as threatened, we can cherish the world in all its splendour and harmony. In this way, Barth avoids the speculation and triumphalism of earlier forms of providentialism. His commitment to the practical dimension of providence is welcome, especially where he combines this with the sense of walking by faith rather than by sight.

Yet the reception has been mixed. Critics of Barth's doctrine of providence have complained that this account is little more than a reheating of seventeenth-century Reformed orthodoxy with its construction of a world already fully coordinated with the divine will.[94] A former pupil who attended Barth's lectures on providence, Dietrich Ritschl argued that his reworking of the *concursus*, with its typical stress on determinism and divine sovereignty in every event, was of little pastoral worth in facing problems of suffering and evil. Too little attention was devoted to Scripture and to thinking of divine providence in relation to empirical history, particularly its most tragic outcomes.[95] Perhaps as a result of dealing with evil in

---

[93] Barth, *Church Dogmatics* III/3, p. 297.

[94] For an informative overview of the reception, see Mark W. Elliott, *Providence Perceived: Divine Action from a Human Point of View* (Berlin: de Gruyter, 2015), pp. 242–7.

[95] Dietrich Ritschl, 'Sinn und Grenze der theologischen Kategorie der Vorsehung', *Zeitschrift für Dialektische Theologie*, 10 (1994), 117–33. Even Otto Weber, an otherwise sympathetic commentator, registers a similar criticism. See *Foundations of Dogmatics*, vol. 1 (Grand Rapids: Eerdmans, 1981), pp. 505–22. See also Christian Link, 'Schöpfung und Versehung' in Michael Beintker (ed.), *Barth Handbuch*

a subsequent paragraph of the *Church Dogmatics*, Barth does not adequately describe this correlation in his providential teaching.[96]

Allied to this concern is the worry that Barth's account lacks a strong promissory note. An eschatological deficit here tends towards an affirmation of each and every state of a Christ-centred universe as having its own rationale under the providence of God. The disposition of hope is understated, with the result that faith is too exclusively focussed on what God has already done, rather than on what God will do. The muting of this eschatological dimension deprives the language of providence of its promissory elements. The 'here and now' is shaped by the 'once for all', and so has a joyous character. But the 'not yet' that provides the content of Christian hope is less well expressed.[97] Past and present mesh, but without giving full expression to those future-tense statements that recur throughout Scripture. Listening to Handel's *Messiah* (to take a composer other than Mozart), one becomes conscious of the extent to which tense is crucial to the different registers of faith. The coming of Christ both fulfils and repeats the promise of God in such a way that faith and hope elide.

Barth's attempt at finding eschatological fulfilment in the mind of God has met with similar resistance. As finite creatures, we live for a time and then pass away. Yet within the life of God, each life remains eternally present, even 'the wing-beat of the day-fly in far-flung epochs of geological time'.[98] The adequacy of this account of eternal life was challenged by his early commentators. The suggestion that our lives are retained in the eternal memory of God does not capture the eschatology of the New Testament with its message of a continued though transformed human existence. G. C. Berkouwer

---

(Tübingen: Mohr Siebeck, 2016), pp. 328–34, esp. p. 333. Elsewhere Link has advocated a transposing of providence to the third article of the faith.

[96] See again Gilkey, 'The concept of providence in contemporary theology', pp. 188–90.

[97] The intention of Jürgen Moltmann's theology of hope is largely corrective in this respect.

[98] Barth, *Church Dogmatics* III/3, p. 90.

identifies this as a flaw in Barth's theology, perhaps to be explained by an overreaction against pagan notions of immortality or a fear that the time allotted to us now for God's service may be undervalued by the prospect of a more blissful post-mortem state.[99]

The principal difficulty in Barth's treatment of providence is one of coherence. He sets out some trenchant criticisms and adjustments of the Reformed tradition which appear to set him on a more radically revisionist trajectory. And yet he returns with enthusiasm to the standard Reformed *concursus*, even to the extent of charging its opponents *de haut en bas* with lack of faith, fear and half-heartedness. This tension is further compounded by his readiness to use the (unbiblical) language of causality in a way that arguably threatens to depersonalise the encounter between and agency of God and creatures. Critics today must raise questions around the stability of this position. The strong criticism of the classical Reformed tradition seems to anticipate a more radical revision of its terms. But in the final analysis, Barth's position reposes upon the categories of Reformed orthodoxy, which makes it difficult to introduce any substantive difference in material content. The use of the threefold distinction and double agency may be inflected, but the basic lineaments of the position are unaltered. We continue to be haunted by a theology that over-determines the will of God in every event, with all the bad outcomes that has entailed.[100]

A comparison with Barth's doctrine of election is instructive here. While the terms of his criticism of the classical position led to its extensive revision, no such outcome is really evident in his handling of providence. Barth's exposition of providence generates several questions. Is the way in which God often improvises with

---

[99] G. C. Berkouwer, *The Triumph of Grace in the Theology of Karl Barth* (Grand Rapids: Eerdmans, 1956), pp. 329–33.

[100] Wolfhart Pannenberg seems to imply the same criticism by stressing that wickedness and evil are not an object of God's will but 'accompanying phenomena' that are conditions for the realisation of a purpose. *Systematic Theology*, vol. II (Grand Rapids: Eerdmans, 1994), p. 167.

creaturely material in Scripture fully reflected in this account? Does it resonate for an age in which we are more reluctant to commit *simpliciter* to the notion that every event is caused by the will of God? Can the personalist themes in his theology be captured by the language of causality? Does the ecumenical consensus against this position require more scrutiny beyond a haughty dismissal? Has Barth here broken sufficiently with philosophical notions of God as perfect being, and the attendant account of providence, which he otherwise deplores in his theology?

Divine sovereignty may require expression in more flexible ways to capture its various scriptural inflections and to consolidate the gains of Barth's handling of providence. Though these need to be set in positive relation, Christological performance does not entail a determinism of every event under the first and third articles of the faith via the traditional abstractions of the *concursus*. The spread of determinism to the impersonal and monolithic terms of the threefold form of providence prevents Barth's account from fully registering the requisite scriptural plurality of forms. This lack of nuancing arises from his reprisal of the categories of Reformed orthodoxy. The consequence is a failure to capture the full range of providential forms, especially with respect to the action of the Spirit.

5.5 Revisionism Type Three: General Providence Only

An alternative, though not wholly dissimilar approach to relational theism, can be found in accounts of general providence which echo the more orthodox deist literature of the eighteenth century. This body of writings is acutely conscious of the problems identified by Gilkey above, while also stressing difficulties around the concept of particular divine action. An instructive example is found in Maurice Wiles's Bampton Lectures of 1986.[101] Characteristically honest

---

[101] Maurice Wiles, *God's Action in the World* (London: SCM, 1986). See also Gordon Kaufman, *Systematic Theology: A Historicist Perspective* (New York: Scribner's, 1968).

and accessible, his reformulation of providence is shaped by two overriding criticisms of earlier tradition. First, traditional notions of divine intervention have been superseded by modern advances in scientific and historical explanation. We cannot attribute an event to God's causality without infringing upon the integrity of other forms of description. The conceptual means for identifying the causal joint linking an event in the natural world with divine agency is not available to us. All traditional accounts seem to founder on this problem. Second, Wiles is adamant that divine action would also generate an inadmissible theodicy problem. If God intervenes in one place to mitigate or avoid a bad outcome, then why not more frequently? Faced by these severe constraints, providence is reduced to a single general act which constitutes the world according to various laws and tendencies. These incline towards providential outcomes without necessitating them in every instance. Where this view differs from process theology is that it appears capable of retaining traditional assumptions around creation and (maybe) eschatology. But what happens in the intervening period is characterised along similar lines, though via a concept of general providence alone.

Wiles is especially scathing in his comments on the metaphysics of process thought. Its panpsychist account of matter depicts significant evolutionary shifts in terms of an innate awareness within organisms of new possibilities. This, he remarks, is 'to add confusion to mystery', so that the results 'lack all credibility'.[102] Admittedly, this incursion of process metaphysics into the discourse of natural science does create some confusion of types of explanation. As an untestable scientific proposal, it exhibits all the risks of a 'God of the gaps' explanation. Yet as a meta-description of the totality of nature, it need not threaten the integrity of scientific explanation, nor does it seem very far removed from the account that Wiles himself offers of the empirical effects of our awareness of a divine spiritual presence. However, it is clear that for Wiles all accounts of particular

---

[102] Wiles, *God's Action in the World*, p. 33.

or special providence fail to offer any adequate specification of the causal joint for divine action.

On his reduced account of providence, the difficulty for Wiles is to make sense of traditional themes such as incarnation, divine–human interaction and prayer. Here he departs from the apparently deist setting of his theology to develop a strong account of divine presence. Throughout the creation, there is an accompanying of the creature that generates a pressure to act in ways consonant with God's overall purposes. Another exponent of this view, Ruth Page, has designated the universal divine accompanying as 'pansyntheism'.[103] In exerting a constant influence upon the created world, especially through self-conscious agents, God can make a difference. Particularly dramatic acts of responsiveness on the part of creatures have a revelatory quality which can remain instructive for subsequent generations. Here the language of disclosure, intervention and incarnation can be reworked in appropriate ways. In the case of petitionary prayer, we should think of a human attuning to the divine presence which can have beneficial effects upon the one who prays. In this respect, prayer makes a difference, though this is to us rather than to God, who remains only its condition. Worship aims at 'a genuinely free human recognition and response to what is God's intention in the creation of the world'.[104]

This account of divine providence has tended to characterise much of liberal Protestantism.[105] It displays a coherence, simplicity

---

[103] Ruth Page, *God and the Web of Creation* (London: SCM, 1996). A former pupil of Wiles, Page seeks to develop this theological position in ways that are less anthropocentric.

[104] Wiles, *God's Action in the World*, p. 103.

[105] Michael Langford perceives this as a typical characteristic of liberal theology. 'According to a liberal view, God may know and control the sweep of history, because this depends on long-term causes and pressures; God may be able to control these without orchestrating every individual event.' Michael J. Langford, *The Tradition of Liberal Theology* (Grand Rapids: Eerdmans, 2014), p. 47. See also Ottati, *Theology for Liberal Protestants*, pp. 313–60.

and intellectual honesty in the face of the leading questions, and it deserves greater attention than has been received in recent years. I suspect that, if pressed, many Christians would assent to something very similar. They are among those who have 'defected in place' from the traditional teaching of divine providence. The preferred model is that of an improvised drama. While the setting and character of the actors is shaped by the author, the actors are given an experimental freedom in which to develop their parts.[106] Those in whom the author's intention finds its clearest expression and fullest response are those around whom the language of revelation is deployed. But this is not to breach the principle of general providence as only a single constitutive action of God.[107] A similar view is articulated by Gordon Kaufman in his combination of general and special providence. If general providence refers to the entirety of nature and history as reflecting a single divine purpose, then special providence denotes those particular events in which that same purpose is disclosed. But the particular forms of providence do not represent a separate sequence of divine actions. In essence, these are human discernments of what is always and everywhere happening, to which in the particular case the character of revelation has been attached. 'Their peculiar significance derives from their providing the indispensable historico-psychological grounding for the appearance and continuance of faith in the purposive and living God, in this way serving as "break-throughs" advancing the historical realization of (God's) purposes.'[108]

---

[106] Wiles, *God's Action in the World*, p. 37.

[107] Ibid., p. 108.

[108] Kaufman, *Systematic Theology*, p. 304. In his later work, Kaufman adopts a more constructivist theology which views 'God' as a human symbol to promote vital moral and spiritual purposes. On this basis, he duly departs from the traditional asymmetric dualism of God as a transcendent and provident maker. On his estimation, this fails to capture our dependence and interconnectedness with the cosmos and other creatures. The symbol of God as creativity rather than as personal creator is preferred. See *Theology for a Nuclear Age* (Philadelphia: Westminster, 1985), p. 43, and *In the Beginning … Creativity* (Minneapolis: Fortress, 2004), p. 124.

The difficulties reside principally in relation to the adequacy of this approach. Although postulating a strong account of divine action at the beginning and (often) the end of creation, this theology appears otherwise to be heavily restrictive in relation to God's *modus operandi*. All forms of intermediate divine action must be appropriated to pneumatologically driven notions of presence and persuasion. As Marilyn McCord Adams complains, this account suggests that God does nothing in particular.[109] Little specification is given to the work of the two hands of God – the Word and the Spirit. Anything more would generate impossible theodicy problems, together with epistemic difficulties of discerning divine agency. This renders traditional descriptions of divine overruling very difficult to sustain, except in some deflated description of the effects of created forces and divine presence. Notions of the Spirit's guidance, prompting and encounter seem under threat here, as does any sense of a divine performance in history that constitutes a point of reference for subsequent description and experience of God. A similar criticism from a different perspective can be found in James Cone's black theology of liberation. Criticising Kaufman, he argues for a stronger account of divine transcendent action against injustice. The liberating work of God in its enablement of human forms of protest requires more than is on offer in Kaufman's account of divine action. This extends in Cone to a wider criticism of traditional accounts of providence – Brunner is his immediate target – which are too ready to assimilate God's will to whatever happens. For Cone, a providentialism that motivates protest and resistance is required to counteract demobilising strategies that advocate acquiescence and

---

[109] Marilyn McCord Adams, 'Evil and the God-who-does-nothing-in-particular' in D. Z. Phillips (ed.), *Religion and Morality* (New York: St Martin's Press, 1996), pp. 107–32. A similar criticism is registered by Kalbryn A. McLean, 'Calvin and the personal politics of providence' in Amy Plantinga Pauw and Serene Jones (eds.), *Feminist and Womanist Essays in Reformed Dogmatics* (Louisville: Westminster John Knox Press, 2006), pp. 107–24.

patience. '[D]ivine providence is seeing divine reality in the present reality of black liberation – no more, no less.'[110]

In addition to this, there may be a conceptual puzzle at the centre of the approach. If God's action is reduced to a single creative act combined with a constant spiritual influence, we have yet to explain how this latter influence is exercised. In the case of human agents, presumably, we should think of a spiritual activity on God's part that impinges either directly upon the human mind or indirectly through generating particular brain states. In either scenario, we must postulate a divine action that changes the way things would otherwise be. Here we may be back with the problem of locating the causal joint.[111] In this respect, the panpsychism of process theology may be at an advantage in offering some account of how divine action is possible. On the model proposed by Wiles, this remains a sheer mystery, so that even the work of the Spirit remains opaque. His juxtaposing of deist and pantheist elements generates an inevitable tension. Yet, if a more interactive account of God's action is to be re-admitted in any case, why not enrich this with a variety of modes that do fuller justice to the testimony of the faith community, especially if there is nothing within the doctrine of God that *a priori* forbids it?

Despite the severe limitations of this position, we may need to recognise the inevitability of a deist element in modern theology.[112] The blanket criticism of its tenets from almost all sides has tended to occlude one permanent element of value. This resides in the recognition that the world has received an orderly form by virtue of an original endowment of natural laws and potentialities. This general providence is ordained by God, though it may sometimes work against us as individuals.[113] The contingencies of nature and history are determined by these laws, so that we are never given a

[110] James H. Cone, *A Black Theology of Liberation* (Maryknoll, NY: Orbis, 1986), p. 86.

[111] I owe this point to a conversation long ago with John McIntyre.

[112] This is argued by Peter Baelz, *Prayer and Providence* (London: SCM, 1968), p. 67.

[113] Here there may also be some common ground with Stoicism, particularly in recognising the need to see the work of God in the grain of the universe. While

free pass. Each event cannot be attributed to some hidden intention of a God who engages in micro-managing the cosmos, beyond the work of conservation. We do not have frequent interpositions, except those of volitional embodied creatures, which suspend or redirect the flows of nature. The world has its parameters which (it seems) even God respects. Even occasional catastrophic events must be viewed as integral to a natural order that at other times works in our favour. Although we may wish to argue that God can act in, through and even against the grain of the universe, we do not expect it to be suspended or abrogated in our interests. This is not merely the result of intellectual scepticism surrounding special interpositions. A moral component is also involved in refusing to attribute a specific divine intentionality to natural catastrophes and other prodigious events. Wesley's reaction to the Lisbon earthquake is no longer an option. In this respect, we need to incorporate elements of deism into any satisfactory account of providence. Although a repristinated deism or modified Stoicism will fail to provide a sufficiently robust and differentiated account of divine action, this single theme will need to be accommodated under the first article. This is of some moral urgency at a time when the stability of the natural environment is increasingly threatened by human activity rather than divine fiat.

5.6 Conclusion

Despite their difficulties, each of the different models explored here has something to contribute to a contemporary reconstruction of providential theology that expresses the various registers of God's work of creation, redemption, interaction and promise. These can be appropriated by a dispersed theology of providence that offers a constellation of approaches under each of the three articles of the faith.

not exhausting the forms of divine providential action, this should be allowed its proper place.

While this generates the challenge of drawing these together with some semblance of coherence, the more pluralist approach favoured in this study has the advantage of registering the various themes and moods that express Christian faith. In the closing chapter, I examine some of the dogmatic expressions of these, together with selected practical themes encompassed in the language of providence.

6 | Providence Reconstructed

Sarah's laughter is faith's constant companion.[1]

6.1 Summation

Several recurrent themes have emerged in the preceding discussion. These are reiterated in the following twelve paragraphs.

i) The theology of providence covers the full range of Christian doctrines. As a dispersed notion, providence attaches in different ways to each of the three articles of the faith. Hence it needs to be variously appropriated to Father, Son and Spirit. Its different forms and manifestations require recognition of the diverse modes of divine action, rather than assimilation and constriction to any one of these. This tracking function of providentialism – as parasitic upon the core doctrines of Christian faith, it derives its form and content from these – should be acknowledged to the extent that it is best handled not as a discrete locus but as an element shared and modulated by all the doctrines.

ii) Where the exposition of providence is undertaken as a subdivision of either the doctrine of God or the doctrine of creation, it suffers from constraints that inevitably distort its expression within other doctrinal loci. This has given rise to an over-determinism of contingent events by the divine will. The establishment of providence at the outset of a systematic theology often results in a failure to provide a satisfactory account of

[1] Ernst Käsemann, *Perspectives on Paul* (London: SCM, 1971), p. 69.

how it is expressed through the work of the Holy Spirit. A lack of pneumatological inflection characterises much of the literature which is (unintentionally) monist in this respect.

iii) Scriptural accounts of divine providence are strikingly diverse, even to the extent of generating tension and confusion. This is to be embraced in the interests of registering the different accentuations of divine providence in creation, redemption, dynamic presence and eschatological fulfilment. If a multi-layered account of providence suffers some loss of systematic coherence, it will gain through greater adequacy to the themes and moods of Christian life and worship. The liturgical celebration of providence is apparent in the seasons of the church's year. Advent is not Lent, Christmas is not Good Friday, Easter is not Pentecost, and Harvest is not Ascension. Yet each displays some aspect of God's providence towards the world.

iv) Since the noun 'providence' and cognate notions such as 'foresight' and 'provision' are substantive and somewhat static notions, we might do better to think more adverbially or adjectivally. Providence depicts the entire series of divine actions that are directed towards the good of creatures. These include ordaining, endowing, blessing, guiding, ruling, forgiving, reconciling, inspiring, prompting, healing, sanctifying and promising. The absence of the term itself from Scripture (and in languages such as Chinese and Japanese) should caution us from overloading one concept with significance as if it were a single divine attribute or creaturely phenomenon. We might say that providence is a theological term that needs to be *narrated* through a series of descriptions of how God relates to creatures, rather than *defined* in any essentialist manner. For this reason, the statement that God acts providentially might be the primary form of a theology of providence.[2]

---

[2] 'When we speak of Providence we are simply speaking of God or of God's action … We are not called upon to show that heaven runs a Ministry of Providence with a

v) Given that providence is a notion attaching to a sequence of divine actions, one can reasonably ask what we contribute by characterising the works of God as providential. Several concerns are relevant here. A theology of providence has the effect of linking 'inner' and 'outer' dimensions of God's rule. By 'inner', we intend the stories of Israel, Jesus and the church, though this need not be exclusive of other historical traditions. With respect to 'outer', we think of the wider dimensions of nature and history, most of which may be unknown and inaccessible to us. 'Inner' and 'outer' need to be configured so that the actions of the God of Jesus are co-extensive with those of God the Creator. One function of a theology of providence is to chart these connections, though without overly systematising these to the detriment of the variety of God's works or the recognition of our narrow epistemological confinement. Another function of providential theology is to signify the goodness of all God's ways. This is a corollary of the doctrine of creation – an account of God's wisdom must relate to the life of the world in its totality. A theology of providence describes the work of God as to our advantage, though not always in ways that we can anticipate or understand. Barth wrote of creation as 'benefit' (*Wohlgetan*).[3] He might equally well have described providence in the same way. God's rule is to our benefit, though not in the pursuit of some private, factional or national self-interest. For this reason, the providence of God is especially a focus of preaching and pastoral care. The discernment of God's action takes place with a view to its practical appropriation as good, purposive and to our benefit. And its comprehensive scope requires consideration of how

separate staff of angelic executives, quite distinct from the Creation Office or the Preservation Office or even (if it is decent so to speak) from the Court of Atonement.' Austin Farrer, *Saving Belief: A Discussion of Essentials* (London: Hodder and Stoughton, 1964), p. 53.

[3] Karl Barth, *Church Dogmatics* III/1 (Edinburgh: T&T Clark, 1958), pp. 330–43.

providence might be understood and exercised in political life and the natural world.

vi) Divine providence takes place in, with, through and sometimes against creaturely forces. This requires us to think of a contingent creation with some 'free play' in which God is constantly active, though not by one mode alone. Here the metaphor of the two hands of God – Word and Spirit – offers a valuable resource. This divine work unfolds temporally within the created world, rather than in the timeless willing of a single block universe. Notions of divine wrestling, struggle and improvisation should not be spirited away as anthropomorphic concessions to our ways of thinking. These have deep scriptural roots and significant pastoral traction. One upshot of this account is that the distinction between divine permission and willing needs to be more robustly maintained than in traditional expressions of Thomism and Calvinism. While this generates a further tension in relation to divine sovereignty, it should be upheld. To this extent, we can learn something from the Orthodox churches, which have always reinforced the distinction, over against the Latin churches, which generally have not. The sovereignty of God should be constructed in promissory terms, rather than in a total control that is everywhere and always exercised. Hence divine determinism might be understood with reference to eschatological outcomes, but not as governing every penultimate event.

vii) The foregoing historical explorations have been important in assessing the different cultural contexts in which providentialist thought has been deployed. The problematising of this material is integral to the claim that some recasting of the theology of providence is now demanded of us. Earlier accounts of providence have been too closely aligned to Stoic philosophy, natural catastrophes, imperial projects, economic forces and unjust institutions. Examples have not been difficult to locate. The fit between divine volition and the order of nature and history has been too tightly calibrated for many centuries. This has left insufficient room for notions of resistance, redemption and promise, often with deleterious political and pastoral consequences. Wolterstorff's passing remark that Calvin's account of providence inclines towards occasionalism is not without force. The perceived need to see each microscopic event as individually foreordained by God – a position that is not without robust argumentative support – presents divine action and creaturely effects as too closely aligned. Secondary causes here tend to become mere ciphers for divine volition, their principal function being to rescue God from direct responsibility for sin and evil. But by loosening the fit between divine volition and contingent occurrence, we are no longer committed to regarding all history as fulfilling a single foreordained plot. This might also liberate us from overestimating our own destiny as agents of historical progress.

viii) A comprehensive theology of providence should reflect on its various registers in Scripture, worship and Christian practice. As a critical task, this involves taking account of the different cultural settings in which Scripture is interpreted and faith practised. Where earlier accounts are found wanting, these should be repaired, revised or replaced. Recognition of theological mobility takes places amid a sustained and respectful conversation with earlier traditions. While systematic coherence remains a desideratum, this should not be prioritised above Christological commitments, a recognition of scriptural and liturgical diversity, or the need for pastoral and political adequacy. Here one can cite the instructive example of David Kelsey's work in theological anthropology. In attending to the practices and convictions of a lived religion with its sacred texts and ritual practices, systematic theology may find itself sometimes displaying an unsystematic appearance.[4] In the case

---

[4] Kelsey writes of a 'systematic unsystematic secondary theology'. See David H. Kelsey, *Eccentric Existence*, 2 vols. (Philadelphia: Westminster John Knox Press, 2009), vol. I, p. 45.

of characterising the works of God in creation, redemption, dynamic presence and eschatological resolution, the theology of providence provides an example *par excellence* of a 'systematic unsystematic' theology.

ix) Notwithstanding the anxieties around earlier descriptions of providence, several features of the classical account need to be accommodated. The tradition is not to be regarded as a set of options that must be relentlessly deconstructed. Nor should it be ignored as if it were of antiquarian interest only. Our task is to appropriate, adapt and reframe *in optimam partem* these earlier formulations within the life of the church. The term 'providence' itself usefully designates the way in which creation is not merely an original and singular event. As the first of God's works, creation introduces a narrative that is marked by divine rule, covenant partnership and constant involvement in the life of the world. This is not a restricted or intermittent relationship but one that is universal and pervasive, though with historically particular outcomes. The traditional expression of providence has sought to express this *creatio continua* alongside and as the necessary complement of *creatio ex nihilo*. In characterising the forms of providence, Christian theologians have rightly invested the concept with a meaning beyond its etymological senses of 'foresight' and 'provision'. The threefold form in Reformed orthodoxy points towards the richness of divine providence as embracing a range of meanings. And, despite their difficulties and limitations, accounts of double agency have the capacity to point towards divine involvement in everything that happens (through notions of preservation, permission and dynamic presence), so that each and every event has a conferred potential for some redeemed outcome. Nevertheless, we should strenuously resist any equation of this with a justification for everything that happens, or the (stronger) view that God positively wills every outcome.

x) The vexed relationship of the theology of providence to theodicy is unavoidable. Questions of suffering and evil now haunt the margins of every paragraph written on divine providence. But it is a mistake to assume that the function of providentialism is to provide the solution to a problem or that a successful theodicy must be one of its essential ingredients. Once again, the history of theology is littered with flawed attempts to explain evil and suffering as encompassed within the providential purposes of God. Nevertheless, the theology of providence cannot ignore traditional theodicies for at least three reasons. First, some of their features (for example, free will and divine restraint) need to be accommodated in any adequate position. Second, an account of providence should not make the problem of evil any worse that it must already be. Some accounts of divine sovereignty, especially those culminating in double predestination, achieved precisely this result. And third, the theology of providence may have a responsibility to expose those points at which all theodicies suffer breakdown. For this last reason, it is a mistake, for both theoretical and pastoral reasons, merely to eschew theodicy altogether as if were a corrupting theological habit. This move may itself promote the wrong posture.

xi) Though numerical divisions are somewhat arbitrary, five dimensions of providence may be discerned in Scripture and tradition. Each of these appears, more or less prominently, in the liturgy, prayers and hymns of the church. (a) The providential framing of the cosmos is evident in its natural regularity, for example in the daily rising of the sun, the seasons of the year (Genesis 8:22) and the abundance of the earth (Psalm 104). (b) Closely related to this same natural order is the wisdom that pervades (optimal) political, economic and domestic practices (Proverbs). These manifestations of divine goodness in both nature and society are celebrated in Psalm 19. This wisdom is the source of our common well-being. But, even as God's wisdom is celebrated as providential, there is a keen awareness that this is threatened by internal and external forces. Everywhere it is beset by temptation and frailty. Our moral weakness, coupled with dangers including disease, famine and invasion, contaminates the natural order and generates a sense of its fragility. Affirmations of cosmic order belong to a beleaguered context. (c) Within the created world, performative actions of God are also attested. These include generating covenant partnerships, the giving of the law, prophetic denunciation and promise, the coming of Christ into the world, and the spread of the church throughout the Gentile world. Each of these actions is providential in establishing God's 'good will to all peoples'. (d) The more elusive language of 'spirit' extends both of these notions, while connecting them in important ways. *Ruaḥ*, a bridge term between God and creation, denotes divine presence and immanence without consequent loss of transcendence. There is no place on earth or in heaven where God's spirit can be evaded (e.g. Psalm 139). In the New Testament, this is identified with the Holy Spirit, who empowers the lives of Christians in the unity of the church. Although its wider cosmic functions are more muted in the epistles, they are developed in the subsequent pneumatology of the church with its more sustained reflection on the links between creation and redemption. As spirit, God is everywhere present and active, but in ways that point to a completion of the other two actions of God. This is illustrated in Aquinas's Trinitarian inflection of creation, where he appropriates diverse but related works to each of the three persons in the origination, imprinting with wisdom, and bringing to completion of the *opera ad extra*.[5] (e) To these three providential movements of God, we should add an eschatological re-creating which fulfils the promissory elements embedded in the performative works; this is

---

[5] Thomas Aquinas, *Summa Theologiae*, 1a.45.7.

already anticipated in the signification of the first Sabbath in Genesis 1. As a further mode of divine action, this should not be assimilated to any of the other three since it involves a *creatio ex vetera* which is neither a second *creatio ex nihilo* nor an evolutionary end point of immanent processes. Although its characterisation is fraught with difficulty – only scattered images can be tentatively proffered – such consummation by divine action is the corollary of Christ's resurrection from the dead. From this brief sketch, there emerges a polyphony of divine actions. Each of these is different; yet all are interwoven to depict a unity of providential outcomes in the divine economy.

xii) These forms of providence are not subject to rational demonstration. No worldview is generated which can be vindicated over against its rivals by virtue of superior explanatory power. As an articulation of a position internal to Christian faith and ecclesial practice, it seeks to display some coherence, pastoral adequacy and avoidance of the difficulties inherent in earlier accounts. Yet this falls some way short of proof, while admitting elements of tension and ambivalence. The discernment of providence is as much a spiritual practice as an intellectual hypothesis. With persistent challenges and threats to God's providential rule, we walk by faith rather than by sight. Sarah's laughter at the divine promise suggests how often providence must work against the grain of plausible expectation.

6.2 A Dogmatics of Providence: Three Examples

Much of what has been attempted represents a preamble to a more adequate theology of providence. To give some material elaboration to the providential dimension of the diverse works of God, the following examples are offered, under each of the three articles of the faith.

6.2.1 *Creatio continua*

The theology of creation is established in the Hebrew Bible by writers who were acutely conscious of the precariousness of what they affirmed. Disturbances to nature and society were frequently visited upon the people, while their own complicity in wrongdoing was a constant source of prophetic criticism. Yet the wonder and beauty of the world were still celebrated in the face of this uncertainty. Indeed, the intensity and pathos of much of this literature owes much to an awareness of fragility. As proclaimed in Genesis 1, the goodness of creation is accentuated by the waters of the deep and the formless void.

This providential dimension of our creation and preservation is illustrated by Julian of Norwich's image of a hazelnut in the palm of her hand. Her contemplation of its small size and insignificance causes her to wonder why it exists and continues in being. As a signifier of all that is made, the hazelnut represents creation in its entirety considered in relation to God.[6] 'I marvayled how it might laste, for me thought it might sodenly have fallen to nawght for littleness. And I was answered in my understanding: "It lasteth and ever shall, for God loveth it. And so hath all thing being by the love of God."'[7] This elicits for Julian a sense of God as maker, keeper and lover of all things.

The anthologising of this famous passage and its use as a liturgical reading risks divorcing it from what has been described as a 'tough doctrine of providence'.[8] A hard-won insight, this is grounded in her vision of the dying Christ as the one who alone can resolve the tension between the goodness of the world and the

---

[6] For comment on the philosophical and religious character of this exploration, see Denys Turner, *Thomas Aquinas: A Portrait* (New Haven: Yale University Press, 2013), pp. 139–41.

[7] Denise N. Baker (ed.), *The Showings of Julian of Norwich* (New York: Norton, 2005), chapter 5, p. 9.

[8] Denys Turner, *Julian of Norwich, Theologian* (New Haven: Yale University Press, 2011), p. 18.

pervasiveness of our sin. In the surrender of self to God, we find the meaning of our existence and preservation, just as Mary did at the annunciation. 'And also our good Lord shewed that it is full great plesaunce to him that a sely sowle come to him naked, pleaynly and homely.'[9] Although there is a risk of too tightly binding the significance of creation to our union with Christ (an example of over-systematising), Julian's hazelnut image points to the way in which God's making and sustaining of the world is an act of great providence. Depicting an intimate relationship, this deserves our wonder and gratitude. And this is an affirmation not borne of facile optimism but through a sense of precariousness. The world might not have existed at all. Creatures might have lacked preservation. But the endurance of the world is a sign that creating and sustaining are providential works of God. A further element of this understanding includes a sense of divine involvement in all created reality. God is invested in the world by virtue not only of its making but also of its keeping and loving. This reveals a benevolent omnipresence comprehending all nature. God's work in everything is well done – it has a right and fitting quality.[10] Intended for her wider audience of 'evenchristen' (ordinary, fellow Christians), Julian presents this neither as the exclusive insight of the philosophical nor as an esoteric vision granted only to a few.[11]

In his study of Aquinas, Denys Turner remarks that Julian's account of divine origination and conservation takes a philosophical form, unlike, say, the poetic insights of Gerald Manley Hopkins

---

[9] Baker, *The Showings of Julian of Norwich*, chapter 5, p. 10. 'And our good Lord showed that it is very great pleasure to him that a blessed soul come to him stripped naked, plainly and intimately.'

[10] Ibid., chapter 11, pp. 20–1. See also Christopher Abbott, *Julian of Norwich: Autobiography and Theology* (Woodbridge: D. S. Brewer, 1999), pp. 147–8.

[11] See Elizabeth Robertson, 'Julian of Norwich's "modernist style" and the creation of audience' in Liz Herbert McAvoy (ed.), *A Companion to Julian of Norwich* (Woodbridge: D. S. Brewer, 2008), pp. 139–53.

in 'God's grandeur'. Yet this distinction also points towards ways in which these different discourses converge on the same conclusion regarding creaturely dependence upon the love of God. In each case, a sense of intense wonder is evoked, resulting in a heightened appreciation of the world. Celebration of God's general providence is not constructed upon a natural theology of the clockwork universe but instead derives from a scripturally embedded sense of wonder, beauty and fragility.

Nevertheless, one might develop the hazelnut image in a way that is less evident in Julian's deliberations. The hazelnut has its distinctive texture, shape and colour. As the fruit of the hazel tree, it can be harvested and eaten for its taste and nutritional properties. Considered as part of the natural environment, the hazelnut displays a structure that is useful and dependable. These material parameters order our daily lives in myriad ways, and set the context within which God's general providence is both revealed and constrained. In preserving the world, God establishes a providential framework within which God must subsequently work. Other forms of providence take place in and through this created order. In this way, God is constrained by the decision to create and conserve. Today these insights are ethically freighted with the growing recognition that we ourselves have a vital role to play in this work of conservation. Our own species can adversely impact the ecosystem and other forms of life, thus reminding us of our interdependence with the created order in which we are situated. The balance of the created world is not simply a given; it is fragile and increasingly disrupted by our ways of life.

6.2.2 Theologia crucis

Luther's theology of the cross presents some formidable challenges for a contemporary providentialism. Several criticisms recur in the literature. With its fear of the last judgement and concentration on the suffering of the crucified, the thought world of late medieval piety has been problematised in different ways. Luther's description of the cross seems to assume an Anselmian model of penal substitutionary atonement. The injunction to follow in the way of the cross can too readily glorify suffering or cast the victims of abuse in a submissive role. Other questions arise in relation to the Latin preoccupation with the crucifixion, as opposed to the incarnation and the resurrection, while many of the nineteenth-century hymns that we sing on Good Friday have become increasingly remote from contemporary piety. And in any case, what are other religions to make of the Christian obsession with the execution of one innocent person?

These questions are not easily sidestepped by turning instead to the teaching and example of the pre-Easter Jesus. The New Testament and the creeds seek to impress upon us the centrality of cross and resurrection. The focus for the evangelists, especially in the Fourth Gospel, is on Christ's passion, while the Pauline epistles view the crucifixion–resurrection sequence as a hinge event in the performance of God's providence. With its 'once for all' significance, this becomes a point of constant return for Christian reflection and worship. Represented above all in the cross, the foolishness of God is the hidden and unexpected enactment of a providential purpose. For all the difficulties that we encounter with Luther's religious intolerance and political misjudgement, he understands how readily Christian thought and piety can retreat from the cross. Although developed in greater depth in his later writings, the *Heidelberg Disputation* (1518) expresses this most memorably. His theology provides a valuable exercise in providentialism precisely because he takes the counter-intuitive character of the crucifixion so seriously. Its foolishness is the focus of sustained concentration, not with a morbid preoccupation on immolation and punishment, but in ways that explore its multi-dimensional significance for faith and practice. God's will is enacted under the appearance of a contrary form – this is God's hiddenness in the flesh of Christ and his cross. Instead of rational speculation, we must accept this with childlike trust.[12]

> He deserves to be called a theologian, however, who comprehends the visible and manifest thing of God seen through suffering and the cross.
>
> A theologian of glory calls evil good and good evil. A theologian of the cross calls the thing what it actually is.[13]

In subsequent writings, Luther explicates this through a range of classical ideas. These include substitutionary atonement; the forgiveness of sins; the wondrous exchange that is accomplished in the totality of Christ's incarnate life and work; the establishment of God's covenant faithfulness; the victory over sin, death and the devil; the hope of the last day; and the comfort afforded us in dying.[14] While the centrality accorded the imputation of Christ's alien righteousness to the sinner may represent a *novum* in Luther's theology, this can be viewed as a way of foregrounding what is already inherent in the apostolic tradition. God's decision to love us is without regard to our worthiness. As our representative, Christ has already suffered and endured for our benefit. He is the one by whom God's covenant with us is upheld. His victory is for us; hence, it is appropriated in faith alone and never earned by any right. As we face our own weakness and mortality, together with the severe limits of our accomplishments, we are confronted by this figure of the crucified Christ as the word and wisdom of God for the world. This requires explication through a series of divine actions that include Christ's coming into the world, his sending by God to accomplish a unique

---

[12] See Robert Kolb, *Martin Luther and the Enduring Word of God: The Wittenberg School and Its Scripture-Centred Proclamation* (Grand Rapids: Baker, 2016), p. 116.

[13] *Heidelberg Disputation*, theses 20–1, in Timothy F. Lull (ed.), *Martin Luther's Basic Theological Writings* (Minneapolis: Fortress, 1989), pp. 30–49 at p. 31.

[14] 'Thus, coherent with the enormous concentration of all his theological work is its great breadth, with the result that all the variety and abundance of the various themes and tasks of theology are retained and in each instance intensively discussed.'

mission, his proclamation of the reign of God, his sacrificial death, his resurrection from the dead and his presence in the church. This representation of the crucified Christ as the whole Christ (*totus Christus*) is one way in which a morbid preoccupation with violence and punishment can be avoided. Commenting on Galatians 1:3 (1535), Luther writes,

> [W]henever you are concerned to think and act about your salvation, you must put away all speculations about the Majesty, all thoughts of works, traditions, and philosophy – indeed of the Law of God itself. And you must run directly to the manger and the mother's womb, embrace this Infant and Virgin's Child in your arms, and look at Him – born, being nursed, growing up, going about in human society, teaching, dying, rising again, ascending above all the heavens, and having authority over all things. In this way you can shake off all terrors and errors, as the sun dispels the clouds. This vision will keep you on the proper way, so that you may follow where Christ has gone.[15]

For Luther, the resurrection of Christ is the necessary accompaniment to the cross, which is radiated by a proper attention to the whole Christ who lives today. In his preaching and commentaries, he repeatedly stresses the incarnate Jesus in his totality. And Jesus' work in crucifixion and resurrection can be distinguished but not separated.[16] His rising from the dead is a victory for the gospel over the law of death. This is good news now and, owing to its promissory character, in the future. The eschatological assurance that is offered is the source and content of Christian hope. A strong eschatological determination is posited, which can neither be jeopardised by God's

---

Bernhard Lohse, *Martin Luther's Theology* (Minneapolis: Augsburg Fortress, 1999), p. 260.

[15] Jaroslav Pelikan (ed.), *Luther's Works*, vol. XXVI (St Louis: Concordia, 1963), p. 30.

[16] For exploration of Luther's frequent return to Romans 4:25 – Christ was handed over to death for our trespasses and was raised for our justification – see Robert Kolb, 'Resurrection and justification: Luther's use of Romans 4,25', *Lutherjahrbuch*, 78 (2011), 39–60.

change of mind nor invalidated by our chronic failures. Again, this has a strong providential cast in Luther's exposition. The hope of our own resurrection inscribes the fear of death. Inverting the order of Psalm 90, he states, 'See how divine majesty is at hand in the hour of death. We say, "In the midst of life we die". God answers, "Nay, in the midst of death we live." '[17]

What is striking about Luther's theological work *inter alia* is the crossover from lectern to pulpit. In repudiating overly speculative approaches to theology – a feature of Calvin's theology also – Luther returns to the written Word of God. But this Word had also to be preached in order that faith might arise and be confirmed in the church; it is directed to the whole people of God. At the core of the Reformation movement, there is a commitment to preaching to the common people (Julian's 'evenchristen' again). And, in focussing on the Bible, Luther found its hermeneutical principle and material content in the theology of the cross.[18] Hence the work of Christ is expounded in ways that accentuate its benefits for us. Lucas Cranach's altarpiece image of Luther in the Stadtkirche in Wittenberg is compelling. Facing his family, friends, students and fellow townspeople, he gestures towards the figure of the crucified Christ, whose loincloths flutter with the breath of the Spirit. Always this is the proclamation of good news. And yet the hiddenness of God in the cross also requires a dismantling of overconfident views of providence that are self-serving, trivial or triumphalist. A reconstruction of God's ways in the world is demanded of us, when the theology of the cross is acknowledged.

Heinrich Bornkamm notes that for us the abiding fear may no longer be hell and eternal punishment.[19] To that extent, we are

---

[17] Quoted by Roland H. Bainton, *Here I Stand: A Life of Martin Luther* (Nashville: Abingdon, 1950), p. 370. See also Lohse, *Martin Luther's Theology*, p. 332.

[18] For further discussion of the significance of preaching in Luther's Wittenberg, see Kolb, *Martin Luther and the Enduring Word of God*, pp. 174–208.

[19] Heinrich Bornkamm, *Luther's World of Thought* (St Louis: Concordia, 1958), pp. 123–4.

separated from Luther's world of thought. But the breakdowns of life – the failed relationships, the irretrievable wrongs, the painful losses endured – continue to haunt us, not least us as we confront our mortality. The crucified and risen Christ is the guarantee of a love that grasps us in the depths and transforms us in spite of who we are. For this reason, the Last Day is to be welcomed and longed for by Christians everywhere. It is the end of our tribulation and the commencement of God's new creation. Luther writes to his wife of that 'dear last day' (*lieber jüngster Tag*) – a fresh dawn for which he longed, rather than the end he had feared in former times.[20] We face death not alone but in the company of God, Christ, the angels and the communion of saints. Bornkamm notes the importance in Lutheran theology of maintaining company with the dying and 'of shouting in their ears' – there are echoes here of Garrigou-Lagrange. 'Now, in this moment, everything that the church of all times and all places, or, as Luther liked to put it, the communion of saints, has of love, intercession, and supporting power is present for him, the lonely individual.'[21] To carry the cross is not to resign oneself passively to the role of victim; instead, we should think of the calling to bear one another's burdens.[22]

Luther's genius resides in his capacity to maintain this exclusive concentration upon cross and resurrection while applying its insights to an array of pastoral contexts. In this respect, the gap between theologian and preacher is reduced to vanishing point. If this makes his work frustrating from the vantage point of systematic theology, we can still profit from its frequent and arresting insights. His theology of the cross should be read as providential. As gospel, it is presented in the form of promise. Through faith, it provides

---

[20] Martin Luther, *Werke: Kritische Gesamtausgabe, Briefwechsel Band 9: 1540–28* (Weimar: Böhlau, 1941), p. 175.

[21] Bornkamm, *Luther's World of Thought*, p. 128.

[22] Joseph Butler once remarked that 'vicarious punishment is a providential appointment of every day's experience'. I owe this quote to William C. Placher, 'Christ takes our place: rethinking atonement', *Interpretation*, 53.1 (1999), 5–20 at 17.

assurance; through hope, it imparts comfort; through love, it enlivens us for the service of God in the church and the world. And in the constant return to this one point, we are reminded that faith can never be assimilated to our own work. Our standing before God remains wholly dependent upon the divine work. In understanding the ways of God, we are brought for the first time to a clearer comprehension of ourselves.[23]

In this theology of cross and resurrection, there is a strong unilateral mode of divine performance that cannot be captured merely by combining first-article themes of order with third-article notions of spiritual inspiration, though these will need to be connected in any adequate account. At this point, moreover, we see why providence is only minimally an *articulus mixtus*. The theology of the cross cannot be adumbrated along philosophical lines, nor easily positioned within a worldview dominated by a Paleyan natural theology. As Hans-Martin Barth suggests, a Feuerbachian would hardly have projected the theology of the cross as a way of expressing our deepest human aspirations.[24] With its distinctively cruciform inflection, divine providence must constantly be rescued from false if tempting formulations that incline towards cosmic optimism, historical progress or depictions of human existence rid of dysteleological suffering and failure.

---

[23] See Paul Althaus, *The Theology of Martin Luther* (Philadelphia: Fortress, 1966), p. 31.

[24] Hans-Martin Barth, *The Theology of Martin Luther: A Critical Assessment* (Minneapolis: Fortress, 2013), p. 86. A possible objection might appeal to Girard's mimetic theory of the scapegoat, which offers an anthropological reading of the work of Christ. As a victim who is punished for our failures, Christ is another scapegoat, the dramatisation of whose innocence should finally end all such practice. Yet the work of Christ as a voluntary 'once for all' sacrifice is ordered towards the acquittal of the guilty and is not simply an egregious human error. Girard's theory does not capture this at all. See for example Placher, 'Christ takes our place', and George Hunsinger, 'The politics of the nonviolent God: reflections on René Girard and Karl Barth' in *Disruptive Grace: Studies in the Theology of Karl Barth* (Edinburgh: T&T Clark, 2000), pp. 21–41.

Theologians have sometimes reached too swiftly for aesthetic analogies which suggest that everything in creation contributes to an overall harmony. The danger here is of transposing moral and religious objections to suffering into artistic descriptions of the shadow in the painting or the discordant note in the music which comprise a richer and more poignant performance. The problem of evil resists such categorisation, for much the same reason as we hold that the end cannot always justify the means. Although an account of the rich tapestry of creation might accommodate a modicum of pain and discomfort to facilitate the emergence of greater goods, such considerations can cope neither with the intensity of some forms of suffering nor with the depravity of some of our actions. The distribution and depth of innocent suffering prevent the easy deployment of a theodicy oriented towards an aesthetic resolution.

This problem notwithstanding, the musical analogy of a *cantus firmus* might serve a theology of providence. Originating in medieval and Renaissance composition, and exemplified par excellence by Bach, the *cantus firmus* establishes a steady and underlying melody to which the other contrapuntal tunes relate, while still displaying their own distinctiveness. By theological analogy, we might accord the story of Jesus a central place without detriment to the many other counterpoint tunes that can exist in positive relation to it, without losing their individuality.

This meta-image can incorporate the diverse polyphonic works of the trinitarian God while also positing some unity amid difference. In one of his last letters, Bonhoeffer writes of the way in which the polyphony of music registers an essential theme of the Christian life. 'Only the polyphony gives your life wholeness, and you know that no disaster can befall you as long as the cantus firmus continues.'[25] The *cantus firmus* belongs to God, reflecting the melody of Christ and his work. The counterpoint can be ours through the Spirit, distinctive

---

[25] Dietrich Bonhoeffer, *Works, Vol. 8: Letters and Papers from Prison*, ed. John W. de Gruchy, trans. Isabel Best (Minneapolis: Fortress, 2010), p. 394. Although there are

and different, yet also contributing to the whole composition by its relation to the *cantus firmus*. For Bonhoeffer, this provided a way of relating a love of created realities to a love of the creator, thus enabling a form of secular Christianity or Christian humanism. But the same analogy might be deployed to signify the way in which a polyphony of providential themes is undergirded by one historical sequence that reflects a particular and definitive form of divine action.[26] Crucifixion and resurrection have a finality in terms of their providing a constant point of reference for the Christian – this enables us to discern an emerging order and wholeness in our lives, yet one that carries the promise of a fuller resolution.

6.2.3 *Veni Creator Spiritus*

The swirling of the breeze as Luther preaches in the Stadtkirche of Wittenberg should caution against any sense that divine action is restricted to one past episode. While its attestation may continue to be the focus of the Word, we also require an account of the Spirit as universal, active and providential. Here I begin with the example of the paradox of grace in Donald Baillie's *God Was in Christ*.[27] Without committing to his construction of providence or attempting to frame an account of the incarnation in these terms, I propose that the paradox of grace expresses a central feature of the Christian life (though its application need not be restricted to

similarities here with Mikhail Bakhtin's notion of polyphony as a literary device which are worth pursuing, I neither borrow from this directly nor repose upon his account.

[26] Although this may invite the charge of an implicit Christomonism, much depends on how one constructs the significance of Jesus. For discussion of the theological uses of the *cantus firmus* image, see David J. R. S. Moseley, ' "*Parables*" and "*Polyphony*": the resonance of music as witness in the theology of Karl Barth and Dietrich Bonhoeffer' in Jeremy S. Begbie and Steven R. Guthrie (eds.), *Resonant Witness: Conversations Between Music and Theology* (Grand Rapids: Eerdmans, 2012), pp. 240–70.

[27] Donald M. Baillie, *God Was in Christ: An Essay on Incarnation and Atonement* (London: Faber, 1948), esp. pp. 114–24.

Christians).[28] What Baillie intends is an exposition of the Pauline remark 'I, yet not I, but the grace of God within me' (1 Corinthians 15:10) to describe the ways in which our best, most personal and fully responsible actions are to be properly attributed to the grace of God alone. 'Never is human action more truly and fully personal, never does the agent feel more perfectly free, than in those moments of which he can say as a Christian that whatever good was in them was not his but God's.'[29]

On a first hearing, this may appear like pious religious sentiment cloaked in technical jargon. Yet, as one of 'the immediate utterances of faith', the paradox of grace is hard to gainsay. In attributing a free and virtuous action to divine grace, we find the grain of truth contained in the otherwise problematic cliché 'there but for the grace of God go I'. This ascription of agency to the Spirit offsets any sense of divine influence as the religious analogue of a performance-enhancing drug. The work of God within us does not merely give us a bit extra, as if it only adds momentum or motivation. Instead, it is better compared to the captivation of the self by a Spirit that makes us free, personal and properly attuned. In this context, the paradox of grace is a more adequate description than any model suggesting a pneumatic additive.

Yet Baillie is correct to note that the attribution of everything to divine grace must run together with an affirmation of human freedom and responsibility. This is the paradox – two well-grounded claims though set in unresolved conceptual tension. A hyper-Augustinianism, which does not properly permit the liberty of

---

[28] The standard charge against Baillie's Christology is that it leans towards adoptionism, though this is clearly not his intention given the stress on the qualitative difference and generative capacity of the paradox of grace in the person of Christ. Notwithstanding its difficulties, the paradox of grace may provide a useful way of imagining an encounter with Christ in his incarnate ministry – this is highly problematic on the standard Chalcedonian model. For a fuller account of his approach to providence, a theme to which Donald Baillie regularly returned, see *Faith in God and Its Christian Consummation* (Edinburgh: T&T Clark, 1927), pp. 288–94.

[29] Baillie, *God Was in Christ*, p. 114.

the will, simply distorts the confession of grace by abrogating the paradox. We require a 'both/and' description rather than an 'either/or' that apportions part to God and part to ourselves. If personal responsibility is a necessary element, this is not the salient factor or the relevant reason that we are inclined to cite for 'whatever is of good report' (Philippians 4:8). The grace of the Spirit before, during and after our own activity is what really counts. This is not to be regarded as the effusion of an over-wrought sanctimony, but as the proper confession of those who find themselves surprised by grace. Its paradoxical features need to be held in tension, if a disavowal of Pelagianism is not to lead inexorably to an overdrawn determinism.

Where Baillie's account is arguably deficient is in the lack of a robust description of the person and work of the Spirit. Although this is remedied rather belatedly in his subsequent treatment of the Trinity and the church, he does not sufficiently foreground the Spirit in relation to the paradox of grace. Recent writers have sought to do this, though the *locus classicus* remains Thomas Aquinas's description of the Spirit's role in the infusion of the habit of charity in the human soul. For Aquinas, there is an indwelling of the Spirit which is distinguished both from the presence of God to all creatures and from the unique hypostasisation of God the Son in Christ. This indwelling of the Spirit in the Christian life generates the supernatural gift of charity. '[I]t is necessary that there be some habit of charity created in the soul, according to which the Holy Spirit is said to dwell in the soul itself.'[30]

William Alston has recently attempted a closer investigation of what might be involved in this notion of spiritual indwelling.[31] He considers an interpersonal model and offers a series of images to

---

[30] Thomas Aquinas, *Sentences*, d.17q.1a. See Peter A. Kwasniewski (ed.), *On Love and Charity: Readings from the 'Commentary on the Sentences of Peter Lombard'* (Washington, DC: Catholic University of America, 2008), p. 10.

[31] William P. Alston, 'The indwelling of the Holy Spirit' in *Divine Nature and Human Language: Essays in Philosophical Theology* (Ithaca: Cornell University Press, 1989), pp. 223–52.

characterise it. These include: i) the fictional notion of two minds sharing the same thoughts and feelings, perhaps by some set of neural connectors; ii) the integration of thoughts and mental compartments that is sometimes achieved through psychothera-peutic treatment; and iii) the collective appreciation of a work of music, a game or a speech that is shared by all the members of a crowd. While these analogies must fall short, they point to ways in which an internal captivation of personality might take place by the Holy Spirit without implying either coercion or overriding of the freedom and spontaneity of the individual. More problemat-ically, Alston seems to suggest that once the Spirit's initiative has been accomplished this will release the self to work towards its appointed goals.[32] This last point seems a dubious characterisation of the Christian life for the reasons adverted to by Baillie. The work of the Spirit is more than an act of initiation and enablement. To describe the increasing saliency of the Spirit in the sanctified life, we are constrained to confess 'I, yet not I.'

In her critique of Alston's account, Marilyn McCord Adams points out that one may be deeply affected by the conditions of the surrounding environment without ever becoming conscious of this.[33] For example, we are not generally aware of the oxygen in the air, despite our constant dependence on it. And in cases of back-ground noises and scents, we may only be dimly conscious of these without being able to describe their content and source. Adams goes on to develop what she describes as the 'interpersonal transac-tion model' as providing an analogy for the indwelling of the Spirit. A therapist may be attuned to a client's mood and feelings. Through this process, the client gradually reaches a deep awareness of her situation and so can experience some healing. An attunement of

---

[32] Ibid., p. 251. Alston's closing position seems to lean too far towards the autonomy of the Christian instead of stressing a union with Christ through the Spirit.

[33] See Marilyn McCord Adams, 'The indwelling of the Holy Spirit: some alternative models' in Peter J. Weigel and Joseph G. Prud'homme (eds.), *The Philosophy of Human Nature in Christian Perspective* (New York: Peter Lang, 2016), pp. 83–99.

emotion and thought can also mark the interaction of lovers and friends. As this happens, each is enriched and strengthened in ways that would be impossible without the interaction. Where the Spirit's indwelling is concerned, Adams is concerned to stress that this is universal and often unconscious.

For much of the time, we may be unaware of being indwelt by God's spirit. Yet when such awareness arises, it takes the form of a realisation of what has been there all along. Vivid and episodic perceptions of presence are revelatory precisely in their disclosure of a reality that is not momentary but enduring. The constancy and persistence of the Spirit are characteristics of our experience of it, though this presence precedes our awareness. For Adams, spiritual indwelling should be considered universal. Since the love of God is comprehensive, we cannot envisage a decision to indwell one person while desisting in the case of others. One weakness of this approach, however, is that it tends to depict the agency of the Spirit primarily in terms of a private indwelling of the Spirit. Such exclusive interiorising of the Spirit fails to register properly our dependence upon other people and our involvement in social practices, as if the real action of God must first take place within me, rather than in the world around me.[34]

To resolve this, an enhanced account of the Spirit – not only as indwelling the believer, but as omnipresent and circumambient – is required. Both models are employed by the New Testament writings, though, as David Kelsey notes, the indwelling of the Spirit is dependent upon its circumambient presence in the church and the world.[35] The latter takes priority, though much of the standard characterisation of the work of the Spirit refers us only to the

---

[34] This is addressed by Adams in a rather different context with reference to the more corporate aspects of divine personality. See Marilyn McCord Adams, *Christ and Horrors: The Coherence of Christology* (Cambridge: Cambridge University Press, 2006), pp. 144–69 at p. 156: 'The whole universe is envisaged as a society of friends, with Christ as center.'

[35] '[N]ot only is it one-sided to ignore the Spirit's environing relation around about us; to do so subverts the way in which New Testament accounts of the Spirit ground its

former.[36] Yet the interior work of the Spirit is often effective in connecting us to the established practices in which the Spirit is already at work in the church and the world. These might include forms of care, education, social witness, administration of justice, and support of the economy. Here the connection with wisdom is apparent, though a dynamic account of divine presence can also designate ways in which the Spirit enables criticism, reform and innovation.

What does this entail for a theology of providence? The action of the Spirit has a providential dimension throughout the New Testament, whether in shaping the church, sending its people, calling and equipping the saints, or generating the 'fruit' listed by Paul in Galatians 5:22–3. As dove of peace, tongues of fire or advocate, the Spirit's activity establishes 'atmospheric conditions' for practices that, shaped by a Christ-like pattern, promote creaturely welfare and so counteract those disruptive and selfish tendencies within our nature. Adams writes: 'It is only to the extent that our defences come down in relation to God that we consciously and unconsciously experience Divine love and resourcefulness enough to let go of our darwinian strategies for self-preservation and accept life as a gift that God can be trusted to keep on giving forever.'[37]

The plea for the theology of the providence to shift emphasis from the first article to the (present and future) work of the Holy Spirit is well made by Christian Link and others.[38] Further reflection on this

intimate relation to human persons' interiorities in its always already being there as those persons' environing context, and not the reverse.' Kelsey, *Eccentric Existence*, vol. I, p. 444.

[36] This may have something to do with the ways in which the functions of spirit (*ruaḥ*) in the Hebrew Bible tended to be appropriated to the Word (*logos*) of God in the New Testament, thus constricting a theology of the third article of the faith. See Alasdair Heron, *The Holy Spirit* (Philadelphia: Westminster, 1983), p. 59.

[37] Marilyn McCord Adams, 'The indwelling of the Holy Spirit', p. 97.

[38] For example, Christian Link, *Schöpfung: ein theologischer Entwurf im Gegenüber von Naturwissenschaft und Ökologie* (Neukirchen-Vluyn: Neukirchener Theologie, 2012), p. 334.

wider corporate dimension of the Spirit is needed – the reluctance of some theologians to explore this may reflect an antipathy towards process metaphysics and its accompanying doctrinal commitments. But a more adequate pneumatology is required in this context, not least for understanding the providential dimension of the third article. This requires more detailed explication of the ways in which spiritual circumambience and indwelling constitute distinct forms of divine influence upon the world. In this way, it illustrates how vital notions of partnership, improvisation and interaction can better be accommodated within a theology of providence, as opposed to more unitarian accounts of primary and secondary causation.

6.3 A Practical Theology of Providence: Prayer, Politics and Suffering

Much of the preceding discussion impinges upon the spiritual life. Existential themes of guidance, order, redemption and promise also disclose the crossover between systematic and pastoral theology. This is especially marked within the treatment of providence. In conclusion, I offer comment on three topics where the curricular division between the doctrinal and the practical has not served us well.

6.3.1 *Prayer*

Petitionary prayer is a regular and frequent feature of the Christian life. And there will be many people outside or on the fringes of the church who maintain an occasional practice of prayer. Given the weekly petitions offered for the church and the world, one wonders what significance is attached to these acts by the occupants of the pews. Some rationale is owed them by their theologians and leaders of worship. This has the twofold task of disabusing people of some of the more frivolous and implausible aspects of prayer while seeking to

offer an account that avoids reduction solely to religious contemplation or meditation. Here the triple themes explored in the previous
section offer some pointers. The practice of prayer should not expect
God to suspend the regular processes of nature. Sometimes this may
disappoint us, but in general many Christians seem to respect and
understand the ways in which divine action can be constructed. At
the same time, the dynamic presence of the Spirit finds opportunities to work in and through nature and society, offering resources
and possibilities for self-conscious agents to respond. These are
patterned according to the life of Christ, which offers direction for
these forms of response. Within the divine–human interaction,
particularly with respect to the work of the Spirit, prayer has an
important place.

As Hendrikus Berkhof once pointed out, treatises on prayer
are quite rare in the history of theology, at least in the western
traditions of the church.[39] Yet the logic of prayer and the variety
of its forms follows directly from considerations of divine providence. God's sovereignty as reflected in the goodness of creation
calls forth our praise and thanksgiving. The covenant partnership
between God and creatures generates a dialogical relationship
marked by address and response. The ministry of Jesus is informed
by a regular habit of prayer, which is transmitted to his disciples.
The indwelling of the Spirit prompts us to pray and directs our
thoughts. A reduction of this plurality of forms to only one mode
of praying is mistaken. There is no single essence or form that can
be identified, whether in terms of contemplation, mystical union
or alignment of self with the divine. While these must have their
place, other forms including petition, intercession and complaint
should be accommodated.

---

[39] Henrikus Berkhof, *Christian Faith: An Introduction to the Study of the Faith* (Grand
Rapids: Eerdmans, 1979), p. 495. For a brief but valuable reflection on the works of
Origin, Gregory of Nyssa and John Cassian on the Lord's Prayer, see Rowan Williams,
Being Christian: Baptism, Bible, Eucharist, Prayer (London: SPCK, 2014), pp. 61–82.

A theology of prayer can readily offer therapeutic justification for regular practice. It is to our advantage that prayer facilitates self-recognition, acceptance of one's condition, and the articulation of fears, anxieties and hopes. The current interest in mindfulness appreciates these therapeutic elements, which can be transposed into more secular forms of meditation. With respect to the practice of intercession, we can offer some rationale in terms of purifying our desires and willing what is good for others. In consciously aligning ourselves with God's good purposes, we expose ourselves to the deeper influence of the Spirit. These are plausible responses to scepticism around the habit of prayer and they should not be neglected by the theologian. And the concept of covenant implies a measure of reciprocity and partnership in which communication is essential. For this reason, a description of divine–human fellowship cannot manage without offering an account of prayer. As far as the Psalms are concerned, God desires our conversation, our requests and even our complaints.[40]

But in praying for the sick, the dispossessed, the war-torn and the dying, we seem to be aiming at more than this.[41] Our prayers are intended to make some positive contribution not only to ourselves but to others, and not merely through our becoming more resolved to support those in need. The practice of intercessory prayer presupposes that it can make a difference to the way in which God acts towards other people. Here problems confront us. Why would God not act alone? Can we really imagine that our requests

---

[40] Vincent Brümmer notes the ways in which prayer is essential to the personal dimension of the divine–human relationship. 'Prayer and the life of fellowship with God are impossible without each other.' *What Are We Doing When We Pray? On Prayer and the Nature of Faith* (Aldershot: Ashgate, 2008), p. 131.

[41] John Cassian describes the range and centrality of intercessory prayer in his classic study. '[T]here are intercessions, which we are also accustomed to make for others when our spirits are fervent, beseeching on behalf of our dear ones and for the peace of the whole world.' 'Ninth conference: on prayer', Boniface Ramsey (ed.), *John Cassian: The Conferences* (New York: Paulist Press, 1997), pp. 323-63 at pp. 337–8.

will incite God to do something which otherwise would remain undone? And what possible mechanism will explain how the transmission of prayer takes effect? The formidable difficulties presented by these questions have sometimes led theologians to stress the role of prayer as submission or attunement, as opposed to making any difference either to God or to the world beyond ourselves. John Oman, to cite one example, stresses the importance of aligning ourselves with God in prayer rather than seeking to interfere with general providence.[42] There is much wisdom in this. The tendency for prayer to become self-serving is too readily apparent. Each of us may be prone to the assumption, more than we might wish to admit, that we can do deals with God or enjoy the capacity to control providence by our good works.

Consider the ways in which human beings appear incurably superstitious. Notions that we can manipulate God (or some pagan surrogate such as fate, destiny or fortune) abound in activities that are inherently unpredictable simply because of their complexity, or because we lack any adequate knowledge of causal processes, or on account of the way in which outcomes are finely balanced. The logo for the National Lottery in the UK is a finger that must single out someone for special favour. We know that sports personalities are inherently superstitious and religious, sometimes because this is believed to give them a competitive advantage. Consider how many substitutes cross themselves before entering the field of play, or prayers that are invoked during the team huddle prior to kick-off, or thanks offered after a goal, a touchdown or final victory. Some golfers will silently pray before making a crucial shot, as if God were likely to reward them for their piety, presumably punishing an opponent

---

[42] See John Oman, 'Prayer in Christ's name' in F. H. Ballard (ed.), *'A Dialogue with God' and Other Sermons by the Late John Oman* (London: James Clarke, 1950), pp. 54–60. 'True confidence in prayer is in knowing that the highest thing we ask for is the thing God has already granted to us' (pp. 59–60). For a useful discussion of this topic, see Philip Clements-Jewery, *Intercessory Prayer: Modern Theology, Biblical Teaching and Philosophical Thought* (Aldershot: Ashgate, 2005), esp. pp. 43–7.

who plays without such invocation. A story is told of the famous baseball catcher Yogi Berra, who waited behind an incoming hitter. When his opponent proceeded to cross himself before receiving the first pitch, Berra quietly said to him, 'Why don't you just let God enjoy the game?' The underlying point is that God does not do deals with us, at least not in this way – sometimes a hard lesson to learn in matters more important than the outcome of a ball game.

An important function of the theology and practice of prayer is to purge us of these deceits. John Oman points out that Jesus renounced such ways in the temptation story.[43] The suspension of the normal processes of nature was a road not taken. And, at other junctures in the gospel story, there is a submission to God's will which is an intrinsic element of prayer. This alignment of self with God is a regular undertaking that involves confession, meditation, purgation, gratitude and the opening of self to the divine presence and purpose. In these ways, the habit of prayer is one important means by which the providence of God is enacted in our lives. Through prayer, we can become the channels of providence for others. Eastern Christianity may be rather better at expressing this, with its focus on the body and its breathing as affording a keener sense of God living within us and through us. And yet, as already noted, prayer is more than a strategy of submission. The task of serving God in the daily round is embedded in all the petitions of the Lord's Prayer. And we are encouraged by apostolic exhortation to make our requests known to God (Philippians 4:6–7). Is this unreasonable? In his essay 'Is life worth living?', William James suggests otherwise: 'I confess that I do not see why the very existence of an invisible world may not in part depend on the personal response which any one of us may make to the religious appeal. God himself, in short, may draw vital strength and increase of very being from our fidelity.'[44]

---

[43] Oman, 'Prayer in Christ's name'.

[44] James, *The Will to Believe and Other Essays*, p. 61. For a similar argument in favour of the realisation of divine purpose through petitionary prayer, see H. H. Farmer, *The*

To address the difficulties that this inevitably presents, we might appeal to some themes that have already surfaced in this study. A world in which God's spirit is a universal and circumambient presence generates the possibility that we can add our own energy through a process of alignment by prayer. This may be what God wants and so permits by virtue of an accompanying of all creation. Being with, for and alongside others, the Holy Spirit can make some difference without suspending natural and social processes. God's presence in and through the physical world may prove enabling, healing and consoling. By adding our own more limited spiritual energy to the divine we can participate in that process and so contribute in some small measure. This modest contribution to the working of God in the world is something that God intends for us. The locus for this reflection on prayer is the third article. For some, this deflated account of divine action in response to prayer will be insufficient. For others, it will continue to present an implausibly 'wacko' view of how prayer works. Yet, the recent sociological research of Robert Wuthnow suggests that this middle ground is inhabited by significant numbers of Christians today.[45] In acknowledging familiar causal processes, they do not seek the interruption of these by invoking spectacular miracles. But in continuing to pray, the dual conviction becomes apparent that this is both important for them and can make some difference to the lives of others, albeit in ways that are mysterious and not well understood. In praying, many people think in terms of God strengthening and assisting the efforts of carers, leaders and peace-makers while also consoling and uplifting those who suffer and are in distress. Enhancement of wisdom, succour and spiritual strength can meaningfully be requested of God for others, even though we remain doubtful about

---

World and God: A Study of Prayer, Providence and Miracle in Christian Experience (London: NIsbet & Co., 1935), p. 138.

[45] Robert Wuthnow, *The God Problem: Expressing Faith and Being Reasonable* (Berkeley: University of California Press, 2012).

the propriety of praying for a sudden cessation of incurable disease, reversal of physical handicap, or change in the climate. This suggests that prayer is not the irrational expectation of random supernatural intrusion, so much as an activity that belong to a wider interpretive scheme concerning the physical and spiritual realms we inhabit. Wuthnow concludes:

> For many people, prayer is habitual. They pray to greet the morning, to start the day on a positive note, to bring their loved ones' needs to God, to calm their frazzled nerves, or to conclude their day. Prayer is often formulaic, especially at their places of worship, reinforcing familiar beliefs about the existence of God. Yet it is also a topic that requires thoughtful interpretation. Prayer tells people there is something that their rational minds can only partially grasp. Prayer itself is one of those things. It offers assurance, but seldom confers certainty. As a man in Georgia observed, 'You pray for safety for your kids and down deep you know they may be safe – and they might not.'[46]

The pneumatological deficit in much western theology has arguably been the result of a failure to accommodate the Trinitarian logic of prayer. The Christian life is 'in the Spirit', whose indwelling prompts us to pray, as in Romans 8: 26–7.[47] This language of prayer moreover requires attention to the Father as creative source and to the Son as redeemer, thus reinforcing rather than derogating from the distinctiveness of the other two persons. Life in the Spirit assumes a triadic structure, though this recognition may have been hampered in the past by ecclesiastical fear of unregulated spiritual

[46] Ibid., p. 89.

[47] I am indebted here to the argument of Sarah Coakley, 'Why three? Some further reflections on the origins of the doctrine of the Trinity' in Sarah Coakley and David A. Pailin (eds.), *The Making and Remaking of Christian Doctrine: Essays in Honour of Maurice Wiles* (Oxford: Clarendon Press, 1993), pp. 29–56. See also her *God, Sexuality and the Self: An Essay 'On the Trinity'* (Cambridge: Cambridge University Press, 2013), pp. 100–51.

enthusiasm allied to a reinforcement of hierarchical authority. Yet the New Testament is replete with references to the Spirit as an active and present reality that is inextricably bound to 'the Christ event'. The dynamics of this interaction require fuller coverage in a theology of providence.

Somewhat ironically, process theologians, who have often been charged with an inadequate account of divine action, have sought to offer a stronger account in this context. Marjorie Suchocki, for example, writes of the way in which our prayers for others can change the total situation in which God works.[48] After observing the importance of prayer as alignment of the self with God, she considers ways in which intercessory prayer changes the world. This is done neither by changing God's mind nor by goading God into activity, but instead by altering the total situation of the world in which God is constantly at work. In a process universe, she argues, these actions of conscious agents make a small difference to the way the world is. This has the dual advantage of making some sense of petitionary prayer while also recognising that its effects are restricted when other factors are taken into account. Our acts of intercession do not suddenly counteract all other forces, but nor

---

[48] Marjorie Hewitt Suchocki, *God, Christ, Church: A Practical Guide to Process Theology* (New York: Crossroad, 1986), pp. 203–10. See also E. Frank Tupper, *A Scandalous Providence: The Jesus Story of the Compassion of God* (Macon, GA: Mercer University Press, 2003), p. 302. I find this a more useful response than the standard defence of petitionary prayer, namely that God has decreed from all eternity sometimes to use our prayers as instruments, i.e. appointed secondary causes, for fulfilling the divine purpose. This has an impressive pedigree in writers including Origen and Aquinas. But it seems a rather contrived solution that belongs to a determinist worldview, since the decree of God to use prayer in this way amounts only to the appearance of reciprocity. For this reason, its practical usefulness seems questionable. Like the Augustinian doctrine of predestination, we may have to forget it most of the time or else consign it to the status of 'high mystery'. See also Brümmer, *What Are We Doing When We Pray?*, pp. 58–9, and Keith Ward, *Divine Action: Examining God's Role in an Open and Emergent Universe* (West Conshohocken, PA: Templeton Foundation Press, 2007), p. 160.

are they delusional in their primary intentionality with respect to making some difference. If this takes us into a realm of uncomfortable speculation, then so be it. Our knowledge of physical processes is not so comprehensive as to exclude this possibility.[49] The regular practice of petitionary prayer, whether corporate or private, is both a command and a blessing that are integral to our relationship with God. In praying, we find ourselves both the passive recipients of providential grace and its agency for others.

6.3.2 Politics

The preceding discussion has pointed to ways in which political readings of providence have tended towards the over-determination of historical events with religious significance. The deleterious effects of this include a triumphalism that can segue into a disregard for other nations, cultures and forms of life. Examples of this are not hard to identify from the eighteenth and nineteenth centuries. But less often noticed are the ways in which more positive constructions of providence were concealed by these theological and homiletical manoeuvres. The ascription of divine punishment to the Lisbon earthquake obscured the heroic work of Pombal and many others in supplying assistance to the stricken and securing the city's defences. Yet this work was surely a better candidate for the exercise of God's will than the earthquake itself. As a form of special providence, good government makes greater sense than natural disaster.

If the failings of the past were evident in ideological support for dubious political projects and actors, the reverse may threaten us today. A theology that is stuck in a denunciatory reverse gear may find it difficult to offer any measure of support or recognition of the

---

[49] 'Whatever else be certain, this at least is certain – that the world of our present natural knowledge *is* enveloped in a larger world of *some* sort of whose residual properties we at present can frame no idea.' James, *The Will to Believe and Other Essays*, p. 54.

providential possibilities of politics. This in turn can result in the absence of moral direction, civic virtue or vocational possibilities in contemporary political life. Instead of the uncritical allegiance of yesteryear, there arises voter apathy, a hollowing out of the public sphere, or a contemptuous cynicism of the political process. How to escape this without repeating past mistakes or finding new forms of collusion remains a challenge for political theology today.

The approaches adopted in Scripture reveal that this problem is hardly new. The Psalms of enthronement extol the potential of kingship for establishing a just and peaceful order in accordance with the law of God. Hence the reign of the king can promote a godly commonwealth. Yet the history of Israel and the preaching of the prophets frequently attest the reality of corruption and disobedi-ence amid those in power and the groups that support them. For this reason, Martin Buber regarded the prophets as the authentic voice of Judaism, offering a hope that transcended the history of their political failure.[50] Within the New Testament, the imperial rule is responsible for the crucifixion of Jesus. The early church endured bouts of persecution and is frequently set in a counter-cultural stance. But, notwithstanding these problems, there remains a sense of political rule as ordained by God with the potential to maintain a measure of justice and peace (Romans 13:1–7; 1 Peter 2:13–17). In the teaching of Jesus, the kingdom of God is a reality already at hand and in-breaking, yet not fully realised and frequently beset with opposition. Since its final accomplishment is eschatological, any interim political regime must be held accountable for its inevitable shortcomings.

Hence, the scriptural precedents already point towards a dialectic of critical deconstruction and positive potential. This has left sub-sequent Christian theology with the task of finding its way between a Manichean dualism on the one side and a Whiggish optimism on the other. In negotiating this course, writers have tended to offset

---

[50] Martin Buber, *On the Bible* (New York: Schocken Books, 1982), 148–150.

the former by appeal to the goodness of physical and social exist-ence coupled with an affirmation of the resurrection of Christ and the activity of the Spirit in the world. To combat the latter, arguments have focussed on the fallenness of creation and the insinuation of personal life and social structures by fallibility, corruption and evil. In reflecting upon the rule of God in world occurrence, Karl Barth notes that there is neither unequivocal affirmation nor negation.[51] This generates a constant responsibility both to negate and to affirm, while also discerning where the balance lies. Hence the prophetic criticism of institutions and political actors also carries the respon-sibility of offering support where this is due and seeking forms of amelioration, rather than merely resting on the far side of negation while continuing to draw a salary.[52]

Examples of courageous protest are easier to identify – these deserve a place of honour and regular celebration. We may view Gandhi, King, Mandela, Tutu and Aung San Suu Kyi as iconic fig-ures through whom God has worked in recent times, whether or not Christian, notwithstanding their previous or subsequent failings. As exemplars of divine providence in history, these have sometimes combined in the face of egregious injustice both prophetic witness and personal commitment. But a politics of providence might seek to discern the hand of God far below the headlines, and often in local forms of action, rather than in the processes and movements that are the customary focus of historical study. If we think of providence as often hidden in unexpected places and agents, then its more positive manifestations may appear more manifold than is generally recognised. There are others who in office have sought to do the right thing, despite the loss of popularity and career

---

[51] Karl Barth, *Church Dogmatics* IV/3 (Edinburgh: T&T Clark, 1962), p. 696.

[52] The contribution of Reinhold Niebuhr continues to be cited, particularly in the USA as an important resource in this setting. See for example Robin W. Lovin, *Reinhold Niebuhr and Christian Realism* (Cambridge: Cambridge University Press, 1995), pp. 158–90. Niebuhr's enduring appeal is evident in the recent film *An American Conscience: The Reinhold Niebuhr Story* (2017), produced by Martin Doblmeier.

opportunity, and those whose diligence and skill have prevented war, alleviated suffering or produced more effective systems of education and health care. Though harder to name, they have exercised an important vocation and have achieved some providential outcomes. John Macmurray points to this in these salutary remarks. 'When we track the state to its lair, what shall we find? Merely a collection of overworked and worried (people), not at all unlike ourselves, doing their best to keep the machinery of government working as well as may be, and hard put to it to keep up appearances.'[53]

The work of conservation is easy to neglect in this context. Yet as a reflection of the divine *conservatio*, it may deserve fuller recognition in a politics of providence, as well as ecological ethics. Towards the end of the first book of *De Regno*, Thomas Aquinas writes of the role of the king in conserving the common good through succession planning, the maintenance of legal systems, and the defence of the realm from external peril.[54] This act of preserving the political community sits alongside the need constantly to seek improvement. The defence and maintenance of institutions amid internal and external pressures can often prevent their collapse and disruption to the detriment of the most vulnerable. Burke's admittedly tendentious metaphor of the cattle quietly grazing in the field gestures in this direction. 'Because half a dozen grasshoppers under a fern make a field ring with their importunate chink, while thousands of great cattle, reposed beneath the shadow of the British oak, chew the cud and are silent, pray do not imagine that those who make the noise are the only inhabitants of the field.'[55]

Conservation, as well as correction, may be a theme much in need of expression at a time of populist politics and sudden geopolitical shifts. A democratic society typically requires an independent

---

[53] John Macmurray, *Persons in Relation* (London: Faber & Faber, 1961), pp. 200–1.

[54] See R. W. Dyson (ed.), *Aquinas: Political Writings* (Cambridge: Cambridge University Press, 2002), pp. 44–5.

[55] Edmund Burke, *Reflections on the Revolution in France*, ed. Frank Turner (New Haven: Yale University Press, 2003), p. 73.

judiciary, fair elections, a free press and other checks and balances that curb power, protect minorities and hold powerful political and economic elites to account. We may underestimate the contribution of those office-bearers whose work has been directed towards a maintenance of such socio-political institutions and the relative order that they can provide. Liable to deconstruction, such ascriptions of providentialism remain dangerous of course. Subsequent developments and exposures may render them ambivalent at best – Suu Kyi may provide a recent example – and history has witnessed too many claims to the quasi-messianic status of political leaders. Yet, for the reasons advanced above, we cannot evacuate the field of all possibility without also denying the presence and activity of God in the temporal world. Although it is not our task to usher in the millennium or to participate in the steady progressivism of liberal systems, there may be ways in which our politics can remain engaged and committed under the providence of God. Although these should shun the grandiose claims of collectivist visions and ideologies of the free market, the alliance with democratic ideals remains worthy of ecclesial support.[56]

6.3.3 Suffering

The theology of providence has too often been self-confident in its assertions surrounding God's ways in the world, as if these could

---

[56] Hans Frei argues along similar lines in his commentary on H. Richard Niebuhr. '[A] gospel of the universal, present, governing glory of God might have more to do with a carefully circumscribed progressive politics than with either a theology of revolution or some other political theology ... One step at a time, no more than that for the task of public theology.' 'H. Richard Niebuhr on history, church and nation' in Ronald F. Thiemann (ed.), *The Legacy of H. Richard Niebuhr* (Minneapolis: Fortress, 1991), pp. 1–23 at p. 23. For further discussion, see Mike Higton, *Christ, Providence and History: Hans W. Frei's Public Theology* (London: T&T Clark, 2004), pp. 167–73. Frei's notion of a figuration of Christ in secular history is not dissimilar to the model of a *cantus firmus* above.

be deduced from or made synonymous with events that are going well for us and our kindred. This generates acute pastoral problems in the face of sudden setback, serious illness or overwhelming tragedy. Too tight a fit between contingent events and the divine will has resulted in an over-determination of suffering as punishment, testing or the means to some foreordained end. To claim that everything is meant to be and must be for the best is unduly acquiescent. Theology and the Christian life must find a way between the sirens of bland optimism and resigned fatalism.

We may want to see every occasion as situated within the scope of God's care, but this is a different thought from the one that sees every event as sent by God. Created forces such as accident, chance, sickness, health and prosperity have their place and exercise their influence but should be complemented by an account of divine wisdom and redemption that finds its paradigm in the cross and resurrection. There is a morning prayer that begins with the words 'we do not know what the day will bring forth, save that the hour for serving thee is always present'.[57] This seems to capture the balance between allowing scope for the changes and chances of our lives, while seeing these as falling inside the greater scope of a divine purpose.

Some people are simply the victims of desperately bad luck or grievous accident or human malevolence. A former student, Helen Jones, was a young woman who came to the University of Aberdeen from Annan, near the town of Lockerbie. As a child, it was her good fortune to have escaped death on the night of 21 December 1988 when Pan Am flight 103 was destroyed overhead. A bright and accomplished student of systematic theology, she graduated with a first-class degree. But while working in London several years later she found herself boarding a tube at King's Cross Station on 7 July 2005, where she was killed by a suicide bomber. There is no theological

---

[57] Although the prayer is attributed to the Unitarian philosopher James Martineau, I have been unable to identify the source.

rationale that can explain why she survived one bombing, only to perish in another. She was in the wrong place at the wrong time, a life suddenly cut short at the age of twenty-eight.

Why has God done this to me, especially when I have tried to lead a faithful and upright life? Such questions seem spontaneous and ineluctable, especially to parents who have lost children, but these should not be allowed to become the occasion for bad theology, even if some people appear to be consoled by the thought of an inscrutable divine volition that foreordains everything that happens. Jesus' remarks about the fate of those who were crushed by the tower of Siloam (Luke 13:4) and his reflection on the man born blind (John 9:3) suggest that there is no direct divine correlation between the merits of our actions and the fate we suffer. Each event may provide a fresh opportunity for serving God or deepening faith, but it is important to distinguish this from the claim that events are directly visited upon us to exercise some finely grained but obscure divine purpose.

At the same time, a theory of providence enters impossible territory if the work of God is seen as favourably disposed to one individual at the expense of another. Here we have an example of believing too much in the wrong things. This is often the reaction of those who survive disasters when others around them perish. Doubtless it is natural to seek an answer to the question 'why me?' And survival can often be a turning point, a moment of crisis that is put to some heroic use in the redirection of a life. But it is claiming too much to portray providence as distributing favours, if this implies that these are deliberately withheld from others in the same situation. Confronted by this thought, Elie Wiesel wrote in the preface to the new translation of his holocaust novel, *Night*:

> There are those who tell me that I survived in order to write this text. I am not convinced … A miracle? Certainly not. If heaven could or would perform a miracle for me, why not for others more deserving than myself. It was nothing more than chance … I only know that

without this testimony, my life as a writer – or my life, period – would not have become what it is: that of a witness who believes he has a moral obligation to try to prevent the enemy from enjoying one last victory by allowing his crimes to be erased from human memory.[58]

Today, it has become customary in this context to denounce the project of theodicy. This is not just profoundly difficult, we are told, but fundamentally mistaken. The Bible offers not theoretical solutions to the problem of evil, but a range of practical responses following the pattern of Christ's life, death and resurrection. Doubtless there are good reasons for not attaching too much significance to our theodicies – these are of limited success and of doubtful practical use. Even if we could come up with a convincing explanation of why God permitted or willed evil, would that help those who make journeys of pain amid the shadows.[59] The spectator might find an intellectually satisfying explanation of the sort demanded by Philo in Hume's *Dialogues*, but the agent is unlikely to use this to good effect. Better, it seems, to admit our ignorance and the limits placed upon our knowledge. In any case, a theodicy can too easily slide into acceptance of the ways things are, thus ignoring the need to defeat evil, rather than to explain it. No answers may be preferable to those that are pastorally counter-productive or lead in wrong directions.

I recall once visiting a woman in my congregation who had a malignant tumour in her jaw. She had suffered too long and the invasive treatment seemed unlikely to arrest her cancer. When I came upon her in the hospital ward, her face was badly disfigured. Tubes had been inserted into both her nose and her mouth. Since

---

[58] Elie Wiesel, *Night* (New York: Hill & Wang, 2006), p. viii.

[59] In what follows, I have been influenced by Nicholas Wolterstorff, *Lament for a Son* (London: SPCK, 2007). 'I have read the theodicies produced to justify the ways of God to man. I find them unconvincing. To the most agonized question I have ever asked I do not know the answer. I do not know why God would watch him fall. I do not know why God would watch me wounded. I cannot even guess' (pp. 67–8).

she could not speak, there was a notepad and pencil at her bedside. I expected her to exchange some initial pleasantries, but she wrote down just one word for me, 'why?' I was struck by the juxtaposition of our situations. She was facing prolonged suffering and death, combined with anxieties, which were to prove well founded, about her husband's capacity to cope on his own. I was a young minister at the outset of my career, and soon to be married. It was a summer's day – the sun was shining on me, but not on her. Though I had received more than a decade of training in philosophy and theology, all I could say to her was 'I don't know'. The only thing that lame answer had going for it was that it was true. She was decent enough to squeeze my hand, as if to say that she did not expect much, and there we remained, both speechless though for different reasons.

What we find in the recent literature instead is a concentration on strategies of discipleship. These are set in dialectical opposition to the classical theodicies, the experiential being preferred to the theoretical. John Swinton writes of listening to the silence, of practising lament and forgiveness, and of showing care and hospitality. Many of these practices do flourish and act in ways that support the sick and the bereaved. 'The church is an embodied theodicy of practice that does not seek to explain how a good, all-loving, all-powerful God could allow evil and suffering, but through its practices and gestures of redemption reveals in concrete, tangible forms the way in which God responds to evil.'[60]

This seems right, though there lurks a danger that more 'practical' responses to the problem of evil will generate their own difficulties. Any meaningful practice must be informed by regular reflection. And, if we are not careful, a response to evil in terms of a discipleship patterned by the crucified and risen Christ may run the risk of an incipient Pelagianism that sets the bar very high for those who experience the worst excesses of suffering and evil. In an older Calvinist mind-set, all one had to do was to 'grin and

---

[60] John Swinton, *Raging with Compassion* (Grand Rapids: Eerdmans, 2007), p. 246.

bear it' because suffering was sent either for our chastisement or for our humility. But an over-stressed insistence on a discipled suffering may impose too much upon those who struggle with sickness, misfortune, guilt and bereavement. Attention to the vicarious sufferings of Christ enables a stress upon the 'once for all' nature of his work, one outcome of which is a yoke that is easier and a burden that is lighter. We are not called to heroic repetition, though some may aspire to this. And, in any case, who are we to prevent people from raising intellectual questions with us about evil? These emerge at hospital bedsides, in grief-stricken homes and in Bible study groups, as well as in the seminary, the university and the pub late at night. A blanket suppression of such questions may be just as pastorally strained as the pedalling of unrealistic solutions.

Some recent work in theodicy has made striking gains in considering ways in which human lives beset by horrendous evils can achieve some great goods that deepen our love for God and our neighbour.[61] In this context, Eleonore Stump points to the importance of second-person knowledge by considering historical narratives rather than sets of philosophical proposition. Exploring the stories of Abraham, Samson, Job and Mary of Bethany, she identifies ways in which the deep disturbances of suffering can sometimes generate vision, action and love, all of which would not have been otherwise realised. This might enable someone to live with the thought that God has permitted a world in which such suffering occurs. In each case, the re-ordering of our heart's desires can lead to a fulfilment which enables us to consider life as a great good even amid its shadows. Evidence of what is now generally described as 'post-traumatic growth' suggests that disruptive and painful episodes can lead to some positive outcomes. These include enhancement of

---

[61] Here I think especially of Marilyn McCord Adams, *Horrendous Evils and the Goodness of God* (Ithaca: Cornell University Press, 2000), and Eleonore Stump, *Wandering in the Darkness: Narrative and the Problem of Suffering* (Oxford: Oxford University Press, 2010).

relationships, a re-ordering of personal priorities coupled with a growth in wisdom and acceptance of vulnerability, and 'alterations in life philosophy such as finding a fresh appreciation for each new day, a sense of what really matters in life, or experiencing a change in spiritual beliefs'.[62] Increasingly documented by researchers, these empirical findings correlate with a providentialism that affirms the possibility of redemption in the face of suffering and evil. While accurate figures are difficult to compute, the incidence may be higher than was previously recognised by research into trauma. Only within the last twenty years or so has post-traumatic growth become a focus of sustained study, though its links with traditional themes of religious transformation are widely recognised.[63]

I find the recent work of Marilyn McCord Adams and Eleonore Stump moving, bold and rigorous. Their success lies in pointing to the ways in which, amid the worst circumstances, people can some-times realise providential possibilities. These are occasions in which divine grace succeeds in our lives. Not everyone is defeated by evil or testifies to the destruction of their faith. On the contrary, occasions of suffering can sometimes generate the most powerful attestations of divine providence. These stories require faithful telling. Post-traumatic growth needs to be recognised in any theology that attests the power of redemption in human lives. For Stump, our 'second-person knowledge' is partly shaped by our encounters with other people and our experience of being befriended, supported and not

---

[62] Stephen Joseph and Kate Hefferon, 'Post-traumatic growth: eudaimonic happiness in the aftermath of adversity' in Ilona Boniwell, Susan A. David and Amanda Conley Ayers (eds.), *Oxford Handbook of Happiness* (Oxford: Oxford University Press, 2013), pp. 926–40 at p. 927. For a theological perspective, see Deborah van Deusen Hunsinger, *Trauma, Gospel, and Pastoral Care* (Grand Rapids: Eerdmans, 2015).

[63] Studies of post-traumatic growth reveal a somewhat bewildering range of 3–99 per cent, depending on types of stress and criteria of measurement. See Mary Beth Werdel and Robert J. Wicks, *Primer on Post-Traumatic Growth* (Hoboken, NJ: John Wiley and Sons, 2012), p. 20.

judged.[64] What it feels like to be loved is not convertible into a philosophical argument but is better expressed in narrative form. To this extent, literature may be a vital resource for philosophical and theological reflection.

The principal difficulty is that this falls well short of constituting an adequate theodicy. Such examples do not produce a cost–benefit analysis that can explain the creation of a world in which such excesses of evil are tolerated. Some forms of stress may profoundly shake us, so leading eventually to positive growth and change. What does not kill us will (sometimes) make us stronger. But in other cases, traumatic stress may shatter people to a point beyond repair. The many lives cut short, overwhelmed or brutalised leave an outstanding surd element that cannot be fully justified by our theodicies. To admit this is not to deny the significance of God's grace in the remarkable resilience of human beings in generating real gains from hardship, illness and loss. Stump's reflections may cause us to wonder if this happens more than we generally realise. As victories of divine providence, these become an important counterpoint to the *cantus firmus* of cross and resurrection. But the drift towards an instrumentalisation of evil should be resisted. Its capacity for destruction cannot be wholly contained or resolved by a worldview in which it constitutes a necessary part of divine design.

Can we speak of everything that happens as willed by God? Classical Reformed dogmatics did this by reference to the threefold pattern of divine action – preservation, concurrence and overruling. But we should speak of the divine will only in a clearly differentiated manner. Insofar as the world is created and sustained by God, it exists in its totality by the divine will. This entails that every event is permitted by God. And, if everything that happens can create an occasion for some redemptive prospect, then we cannot say that any

---

[64] Here she distinguishes between Dominican and Franciscan approaches as types, arguing both for their importance and for their complementarity. See Stump, *Wandering in the Darkness*, pp. 39–63.

event lies irrevocably outside the providential rule of God. But what must also be said, and more clearly than before, is that the nature and purpose of God's action produce a set of criteria by which the divine will is to be measured. And, in this respect, there is clearly much that happens that cannot be said to be the will of God. In eschewing any appeal to inadequate, implausible and offensive explanations, we should admit that there is a surd element in life that remains incomprehensible. While this generates tensions with other theological commitments, we do better to locate these here and not elsewhere. As P. T. Forsyth maintained in another context, it comes down to a choice of difficulties.[65] And in making the choice, we do well also to concede the speculative limits of Christian theology, and to acknowledge its practical character. Though the streetlights trained on the road in front of us leave the surrounding countryside in darkness, we may find sufficient light for the journey ahead.

The main lines of argument have already been set out in the opening section of this chapter. As an exercise in systematic theology, this book will prove frustrating to those who seek greater conceptual coherence. Consistency is not lightly to be eschewed, nor should philosophical rigour be abandoned. Yet the search for a greater adequacy to the range of scriptural themes and the contexts of lived religion has resulted in some losses of systemic unity as the historical forms of providentialism are assessed and reconstructed. While registering a protest against some classical expressions, I have sought to recapture elements of these in an account that somewhat differently accommodates several themes – hence a polyphony (not a cacophony) that views God's providential action in multiple ways.

---

[65] P. T. Forsyth, *The Person and Place of Jesus Christ* (London: Hodder & Stoughton, 1910), p. 294.

Bibliography

Abbott, Christopher. *Julian of Norwich: Autobiography and Theology* (Woodbridge: D. S. Brewer, 1999).

Achituv, Yosef. 'Theology and the Holocaust: the presence of God and divine providence in history from the perspective of the Holocaust' in Steven T. Katz (ed.), *The Impact of the Holocaust on Jewish Theology* (New York: New York University Press, 2005), pp. 275–86.

Adams, Marilyn McCord. *Christ and Horrors: The Coherence of Christology* (Cambridge: Cambridge University Press, 2006).

'Evil and the God-who-does-nothing-in-particular' in D. Z. Phillips (ed.), *Religion and Morality* (New York: St Martin's Press, 1996), pp. 107–32.

Horrendous Evils and the Goodness of God (Ithaca: Cornell University Press, 2000).

'The indwelling of the Holy Spirit: some alternative models' in Peter J. Weigel and Joseph G. Prud'homme (eds.), *The Philosophy of Human Nature in Christian Perspective* (New York: Peter Lang, 2016), pp. 83–99.

Alcinous. *Handbook of Platonism*, ed. John Dillon (Oxford: Oxford University Press, 1993).

Alexander of Hales. *Doctoris irrefragabilis Alexandri de Hales Ordinis minorum Summa theologica*, vol. 1 (Florence: Quaracchi, 1924).

Allen, Diogenes. 'Faith and the recognition of God's activity' in Brian Hebblethwaite and Edward Henderson (eds.), *Divine Action: Studies Inspired by the Philosophical Theology of Austin Farrer* (Edinburgh: T&T Clark, 1990), pp. 197–210.

Alston, William P. 'The indwelling of the Holy Spirit' in *Divine Nature and Human Language: Essays in Philosophical Theology* (Ithaca: Cornell University Press, 1989), pp. 223–52.

Althaus, Paul. *The Theology of Martin Luther* (Philadelphia: Fortress, 1966).

Altmann, Alexander. 'Providence: in medieval Jewish philosophy' in Fred Skolnik (ed.), *Encyclopaedia Judaica*, 2nd edn (Detroit: Macmillan Reference, 2007), vol. XVI, pp. 649–51.

Aplin, Lucy M., Farine, Damien R., Morand-Ferron, Julie, Cockburn, Andrew, Thornton, Alex and Sheldon, Ben. C. 'Experimentally induced innovations lead to persistent culture via conformity in wild birds', *Nature* 518 (26 February 2015), 538–41.

Appleton, Naomi. *Narrating Karma and Rebirth: Buddhist and Jain Multi-Life Stories* (Cambridge: Cambridge University Press, 2014).

Aquinas, Thomas. *Catena Aurea*, ed. J. H. Newman, vol. I.III (London: J. G. F. & G. Rivington, 1842).

The Literal Exposition of Job: A Scriptural Commentary Concerning Providence, trans. Anthony Damien (Atlanta: Scholars' Press, 1989).

Opera Omnia, 25 vols. (Parma, 1852–73).

The Power of God, trans. Richard J. Regan (Oxford: Oxford University Press, 2012).

Summa Contra Gentiles, trans. J. F. Anderson (Notre Dame, IN: University of Notre Dame Press, 1975).

Summa Theologiae, Blackfriars edn, 61 vols., Latin and English with notes and introductions (London: Eyre & Spottiswoode, and New York: McGraw-Hill Book Company, 1964–80).

Aristotle. *Meteorologica*, trans. H. D. P. Lee (London: Heinemann, 1952).

Asselt, Willem J. van, Bac, J. Martin and Velde, Roelf T. te. *Reformed Thought on Freedom: The Concept of Free Choice in Early Modern Reformed Theology* (Grand Rapids: Baker, 2010).

Augustine. *City of God*, trans. Henry Bettenson (Harmondsworth: Penguin, 1972).

'Divine providence and the problem of evil' in Robert P. Russell (ed.), *Writings of St Augustine*, vol. 1 (New York: CIMA Publishing, 1948).

Baelz, Peter. *Prayer and Providence* (London: SCM, 1968).

Baillie, Donald M. *Faith in God and Its Christian Consummation* (Edinburgh: T&T Clark, 1927).

God Was in Christ: An Essay on Incarnation and Atonement (London: Faber, 1948).

Bainton, Roland H. *Here I Stand: A Life of Martin Luther* (Nashville: Abingdon, 1950).

Baker, Denise N. (ed.). *The Showings of Julian of Norwich* (New York: Norton, 2005).

Barclay, John M. G. 'Article review: *Paul and the Faithfulness of God*', *Scottish Journal of Theology*, 68.2 (2015), 235–43.

Barth, Hans-Martin. *The Theology of Martin Luther: A Critical Assessment* (Minneapolis: Fortress, 2013).

Barth, Karl. *Church Dogmatics*, eds. and trans. G. W. Bromiley and T. F. Torrance, vols. I–IV (Edinburgh: T&T Clark, 1956–75).

Basinger, David. *Divine Power in Process Theism: A Philosophical Critique* (Albany, NY: State University of New York, 1988).

Bavinck, Herman. *Reformed Dogmatics, Volume 2: God and Creation* (Grand Rapids: Eerdmans, 2009).

Beardslee III, John W. (ed.). *Reformed Dogmatics* (New York: Oxford University Press, 1965).

Benson, Bruce Ellis. 'Improvising texts, improvising communities: jazz, interpretation, heterophony, and the *ekklesia*' in Jeremy S. Begbie and Steven R. Guthrie (eds.), *Resonant Witness: Conversations Between Music and Theology* (Grand Rapids: Eerdmans, 2011), pp. 295–322.

Bergjan, Silke-Petra. *Der Fürsorgende Gott* (Berlin: De Gruyter, 2002).

Berkhof, Hendrikus. *Christian Faith: An Introduction to the Study of the Faith* (Grand Rapids: Eerdmans, 1979).

Berkouwer, C. G. *The Providence of God* (Grand Rapids: Eerdmans, 1962).
  The Triumph of Grace in the Theology of Karl Barth (Grand Rapids: Eerdmans, 1956).

Berlin, Isaiah. *Russian Thinkers* (London: Penguin, 1978).

Bernasconi, Robert. 'Kant as an unfamiliar source of racism' in Julie K. Ward and Tommy L. Lott (eds.), *Philosophers on Race: Critical Essays* (Oxford: Blackwell, 2002), pp. 145–66.

Besterman, Theodore. *Voltaire* (London: Longmans, Green & Co, 1969).

Blair, Hugh. 'Of our present ignorance of the ways of God' in David Fergusson (ed.), *Scottish Philosophical Theology* (Exeter: Imprint Press, 2007), pp. 79–86.
  'On the love of our country' in *Sermons*, vol. V (London, 1808), pp. 114–39.

Blumenfeld, David. 'Perfection and happiness in the best possible world' in Nicholas Jolley (ed.), *Cambridge Companion to Leibniz* (Cambridge: Cambridge University Press, 1995), pp. 382–410.

Boethius. *The Consolation of Philosophy*, trans. V. E. Watts (Harmondsworth: Penguin, 1969).

Bonhoeffer, Dietrich. *Works, Vol. 8: Letters and Papers from Prison*, ed. John W. de Gruchy, trans. Isabel Best (Minneapolis: Fortress, 2010).

Bornkamm, Heinrich. *Luther's World of Thought* (St Louis: Concordia, 1958).

Bouteneff, Peter C. 'The two wills of God: providence in St John of Damascus', *Studia Patristica*, 42 (2006), 291–96.

Brackenridge, R. Douglas. 'The "Sabbath War" of 1865–66: the shaking of the foundations', *Records of the Scottish Church History Society*, 16 (1969), 143–67.

Brightman, E. S. 'The Lisbon earthquake: a study in religious valuation', *American Journal of Theology*, 23.4 (1919), 500–18.

Broadie, Alexander. *The Scottish Enlightenment* (Edinburgh: Birlinn, 2001).

Brooke, John and Cantor, Geoffrey. *Reconstructing Nature: Engagement of Science and Religion* (Edinburgh: T&T Clark, 1998).

Brooke, John Hedley. 'Natural law in the natural sciences: the origins of modern atheism?', *Science and Christian Belief*, 4:2 (1992), 83–103.

'The relations between Darwin's science and his religion' in John Durant (ed.), *Darwinism and Divinity: Essays on Evolution and Religious Belief* (Oxford: Blackwell, 1985), pp. 40–75.

Brouwer, Rinse H. Reeling. *Karl Barth and Post-Reformation Orthodoxy* (Farnham: Ashgate, 2015).

Brown, Stuart. 'The regularization of providence in post-Cartesian philosophy' in Robert Crocker (ed.), *Religion, Reason and Nature in Early Modern Europe* (Dordrecht: Kluwer, 2001), pp. 1–16.

Brown, Stewart J. *Providence and Empire 1815–1914* (Harlow: Longman, 2008).

'William Robertson (1721–1793) and the Scottish Enlightenment' in Stewart J. Brown (ed.), *William Robertson and the Expansion of Empire* (Cambridge: Cambridge University Press, 1997), pp. 7–35.

Bruce, A. B. *The Providential Order of the World* (New York: Scribner's, 1905).

Brueggemann, Walter. *Theology of the Old Testament: Testimony, Dispute, Advocacy* (Minneapolis: Fortress, 1997).

Brümmer, Vincent. 'Farrer, Wiles and the causal joint', *Modern Theology*, 8 (1992), 1–14.

What Are We Doing When We Pray? On Prayer and the Nature of Faith (Aldershot: Ashgate, 2008).

Buber, Martin. *On the Bible* (New York: Schocken Books, 1982).

Bullinger, Heinrich. *Decades*, vol. IV, ed. Thomas Harding (Cambridge: Cambridge University Press, 1851).

Burke, Edmund. *Reflections on the Revolution in France*, ed. Frank Turner (New Haven: Yale University Press, 2003).

Burns, William. *An Age of Wonders: Prodigies, Politics and Providence in England 1657–1727* (Manchester: Manchester University Press, 2002).

Burrell, David B. *Freedom and Creation in Three Traditions* (Notre Dame, IN: University of Notre Dame Press, 1993).

Towards a Jewish–Christian–Muslim Theology (Oxford: Wiley Blackwell, 2011).

Byrne, Peter. *Natural Religion and the Nature of Religion* (London: Routledge, 1989).

Calvin, John. *Commentary on the Book of Psalms*, vol. IV, trans. James Anderson (Grand Rapids: Baker, 1989).

A Harmony of the Gospels: Matthew, Mark and Luke, ed. D. W. Torrance and T. F. Torrance, 3 vols. (Edinburgh: St Andrew Press, 1972).

Institutes of the Christian Religion, trans. Ford Lewis Battles (Philadelphia: Westminster Press, 1960).

Institutes of the Christian Religion: 1541 French Edition, trans. Elsie Anne McKee (Grand Rapids: Eerdmans, 2009).

Carter, J. Kameron. *Race: A Theological Account* (New York: Oxford University Press, 2008).

Cartwright, Nancy. *The Dappled Universe: A Study of the Boundaries of Science* (Cambridge: Cambridge University Press, 1999).

Cassian, John. 'Ninth conference: on prayer' in Boniface Ramsey (ed.), *John Cassian: The Conferences* (New York: Paulist Press, 1997), pp. 323–63.

Cave, Alfred A. 'Canaanites in a promised land: the American Indian and the providential theory of empire', *American Indian Quarterly*, 12.4 (1988), 277–97.

Chalmers, Thomas. *On the Power, Wisdom and Goodness of God as Manifested in the Adaptation of External Nature to the Moral and Intellectual Constitution of Man* (London: Pickering, 1833).

Chambers, William and Chambers, Robert. *Chambers's Journal*, 6th series, 1, (1897–8).

Chappell, David L. *A Stone of Hope: Prophetic Religion and the Death of Jim Crow* (Chapel Hill: University of North Carolina Press, 2005).

Charry, Ellen. *God and the Art of Happiness* (Grand Rapids: Eerdmans, 2010).

Clarke, M. L. *Paley: Evidences for the Man* (London: SPCK, 1974).

Clarke, Samuel. *A Demonstration of the Being and Attributes of God and Other Writings* (Cambridge: Cambridge University Press, 1998).

'A discourse concerning the unchangeable obligations of truth and certainty of the Christian revelation' in *The Works of Samuel Clarke*, ed. Benjamin Hoadly, 4 vols. (Bristol: Thoemmes, 2002), vol. 11, pp. 595–733.

Clayton, Philip. *God and Contemporary Science* (Edinburgh: Edinburgh University Press, 1997).

Clement, Stromateis in Alexander Robertson and James Donaldson (eds.), *Ante-Nicene Fathers*, 10 vols. (Edinburgh: T&T Clark, 1985–7), vol. 11.

Clements-Jewery, Philip. *Intercessory Prayer: Modern Theology, Biblical Teaching and Philosophical Thought* (Aldershot: Ashgate, 2005).

Coakley, Sarah. *God, Sexuality and the Self: An Essay 'On the Trinity'* (Cambridge: Cambridge University Press, 2013).

Sacrifice Regained: Evolution, Cooperation and God (Oxford: Oxford University Press, in press 2018).

'Why three? Some further reflections on the origins of the doctrine of the Trinity' in Sarah Coakley and David A. Pailin (eds.), *The Making and Remaking of Christian Doctrine: Essays in Honour of Maurice Wiles* (Oxford: Clarendon Press, 1993), pp. 29–56.

Cobb Jr, John B. and Griffin, David Ray. *Process Theology: An Introductory Exposition* (Philadelphia: Westminster, 1976).

Cochrane, A. C. (ed.). *Reformed Confessions of the Sixteenth Century* (Philadelphia: Westminster John Knox Press, 2003).

Cone, James H. *A Black Theology of Liberation* (Maryknoll, NY: Orbis, 1986).

Cottingham, John. *Descartes* (Oxford: Blackwell, 1986).

Darwin, Francis (ed.). *Life and Letters of Charles Darwin: Vol. II* (London: John Murray, 1888).

Davies, Brian. *Thomas Aquinas's Summa Contra Gentiles: A Guide and Commentary* (New York: Oxford University Press, 2016).

The Thought of Thomas Aquinas (Oxford: Oxford University Press, 1992).

de Boer, Martinus C. 'Cross and cosmos in Galatians' in David J. Downs and Matthew L. Skinner (eds.), *The Unrelenting God: God's Action in Scripture, Essays in Honor of Beverly Roberts Gaventa* (Grand Rapids: Eerdmans, 2013), pp. 208–25.

Dempsey, Michael. 'Providence, distributive justice and divine government in the theology of Thomas Aquinas', *New Blackfriars*, 90 (2009), 365–84.

Dennett, Daniel. *Darwin's Dangerous Idea* (New York: Touchstone, 1995).

Dorrien, Gary. 'Modernism as a theological problem: the theological legacy of Langdon Gilkey', *American Journal of Theology & Philosophy*, 28.2 (2007), 64–94.

Dowey Jr, Edward A. *A Commentary on the Confession of 1967 and Introduction to the 'Book of Confessions'* (Philadelphia: Westminster, 1968).

Dragona-Monachou, Myrto. 'Divine providence in the philosophy of the empire', *Aufsteig und Niedergang der Römischen Welt, Teil II*, 36.7 (1994), 4417–90.

Duns, John. *Science and Christian Thought* (London, 1866).

Dyson, R. W. (ed.). *Aquinas: Political Writings* (Cambridge: Cambridge University Press, 2002).

Elliott, Mark. *The Heart of Biblical Theology: Providence Experienced* (Farnham: Ashgate, 2012).

Providence Perceived: Divine Action from a Human Point of View (Berlin: de Gruyter, 2015).

Ellis, George. 'Ordinary and extraordinary divine action' in Robert John Russell, Nancey Murphy and Arthur R. Peacocke (eds.), *Chaos and Complexity: Scientific Perspectives on Divine Action* (Vatican City: Vatican Observatory Publications, and Berkeley: Center for Theology and the Natural Sciences, 1997), pp. 359–95.

Endō, Shūsaku. *Silence*, trans. William Johnston (New York: Picador, 2016).

Eze, E. C. (ed.). *Race and the Enlightenment: A Reader* (Oxford: Blackwell, 1997).

Fakhry, Majid. *A History of Islamic Philosophy* (New York: Columbia University Press, 1970).

Farmer, H. H. *The World and God: A Study of Prayer, Providence and Miracle in Christian Experience* (London: Nisbet & Co., 1935).

Farrer, Austin. *Faith and Speculation: An Essay in Philosophical Theology* (Edinburgh: T&T Clark, 1988).

   Saving Belief: A Discussion of Essentials (London: Hodder and Stoughton, 1964).

Fergusson, David. *Creation* (Grand Rapids: Eerdmans, 2014).

   'Providence' in Paul Dafydd Jones and Paul T. Nimmo (eds.), *The Oxford Handbook to Karl Barth* (Oxford: Oxford University Press, in press).

Flint, Thomas P. *Divine Providence: The Molinist Account* (Ithaca: Cornell University Press, 1998).

   'Two accounts of providence' in Thomas V. Morris (ed.), *Divine and Human Action: Essays in the Metaphysics of Theism* (Ithaca: Cornell University Press, 1988), pp. 147–81.

Ford, Lewis S. *The Lure of God: A Biblical Background for Process Theism* (Philadelphia: Fortress, 1978).

Foster, Paul. *Colossians* (London: Bloomsbury T&T Clark, 2016).

Forsyth, P. T. *The Person and Place of Jesus Christ* (London: Hodder & Stoughton, 1910).

Frame, John M. *No Other God: A Response to Open Theism* (Phillipsburg, NJ: P&R Publishing, 2001).

Freddosos, Alfred J. 'Medieval Aristotelianism and the case against secondary causation in nature' in Thomas V. Morris (ed.), *Divine and Human Action: Essays in the Metaphysics of Theism* (Ithaca: Cornell University Press, 1988), pp. 74–118.

Frei, Hans. 'H. Richard Niebuhr on history, church and nation' in Ronald F. Thiemann (ed.), *The Legacy of H. Richard Niebuhr* (Minneapolis: Fortress, 1991), pp. 1–23.

Fretheim, Terence E. *God and World in the Old Testament: A Relational Theology of Creation* (Nashville: Abingdon, 2005).

Freud, Sigmund. *The Future of an Illusion* (London: Hogarth Press, 1928).

Frick, Peter. *Divine Providence in Philo of Alexandria* (Tübingen: Mohr Siebeck, 1999).

Friedman, Milton and Friedman, Rose. *Free to Choose* (London: Secker and Warburg, 1980).

Furley, David. 'Cosmology' in Leimpe Algra, Jonathan Barnes, Jaap Mansfeld and Malcolm Schofield (eds.), *Cambridge History of Hellenistic Philosophy* (Cambridge: Cambridge University Press, 1999), pp. 412–51.

Gannsle, Gregory E. (ed.). *God and Time: Four Views* (Downer's Grove, IL: IVP, 2001).

Garrigou-Lagrange, Reginald. *Providence*, trans. Bede Rose (London: Herder, 1937).

Gaventa, Beverley Roberts. *When in Romans: An Invitation to Linger with the Gospel According to Paul* (Grand Rapids: Baker, 2016).

Geach, Peter. *Providence and Evil* (Cambridge: Cambridge University Press, 1977).

Gelber, Hester Goodenough. 'Providence' in Robert Pasnau (ed.), *The Cambridge History of Medieval Philosophy*, 2nd edn (Cambridge: Cambridge University Press, 2014), pp. 761–72.

Gentile, Emilio. *Politics as Religion* (Princeton: Princeton University Press, 2006).

Gerrish, Brian. 'Creation and covenant', *Interpretation*, 16 (1962), 216–20.

    The Old Protestantism and the New (Edinburgh: T&T Clark, 1982).

    'The place of Calvin in Christian theology' in Donald McKim (ed.), *Cambridge Companion to John Calvin* (Cambridge: Cambridge University Press, 2004), pp. 291–304.

Giberson, Karl W. (ed.). *Abraham's Dice: Chance and Providence in the Monotheistic Traditions* (New York: Oxford University Press, 2016).

Gilkey, Langdon B. 'The concept of providence in contemporary theology', *Journal of Religion*, 43.3 (1963), 171–92.

    Reaping the Whirlwind: A Christian Interpretation of History (New York: Seabury, 1976).

Goris, Harm. 'Divine foreknowledge, providence, predestination and human freedom' in Rik Van Nieuwenhove and Joseph Wawrykow (eds.), *The Theology of Thomas Aquinas* (Notre Dame, IN: Notre Dame Press, 2005), pp. 99–122.

Gorringe, T. J. *God's Theatre: A Theology of Providence* (London: SCM, 1991).

Gould, Stephen Jay. *Wonderful Life: The Burgess Shale and the Nature of History* (New York: Norton, 1989).

Gourevitch, Victor. 'Rousseau on providence', *Review of Metaphysics*, 53.3 (2000), 565–611.

Green, Christopher. *Doxological Theology: Karl Barth on Divine Providence, Evil, and the Angels* (London: T&T Clark, 2012).

Griffin, David Ray. *Evil Revisited: Responses and Reconsiderations* (Albany, NY: State University of New York, 1991).

'Process theology and the Christian good news: a response to classical free will theism' in John B. Cobb Jr and Clark H. Pinnock (eds.), *Searching for an Adequate God: A Dialogue Between Process and Free Will Theists* (Grand Rapids: Eerdmans, 2000), pp. 1–38.

Grintz, Yehoshua M. 'Providence: in the Talmud' in Fred Skolnik, *Encyclopaedia Judaica*, 2nd edn (Detroit: Macmillan Reference, 2007), vol. XVI, p. 649.

Grundlach, Bradley J. *Process and Providence: The Evolution Question at Princeton, 1845–1929* (Grand Rapids: Eerdmans, 2013).

Gunton, Colin E. *Becoming and Being: The Doctrines of God in Charles Hartshorne and Karl Barth* (Oxford: Oxford University Press, 1978).

The Triune Creator (Edinburgh: Edinburgh University Press, 1998).

Guyatt, Nicholas. *Providence and the Invention of the United States 1607–1876* (Cambridge: Cambridge University Press, 2007).

Habel, Norman C. 'In defense of God the sage' in Leo. Perdue and W. Clark Gilpin, (eds.), *The Voice from the Whirlwind: Interpreting the Book of Job* (Nashville: Abingdon, 1992), pp. 21–38.

Haleem, M. Abdel. 'Early *kalām*' in Seyyed Hossein Nasr and Oliver Leaman (eds.), *History of Islamic Philosophy*, Part I (London: Routledge, 1996), pp. 71–88.

Harrison, Peter. 'Evolution, providence and the nature of chance' in Karl W. Giberson (ed.), *Abraham's Dice: Chance and Providence in the Monotheistic Traditions* (New York: Oxford University Press, 2016), pp. 260–90.

Harvey, Paul. *Christianity and Race in the American South: A History* (Chicago: University of Chicago Press, 2016).

Hasker, William. *Providence, Evil and the Openness of God* (London: Routledge, 2004).

'Response to David Ray Griffin' in John B. Cobb Jr and Clark H. Pinnock (eds.), *Searching for An Adequate God: A Dialogue Between Process and Free Will Theists* (Grand Rapids: Eerdmans, 2000), pp. 39–52.

Hebblethwaite, Brian. *The Philosophical Theology of Austin Farrer* (Leuven: Peeters, 2007).

Hegel, G. H. F. *Lectures on the Philosophy of World History*, ed. Robert E. Brown and Peter C. Hodgson, 2 vols. (Oxford: Clarendon Press, 2011). *Philosophy of Right*, trans. T. M. Knox (Oxford: Clarendon, 1952).

Helm, Paul. *The Eternal God*, 2nd edn (New York: Oxford University Press, 2010).

Henderson, Edward. 'Double agency and the relation of persons to God' in Douglas Hedley and Brian Hebblethwaite (eds.), *The Human Person in God's Word: Studies to Commemorate the Austin Farrer Centenary* (London: SCM, 2006), pp. 38–64.

Hengstmengel, Joost. 'Divine Oeconomy: The Role of Providence in Earl-Modern Economic Thought Before Adam Smith', PhD thesis, Erasmus University Rotterdam (2015).

Heppe, Heinrich. *Reformed Dogmatics*, trans. G. T. Thomson (London: Allen & Unwin, 1950).

Herbert, George. 'Easter' in *The Complete English Poems* (Harmondsworth: Penguin, 1991), p. 37.

Heron, Alasdair. *The Holy Spirit* (Philadelphia: Westminster, 1983).

Higton, Mike. *Christ, Providence and History: Hans W. Frei's Public Theology* (London: T&T Clark, 2004).

Hill, Lisa. 'The hidden theology of Adam Smith', *European Journal of the History of Economic Thought*, 8:1 (2001), 1–29.

Hilton, Boyd. *The Age of Atonement: The Influence of Evangelicalism on Social and Economic Thought, 1795–1865* (Oxford: Clarendon, 1988).

'Chalmers as political economist' in A. C. Cheyne (ed.), *The Practical and the Pious: Essays on Thomas Chalmers (1780–1847)* (Edinburgh: St Andrew Press, 1985), pp. 141–56.

Hodge, Charles. *Systematic Theology*, 3 vols. (Grand Rapids: Eerdmans, 1989).

What is Darwinism? And Other Writings on Science & Religion, ed. Mark N. Noll and David A. Livingstone (Grand Rapids: Baker, 1994).

Hodgson, Peter C. *God in History: Shapes of Freedom* (Nashville: Abingdon, 1989).

Shapes of Freedom: Hegel's Philosophy of World History in Theological Perspective (Oxford: Oxford University Press, 2012).

Hoenecke, Adolf. *Evangelical Lutheran Dogmatics*, vol. II, trans. Richard A. Krause and James Langebartels (Milwaukee: Northwestern Publishing House, 2009).

Hopkins, Jasper. *Nicolas of Cusa's Dialectical Mysticism: Text, Translation and Interpretive Study of De Visione Dei* (Minneapolis: Arthur J. Banning Press, 1985).

Houlgate, Stephen. *An Introduction to Hegel: Freedom, Truth and History*, 2nd edn (Oxford: Blackwell, 2005).

Hume, David. 'The idea of a perfect commonwealth' in *Essays Moral, Political, and Literary* (Edinburgh, 1742), Part II, essay XVI.

Hunsinger, Deborah van Deusen. *Trauma, Gospel, and Pastoral Care* (Grand Rapids: Eerdmans, 2015).

Hunsinger, George. 'The politics of the nonviolent God: reflections on René Girard and Karl Barth' in *Disruptive Grace: Studies in the Theology of Karl Barth* (Edinburgh: T&T Clark, 2000), pp. 21–41.

Illingworth, J. R. 'The problem of pain' in Charles Gore (ed.), *Lux Mundi* (London: J. Murray, 1889), pp. 113–26.

Israel, Jonathan. *The Democratic Enlightenment: Philosophy, Revolution and Human Rights 1750–1790* (Oxford: Oxford University Press, 2011).

Iverach, James. *Evolution and Christianity* (London: Hodder & Stoughton, 1894).

James, William. *The Will to Believe and Other Essays in Popular Philosophy* (New York: Longmans, Green & Co., 1897).

Jensen, Alexander S. *Divine Providence and Human Agency: Trinity, Creation and Freedom* (Aldershot: Ashgate, 2014).

John of Damascus, 'Exposition of the Orthodox faith' in *Nicene and Post-Nicene Fathers*, 2nd series (New York: Scribner's, 1899), vol. IX, pp. 41–2.

Johnson, Luke Timothy. *Reading Romans: A Literary and Theological Commentary* (New York: Crossroad, 1997).

Johnson, Niall. *Britain and the 1918–19 Influenza Pandemic: A Dark Epilogue* (London: Routledge, 2006).

Jones, Gareth Stedman. *Karl Marx: Greatness and Illusion* (London: Allen Lane, 2016).

Joseph, Stephen and Hefferon, Kate. 'Post-traumatic growth: eudaimonic happiness in the aftermath of adversity' in Ilona Boniwell, Susan A. David and Amanda Conley Ayers (eds.), *Oxford Handbook of Happiness* (Oxford: Oxford University Press, 2013), pp. 926–40.

Justin Martyr. First Apology in Alexander Robertson and James Donaldson (eds.), *Ante-Nicene Fathers*, 10 vols. (Edinburgh: T&T Clark, 1985–7), vol. I.

Kant, Immanuel. 'Idea for a universal history with a cosmopolitan aim' in *Anthropology, History and Education*, ed. Robert B. Louden and Guenther Zoeller (Cambridge: Cambridge University Press, 2007), pp. 108–20.

Käsemann, Ernst. *Perspectives on Paul* (London: SCM, 1971).

Kaufman, Gordon. *In the Beginning ... Creativity* (Minneapolis: Fortress, 2004).

Systematic Theology: A Historicist Perspective (New York: Scribner's, 1968).

Theology for a Nuclear Age (Philadelphia: Westminster, 1985).

Kaveny, Cathleen. *Prophecy Without Contempt: Religious Discourse in the Public Square* (Cambridge, MA: Harvard University Press, 2016).

Keller, Catherine. *On the Mystery: Discerning God in Process* (Philadelphia: Fortress, 2008).

Kelsey, David H. *Eccentric Existence*, 2 vols. (Philadelphia: Westminster John Knox Press, 2009).

Kennedy, Darren. *Providence and Personalism: Karl Barth in Conversation with Austin Farrer, John Macmurray and Vincent Brümmer* (New York: Peter Lang, 2011).

Kendrick, T. D. *The Lisbon Earthquake* (Philadelphia: Lippincott, 1955).

Kimble, Kevin and O'Connor, Timothy. 'The argument from consciousness revisited' in Jonathan Kvanvig (ed.), *Oxford Studies in the Philosophy of Religion*, vol. III, (Oxford: Oxford University Press, 2011), pp. 110–41.

Kirkpatrick, Frank. *The Mystery and Agency of God: Divine Being and Action in the World* (Minneapolis: Fortress, 2014).

Kolb, Robert. *Martin Luther and the Enduring Word of God: The Wittenberg School and Its Scripture-Centered Proclamation* (Grand Rapids: Baker, 2016).

'Resurrection and justification: Luther's use of Romans 4,25', *Lutherjahrbuch*, 78 (2011), 39–60.

Kwasniewski, Peter A. (ed.). *On Love and Charity: Readings from the 'Commentary on the Sentences of Peter Lombard'* (Washington, DC: Catholic University of America, 2008).

Langford, Michael J. *The Tradition of Liberal Theology* (Grand Rapids: Eerdmans, 2014).

Leftow, Brian. *Time and Eternity* (Ithaca: Cornell University Press, 1991).

Leibniz, G. W. *Theodicy*, ed. Austin Farrer (London: Routledge & Kegan Paul, 1951).

Leith, John. *John Calvin's Doctrine of the Christian Life* (Louisville: Westminster/John Knox, 1989).

Levenson, Jon D. *Creation and the Persistence of Evil: The Jewish Drama of Divine Omnipotence* (San Francisco: Harper & Row, 1988).

Lincoln, Andrew T. *Ephesians: Word Bible Commentary*, vol. XLII (Dallas: Word Book, 1990).

Lindsay, Mark R. *Barth, Israel and Jesus: Karl Barth's Theology of Israel* (Farnham: Aldershot, 2007).

Link, Christian. *Schöpfung: ein theologischer Entwurf im Gegenüber von Naturwissenschaft und Ökologie* (Neukirchen-Vluyn: Neukirchener Theologie, 2012).

'Schöpfung und Versehung' in Michael Beintker (ed.), *Barth Handbuch* (Tübingen: Mohr Siebeck, 2016), pp. 328–34.

Livingston, James C. *Religious Thought in the Victorian Age* (London: T&T Clark International, 2006).

Livingstone, David N. *Darwin's Forgotten Defenders: The Encounter Between Evangelical Theology and Evolutionary Thought* (Grand Rapids: Eerdmans, 1987).

Dealing with Darwin: Place, Politics and Rhetoric in Religious Engagements with Evolution (Baltimore: Johns Hopkins University Press, 2014).

'Public spectacle and scientific theory: William Robertson Smith and the reading of evolution in Victorian Scotland', *Studies in History and Philosophy of Biological and Biomedical Sciences*, 35 (2004), 1–29.

Lloyd, Genevieve. 'Providence as progress: Kant's variations on a tale of origins' in Amélie Oksenberg Rorty and James Schmidt (eds.), *Kant's Idea for a Universal History with a Cosmopolitan Aim: A Critical Guide* (Cambridge: Cambridge University Press, 2009), pp. 200–15.

Providence Lost (Cambridge, MA: Harvard University Press, 2008).

Locke, John. *The Reasonableness of Christianity As Delivered in the Scriptures*, ed. John C. Higgins-Biddle (Oxford: Oxford University Press, 1999).

Lohse, Bernhard. *Martin Luther's Theology* (Minneapolis: Augsburg Fortress, 1999).

Long, A. A. 'Freedom and determinism in the Stoic theory of human action' in A. A. Long (ed.), *Problems in Stoicism* (London: Athlone Press, 1971), pp. 75–113.

Long, A. A. and Sedley, D. N. *The Hellenistic Philosophers*, vol. 1 (Cambridge: Cambridge University Press, 1987).

Louden, Robert B. *Kant's Human Being: Essays on His Theory of Human Nature* (New York: Oxford University Press, 2011).

Louth, Andrew. *Maximus the Confessor* (London: Routledge, 1996).

'Pagans and Christians on providence' in J. H. D. Scourfield (ed.), *Texts and Culture in Late Antiquity: Inheritance, Authority, and Change* (Swansea: Classical Press of Wales, 2007), pp. 279–98.

St John Damascene (Oxford: Oxford University Press, 2002).

Lovin, Robin W. *Reinhold Niebuhr and Christian Realism* (Cambridge: Cambridge University Press, 1995).

Lucas, John R. 'Foreknowledge and vulnerability of God' in Godfrey Vesey (ed.), *The Philosophy in Christianity, Royal Institute of Philosophy Lecture Series* 25 (Cambridge: Cambridge University Press, 1989), pp. 119–28.

Freedom and Grace (London: SPCK, 1976).

The Future: An Essay on God, Temporality and Truth (Oxford: Blackwell, 1989).

Treatise on Time and Space (London: Methuen, 1973).

Luther, Martin. Heidelberg Disputation in Timothy F. Lull (ed.), *Martin Luther's Basic Theological Writings* (Minneapolis: Fortress, 1989), pp. 30–49.

Werke: Kritische Gesamtausgabe, Briefwechsel Band 9: 1540–28 (Weimar: Böhlau, 1941).

Macaskill, Grant. 'History, providence and the apocalyptic Paul', *Scottish Journal of Theology*, 70.4 (2017), 409–26.

Macleod, Alastair. 'Invisible hand arguments: Milton Friedman and Adam Smith', *Journal of Scottish Philosophy*, 5.2 (2007), 103–17.

MacIntyre, Alasdair. 'A partial response to my critics' in John Horton and Susan Mendus (eds.), *After MacIntyre* (Notre Dame, IN: University of Notre Dame Press, 1994), pp. 283–304.

Macmurray, John. *Persons in Relation* (London: Faber & Faber, 1961).

Martin, Dale B. *Inventing Superstition: From the Hippocratics to the Christians* (Cambridge, MA: Harvard University Press, 2004).

Martin, David. 'Economics as ideology: on making "the invisible hand" visible', *Review of Social Economy*, 48.1 (1990), 272–87.

A *Sociology of English Religion* (London: Heinemann, 1967).

Mawson, T. G. *Belief in God* (Oxford: Oxford University Press, 2005).

Maximos the Confessor, *On Difficulties in the Church Fathers: The Ambigua, Vol. 1*, (ed.) Nicholas Constas (Cambridge, MA: Harvard University Press, 2014).

Mayhew, Robert. 'The Theology of the *Laws*' in Christopher Bobonich (ed.), *Plato's 'Laws': A Critical Guide* (Cambridge: Cambridge University Press, 2010), pp. 197–216.

McCormack, Bruce L. 'The actuality of God: Karl Barth in conversation with open theism' in Bruce L. McCormack (ed.), *Engaging the Doctrine of God: Contemporary Protestant Perspectives* (Grand Rapids: Baker, 2008), pp. 185–242.

McFarland, Ian A. *From Nothing: A Theology of Creation* (Louisville: Westminster John Knox Press, 2014).

McGrath, Alister. *Darwin and the Divine: Evolutionary Thought and Natural Theology* (Oxford: Wiley-Blackwell, 2011).

McLean, Kalbryn A. 'Calvin and the personal politics of providence' in Amy Plantinga Pauw and Serene Jones (eds.), *Feminist and Womanist Essays in Reformed Dogmatics* (Louisville: Westminster John Knox Press, 2006), pp. 107–24.

McTaggart, J. M. E. 'The unreality of time' in *Philosophical Studies* (London: Arnold, 1934), pp. 110–31.

Migliore, Daniel. *Faith Seeking Understanding* (Grand Rapids: Eerdmans, 1991).

Minutes of the Annual Conference of the Methodist Church (London: Methodist Publishing House, 1936).

Mitchell, Basil. 'Introduction' in Douglas Hedley and Brian Hebblethwaite (eds.), *The Human Person in God's Word: Studies to Commemorate the Austin Farrer Centenary* (London: SCM, 2006), pp. 1–13.

Moberly, R. W. L. *Old Testament Theology: Reading the Hebrew Bible as Christian Scripture* (Grand Rapids: Baker, 2013).

Moltmann, Jürgen. *God in Creation* (London: SCM, 1985).

Moore, Aubrey. 'The Christian doctrine of God' in Charles Gore (ed.), *Lux Mundi* (London: J. Murray, 1889), pp. 57–109.

Science and the Faith (London: Kegan Paul, 1889).

Moore, James. 'Deconstructing Darwinism: the politics of evolution in the 1860s', *Journal of the History of Biology*, 24 (1991), 353–408.

Moore, Susan Hardman. *Pilgrims: New World Settlers and the Call of Home* (New Haven: Yale University Press, 2007).

Morris, Simon Conway. 'Evolution and convergence: some wider considerations' in Simon Conway Morris (ed.), *The Deep Structure of Biology: Is Convergence Sufficiently Ubiquitous to Give a Directional Signal?* (West Conshohocken, PA: Templeton Press, 2008), pp. 46–67.

Moseley, David J. R. S. ' "*Parables*" and "*Polyphony*": the resonance of music as witness in the theology of Karl Barth and Dietrich Bonhoeffer' in Jeremy S. Begbie and Steven R. Guthrie (eds.), *Resonant Witness: Conversations Between Music and Theology* (Grand Rapids: Eerdmans, 2012), pp. 240–70.

Mossner, E. C. 'Deism' in Paul Edwards (ed.), *Encyclopaedia of Philosophy*, 8 vols. (New York: Macmillan, 1967), vol. 11, p. 335.

Muller, Richard A. *Post-Reformation Reformed Dogmatics, Volume Three: The Divine Essence and Attributes* (Grand Rapids: Baker, 2003).

Mullins, Ryan. *The End of the Timeless God* (Oxford: Oxford University Press, 2016).

Murphy, Nancey. *Bodies and Souls, or Spirited Bodies* (Cambridge: Cambridge University Press, 2006).

Murray, Michael J. *Nature Red in Tooth and Claw: Theism and the Problem of Animal Suffering* (Oxford: Oxford University Press, 2008).

Nadler, Stephen. 'Conceptions of God' in Desmond M. Clarke and Catherine Wilson (eds.), *Oxford Handbook of Philosophy in Early Modern Europe* (Oxford: Oxford University Press, 2011), pp. 525–47.

Spinoza's Theory of Divine Providence: Rationalist Solutions, Jewish Sources (Budel, The Netherlands: Damon, 2005).

Nagel, Thomas. *Mind and Cosmos: Why the Materialist Neo-Darwinian Conception of Nature Is Almost Entirely False* (New York: Oxford University Press, 2012).

Naphy, William. 'Calvin's Geneva' in Donald McKim (ed.), *Cambridge Companion to John Calvin* (Cambridge: Cambridge University Press, 2004), pp. 25–37.

Neil, Bronwen. 'Divine providence and the gnomic will before Maximus' in Pauline Allen and Bronwen Neil (eds.), *Oxford Handbook to Maximus the Confessor* (Oxford: Oxford University Press, 2015), pp. 235–52.

Neiman, Susan. *Evil in Modern Thought: An Alternative History of Philosophy* (Princeton: Princeton University Press, 2002).

Nemesius. *On the Nature of Man*, trans. R. W. Sharples and P. J. van der Eijk (Liverpool: Liverpool University Press, 2008).

Newman, John Henry. *The Idea of a University* (London: Longman, Green & Co, 1907).

Noll, Mark A. *The Civil War as a Theological Crisis* (Chapel Hill: University of North Carolina Press, 2006).

'"Wee shall be as a citty upon a hill": John Winthrop's non-American exceptionalism', *Review of Faith and International Affairs*, 10:2 (2012), 5–11.

Nowak, Martin A. 'Five rules for the evolution of cooperation' in Martin A. Nowak and Sarah Coakley (eds.), *Evolution, Games and God: The Principle of Cooperation* (Cambridge, MA: Harvard University Press, 2013).

Oberman, Heiko A. *The Two Reformations: The Journey from the Last Days to the New World* (New Haven: Yale University Press, 2003).

Oliver, Simon. 'Augustine on creation, providence and motion', *International Journal of Systematic Theology*, 18.4 (2016), 379–98.

Oman, John. 'Prayer in Christ's name' in F. H. Ballard (ed.), *'A Dialogue with God' and Other Sermons by the Late John Oman* (London: James Clarke, 1950), pp. 54–60.

Oord, Thomas Jay. *The Uncontrolling Love of God: An Open and Relational Account of Providence* (Downer's Grove, IL: IVP, 2015).

Origen. *De Principiis*, in Alexander Robertson and James Donaldson (eds.), *Ante-Nicene Fathers*, 10 vols. (Edinburgh: T&T Clark, 1985–7), vol. IV.

Oslington, Paul. 'Divine action, providence and Adam Smith's invisible hand' in Paul Oslington (ed.), *Adam Smith as Theologian* (London: Routledge, 2011), pp. 61–76.

Ottati, Douglas T. *Theology for Liberal Protestants: God the Creator* (Grand Rapids: Eerdmans, 2012).

Padgett, Alan G. *God, Eternity and the Necessity of Time* (Basingstoke: Macmillan, 1992).

Pagden, Anthony. *Lords of All the World: Ideologies of Empire in Spain, Britain and France c1500–c1800* (New Haven: Yale University Press, 1995).

Page, Ruth. *God and the Web of Creation* (London: SCM, 1996).

Pailin, David A. *God and the Processes of Reality: Foundations of a Credible Theism* (London: Routledge, 1989).

Paley, William. *Natural Theology* (New York: American Tract Society, 1881).

Pannenberg, Wolfhart. *Systematic Theology*, vol. II (Grand Rapids: Eerdmans, 1994).

Paul, Diane B. 'Darwinism, social Darwinism and eugenics' in Jonathan Hodge and Gregory Radick (eds.), *Cambridge Companion to Darwin* (Cambridge: Cambridge University Press, 2003), pp. 214–39.

Peddicord, Richard, OP, *The Sacred Monster of Thomism: An Introduction to the Life and Legacy of Reginald Garrigou-Lagrange* (South Bend, IN: St Augustine's Press, 2005).

Pederson, Ann. *God, Creation and All that Jazz: A Process of Composition and Improvisation* (St Louis: Chalice Press, 2001).

Pelikan, Jaroslav (ed.), *Luther's Works*, vol. XXVI (St Louis: Concordia, 1963).

Phillips, Paul T. *A Kingdom on Earth: Anglo-American Social Christianity 1880–1940* (University Park, PA: Pennsylvania State University Press, 1996).

Phillipson, Nicholas. 'Providence and progress: an introduction to the historical thought of William Robertson' in Stewart J. Brown (ed.), *William Robertson and the Expansion of Empire* (Cambridge: Cambridge University Press, 1997), pp. 55–73.

Pictet, Benedict. *Christian Theology*, trans. Frederick Reyroux (London: Seeley and Burnside, 1834).

Pinnock, Clark. *Most Moved Mover: A Theology of God's Openness* (Grand Rapids: Baker, 2001).

'Systematic theology' in Clark Pinnock, Richard Rice, John Sanders, William Hasker and David Basinger, *The Openness of God: A Biblical Challenge to the Traditional Understanding of God* (Downer's Grove, IL: IVP, 1994), pp. 101–25.

A Wideness in God's Mercy: Jesus Christ in a World of Religions (Grand Rapids: Zondervan, 1992).

Pinnock, Clark, Rice, Richard, Sanders, John, Hasker, William and Basinger, David. *The Openness of God: A Biblical Challenge to the Traditional Understanding of God* (Downer's Grove, IL: IVP, 1994).

Placher, William C. 'Christ takes our place: rethinking atonement', *Interpretation*, 53.1 (1999), 5–20.

The Domestication of Transcendence (Louisville: Westminster John Knox, 1996).

Plantinga, Alvin. 'What is "intervention"?', *Theology and Science*, 6.4 (2008), 369–401.

Plato. *Laws*, in Edith Hamilton and Huntington Cairns (eds.), *Collected Dialogues of Plato, Vol. iv* (Princeton: Princeton University Press, 1961).

Plotinus. *Enneads 3*, ed. and trans. A. H. Armstrong (London: Heinemann, 1967).

Poirier, Jean-Paul. 'The 1755 Lisbon disaster, the earthquake that shook Europe', *European Review*, 14.2 (2006), 169–80.

Polkinghorne, John. *Belief in God in an Age of Science* (New Haven: Yale University Press, 1998).

'Divine action: some comments', *Science and Christian Belief*, 24.1 (2012), 31–2.

Science and Providence: God's Interaction with the World (London: SCM, 1989).

Science and Religion in Quest of Truth (London: SPCK, 2011).

Pope, Alexander. *An Essay on Man* (Edinburgh, 1797).

Pope, Stephen J. *Human Evolution and Christian Ethics* (Cambridge: Cambridge University Press, 2007).

Porter, Andrew. '"Commerce and Christianity": the rise and fall of a nineteenth-century missionary slogan', *Historical Journal*, 28.3 (1985), 597–621.

Posti, Mikko. 'Divine providence in medieval philosophical theology, 1250–1350', unpublished PhD thesis, University of Helsinki (2017).

https://helda.helsinki.fi/bitstream/handle/10138/228641/DIVINEPR. pdf? sequence=1

Rainy, Robert. *Evolution and Theology* (Edinburgh: Maclaren and Macniven, 1874).

Rauschenbusch, Walter. *A Theology for the Social Gospel* (Nashville: Parthenon Press, 1978).

Reichenbach, Bruce R. *Divine Providence: God's Love and Human Freedom* (Eugene, OR: Cascade, 2016).

Rigby, Cynthia L. 'Providence and play', *Insights: The Faculty Journal of Austin Theological Seminary*, 126.2 (2011), 10–18.

Rist, John. 'Plotinus and Christian philosophy' in Lloyd P. Gerson (ed.), *Cambridge Companion to Plotinus* (Cambridge: Cambridge University Press, 2006), pp. 386–414.

Stoic Philosophy (Cambridge: Cambridge University Press, 1969).

Ritschl, Dietrich. 'Sinn und Grenze der theologischen Kategorie der Vorsehung', *Zeitschrift für Dialektische Theologie*, 10 (1994), 117–33.

Roberts, Jon H. 'That Darwin destroyed natural theology' in Ronald Numbers (ed.), *Galileo Goes to Jail: And Other Myths about Science and Religion* (Cambridge, MA: Harvard University Press, 2009), pp. 161–9.

Robertson, Elizabeth. 'Julian of Norwich's "modernist style" and the creation of audience' in Liz Herbert McAvoy (ed.), *A Companion to Julian of Norwich* (Woodbridge: D. S. Brewer, 2008), pp. 139–53.

Robertson, William. *History of America* (Edinburgh, 1777).

The Situation of the World at the Time of Christ's Appearance, and Its Connexion with the Success of His Religion Considered (Edinburgh, 1755).

Robinson, Marilynne. *Lila* (London: Virago, 2014).

Rogerson, John. 'Can a doctrine of providence be based on the Old Testament?' in Lyle Eslinger and Glen Taylor (eds.), *Ascribe to the Lord: Biblical and Other Studies in Memory of Peter C. Craigie* (Sheffield: JSOT, 1988), pp. 529–43.

Rousseau, Jean-Jacques. 'Letter to Voltaire' in Victor Gourevitch (ed.), *The Discourse and Other Early Political Writings* (Cambridge: Cambridge University Press, 1997), p. 241.

Rubinstein, Richard L. *After Auschwitz: History, Theology and Contemporary Judaism*, 2nd edn (Baltimore: Johns Hopkins University Press, 1992).

Ruse, Michael. *Charles Darwin* (Oxford: Blackwell, 2008).

Russell, Robert John, Murphy, Nancey and Peacocke, Arthur R. (eds.). *Chaos and Complexity: Scientific Perspectives on Divine Action* (Vatican City: Vatican Observatory Publications, and Berkeley: Center for Theology and the Natural Sciences, 1997).

Sanders, John. *The God Who Risks: A Theology of Divine Providence*, 2nd edn (Downer's Grove, IL: IVP, 2007).

'Why Oord's essential kenosis model fails to solve the problem of evil while retaining miracles', *Wesleyan Theological Journal*, 51.2 (2016), 174–87.

Saunders, Nicholas. 'Does God cheat at dice? Divine action and quantum possibilities', *Zygon*, 35.3 (2000), 517–44.

Schleiermacher, F. D. E. *The Christian Faith*, trans. H. R. Mackintosh and J. S. Stewart (Edinburgh: T&T Clark, 1928).

Schmid, Heinrich. *The Doctrinal Theology of the Evangelical Lutheran Church*, trans. Charles E. Hay and Henry E. Jacobs (Philadelphia: United Lutheran Publication House, 1889).

Schotroff, W. 'R'h – to see' in Ernst Jenni and Claus Westermann (eds.), *Theological Lexicon of the Old Testament*, vol. III (Peabody, MA: Henrickson, 1990), pp. 1176–83.

Schreiner, Susan E. *Where Shall Wisdom Be Found? Calvin's Exegesis of Job from Medieval and Modern Perspectives* (Chicago: University of Chicago Press, 1994).

Scruton, Roger. *The Face of God* (London: Continuum, 2012).

Seitz, Christopher R. *Colossians* (Grand Rapids: Brazos, 2014).

Seneca. 'De providentia' in *Moral Writings*, ed. John Basore, Loeb Classical Library (London: Heinemann, 1928).

Sharples, Robert. 'Fate, prescience and free will' in John Marenbon (ed.), *The Cambridge Companion to Boethius* (Cambridge: Cambridge University Press, 2009), pp. 207–27.

Sher, Richard. *Church and University in the Scottish Enlightenment: The Moderate Literati of Edinburgh* (Edinburgh: Edinburgh University Press, 1985).

'Witherspoon's *Dominion of Providence* and the Scottish jeremiad tradition' in Richard B. Sher and Jeffrey R. Smitten (eds.), *Scotland and America in the Age of the Enlightenment* (Edinburgh: Edinburgh University Press, 1990), pp. 46–64.

Sibbes, Richard. 'The soul's conflict with itself, and victory over itself by faith' in *Complete Works*, ed. Alexander B. Grosart, 7 vols. (Edinburgh: James Nichol, 1862–4), vol. I, pp. 119–214.

Silva, Ignacio. 'John Polkinghorne on divine action: a coherent theological evolution', *Science and Christian Belief*, 24.1 (2012), 19–30.

'Revisiting Aquinas on providence and rising to the challenge of divine action in nature', *Journal of Religion* 94.3 (2014), 277–91.

'Thomas Aquinas holds fast: objections to Aquinas within today's debate on divine action', *Heythrop Journal*, 54, (2013), 658–67.

Smith, Adam. *An Enquiry into the Nature and Causes of the Wealth of Nations*, ed. R. H. Campbell, A. S. Skinner and W. B. Todd (Oxford: Clarendon Press, 1979).

Theory of Moral Sentiments, ed. R. P. Hawley (London: Penguin, 2009).

Smith, Craig. *Adam Smith's Political Philosophy: The Invisible Hand and Spontaneous Order* (London: Routledge, 2006).

Snape, Michael. *God and the British Soldier: Religion and the British Army in the First and Second World Wars* (London: Routledge, 2005).

Sober, Elliott. 'Remarkable facts: ending science as we know it' [review of Thomas Nagel's *Mind and Cosmos*], *Boston Review* (November/ December 2012), pp. 50–5.

Southgate, Christopher. *The Groaning of Creation* (Louisville: Westminster John Knox, 2008).

Spence, Martin. *Heaven on Earth: Reimagining Time and Eternity in Nineteenth-Century British Evangelicalism* (Eugene, OR: Wipf and Stock, 2015).

Spencer, John. *Discourse Concerning Prodigies* (London, 1663).

Spinoza, Benedict de. *Ethics*, ed. and trans. Edwin Curley (London: Penguin, 1994).

'The theological-political treatise' in Edwin Curley (ed.), *Collected Works of Spinoza*, vol. II (Princeton: Princeton University Press, 2016), pp. 65–354.

Suchocki, Marjorie Hewitt. *God, Christ, Church: A Practical Guide to Process Theology* (New York: Crossroad, 1986).

In God's Presence: Theological Reflections on Prayer (St Louis: Chalice Press, 1996).

Stanley, Brian. '"Commerce and Christianity": providence theory, the missionary movement, and the imperialism of free trade, 1842–1860', *Historical Journal*, 26.1 (1983), 71–94.

Stannard, David E. *American Holocaust: The Conquest of the New World* (New York: Oxford University Press, 1992).

Stead, Christopher. *Philosophy in Christian Antiquity* (Cambridge: Cambridge University Press, 1994).

Stephens, W. P. 'Election in Zwingli and Bullinger: a comparison of Zwingli's Sermonis de Providentia Dei Anamnema (1530) and Bullinger's Oratio de Moderatione Servanda *in* Negotio Providentiae, Praedestinationis, Gratiae et Liberi Arbitrii (1536)', *Reformation and Renaissance Review*, 7 (2005), 42–56.

The Theology of Huldrych Zwingli (Oxford: Clarendon Press, 1986).

Strawson, Galen. *The Subject of Experience* (Oxford: Oxford University Press, 2017).

Stump, Eleonore. *Wandering in the Darkness: Narrative and the Problem of Suffering* (Oxford: Oxford University Press, 2010).

Sullivan, Robert E. *John Toland and the Deist Controversy* (Cambridge, MA: Harvard University Press, 1982).

Sweetman, Brendan. *Evolution, Chance and God: Understanding the Relationship Between Evolution and Religion* (London: Continuum, 2015).

Swinton, John. *Raging with Compassion* (Grand Rapids: Eerdmans, 2007).

Tanner, Kathryn. *God and Creation in Christian Theology: Tyranny or Empowerment* (Oxford: Blackwell, 1988).

Taylor, Charles. *A Secular Age* (Cambridge, MA: Belknap Press of Harvard University Press, 2007).

Temple, Frederick. *The Relations Between Religion and Science* (London: Macmillan, 1884).

TeSelle, Eugene. *Augustine: The Theologian* (New York: Herder and Herder, 1970).

Theodoret of Cyrus, *On Divine Providence*, trans. Thomas Halton (New York: Newman Press, 1988).

Theophilus of Antioch. To Autolycus in Alexander Robertson and James Donaldson (eds.), *Ante-Nicene Fathers*, 10 vols. (Edinburgh: T&T Clark, 1985–7), vol. II.

Thiselton, A. C. *First Epistle to the Corinthians* (Grand Rapids: Eerdmans, 2000).

Thomson, J. Arthur and Geddes, Patrick. *Evolution* (London: Williams & Norgate, 1912).

Thornwell, James Henley. 'The Christian doctrine of slavery' in John B. Adger and John L. Girardeau (eds.), *Collected Writings of James Henley Thornwell*, vol. IV (New York: Carter, 1873), pp. 398–436.

Topham, Jonathan. 'Science and popular education in the 1830s: the role of the Bridgewater Treatises', *British Journal for the History of Science*, 25 (1992), 397–430.

Tracy, Thomas. 'Divine action, created causes, and human freedom' in Thomas Tracy (ed.), *The God Who Acts: Philosophical and Theological Explorations* (University Park, PA: Pennsylvania State University Press, 1994), pp. 77–102.

'Scientific vetoes and the hands-off God: can we say that God acts in history?', *Theology and Science*, 10.1 (2012), 55–80.

Tupper, E. Frank. *A Scandalous Providence: The Jesus Story of the Compassion of God* (Macon, GA: Mercer University Press, 2003).

Turner, Denys. *Julian of Norwich, Theologian* (New Haven: Yale University Press, 2011).

Thomas Aquinas: A Portrait (New Haven: Yale University Press, 2013).

Turner, Frank M. 'The Victorian conflict between science and religion: a professional dimension', *Isis*, 69 (1978), 356–76.

Turretin, Francis. *Institutes of Elenctic Theology*, vol. I, trans. George Musgrave Giger (Phillipsburg, NJ: P&R Publishing, 1992).

Udías, Agustín. 'Earthquakes as God's punishment in 17th- and 18th-century Spain' in M. Kölbl-Ebert (ed.), *Geology and Religion: A History of Harmony and Hostility* (London: Geological Society, 2009), pp. 41–8.

Updike, John. *Memories of the Ford Administration* (New York: Alfred Knopf, 1992).

van Asselt, Willem J. *The Federal Theology of Johannes Cocceius (1603–1669)* (Leiden: Brill, 2001).

van Huyssteen, Wentzel. *Alone in the World? Human Uniqueness in Science and Theology* (Grand Rapids: Eerdmans, 2006).

Vanstone, W. H. *Love's Endeavour, Love's Expense* (London: Darton, Longman and Todd, 1977).

Venema, Cornelis P. *Heinrich Bullinger and the Doctrine of Predestination: Author of 'The Other Reformed Tradition'?* (Grand Rapids: Baker, 2002).

Verbeke, Gerard. *The Presence of Stoicism in Medieval Thought* (Washington DC: Catholic University Press, 1983).

Viner, Jacob. *The Role of Providence in the Social Order* (Philadelphia: American Philosophical Society, 1972).

Voltaire. 'Poem on the Lisbon disaster; or an examination of the axiom, "All is well"' in Joseph McCabe (ed.), *Toleration and Other Essays by Voltaire* (New York: Putnam's, 1912), pp. 255–63.

Walsh, Denis. 'Teleology' in Michael Ruse (ed.), *Oxford Handbook of Philosophy of Biology* (Oxford: Oxford University Press, 2008), pp. 113–37.

Walsham, Alexandra. *Providence in Early Modern England* (Oxford: Oxford University Press, 1998).

Walt, Stephen M. 'The myth of American exceptionalism', *Foreign Policy*, 189 (2011), 72–5.

Walzer, Michael. *The Revolution of the Saints: A Study in the Origins of Radical Politics* (London: Weidenfeld and Nicolson, 1966).

Ward, Keith. *Divine Action: Examining God's Role in an Open and Emergent Universe* (West Conshohocken, PA: Templeton Foundation Press, 2007).

Rational Theology and Creativity of God (Oxford: Blackwell, 1982).

Ware, Bruce A. *God's Lesser Glory: The Diminished God of Open Theism* (Wheaton, IL: Crossway, 2000).

Watt, W. Montgomery. *Free Will and Predestination in Early Islam* (London: Luzac, 1948).

Weber, Otto. *Foundations of Dogmatics*, vol. I (Grand Rapids: Eerdmans, 1981).

Weiner, Jonathan. *The Beak of the Finch: The Story of Evolution in Our Time* (New York: Random, 1994).

Wells, Sam. *Improvisation: The Drama of Christian Ethics* (Grand Rapids: Brazos, 2004).

Werdel, Mary Beth and Wicks, Robert J. *Primer on Post-Traumatic Growth* (Hoboken, NJ: John Wiley and Sons, 2012).

Wesley, John. 'Serious thoughts occasioned by the late earthquake at Lisbon' in John Emory (ed.), *The Works of Rev John Wesley*, 7 vols. (New York: Carlton and Porter, 1856), vol. VI, pp. 238–47.

White, Vernon. *Purpose and Providence: Taking Soundings in Western Thought, Literature and Theology* (London: T&T Clark, 2015).

Whitehead, Alfred North. *Process and Reality* (New York: Free Press, 1978).

Whitehouse, W. A. *Creation, Science and Theology: Essays in Response to Karl Barth* (Edinburgh: T&T Clark, 1981).

Wickham, E. R. *Church and People in an Industrial City* (London: Lutterworth, 1957).

Wiesel, Elie. *Night* (New York: Hill & Wang, 2006).

Wilberforce, Samuel. *Speeches on Missions* (London, 1874).

Wildman, Wesley. 'The divine action project 1988–2003', *Theology and Science*, 2.1 (2004), 31–75.

Wiles, Maurice. *God's Action in the World* (London: SCM, 1986).

Wilkinson, Alan. *The Church of England and the First World War* (London: SPCK, 1978).

Williams, Rowan. *Being Christian: Baptism, Bible, Eucharist, Prayer* (London: SPCK, 2014).

'Reply [to Marilyn McCord Adams]: redeeming sorrows' in D. Z. Phillips (ed.), *Religion and Morality* (New York: St Martin's Press, 1996), pp. 132–48.

Tokens of Trust: An Introduction to Christian Belief (Norwich: Canterbury Press, 2007).

Winston, David. *The Wisdom of Solomon*, Anchor Bible vol. XLIII (New York: Doubleday, 1979).

Wisdom, John. 'Gods', *Proceedings of the Aristotelian Society*, 45 (1944–5), 185–206.

Witherspoon, John. 'The dominion of providence over the passions of men' in *Collected Works*, vol. V (Harrisonburg: Sprinkle, 2005), pp. 17–42.

Wollaston, William. *The Religion of Nature Delineated* ([London], 1722).

Wolterstorff, Nicholas. 'God and darkness in Reid' in Joseph Houston (ed.) *Thomas Reid: Context, Influence, Significance* (Edinburgh: Dunedin Academic Press, 2004), pp. 77–102.

'If God is good and sovereign, why lament?', *Calvin Theological Journal*, 36 (2001), 42–52.

Inquiring about God (Cambridge: Cambridge University Press, 2010).

Lament for a Son (London: SPCK, 2007).

Thomas Reid and The Story of Epistemology (Cambridge: Cambridge University Press, 2001).

'The wounds of God: Calvin's theology of social justice' in *Hearing the Call: Liturgy, Justice, Church, and World* (Grand Rapids: Eerdmans, 2011), pp. 114–32.

Wood, Charles. *The Question of Providence* (Louisville: Westminster John Knox Press, 2008).

Wright, David F. 'Calvin's Pentateuchal criticism: equity, hardness of heart, and divine accommodation in the Mosaic harmony commentary', *Calvin Theological Journal*, 21 (1986), 33–50.

Wright, N. T. *Paul and the Faithfulness of God* (Minneapolis: Fortress, 2013).

Wuthnow, Robert. *The God Problem: Expressing Faith and Being Reasonable* (Berkeley: University of California Press, 2012).

Zbaraschuk, G. Michael. *The Purposes of God: Providence as Process-Historical Liberation* (Eugene, OR: Pickwick, 2015).

Zwingli, Huldrych. *On Providence and Other Essays*, ed. William John Hinke (Durham, NC: Labyrinth Press, 1983).

Names Index

Adams, Marilyn McCord, 293, 316–22, 334–42
Alcinous, 16
Alexander of Hales, 61
Alston, William, 318, 319
Aquinas, Thomas, 38, 62, 63–77, 92, 108, 128, 175, 189, 225, 226, 246, 276, 304, 307, 318, 333
Aristotle, 13, 128, 131
Augustine, 7, 9, 38, 48, 49, 51, 67, 75, 85, 88, 133, 142, 175, 276

Baillie, Donald, 316–22
Barth, Hans-Martin, 314
Barth, Karl, 250, 271–89, 299, 332
Bavinck, Herman, 249
Bergjan, Silke-Petra, 45
Berkhof, Hendrikus, 323
Berkouwer, G. C., 246–52, 287
Berlin, Isaiah, 150
Blair, Hugh, 135, 137
Blumenfeld, David, 123
Boethius, 60
Bonhoeffer, Dietrich, 315
Bornkamm, Heinrich, 312
Broadie, Alexander, 119
Bruce, A. B., 152
Buber, Martin, 331
Bullinger, Heinrich, 83, 92

Calvin, John, 84–101, 108, 175, 225, 226, 272, 282
Chalmers, Thomas, 155, 160, 161
Clarke, Samuel, 10, 116, 117
Clayton, Philip, 227

Clement of Alexandria, 43
Cone, James, 293

Darwin, Charles, 167, 169, 183, 185, 196, 201
Davies, Brian, 69
Dempsey, Michael, 74
Dowey, Edward, 80
Duns, John, 167

Ellis, George, 220
Endō, Shūsaku, 260

Farrer, Austin, 73, 246–52
Forsyth, P. T., 342
Fretheim, Terrence, 33, 35
Freud, Sigmund, 2

Garrigou-Lagrange, Reginald, 65, 82, 246–52
Geach, Peter, 261
Geddes, Patrick, 197
Gentile, Emilio, 164
Gerrish, Brian, 100, 285
Gilkey, Langdon, 241, 242, 245, 256
Goris, Harm, 67
Gorringe, T. J., 262
Gould, Stephen Jay, 180
Guyatt, Nicholas, 146

Hegel, G .F. W., 148, 149, 166
Hodge, Charles, 99, 168, 195, 197

Illingworth, J. R., 209
Iverach, James, 206

James, William, 261, 326
John of Damascus, 52, 55, 57, 62

Subject Index

agency
  divine, 11, 17, 23, 29, 42, 72, 114, 127, 177,
    219, 257, 265, 288, 317, 320
  double, 51, 59, 66, 68, 72, 75, 107, 129,
    217–40, 277, 302
  human, 45, 55, 173, 202, 330
  primal, 75
anthropomorphism, 27
Arminianism, 92–101, 266, 275
assurance, 25, 78, 81, 102, 104, 140, 247, 311,
  314, 328
Augustinianism, 59, 64, 66, 103, 198
  hyper, 317
authority, 53, 311, 329

beauty, 8, 24, 46, 89, 96, 100, 113, 120, 185,
  192, 197, 253, 306, 308
Buddhism, 2

causality, 46, 60, 63, 65, 82, 84–92, 93, 128,
  180, 274, 288, 289–95
  and effect, 70
  creaturely, 67, 71
  natural, 59
  primary, 64, 65, 68, 172, 211,
    225, 261
  secondary, 30, 49, 64, 68, 132
  voluntary, 51
chance, 15, 30, 43, 49, 57, 63, 85, 88, 96,
  106, 169, 179, 195, 225, 335
chaos theory, 171, 221, 224, 230
church, 43–58, 100, 116
  contemporary, 4, 244, 249, 300, 303,
    304, 313, 322
  history of, 1, 124, 132, 140, 162,
    279, 331

theology, 40, 79, 85, 95, 177, 210, 216,
  232, 239, 277, 279, 284, 299, 304, 311,
  318, 321, 338
concursus, 84–101, 102, 172, 256, 286, 288
conservation, 113, 236, 274, 295, 307, 333
contingency, 30, 53, 60, 64, 67, 82, 96, 101,
  132, 169, 172, 180, 199, 225, 232
cosmological argument, 65, 246, 273
creation, 1, 9, 21, 26, 28, 32, 40, 50, 63, 65, 67,
  71, 73, 78, 97, 129, 167, 188, 191, 193, 195,
  203, 212, 219, 225, 230, 238, 244, 254,
  261, 274, 282, 291, 297–316, 323, 332, 341
  continuous, 23–7, 53, 84, 93, 177, 268, 306
  ex nihilo, 9, 70, 256, 276
  orders, 51
  theology of, 22, 251, 306

Daoism, 2
Darwinism, 8, 168, 181, 190–5, 206, 207–17
deism, 9, 22, 68, 73, 85, 110–32, 157, 190–5,
  220, 245, 254, 295
  and creation, 72
design argument, 65, 114, 118, 181, 185, 191,
  192, 205, 246
destiny, 15, 19, 43, 49, 64, 67, 141, 266,
  301, 325
determinism, 2, 7, 9, 15, 27, 44, 49, 51, 58,
  59, 65, 73, 75, 76, 89, 99, 169–72, 226,
  234, 238, 250, 261, 265, 271, 275, 277,
  286, 289, 297, 318
  and chance, 190–215
divine action, 11, 21, 23–32, 42, 51, 63–77,
  88, 91, 107, 128, 129, 131, 167, 171, 172,
  177, 199, 217–40, 271–89, 297–316, 323,
  327, 329, 341
dualism, 7, 22, 331

374